I0114654

LONG JOURNEY HOME

LONG JOURNEY HOME

ORAL HISTORIES OF CONTEMPORARY DELAWARE INDIANS

EDITED BY JAMES W. BROWN AND RITA T. KOHN
PHOTOGRAPHS BY JAMES W. BROWN

INDIANA UNIVERSITY PRESS
BLOOMINGTON AND INDIANAPOLIS

Frontis: Forrest Yearout in a Gourd Dance with grandsons Noah (near) and Matthew Yearout at the 2006 Delaware Powwow near Copan, Oklahoma. The Gourd Dance is a man's dance performed by tribal warrior societies or service veterans and their relatives. Forrest Yearout wears the traditional gourd sash over his shoulders. Eagle feather or Hawk fans are held in the left hand while a gourd or saltshaker rattle shakes in rhythm to the gourd song and drum. Yearout's fan is made from a Red-tailed Hawk wing.

The graphic device used on the opposite page and throughout the book was made by James Brown from an original design by Delaware artist and silversmith Don Secondine. It was drawn from a silver brooch made by Secondine and is used by permission. Secondine's oral history may be found in the contemporary history section of the book.

This book is a publication of

Indiana University Press
601 North Morton Street
Bloomington, IN 47404-3797 USA

http://iupress.indiana.edu

Telephone orders	800-842-6796
Fax orders	812-855-7931
Orders by e-mail	iuporder@indiana.edu

© 2008 by James W. Brown and Rita T. Kohn
All rights reserved

No part of this book may be reproduced or utilized in any form or by any means, electronic or mechanical, including photocopying and recording, or by any information storage and retrieval system, without permission in writing from the publisher. The Association of American University Presses' Resolution on Permissions constitutes the only exception to this prohibition.

The paper used in this publication meets the minimum requirements of American National Standard for Information Sciences—Permanence of Paper for Printed Library Materials, ANSI Z39.48-1984.

Manufactured in China

Library of Congress Cataloging-in-Publication Data

Long journey home : oral histories of contemporary Delaware Indians / edited by James W. Brown and Rita T. Kohn ; photographs by James W. Brown.
    p. cm.
  Includes bibliographical references and index.
  ISBN-13: 978-0-253-34968-2 (cloth)
  1. Delaware Indians—History. 2. Delaware Indians—Biography. 3. Delaware Indians—Portraits. I. Brown, James W. (James William), 1945– II. Kohn, Rita T.
  E99.D2L66 2008
  974.004'97345—dc22

                                                                        2007030436

1 2 3 4 5   13 12 11 10 09 08

INDIANA UNIVERSITY PRESS
GRATEFULLY ACKNOWLEDGES A MAJOR GIFT FROM
CONOCOPHILLIPS COMPANY IN SUPPORT OF
PUBLICATION OF THIS BOOK.

OTHER CONTRIBUTORS INCLUDE
KAREN BRAECKEL AND JOHN BRAECKEL,
JAMES AND REBECCA BROWN,
BRIAN BROWN, JENNIFER BROWN,
JOSHUA ECKERT, BLAKE EGAN,
JOHN AND MAGGIE HILLERY,
HOOSIER STATE PRESS ASSOCIATION,
RITA KOHN, DEBORAH PERKINS,
ROBERTS DISTRIBUTORS,
SCHOOL OF JOURNALISM IUPUI,
THOMAS AND SUSIE SAMS,
AND DAVID AND DONNA SEASE.

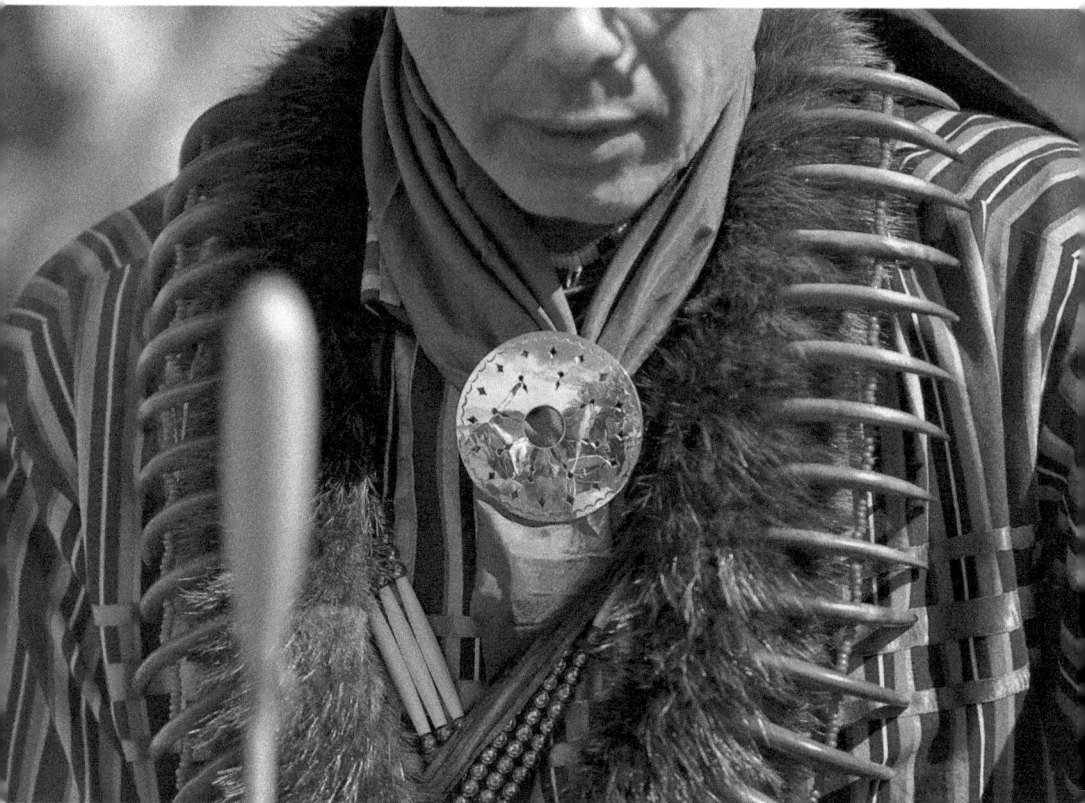

Don Secondine sings for school children visiting Conner Prairie Living History Museum in Fishers, Indiana. Secondine, a Delaware artist and silversmith, made the scarf slide he wears.

To

The Lenape Ancestors

and

Elders

who kept alive the ideals

and vision of

the Grandfather People

CONTENTS

FOREWORD

IN THE LATE EIGHTEENTH CENTURY, the Delaware Tribe was on the frontier of the growing United States in Ohio; the Treaty of Greenville in 1795 brought the tribe into Indiana, where they lived on land occupied by the Miamis. This began a twenty-five-year time of trial and desperation for those tribes in the period before Indiana became a state in 1816.

While living in Indiana the Delawares were a friendly tribe, but the steady growth of the white population moving from the East was a harbinger that the Delawares would be facing another move further west into Missouri, then Kansas, then Indian Territory, which later became the state of Oklahoma.

The story of the Delaware Nation, also known as the Lenape, is a tale of great suffering and tribulation, but it was also a time that made the Delaware people strong in their reserve and resolve to honor their ancestors and maintain and preserve their way of life.

The stories contained in these pages have many things to tell: the pride of a people, their personal histories, their determination to remain who they were and are as a people. Many of the stories have been edited for brevity's sake, but they are indicative of the resolve and love of their tribe. The early recorded stories relate the stories of the tribe to its present form, and the later stories relate the stories of the people today.

The early history of Indiana is the story of mostly peaceful times between the whites and Indians and the accelerated growth of the country. The tribes were moving further west, and great stretches of rich fertile farmland became available. A new chapter of history awaited the Delawares, but the legacy of their stay in Indiana remains a valuable history of the state's early years.

Sometimes we as individuals take our heritage for granted, and we do not learn the lessons of history. The study of our heritage can truly tell us why we are who we are today. Take the time to remember and honor your ancestors and their history.

I want to express my thanks to Rita Kohn and Jim Brown for their tireless work and efforts in creating this work.

Long may the Delaware Tribe live.

MICHAEL PACE

Grant Johnson (top),
Skye Scimeca, and Trey Johnson
are dressed to dance at the 2007
Delaware Powwow near Copan,
Oklahoma. They are the
continuity of tradition.

PREFACE: HOME

HOME, FOR THE LENAPE, named the Delaware Indians by the Euro-Americans, can be represented as a westward-moving diorama within the depiction of what is now the United States of America. It can be viewed as the sorry legacy of displacing indigenous people from their homeland and promised sanctuaries through a series of broken treaties, inter-tribal hostilities, and outright theft.

Home, for the Lenape, also can be seen as a portrait of a people determined to establish a place, within traditional contexts, wherever they were forced to flee or settle. It is this vibrancy that the authors found through the images and words of the individuals whose memories and memoirs appear in this book. Over time, the abode of one's family has, in an everyday sense, replaced the tribal town, the abiding place of ancestry. Yet, the original values and role within the indigenous culture have been retained and, in some instances, regained across two centuries and over half a continent. The Lenape were forced from their lucrative, stable way of life to become sojourners at the forefront of Euro-American encroachment. Their resilience in the face of so much dislocation is a testament to a people determined to maintain their heritage and unique identity under even the most trying circumstances.

Long Journey Home brings forward the stories of Lenape (Delaware Indians) through first-person accounts spanning post–Civil War events to the present. The authors have allowed personal and tribal events over time and place to unfold through speakers, presented in alphabetical order within the four periods of collecting oral histories. Each entry is a stand-alone memoir. Read all the way through, the diverse parts delineate a group representation, sometimes with overlays, sometimes with blurred images, but always clearly identifiable as the Grandfather People, the peacemakers. The authors made no attempt to censor or explicate. A critic may deem this as haphazard scholarship if judged as a deviation from the usual way of presenting the American Indian story. However, we feel there is value in the naturalness of a conversational approach where the readers can be active participants, picking up points and making connections on their own. We feel this book represents communion between teller and listener in the tradition of oral transmittal.

Long Journey Home grew out of the pan–Great Lakes Woodland Indian oral histories presented in *Always a People,* published by Indiana University Press in 1997. When readers commented they were most surprised to learn the Delawares had that much "history" in the state of Indiana, it seemed essential to bring forward the legacy that has been hidden, overlooked, denied. The intent became to bring readers up to date, 180 years since forced removal, with the Delawares, whose eighteenth- and nineteenth-century towns remain as sites of cities and towns along Indiana's West Fork of the White River. We wondered, what are the great-great-great-great-great-great-grandchildren of the founders of Anderson, Muncie, Noblesville, Strawtown, Conner's trading post, Nancytown, and other communities doing today? Where are they now living? What memories from the eastern seaboard displacement into Pennsylvania and the series of sojourns in Ohio, Indiana, Missouri, Kansas, and Indian Territory have been handed down and remain as part of the tribe's unique memory? What are the reactions to recent reconciliation meetings and events by residents of the places from which Delawares were removed?

From 1998 to 2002, throughout the tenures of Chief Curtis Zunigha and Chief Dee Ketchum, James W. (Jim) Brown and Rita T. Kohn conducted a series of interviews with contemporary descendants of the White River (Indiana) Delawares both in and around Bartlesville, Oklahoma, and during tribal member visits to Indiana, particularly at Conner Prairie in Fishers, Indiana, where an early nineteenth-century living-history Lenape village and trading post have been functioning as a national attraction, and at the Eiteljorg Museum of American Indians and Western Art in Indianapolis. Throughout, Jim Brown recorded visual images on video and still photography.

Three of the subjects interviewed became colleagues. Deborah Nichols-Ledermann and James A. (Jim) Rementer bring intimacy as public scholars who are members of the Delaware Tribe of Indians of Bartlesville, Oklahoma, the latter as an adopted member into the family of Mrs. Nora Thompson Dean (Touching Leaves), the renowned fluent Delaware speaker and linguist. Deborah Nichols-Ledermann and Jim Rementer bring forward the oral histories from the 1930s Indian Pioneer History Project of Oklahoma and the 1968 and 1995 interviews by private individuals, along with providing the overview history. Michael (Mike) Pace reviewed the entire manuscript, verified content as accurate after making corrections where errors of spelling and context occurred. A direct descendant of White River Delawares, Mike Pace has been assistant chief and a member of the Cultural Committee.

One foreseen problem in undertaking a book of oral histories is that of choosing subjects. By narrowing the scope to descendants of Chief William Anderson and related White River Delawares, who were removed from Indiana as a result of the 1818 Treaty of St. Mary's, we hoped to inspire others to undertake their own books to give voice and visibility to other groups of Delawares whose tribal centers are in Canada and other parts of the United States.

Decisions for inclusion in *Long Journey Home* are based on Bartlesville Delaware tribal members' respect for the feelings of elders who keep in mind the sacrifices made by those who had to move from their homeland, who made the hard decisions for survival, and who suffered the pain to sustain their tribal identity. The people whose oral histories appear in this book are descendants of the Lenape who traveled 1,500 miles across this continent over a period of some two hundred years. Each of the speakers has continued identity and enrollment as a member of the Delaware Tribe of Indians of Bartlesville, Oklahoma. Those Lenape who quit the tribe by remaining behind, by personal choice, during any of the several moves from the eastern seaboard to present-day Oklahoma may now have descendants identifying themselves as Lenape. But, according to some enrolled tribal members, these individuals are not truly Lenape in the sense of continuity with community. Because they have lived apart from the cohesive tribe, they do not possess or represent the tribal values and ideals the Lenape of Bartlesville have retained by living as a community. To explain to themselves and to non-Lenape people what it is to be Lenape, tribal members remind all others who now come forward with some distant story of having Delaware ancestry that a common experience is an essential element. Although we recognize that those who stayed behind certainly suffered, their stories are separate from the official tribal story.

For enrolled Lenape, honoring ancestors means more than claiming DNA. Being Delaware means having stayed with the tribe above individual considerations. This is what Annette Ketchum has spoken of in regard to Mekinges, the wife of William Conner. Mekinges probably could have remained in Indiana in 1820, as could their children. Yet, she and her children chose to leave with their Lenape family, giving up a comfortable home and a lucrative trading post, in which Mekinges and the older sons seem to have had a major role. During a visit to Indianapolis in 2003, Annette Ketchum said, "Mekinges is the role model down to me, and from me to my daughters and granddaughters. Being a part, staying with, going with the tribe is most important."

However, living someplace other than Bartlesville does not disqualify someone from having continued identity. Families and individuals whose ancestors made the move to Indian Territory are enrolled members. They retain that enrollment wherever they move. As children are born, their names are added to the original ancestor's lineage. In most cases, individuals who move away from Bartlesville further retain their identity through visits to Bartlesville, attendance at powwows and Delaware Days, practicing their culture at home, and, in many cases, returning to Oklahoma upon retirement to participate in tribal leadership. Thus, readers will find inclusion based on Lenape heritage is narrowly defined but is broadly represented geographically.

Another known aspect of oral histories is in possible variances of "facts" between what already exists in books or between two or more subjects whose memories and points of view may overlap but not exactly fit together. The authors have tried to provide context for the differences through notes within the text.

A third challenge for the general reader is in the way the Lenape, and American Indians generally, relate stories. Past is present and future. The speaker is part of what happened and what will happen, in a time-travel reality; the words and actions of old chiefs are as essential today as in 1820. The massacre of nearly an entire population of Moravian Delawares is as heartrending now as in the eighteenth century to the few survivors, who are the ancestors of the present-day Lenape. Immediacy, rather than detachment, is the way of thinking and talking. Decisions made today affect seven generations hence while decisions made seven generations prior are impacting Lenape today.

A fourth challenge is deciding when and to what extent a term or event or item of material culture alluded to by a speaker needs to be amplified for the general reader to gain appropriate context. The authors have resigned themselves to being faulted for omissions and commissions in this regard.

And although each reader may bring pre-conceived notions of some kind or another, the authors hope readers will come away with broader perspectives, deeper understandings, different questions. For example, the contemporary American Indian as warrior has diverse connotations. For non-Indians it can be a fearsome idea fueled by fantastic tales of atrocities and Hollywood hype depicting "frontier" clashes. For Delawares, like other American Indians, service to the United States is embracing one's ancestry in defense of this place. Since the War for Independence, American Indians have been serving in all branches of the armed forces in proportions far greater than any other ethnic or cultural group. As American Indians have been denied full citizenship, full rights, and full justice, it's hard to understand why until the reader comprehends the love for the land, the loyalty to "turtle island," the responsibility as the Grandfather People—the designation which the Delawares are accorded by other American Indian tribes.

Regarding choices of style and content of the oral histories, the authors use spellings and information in accordance with Delaware Indian preferences. Following transcription of the oral histories collected by Rita Kohn and Jim Brown, each set of typed pages was sent to the subject for verification. Following revision, the copy was mailed for a second verification. Deborah Nichols-Ledermann, Jim Rementer, and Mike Pace then also read each for final verification. The transcribed oral histories from the 1930s,[1] 1968, and 1995 initially were re-typed and verified by Deborah Nichols-Ledermann and Jim Rementer and edited by Rita Kohn and Jim Brown. Nevertheless, although every effort was made to be error-free, it is inevitable that errors will slip in or fail to drop out. In such cases, the authors welcome correspondence so postings on the *Long Journey Home* website can be updated.[2]

In giving voice to the continuing impact of the Delawares on Indiana State, through place-names, historical figures, and cultural legacies, their singular case has taken on universality because the Delawares have equally impacted at least seven other states in which they resided and built an economic, political, and social structure with equally lasting imprints. In seeking answers to how a group's cultural heritage is kept alive and transmitted when all outside forces are bent on quashing that uniqueness, it became clear how interconnected the Delaware story is with people worldwide caught in the cycles of "ethnic cleansing."

And, obliquely, the Delaware story brings even greater poignancy to that of African Americans whose inability to trace heritage to a place, a patrimony/matrimony, a singular oral story, leaves them bereft of a solid connection to home. A video-documentary grew from these inferences. *Long Journey Home* premiered during April 2003 on WFYI Public Television in Indianapolis and soon appeared throughout Indiana. National broadcasting commenced April 2004.

Throughout, the intent has been to bring honor to all indigenous people while enabling one group to emerge as a multi-dimensional, multi-faceted society existing side by side with the other ethnic groups now composing these United States of America. We take a moment now to mourn the passing of Leonard Thompson in 2002 and Joanna J. Nichol in 2004. "Leonard Thompson took it upon himself to be sure the knowledge he held about a culture that had suffered great abuse, and was under great duress over time, was communicated to another generation. In that way he did much to protect that which has defined the Delawares through time immemorial and that will continue to define them in the future," said W. Richard West Jr., director of the Smithsonian's National Museum of the American Indian. "Individual Indians need to value in ways that we have not before, probably because we were not permitted to do so, the cultural knowledge which comes to us from our Elders. They are treasures among us, and we should treat every one of them as a precious gift." The obituary of Joanna Nichol described her "often-colorful life," including service as a volunteer public school teacher and long-time member of the Bartlesville Indian Women's Club. "She never met a stranger."

A final comment regarding this book. Although the documentary was made possible through a generous grant from the Nina Mason Pulliam

Charitable Trust, and additional funding was received from the Indiana Arts Commission–National Endowment for the Arts and WFYI-Teleplex, the authors have supported the research and writing of this book, with critical but minimal support from the Indiana University School of Journalism at Indiana University–Purdue University Indianapolis.

Nevertheless, the enormous value surrounding this book is the network of partnerships and the creation of a series of related activities to bring visibility to the Delaware Indian story along Indiana's White River. Among programs surrounding the premiere of the documentary is one which is to become an ongoing central Indiana project. "Share-a-Legacy: Neighborhood Reflections" invites everyone to uncover the structures and land uses that preceded the buildings and open spaces currently in existence. A program of uncovering relevant sites and mounting historical markers of the Delaware sojourn will follow, as will more exhibitions, community-based programs, dramatic and dance productions, and much needed classroom materials on the Delaware experience in Indiana. Some of the subjects have been inspired to expand their oral histories into their own books. Others plan to develop a national Delaware Heritage Trail to promote the significant contributions of Delawares as city and town founders from New York City to Bartlesville, Oklahoma.

The central issue of *Long Journey Home* deals with giving voice to a people who have been overlooked, yet whose story on the North American continent precedes Euro-American intervention in their lives. Through the oral histories we learned that while the mainstream culture has been moving toward individual isolation, the Delawares of Bartlesville have been coming closer together as a community through a vibrant emergence of cultural activities, educational programs, and political activism. We learned, too, new meanings of tenacity and adaptation. We set out to honor, yet we became recipients of honor—the words, friendships, and teachings have enriched our lives. For this we say *wanishi*—thank you.

JAMES W. BROWN
RITA T. KOHN
INDIANAPOLIS, INDIANA

---

1. These interviews are included with permission of the agencies where they are housed.
2. See http://brownimages.com.

ACKNOWLEDGMENTS

THE DELAWARES WHOSE PHOTOGRAPHS and words make up this book merit our collective appreciation, as do the collectors and transcribers of the 1936, 1968, and 1995 interviews. The subjects of these earlier oral histories most certainly had no idea their contributions would make their way into a book published in the twenty-first century. Perhaps it truly is a long journey home for them to have their stories included with the oral histories collected from 1998 to 2004.

Dee and Annette Ketchum undertook the interviews and transcriptions for the oral histories of Ed Wilson and Will Wilson. Dee and Annette equally assisted in verification of the Indiana Historical Bureau website: Delaware Tribe of Indians.[1]

James A. Rementer and Deborah Nichols-Ledermann earn sincere thanks for locating the earlier oral histories. They have been generous, meticulous historians and guardians of the Delaware culture on many fronts and levels. Their contributions include the brief history, which provides the oral histories with context, and the verification and explication of the earlier oral histories. They spent countless hours and resources toward the improvement of this book.

Michael Pace verified the entire manuscript, bringing to it his broad knowledge of the Delawares and his wonderful sense of humor. His fastidious editing ensures accuracy while honoring human memory and divergent points of view.

Curtis Zunigha initially championed the project, providing both his expertise in collecting stories and the backing of his office as elected chief of the Delaware Tribe of Indians. Chief Zunigha had been part of the earlier oral history project, *Always a People,* published by Indiana University Press in 1997, and the four *Woodland Adventures* picture books published by Children's Press in 1995.

Dee Ketchum, upon his election as chief, embraced the "Long Journey Home" project, by then broadened. Chief Ketchum and his wife, Annette Martin Ketchum, unstintingly shared their home, family campsite, family archives, expertise, and friendship. During development and filming of the Emmy Award–winning video documentary *Long Journey Home,*[2] the extended Ketchum family with grace, honesty, and kindness welcomed the production team from WFYI Public Television of Indianapolis.

The staff at the headquarters of the Delaware Tribe in Bartlesville were of help in providing space for interviews. Equally, in Fishers at Conner Prairie Living History Museum and in Indianapolis at the Eiteljorg Museum of American Indians and Western Art, the Indiana Historical Society and Indiana State Museum, and WFYI Public Television, personnel provided assistance for interview space and historical data in their archives.

The bulk of the research was undertaken at the William Henry Smith Memorial Library and Indiana Historical Society at the Indiana History Center, and the archives at the Indiana Historical Bureau, Eiteljorg Museum, Conner Prairie, and the Indiana Department of Natural Resources. In addition, important background information was provided by the staffs and through the collections at the Bartlesville Public Library and the Delaware Tribe of Indians in Bartlesville, Oklahoma, as well as the Wyandotte County Historical Society and Museum in Bonner Springs, Kansas.

A trip along the West Fork of the White River, with stops at all the known sites of original Delaware villages, was first undertaken with Peg Williams and Thomas D. Kohn, and later with Michael Atwood and Tony Williams.

Considerable assistance in transcribing came from Indiana University School of Journalism at Indianapolis staff, including Sandra Herrin, Peg Williams, Lynn Johnson, and Jennifer Woolfolk, and students, including Meridith Hayden, Andrea Larrea, Carly Nation, and Monique Webster.

Initial permission to undertake the project was given by the members of the Indiana Governor's Commission on American Indians.

Throughout, the belief in the value of the project by the staff at Indiana University Press has sustained us. Special thanks go to John Gallman, Peter-John Leone, and especially Robert Sloan. The unknown readers of the initial manuscript provided important feedback, which we hope has been addressed. Jane Curran was expert at copyediting. Miki Bird and Anne Teillard-Clemmer helped manage the manuscript at Indiana University Press. Dan Pyle was production coordinator and Tony Brewer was composition coordinator. Mary Blizzard brought her design talent to the book, making it a visual delight.

Friends and colleagues who have afforded constant cheer include John Ahlhauser, Mary K. Baumann, Pam Bennett, Jonas Bjork, Trevor Brown, Will Counts, Walt Craig, Bob Dittmer, Chris Feola, Phil Gibson, Jim Grim, Jody Grober, Mark Haab, Andrew G. Hein, Jon Henricks, Maggie Hillery, Will Hopkins, C. William Horrell, Paul Lester, Bill Lutholtz, Pat McKeand, Hank Nuwer, Lori Nye, Deb Perkins, Dani Pfaff, Nelson Price, Sherry Ricchiardi, Steve Sweitzer, Clayton Taylor, James Utterback, and Ralph Veal.

Brian Matsumoto of Canon U.S.A. has also been very helpful.

For our families, who put up with our constant going away and coming home with yet more work, we offer this book as their reward. Rebecca Brown has been bedrock support for James W. Brown. She has traveled with him for photo shoots and has entertained Delawares when they have visited Indiana, which their ancestors called home. Without her support and understanding, this book could not have been completed. Jennifer and Brian Brown have always supported their dad's creative efforts, and Sharon, Martin, and Thomas Kohn have supported their mom's efforts. Thanks.

Throughout the past eight years, we have shared a remarkable journey. In the initial "brain drain" experienced by Indiana, the Delawares were forcibly removed from the state in 1821; this collection is a significant journey home of the words of their descendants.

---

1. See http://www.statelib.lib.in.us/WWW/ihb/delaware/intro2.html.
2. *Long Journey Home* video documentary available through ctaylor@wfyi.org.

Clayton and Jake Sears dance with their grandfather Dee Ketchum at the 2007 Delaware Powwow near Copan, Oklahoma.

INTRODUCTION
HISTORICAL INFORMATION ABOUT THE LENAPE

DEBORAH NICHOLS-LEDERMANN AND
JAMES A. REMENTER (MOOSH-HAH-KWEE-NUND)

FOR MORE THAN 12,000 YEARS, the region that is now southeastern New York, all of New Jersey, eastern Pennsylvania, and the northern part of the state of Delaware was home to groups of Lenape (Delaware) Indians. When first encountered by Europeans in 1524 the Lenape were not a single political entity; rather they lived in a series of separate, autonomous communities.

The Lenape subsisted through a combination of hunting, fishing, and farming. Linked through a network of trade, marriages, and ceremonies, the villages shared similar customs and spoke closely related dialects. Those who lived in what is now lower New York and northern New Jersey spoke dialects of what is today referred to as Munsee. Those who lived along the lower Delaware River spoke dialects of what is today called Unami. All the groups used the term "Lenape," which means "Common Person" or, collectively, "Common People" or, as many now prefer, "The People." After Delaware Bay and the associated river were named for Lord De la Warr (an English colonial governor of Virginia), the Lenape generally became known as Delaware Indians. They were also known as the "Grandfather Tribe," based upon their position of ancient lineage among the Algonquian tribes.

The arrival of Dutch, Swedish, and English settlers during the seventeenth century ushered in a time of unparalleled suffering for the Lenape. Entire communities were wiped out by epidemics of smallpox, measles, and other Old World diseases for which they had no immunity. It is estimated that by the eighteenth century an original population of possibly 25,000 Delawares had been reduced to only a few thousand.

As an unstoppable tide of European settlers cut down woodlands, dammed streams, and killed the game animals, increasing pressure was placed on remnant Lenape communities to sell their lands and emigrate westward. There were tensions between the two vastly different lifestyles from the beginning, although the Lenape in the northern part of their homeland seem to have suffered the worst. In 1643, the governor of New Netherland, who was a notorious Indian hater, ignited more than two decades of sporadic warfare by massacring hundreds of Lenape in their sleep. The Lenape in the southern part of the Lenape homeland seem to initially have had a more peaceful coexistence with their European neighbors until greed for more land generated hostilities and those Lenape were pushed westward.

By the late seventeenth and early eighteenth centuries an enormous exodus of Native peoples from their eastern homes was taking place. Thousands of refugees coalesced in the Susquehanna and Ohio Valleys to form what became known as the Delaware Nation. The Delaware Nation was the first Indian Nation to sign a treaty with "the thirteen fires," as they called the newly formed United States government. Some Lenape held dreams of and proposed to Congress the concept of an Indian state headed by the Delaware Tribe. Others, remembering the bloody slaughter of innocent friends and family, doubted the sincerity of Americans and chose to support the British.

Following the American Revolution, the Delaware Nation was scattered to the four winds. Most of the Munsee-speaking Delawares were offered refuge by the British in Ontario, Canada. Today their descendants can be found at Moraviantown (so named because these Delawares were converts of the Moravian missionaries), at Munceytown, and at Six Nations Reserve. Other Munsee Delawares joined the Stockbridge Mahicans now living near Bowler, Wisconsin, and a few journeyed west with the Unami Delawares. Another group which had separated from the main body of the Delawares in 1789 ultimately settled near the Caddo Indians at Anadarko, Oklahoma.

The Unami, who had largely supported the Americans, continued on a trek that was to take them far beyond the Mississippi. During a series of forced migrations westward over the next century and a half, the group of Lenape now located in northeastern Oklahoma were forced to settle for a while in central and western Pennsylvania, Ohio, Indiana, eastern Missouri, and southwestern Missouri. By 1830 they were settled on a reserve in eastern Kansas, which placed them in the direct path of immigrants on the trails to California and Oregon. In addition, the tribe found itself surrounded by the dangerous turmoil of opposing forces in the pre–Civil War drama known as "Bleeding Kansas." Throughout these years, the Delawares became a legendary thread in the tapestry of the West, marketing their skills as trappers for the Rocky Mountain fur companies; as military guides, interpreters, scouts, hunters, and spies in the Seminole, Mexican, and western Indian wars; as wagon train guides and freight haulers; and finally as valuable U.S. allies as Union soldiers in the Civil War.

During the Kansas period, the Lenape suffered increasing pressures to their cultural and religious traditions. Tribal members were encouraged to abandon their long history of hunting over a wide range of territory in favor of raising domestic livestock and crops. Traditional practices of communal tribal lands were transformed to individual ownership of allotments. Government leaders, Indian agents, and missionaries actively advocated conversion to Christian religion and education in mission schools, discouraging the more traditional Big House church rites and form of spirituality.

In 1866, as settlers once again illegally squatted upon their land, stealing timber and livestock, the Delawares submitted to local and federal government pressure to move from Kansas to Indian Territory (present-day Oklahoma). Tribal members found they were forced to choose between selling their reservation in Kansas to the land developers and railroad companies and moving to Indian Territory or abandoning their national and tribal identity to remain in Kansas as U.S. citizens. Most chose to preserve their tribal identity, once more sacrificing their homes and lands to the appetite of oncoming whites.

The Delaware Nation in Kansas entered into negotiations with the Cherokee Nation to purchase a parcel of land ten miles wide and thirty miles long on the western border of the Cherokee Nation for their reservation. Settlement on Cherokee lands, however, proved to be a most painful and destructive relocation. The Delawares began moving to Indian Territory in the winter of 1867–68. A group composed of about one-third of the tribe protested the move by remaining in Kansas near Lawrence, refusing to resettle in the geographic boundaries of the Cherokee Nation. The proceeds from the sale of their lands and homes were withheld from them by the Indian agent until their homeless and starving condition forced them to agree to leave Kansas and move to Indian Territory in the summer of 1868.

Factions of the Cherokee and former southern tribes who inhabited Indian Territory had joined the Confederate forces during the Civil War. They were still hostile to the pro-Union Delawares. The Osage Tribe was settled to the west of the chosen Delaware area, and boundary disputes arose between the two groups. Postwar Indian Territory was a violent, corrupt, and dangerous place. The removal journey and environmental change brought about sickness. Prices for food were high, and floods came, wiping out new homes and crops. At least a hundred persons (out of a tribal population of roughly a thousand) died during the trip and the first year of resettlement.

Dissatisfaction with available lands, ownership disputes, and the feeling that they were not being adequately represented in their tribal government motivated a group of nearly three hundred Delawares to move in 1871 to the Peoria Reserve within the Quapaw Agency along the Neosho River in northeastern Oklahoma (now Ottawa County). The U.S. government stepped in to try to smooth things over and to avoid having the whole tribe repudiate the 1867 treaty that government officials had so carefully crafted to conveniently place the Delaware Tribe under the jurisdiction of the Cherokee Agency.

The Delawares eventually became settled in districts along three main rivers, under the political influence of several cultural/religious factions. Those who followed the leadership of James Ketchum, a Delaware Methodist minister, and Henry Tiblow, the Delaware interpreter in Kansas, settled along the Grand River in what is the modern-day area of Craig County, Oklahoma. Many of their former farms are now under the waters of the Grand Lake of the Cherokees. Those who followed the leadership of Charles Journeycake, a Baptist minister, and other modernists settled around the Verdigris/Lightning Creek area in what is now Nowata County, Oklahoma. The Oologah Reservoir now covers some of these lands. A third group composed of some of the more traditional tribal families settled in the Caney River area in what is now Washington County, Oklahoma. Records from tribal general councils held in the early 1900s show that representatives from each of these tribal districts had to be present for the council to conduct tribal business.

In 1895, following the death of acting chief Charles Journeycake, the tribe began directing its business under the leadership of a business committee. Though it was composed of men from historically leading families, the committee members were approved by the U.S. government. Together, the business committee and the tribe's general council made decisions affecting the Delaware Tribe. From 1867 to the present the tribe has fiercely battled both the Cherokee Nation and the federal government to protect the property and legal rights of its members, including the Delaware Tribe's right of self-governance.

In 1907, the Lenape people were allotted lands throughout the Cherokee Nation as part of the General Allotment Act supervised by the Dawes Commission. For the Delaware people, this was another period of social and cultural upheaval. An oil boom turned northeastern Oklahoma into a land of both real and imaginary overnight fortunes populated by land speculators, lease-hungry oilmen, and poor oil field laborers. Tribal members again faced an influx of outsiders to their territory and had to fight legal battles for their homes even though many were unable to read, write, or even speak English. The allotment process sometimes scattered tribal members even further throughout the Cherokee Nation, making social and cultural activities more difficult.

Dividing the territory into individual allotments resulted in the loss of many Delaware lands and homes. The Allotment Act was actually a government plan to acquire more Indian lands under the guise of helping the Indians. The Great Depression in 1929 and the following "dust bowl" days brought great hardship to the oil industry and to agriculture. Many people were unable to sustain their families, and nearly 10 percent of the population of Oklahoma left the state in search of jobs. Farms were mortgaged and lost by tribal members who had no real concept of foreclosure.

Throughout the twentieth century, the Lenape were continually challenged to preserve the proud memory of their traditional religious and cultural ceremonies, dances, language, music, clothing, games, and stories. But the sad consequence of so many moves over several centuries has been the near loss of the language and traditions. The Delaware Tribe, which has its headquarters in Bartlesville, Oklahoma, presently has a population of more than ten thousand members. Many live scattered in the non-Indian communities throughout northeastern Oklahoma, and people of Lenape descent can be found in virtually every state of the Union. In addition to volunteering during the Civil War, the Lenape have served in the U.S. military in every war or conflict from World War I up to the present, but there is a certain irony that the Lenape who fought and died in World War I and preceding wars were not, until 1924, even considered citizens of the United States.

New customs have evolved over the last decades, including the annual powwow in the spring and Delaware Days in the fall, when many tribal members make the long journey home to join their families for dancing, games of Indian football, traditional cooking, and long evenings of camaraderie sitting around the Indian camps that dot the powwow grounds. Each year brings the opportunity for the elders to pass on the gift of knowledge to the younger generation of Lenape, knowing that time is short and things not shared may be lost forever in the future. The Lenape face the twenty-first century with concern and renewed hope for the preservation of their ancient and distinct identity.

FOLLOWING PAGE:

Mike Pace explains the use of wampum belts during colonial times to children visiting Conner Prairie Living History Museum. Pace's shirt shows the delicate ribbon work for which Delaware women are known. His turban is made from otter hide.

PART 1.
INDIAN PIONEER
COLLECTION

ABOUT THE COLLECTION

In 1936, the [Oklahoma Historical] society teamed with the history department at the University of Oklahoma to get a Works Progress Administration (WPA) writers' project grant for an interview program.[1] The project employed more than 100 writers scattered across the state, with headquarters in Muskogee, where Grant Foreman served as project director. Asked to "call upon early settlers and (record) the story of the migration to Oklahoma and their early life here," the writers conducted more than 11,000 interviews, edited the accounts into written form, and sent them to the project director who completed the editorial process and had them typed into more than 45,000 pages. When assembled, the Indian Pioneer Papers consisted of 112 volumes, with one set at the university, the other at the society. There are only two complete bound sets of originals. The interviews that follow are presented here in the form as they were originally edited by Grant Foreman.

Bob L. Blackburn, "Battle Cry for History:
The First Century of the Oklahoma Historical Society,"
n.d., Oklahoma Historical Society, 5 Oct. 1998

1. http://www.okhistory.org/battlcry.htm.

Kenny Brown leads the Delaware Tribe
of Indians color guard for
the grand entry of the 2006
annual powwow near Copan,
Oklahoma.

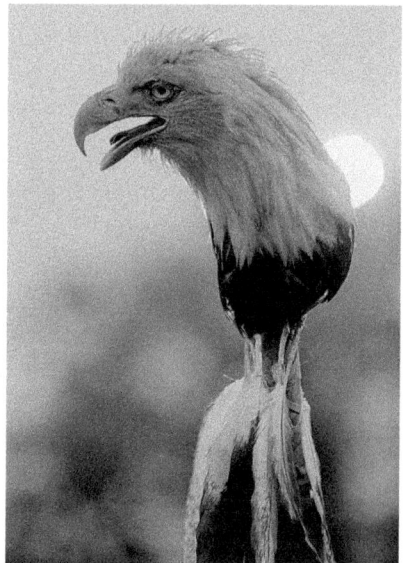

Eagle head staff used by the Broken
Arrow, Oklahoma, color
guard at the 2006 Delaware
Powwow.

HENRY ARMSTRONG

Born October 1870, about one mile east of what is now
Bartlesville, Oklahoma
Date of Interview: May 19, 1937, at his home at 131 North
Choctaw, Bartlesville, Oklahoma

[Field worker's notes:

Father: Arthur Armstrong. The Delaware roll shows he was born in 1840.[1] His parents were on a hunting field trip from Ohio. Arthur was born near Skiatook, Indian Territory. He came to the Indian Territory with the Shawnee and Delaware Indians from Wyandotte County, Kansas, in the spring of 1867.[2] He was a full-blood Delaware Indian and served as a Union Soldier with the 6th Kansas Cavalry in the Civil War and was a strong Republican. He died November 18, 1919 and is buried in White Rose Cemetery [Bartlesville, Oklahoma].

Mother: Nancy Ketchum Armstrong, daughter of a Delaware chief,[3] was born in Wyandotte County, Kansas. The Delaware roll taken February 7, 1867, at Leavenworth, Kansas, showed her age as 22 years old. According to this roll, she was born in 1845. She died at the age of 28 years, near Bartlesville, Oklahoma, and is buried in the Beck Cemetery, located one-half mile north of the county farm, east of Bartlesville.]

The Delaware roll shows the date of my birth as October, but my father said I was born in July when the plums were ripe.

When my parents came to Indian Territory, they settled at what is now the east edge of Bartlesville, Oklahoma. Our house was located on the banks of Armstrong Lake, where the Hutchison power house now stands. Our home was a twelve-by-fourteen-foot log house. The logs were put together with mud and the windows were four-panes in a sash about two-feet-square. We had a large fireplace for heating and cooking.

Our furniture was all homemade. A tree was split, hewn and smoothed for bed posts and rails, and we had no springs. We cut hay or straw and filled a large sack or straw tick for a mattress. Our chairs were blocks of wood cut

---

1. The Delaware lived in Kansas Territory in 1840.
2. The treaty for removal was signed in the spring of 1867, but the actual move did not begin until winter 1867–68.
3. Nancy Ketchum Armstrong was a granddaughter of a Delaware chief.

from the tree trunk with four legs bored into them. We had no tables but spread a blanket on the floor or ground and sat around it on the ground to eat. We had no floors in our home.

After my mother's death, my father married Nancy Jackson, daughter of Colonel Jackson who lived on Cotton Creek, east of Copan. My step-mother died August 7, 1890, and two years later he married Maggie Davis, who is still living in Bartlesville.

When my parents settled in the Indian Territory there were no schools in this part of the Territory. In 1875 my father built the first school house lo-cated one-half mile north of the present County Farm, on Coon Creek. This building was of native lumber, and there were about fifteen white, Indian and Negro children enrolled. This was a subscription school and the parents paid one dollar a month for each child. The first teacher was Mrs. Frank Bel-lows, whose husband was postmaster at the Bartles store.

In about 1886 my father built a log building at the north end of what is now Seneca Avenue. This was used for a school and nondenominational Sunday school for whites, Indians and Negroes.

Later, as the country became more settled and the log building was too small to accommodate the increasing population, my father built a box school house across the street, west of where the city barn is now located on the north end of Delaware Avenue. This building was used for several years as a school house and church. The new town of Bartlesville on the south side of Caney River soon outgrew the small school house and the neighbors, led by J. C. Brooks, took donations and bought native lumber from Jim Stokes' mill west of Dewey and built a larger school house. This was located at what is now Garfield School at 6th Street and Cherokee Avenue. The first teacher was Lizzie Bryant from Kansas. Our second teacher was Emma Hobert, also from Kansas. Other early-day teachers were Carrie Armstrong Overlees, Al-ice Wilson and Albert Rupert. The attendance had increased to twenty-two pupils.

The Cherokee government hired a teacher for the Indian children and the white children were to pay one dollar a month tuition. The teacher was Ida Collins. In about 1905 the Garfield building was erected.

Billy Johnstone, George B. Keeler, Jake Bartles and my father made the largest donations for the early-day education of Bartlesville.

The first Sunday school I can remember in our vicinity was in 1886, held in a house one-fourth mile south of the Nelson Carr home, northwest of what is now Dewey, Oklahoma. There was an attendance of about fifteen and we had one Testament and four hymn books. Each would read a verse from the Testament and pass it on to the next one. Two of our preachers were Billy [William] Adams, of Alluwe, and O. P. Ceberly. They were both Baptist ministers.

The best posted minister I ever heard was C. B. Gray, a Baptist preach-er. The Gray family lived north of Armstrong Lake, east of town where they had cleared the timber from the land for cultivation. Northeast Bartlesville is now located on this land.

One night in the rainy season the lake overflowed. Mr. Gray had sat up most of the night watching the lake and had dropped off to sleep; when he awakened the water was in the house. The floor boards were not nailed down and were floating. His two sons, John and Jim, son-in-law Josh Thompson, and nephew George Martin were awakened and they all waded out in water waist deep. Mr. Gray had a large trunk of clothes and he carried it out on his shoulder. George Martin was lost and climbed a tree where he spent the night. The next morning he saw an opossum and snake in the same tree, just above him. It was noon before the rescue party, Frank Bellows and T. J. Garlic, arrived with a boat from Bartles' store.

The first church was built at Silver Lake, south of Bartlesville, by Billy Adams. This church was for white people and Indians. Until this time all the churches and Sunday schools had been nondenominational and the Negroes were allowed to attend. The Silver Lake Church was of Baptist denomination. I remember a Negro woman, Mary Beck, attended our meetings at Post Oak and Cotton Creek churches, and she could certainly sing and shout. The Beck Cemetery, east of Bartlesville, was named in her memory. There are five Osage Indian graves on the banks of the Armstrong Lake but they cannot be located now. The Osages buried their dead on top of the ground and covered them with rocks.

We had a synagogue [Big House Church] on Coon Creek where we held meetings in October of each year. These meetings lasted twelve days. I remember a Delaware Indian woman, Mrs. Blackwing Anderson, told us at the synagogue [Big House Church] meeting one time, many years ago of a dream she had. She dreamed of a white road, from east to west and from north to south. She warned us to stay off this road for there would be many killed on it. This was the prediction of the paved highways and the accidents that occur on them now.

The horse races of the early days were honest; the best horse always won. Ola Wilhite owned the best race horse in the community and we thought it could not be beaten. One time a man camped near the Bartles mill for a few days and he heard of Wilhite's horse. He went to the Bartles store one day and asked Sam Bopst about the horse and Sam told him it could not be beaten and asked if he had anything that could run. He said, "I have a nag I gallop sometimes." A race was matched for six hundred yards and the race was to be run where Dewey, Oklahoma, is now located, four miles north of Bartlesville. When he arrived with his horse, it was very ordinary looking and was swaybacked. John McCallister, Sam Bopst and several others were placing their bets on the Wilhite horse, when Albert Curleyhead asked Frank Lenno, an Indian, which horse would win. Lenno pointed out some good points about the swayback and said it would win, however, he never bet on a horse race, not even his own horse. Curleyhead bet on the swayback and the others bet on the Wilhite horse. The owner of the swayback said he did not have any money but put up a shot gun and $5.00. The day of the race he had a big roll of bills and bet heavily. His jockey was a little Negro boy, and Albert Lane rode the Wilhite horse. When the old man brought his horse out it could hardly walk but when it was led out onto the track and the little Negro boy was seated in the saddle, the horse "flew." The swayback won and the local boys were a sorry bunch.

When I was about fourteen years old, I was herding cattle for George Brazee for ten cents a day. He had a horse-power threshing machine and did threshing here in Kansas. I had a little bald-faced pony that could step pretty lively, and I had been running a few races for tobacco and handkerchiefs. My father was a peculiar man and he did not approve of races, so I ran my pony secretly. Mr. Brazee was threshing for Joe Nels, south of Havana, Kansas, and matched a race for my pony with a fellow named Stafford. This race was run at a little place, Jayhawk, Kansas, which is not in existence now. The sunflowers were nine feet high and the August sun was fierce, but there were about two hundred there. My pony won the race and Jim Sippy, a heavy loser wanted it run over, but it was not.

I was working near Post Oak, north of Dewey and matched a race for my pony. I bet my Winchester against a cow and won but I did not take the cow, because of my secret from my father. J. C. Ross, a preacher and friend of our family, told my father about this race and one morning while I was grooming the pony my father came to the barn, he commented on the pony and asked what I would take for him. I told him Jack Johnson had offered me $100.00 for the pony and he advised me to take it. I did this but it was a big sacrifice for me to sell. I took the money home and gave it to my father and he bought cattle for me and this gave me my first start. My father then explained to me the reason he objected to horse races. Chief Journeycake owned a good horse at Leavenworth, Kansas, in the early days at the fort. He would not bet on a race, but would run his horse for the sport of the race. He matched a race with the soldiers at the fort and his horse won. After this the soldiers would borrow the horse and match races for it.

A man named Walker camped near the fort one night. He had a team of poor horses, chain harness, and old dilapidated wagon with a cultivator tied behind, and an extra horse which followed behind. That evening he went to the fort and engaged in a game of cards and chuck-a-luck.[4] He told

---

4. Chuck-a-luck is played using three dice thrown from a metal hourglass-shaped container.

them he had a race horse and would like to match a race if they had anything that could run. They borrowed the Journeycake horse and made up a purse of about $700.00 for their horse. He told them he did not have any money but when the betting started he had a big roll of bills. Two days before the race, two strangers arrived at the fort and looked both horses over but said nothing. The Journeycake horse won the race by a fraction and the soldiers wanted to match another race. He told them he would talk it over with them the next morning. When they went to the camp the next day, all they found was a pile of ashes and the old cultivator. It was the soldiers' opinion that the strangers owned the horse and furnished the money for the old man to bet.

Jake Bartles raised the first wheat in this vicinity and in the early nineties he raised a bumper crop. Colonel Norwood lived on the Bartles place and raised wheat on an extensive plan. N. F. Carr was really the founder of the mill site in Old Bartlesville. He tried to establish a mill in the bend of Caney River and cut a tunnel across the neck of the bend, but soon gave it up. Jake Bartles saw the advantages of this location and in 1877 built a dam across the river and established the mill. He bought a quarry on Liza Creek, north of the mound in what is now west Bartlesville. I helped haul rock from this quarry for the dam about the same time I herded cattle for Mr. Brazee. I learned to chew tobacco, swear and shoot while working for these men. I could shoot a horse fly from the back of a steer with a rifle and never touch the steer.

The wheat buyers were Johnstone and Keeler, Bartles and Bradley and Bryant. Jesse Overlees and Albert Rupart established a lumber yard at the corner of Third Street and Cherokee Avenue, which is the present location of the Overlees-Kruse Lumber Yard.

My father was a member of the Cherokee Council and when the Indians wanted the land allotted he opposed it. I remember we were at the Fourth of July picnic on the Joe Parker place on Brush Creek, north of Dewey and the question of the allotment was discussed. My father was asked his views and he discarded his coat and tie, climbed up on a wagon and made a wonderful speech. He told them the restriction would be lifted in a few years, and the Indians would soon sell their land and in a few years they would be penniless. He spoke of the future for the younger generation and his predictions have come true. In conclusion of his speech, he told them if they still wanted the land allotted, he would help them. The land was sectionized and each given his allotment. Out of the eight hundred Delawares who received allotments, there are only about two hundred who have their homes now. The registered Delaware Indians had the same rights as the native born Cherokee and received one hundred acres as their allotment. My allotment was eighty acres north of the Caney River where the Cudahy Refinery Plant now stands. If the land was exceptionally good, the allotment was not so large as the valuation was higher. Our agency was located at Muskogee, Oklahoma, where it is still in existence.

My father came to the Indian Territory with the first Delaware Indians from Wyandotte County, Kansas. The Delawares are divided into three clans, the Turtle, Wolf and Turkey Clans. We belong to the Turtle Clan. The Wyandotte, Seneca, Muncy [Munsee], and Stockbridge Indians settled in the Indian Territory about the same time the Delawares came here.

In 1890, I married Jane Chapman, a white woman, and we have three children, one daughter and two sons living.

I am a strong believer in dreams and I believe if something happens, though many miles away, it will be revealed to us in a dream. I have dreamed things concerning my family and I know the dreams have come true. I believe when the eyelid flutters it is a warning of some unexpected happening.

My father owned the building on Second and Johnstone, where the Malthy Brothers Hardware Store now stands, two buildings on the northwest corner of Second Street and Dewey Avenue, one building east of the Elks Club on Second Street, and the vacant lot at Second and Osage. He sold the Capital Hill Addition of 55 acres for $55,000.00. He added the Armstrong first, second, third, fourth additions to Bartlesville. My father was uneducated and signed his name with an X but he was a very intelligent man.

I have some silver ornaments worn by my grandmother over a hundred years ago. They are about the size of a silver dollar, and she wore six down the outside of each legging. My father gave these ornaments to me in 1903. I think there are two of them left and my daughter has them now. I have a Bible printed in the Delaware language.

Date of death not found.

This interview was done by field worker Alene D. McDowell.
The original document appears on pages 430–443 in volume 12 of
the Indian Pioneer History Project.

Rosa Stephenson Conner

Born October 3, 1866
Date of Interview: May 11, 1937

My name is Rosa Stephenson Conner. I live at 243 South Fifth Street, Vinita, Oklahoma. I was born October 3, 1866, at Wyandotte, Kansas. My father, a Delaware Indian, was named Andrew Stephenson. My mother's name was Mary Tiblow, also a Delaware Indian. My grandfather's name was Henry Tiblow, a Delaware Indian, who spoke seven different languages, English and French and five Indian languages. All of the above and their families came to the Indian Territory in 1868, with the Delaware tribe of Indians and bought an equal right with the Cherokee tribe of Indians.

My grandfather, Henry Tiblow, bought the famous old brick building, built and owned by Johnson Thompson, before the Civil War from Mr. Thompson, himself. It was located on the south bank of the Grand River, in Delaware District, Cherokee Nation, now about seven miles southwest of the present site of Ketchum, in Mayes County, Oklahoma. My father, Andrew Stephenson, bought land and settled a mile and a half east of the old brick building. James Ketchum, another Delaware, who came here with us, step-father of my husband, bought the other old brick house, on the north side of the Grand River. It was owned by Dr. Joe Thompson, son of Johnson Thompson, who lives at Tahlequah. [See also the T. Wyman Thompson interview for further references to this house. Page 35.]

Johnson Thompson, an early-day merchant who operated a store in Delaware District for years before Vinita or any other town was established in the northern part of the Indian Territory, built the two brick houses for a store and residence. They were built two story, and were very stylish houses in their day. During the [Civil] war the Thompsons abandoned the places and went to the Choctaw Nation and stayed for the duration of the war, but came back and retained the places after the war. While they were gone the houses stood idle and anyone who came along camped there, and after the slaves were freed, the slaves camped there in great droves.

Thompson sold the places to the above two men [Henry Tiblow and James Ketchum], who were the sole owners up to the time of their death. The places then went to their heirs, and just a few years back were sold to the Hydro Electric Dam Company, and will go under water when the Grand River Dam is built, near Ketchum. T. C. Bowling, of Pryor, Mayes County, Oklahoma, is now custodian of the two places. Several years ago a cyclone struck these two houses and blew the top story off. The one on the south side of the river was torn down to the first story and re-covered, and made into a bungalow, but the one on the north side was so badly wrecked by the storm that it was never rebuilt. The bricks were sold to Henry L. Crouch, Vinita, R. F. D. 3, who built a beautiful brick bungalow out of them. The brick used in these two houses were made on the ground where the houses were built.

My grandfather, Henry Tiblow, was a famous interpreter among the Delaware tribe. There was a large settlement of Delawares in Nowata County, then Cooweescoowee District, and he was gone most of his time, acting as interpreter among his people. They sent him to Washington in that capacity on several different occasions. He died in 1878 and was buried in Nowata County. [Note: Henry Tiblow also ran a ferry on the Kansas River for a time. The present town of Bonner Springs, Kansas, was originally named Tiblow.]

There were no schools on the south side of Grand River, as the hills soon set in and there was nothing but hills and mountains. My sister Mary and I rode horse-back to school six or seven miles, and we had to cross Grand River to get to a school they called "Contention School." The teachers were most all men those days. Three of them I remember were Mr. Davenport, Mr. Thompson and John E. (Red Cloud) Duncan. Two of the women teachers were Ninnie Cornatzer and Rachel Rogers. When the river was up, we boarded with the family of Robert Daniel, at one time Assistant Chief of the Cherokee Nation. A boy by the name of John Barbee, who stayed with my grandfather, went to school with us and helped us get across the river. In later years a ferry boat was put in and we crossed the river on the ferry boat.

In 1884 I was married to Silas Conner[1] [born 1860], step-son of James Ketchum, for whom the town of Ketchum is named. We are the parents of two children; Oliver [born 1890] and Mamie [born 1888], the latter of whom married George Gay. My husband was a stock buyer and shipped his cattle and hogs to the Kansas City market. He died and was buried in the Ketchum cemetery.

There is a private cemetery on the old Ketchum place, where Mr. James Ketchum is buried, but his wife, who lived to be 111 years old, died after the place had been sold to the Hydro Electric Company for the Grand River dam (the whole place will go under water), so they buried her in the new Ketchum Cemetery, one mile east of the town of Ketchum.

Date of death not found.

Interview by James R. Caselowry. The original document appears on pages 208–212 in volume 2 of the Indian Pioneer History Project.

---

1. Silas Hamilton Conner was a grandson of Harry Hamilton Conner, the second son of Mekinges and William Conner. Harry was born about 1806 at the Conner trading post on the White River (west fork) in Indiana Territory.

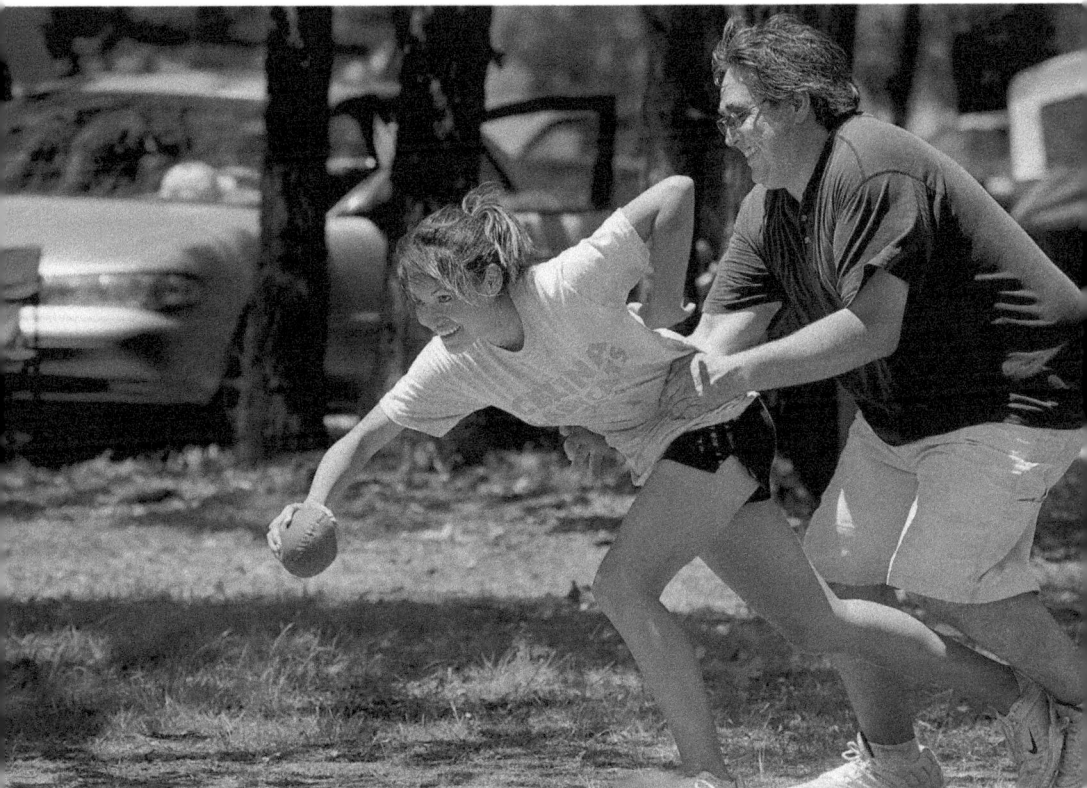

A vigorous game of Indian football pits women against men. Men can only move and score the soft, deerskin ball by kicking and on defense can only block. Women can do offense or defense in any way. Michael Gabbard attempts to stop his daughter Janeé from running with the ball. The women often win.

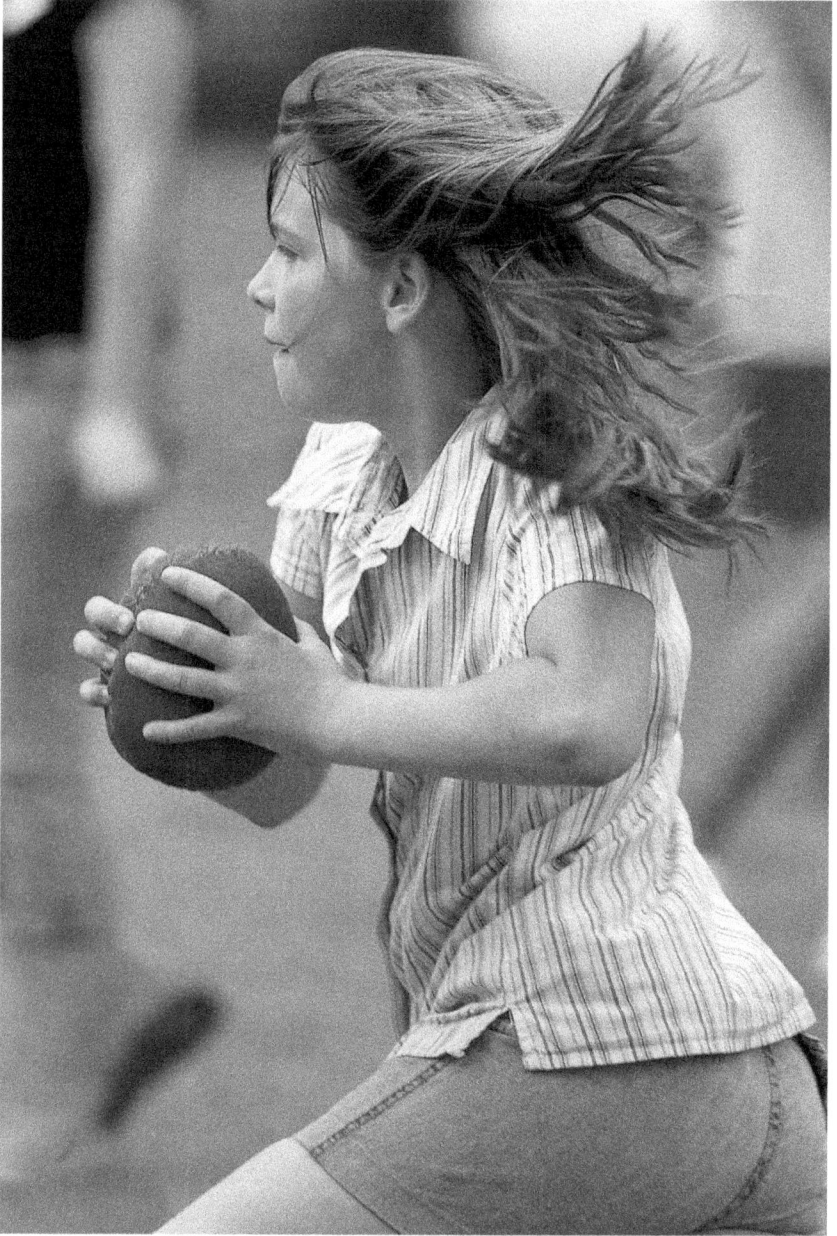

Indian football has moments of exciting bursts of speed. At other times, it looks much like a rugby scrum with many people trying to pry the ball away from whoever has it.

KATIE (WHITETURKEY) DAY (KA-TEL-MAH)

Born 1862
Date of Interview: April 21, 1937

Among the first to agree to move to the Indian Territory were the Delaware Indians and they purchased the right to settle in the Cherokee Nation and became citizens. I was among the Delaware Indians transferred to the Indian Territory from Wyandotte County, Kansas, in 1867, when I was five years old. I was born at Lawrence, Kansas, in 1862, where my parents lived until I was five years of age. At the time we were transferred to Indian Territory there were seven children in our family and there were two born after we came to this country. I had five brothers and three sisters.

[Interviewer's notes: Father, Simon Whiteturkey, a full-blood Delaware Indian, died near Bartlesville at the age of 48 years and is buried in the Silver Lake Cemetery south of Bartlesville. Mother's name not known. She was a full-blood Delaware, died near Bartlesville at the age of 74 years and is buried in the Silver Lake Cemetery.][1]

My father was known as Simon Whiteturkey but his name was really Whiteturkey Simon. After we were settled and started to school the teacher enrolled us as "Whiteturkey" and we have always been known by that name. My parents first settled at Baxter Springs, Kansas, when they were brought here from the east, then moved to Wyandotte County, near Lawrence [Kansas], then moved to Indian Territory. There were about twenty-five or thirty families brought to Indian Territory at the time we made the trip. We came in a hack or light weight carriage and some of the other families drove buggies, wagons, and ox-drawn wagons, and some were horseback. Our food supplies were transported in a large covered wagon drawn by six yoke of oxen. We would camp about noon and the supplies would not arrive until sundown. The oxen traveled very slow.

---

1. According to Cranor, Kik Tha We Nund, pp. 87–88, Simon was born about 1826 in Missouri, grew up in Kansas. He first married Much o loo thee, a daughter of Chief Anderson Sarcoxie. After she died in 1867, Simon married Much o loo thee's sister, Nah wah cum she (Carry), who was born in 1836 in Kansas, according to the Rolls. She died July 1912, known as "Grandma Whiteturkey," according to Cranor, Some Old Delaware Obituaries, p. 71.

A Delaware family named Wahooney[2] was with us, who had one child, a boy 19 years old. After we had eaten our noon meal, this boy rode away on his pony to look for some horses that had strayed away. It was snowing hard and when he was not back in camp early they thought he might have gotten lost. He was gone all afternoon and about sundown they heard a shot and his mother became worried. He did not return that night and early the next morning the men started to look for him. They found him not far from the camp, he had been robbed, scalped and stripped of his clothes by the Osage Indians. He was lying face down in the snow with a soldier's blue overcoat thrown over him. This was a gruesome sight and put a terrible fear in our little band for the safety of our lives. This boy was buried near the camp where we were stationed at the Forks of Caney Cemetery. He was the first person buried in this cemetery and it is the oldest cemetery in Washington County. It is located northwest of Bartlesville.

When we first arrived in the Indian Territory we camped in the Forks of Caney for a while, then moved about one and one-half miles south of Bartlesville on what is now Highway 75. My parents were each allotted 160 acres and my father bought a house for $30.00 and we lived in this house for a while, then moved to a log house, which had one long room, where we lived for two years. When I was 15 years old my father built a seven room frame house. We children all grew to manhood and womanhood in this house. Our family have lived on this place for sixty years and my brother George's widow, Mrs. Katie Whiteturkey, lives there at the present.

My father and brothers were prosperous farmers and they operated on a large scale. The land was exceptionally good and the corn and wheat crops were abundant. Corn sold for 15 cents per bushel. We also raised hogs, cattle, and horses. Our water supply was obtained from the little creek on our farm, Whiteturkey Creek. We used this water for drinking purposes and it was very cold. Our dining table was a long, homemade table and reached across the end of the room and we used tin cups and plates. We had chinaware, but seldom ever used it.

The closest trading post was Baxter Springs, Kansas, and it would take a week to make a trip for supplies. In 1873 Jacob Bartles came to Indian Territory and established a saw mill at Yellow Leaf Ford on the Verdigris river. Later he established a general store on the banks of Turkey Creek, then moved to Silver Lake. A few years later when he saw Nelson Carr trying to

---

2. Julia Hall, page 21, also mentions a Wah hooney family. They were not the same family as that of George Washington, but perhaps were somehow related.

establish a flour mill in the bend of the Caney River, where to get power it was only necessary to build a dam across and cut a sluiceway across the short neck of the bend, he realized this was a favorable location for a town site. He established a store and flour mill and later a blacksmith shop on this location and this was our first real trading post.

I received my early education in a little Cherokee Indian schoolhouse located near Silver Lake, which schoolhouse was later used as a Baptist church, known as the Delaware Baptist Church, now Silver Lake Baptist Church; however, this church is now located a mile east of the original church. Mrs. Carrie Overlees was one of my teachers. I was later sent to a boarding school at Baxter Springs, Kansas, and completed my meager education. We had very little education in those days.

Our clothes were all handmade and the women and girls' dresses were made to fit tight in the waist with skirts gathered full. The Indians had lots of money, because they had no place to spend it. We paid $10.00 a hundred for flour and $6.00 a hundred for meal. My brothers would go to Osage County on hunting trips and stay for a week or ten days and would bring great quantities of fresh venison, quail, and wild turkeys.

My brother, Albert Whiteturkey, was married to Jennie Johnson for eight years and after their separation she married a Cherokee Indian named Gilstrap who was an outlaw. After he was killed, she married Ernest Lewis, another outlaw, who was killed Statehood Day in Bartlesville, and then she married Emmett Dalton a few years later. Emmett was the youngest of the notorious "Dalton gang." The Dalton boys used to camp near our place and have eaten with us many times. They were always very friendly and nice with our family.

In 1888 I was married to James Day, a full-blood Delaware, at the Alluwe Baptist Church, by Reverend Richard Adams [William Adams, the father of Richard, was the minister]. My allotment was located south of Bartlesville, Cherokee Nation, and our first home was a log house built on my allotment about two and one-half miles south of Bartlesville on what is now Highway 75. This house was on the west side of the road and stood there many years, until someone burned it a few years ago. We lived in this house a number of years, then built a seven room house on the east side of the road and about one-half mile south of the old house where I now live. I have lived in this house for twenty-seven years and I still own 80 acres of my allotment where this house is located. When we built this house, the land was not laid out in sections and when the land was surveyed my house is located about one-quarter mile east of Highway 75 and faces the highway, the road running east and west is on the south side of my house. Our family consisted of seven children, all deceased except two. My husband died many years ago and is buried in the Silver Lake Cemetery, located about one mile west of my home.

The first wagon bridge was a swinging bridge across Caney River, located on my place about the same location as the bridge on State Highway 23 now. This is one mile west of U.S. Highway 75. There is a log house located on the banks of Little Caney River, west of Copan where we used to hold camp meetings for three or four weeks. It was about 15 miles to this house and it would take us all day to make the trip. This house still stands in the same location.

One day Mr. Day and I went to the Bartles store for supplies and a Delaware, Frank Lenno, was loading his gun to kill Gilstrap, the outlaw, who was reported coming to the store. Mr. Day tried to keep down trouble and when he saw Lenno was determined and his efforts to reason with him failed he took our baby and ran out of the store out of firing range. I also ran for cover and hid behind a barrel. When Gilstrap came into the store Lenno shot him, killing him instantly. This happened about one year after the store was opened.

I do not know much about the Osage Indians because they were not friendly with the other tribes, but I remember when an Osage died the mourners would face the east and cry before sunup.

When I was about fifteen years of age, as services were being held in a log church at Silver Lake, Frank Rogers and George Shelley, white men, and an Osage named Akin and a Cherokee named Elmer Brown attacked the church, killing John Sarcoxie, a Delaware, one of the guards. Immediately the whole congregation grabbed their firearms and pursued the invaders. Rogers was killed outright in a running fight by Bill Halfmoon. Shelley and Akin were captured and Brown made his escape. They were all drunk when they came looking for trouble. George Keeler hauled Rogers' body away and buried it. The two prisoners were taken in charge by the tribe and, of course, executed. What the manner of execution was or what became of their bodies is not known to this day, except perhaps by some member of the tribe who would never tell.

We had many exciting things happen in those days, we had lots of hardships and privations but we were happy. My children have their homes on their allotments near me and although I live alone I see them every day.

[Comments by Alene D. McDowell, field worker conducting the interview: Mrs. Day is very jolly and interesting and, in spite of her advanced years, seems to be hale and hearty. She remarked to the field worker she would like to walk to town, a distance of three miles, with her. Mrs. Day has passed her 74th milestone but is very active for one of her years. Mrs. Day gives us this story from her heart and enjoys talking about the early days and wants to help the younger generation understand the hardships of their forefathers, the builders of Oklahoma. She gave her name in Delaware as Ka-tel-mah Day.]

All senses are involved with the making of fry bread. Each tribe has its identifying way of making fry bread. Winning the competition is an honor, but with winning goes the responsibility of hosting the competition the next year.

A song showing the sense of humor of the Delaware rewards fry bread competition winners. Usually a new verse is added every year.

THE FRY BREAD SONG

INDIAN PEOPLE LOVE THAT FRY BREAD
YOU ARE THE CHAMPION, FRY BREAD CHAMPION
HOW DID YOU DO IT, WE KNOW YOU CHEATED
YOU PAID OFF THE JUDGES, WE SAW YOU DO IT
QUIT YOUR BRAGGEN, GO BACK TO YOUR CAMP
YOU CALL THAT FRY BREAD, WE CALLEM DOORSTOPS
WHO THE HELL MADE THIS, IT STUCK IN MY THROAT
DON'T DRINK WATER, YOU'LL GO TO SWELLEN
ALL YOU LOSERS, QUIT YOUR BITCHEN

Katie Whiteturkey Day died May 1940, at age 78. She is buried at Silver Lake Cemetery in the Delaware tribal burial ground. She was survived by a daughter, Nora Layton; a son, Clarence; a brother, Sam Whiteturkey; and three grandchildren and one great-grandchild, all of Bartlesville; and one sister, Mrs. Lillie Fugate of Dewey. See Cranor, Some Old Delaware Obituaries, p. 23.

Interview by Alene D. McDowell. The original document appears on pages 471–479 in volume 2 of the Indian Pioneer History Project.

Mary Gene Galloway congratulates her friend Oleta Mahan after learning they are the 42nd Delaware Fry Bread Champions. Ella Pace and Annette Ketchum are cheering them on.

Oleta Mahan and Mary Gene Galloway are subjected to the fry bread song.

JULIA A. HALL

Born 1852, in Kansas
Date of Interviews: first interview, May 16, 1937;
second interview, July 16, 1937
Daughter of George Washington; husband was William Hall.

FIRST INTERVIEW

How well I can remember how my people would send all their young boys away out in the woods after they reached a certain size, as we went by size in those days, not by age. The older men would teach the young boys how to shoot bows and arrows and how to build fires by using flint rock or by rubbing two sticks together, and how to cook their game on camp fires and we would have our Indian worships or our stomp dances, for the stomp dances were what we call our worshiping God [Big House Church], and we looked upon those dances as great things and I believe the people in those days took the stomp dances more seriously than they take the churches in the present times.

At those stomp dances the men would pick out all the boys who were large enough and get them together and give them all a good talking to and tell them what they were to do and tell them that the older men were going to send them away to make warriors out of them, and they then would send the boys into the woods and sometimes they would be gone as long as six months at a time. Then at any time any one of these boys had a dream, he was to come in and tell the older people his dream and they in turn would tell the meaning of the dream; it was said that these boys saw the white man coming ten years before he came. The older people in those days believed that after a boy reached a certain size he would not have these dreams and that the Great White Father would not give them visions; then they would call the boys to [them] and they were called warriors. At any time one of these boys could not make his own way out in the woods and stay until he was called in, he was called a poor warrior and was not cared for even by his own people.

SECOND INTERVIEW

It was in the year of 1853 that, one day in September, a man by the name of John C. Fremont started from West Port, Missouri, a place near

Kansas City, Missouri, to make a trip back to California for the government.[1] In fact, he was trying to blaze out a trail to California, and took along about three hundred people. In the group he took ten Delaware Indians as scouts and hunters. Here are the names of those he took along: George Washington, Andy Miller, James Harrison, Wa-hoo-ney, John Moses, Jacob Eneas, Good Traveller, Solomon Everett, John Smith and James Wolf.

The following is a true copy of the agreement that Mr. Fremont drew up and which was signed by him and a man by the name of Jim Secondine. Secondine was then chief of the Delawares at the time this trip was made.[2]

The Agreement is as follows and stated that Jim Secondine was to furnish John C. Fremont with ten Delaware hunters all good men:

> *Westport, Missouri, September 16, 1853.*
>
> *I have this day made arrangements through Jim Secondine by which ten Delaware hunters (good men) are to accompany me on my journey to California and back to this country. The ten Delawares are to furnish their own animals also, and are each to be paid two dollars ($2.00) a day. They are to provide themselves with good animals, and if any of the animals should die upon the road, I am to pay for the loss. They will, of course, be furnished by me with ammunition and saddles which are furnished to them by me, all at my cost.*
>
> *—Signed "John C. Fremont"*

[The following is a combination of remarks inserted by the interviewer into the continued narrative by Julia Hall.]

The people who made the trip had some dreadful times before they got back to this country. They were snow-bound in from fifteen to thirty feet of snow, and almost starved to death. They would be sitting around the fire and would get so hungry that they would take out their hunting knives and cut a piece out of the tops of their boots, and put it on a stick and hold it over the fire and cook it a little and eat it. They even killed some of their horses

---

1. An account of this trip and the incredible hardships Fremont's men endured are chronicled by S. N. Carvalho (Carvalho, 1954), a photographer who accompanied them as far as Utah. Carvalho states ten Delaware accompanied Fremont but mentions only the names of Captain Wolff, Washington, Welluchas, Soloman, and Moses. Julia Hall states that George Washington's original name was Wa-hoo-ney, but there was a separate and different Delaware by the name of Wa-hoo-ney on this trip and on the Delaware rolls.

2. Capt. Ketchum was principal chief at this time. James Secondine was not listed as a chief, but a sketch of him made on his 1845–46 journey with Fremont labels him as "Head War Chief of the Delaware Tribe" (Cranor, n.d. 68).

and mules and ate them. A lot of the animals starved or froze to death before they got to their destination. In fact, they got through the trip with just one white mule which belonged to Wa-hoo-ney. This man, Wah-hoo-ney, is father to Mrs. Julia Hall and he had no other name than Wa-hoo-ney until, however, Fremont named him George Washington, also the name of Mrs. Hall's brother, because he was a good scout, and a brave man. [See Cyrus Washington interview, page 41 for another account of this name.] Mrs. Hall said she well remembered her father telling of one time on the trip that he ran a buffalo into camp and killed it right in front of Mr. Fremont. Another time they were all snow-bound and out of something to eat, and Wa-hoo-ney and three other men went out and were trying to kill something to eat when they found a large cave. In this cave, they found three big black bears, but all they had taken along was their war clubs and hunting knives. Each one of the men would take his turn in going into the cave and killing a bear. After they had killed all three of the bears, they all had a good feast. Then they went back to camp and told the rest of the people what they had killed. Most of the men folks broke out in a run to reach the cave and get the meat. They brought it into camp and that night everybody had a good feed. Mr. Fremont was a good man for they never ate a meal without his returning thanks. When Mr. Fremont and his crowd got to California most all of the people were so hungry that the first thing Mr. Fremont did was to go to a hotel and order a bunch of chickens killed. He wanted a pot of soup made, and while they were killing the chickens in the back yard of the hotel some of the men folks would lay down and drink the blood from off the ground.

This is a copy out of a paper at Fairland, of the death of George Washington or Wa-hoo-ney at his residence near Fairland, Indian Territory, at three o'clock AM, October 24, 1892:

"George Washington, Delaware Chief, and for years a scout on the plains. Mr. Washington was General Fremont's chief scout and guide when he made his first trip across the plains away back in the forty's. He was one of the Lenne lenapa of Cooper, in his Leather Stocking series of novels, and has now gone over to join his old commander on the other shore. He died of old age, having been blind for years. Deceased requested that his old unique tomahawk and pipe combined, weasel skin tobacco pouch and knife be buried with him and his feet turned westward."

Mrs. Hall died in 1942.

Interviews by Alfred F. Hicks at Nowata, Oklahoma. The original documents appear on pages 68–69 in volume 60 and pages 279–283 in volume 63 of the Indian Pioneer History Project.

Whitney Thomas and Hannah Sears receive their first eagle feather fans made by their grandparents, former chief Dee Ketchum and tribal council member Annette Ketchum.

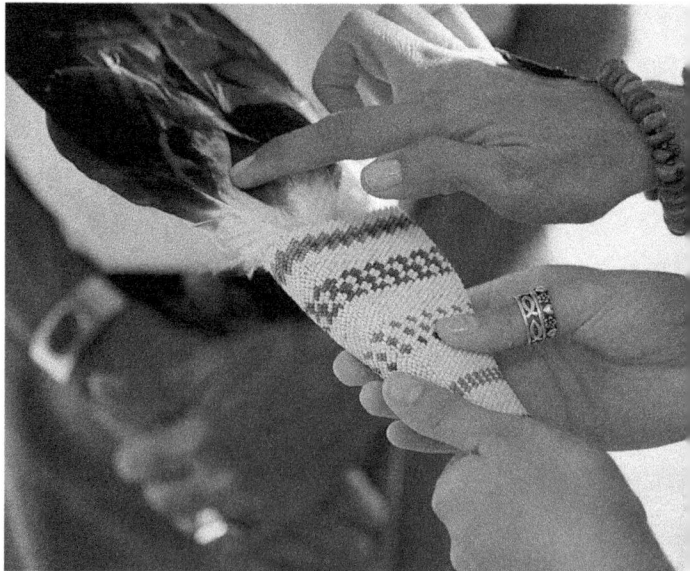

SOL C. KETCHUM

Born January 22, 1861
Date of Interview: June 9, 1937, in Vinita, Oklahoma

My name is Sol C. Ketchum. I was born January 22, 1861, in Wyandotte County, Kansas. I now live at Vinita, R. F. D. S., Oklahoma.

My father's name was Lewis Ketchum. He was born in 1808 on the Delaware Reservation in Ohio, near Sandusky. My grandfather's name was George Ketchum. He also lived on the Delaware Reservation in Pennsylvania, but died among the Delawares on the Caney River near Bartlesville, at the age of 100 years. My father lived to be 96 years old, and died on his allotment ten miles southeast of Vinita, Craig County, in 1904.[1]

My mother's maiden name was Elizabeth Zeigler, half Delaware and half German.

While my father was growing up he lived near Sandusky, Ohio; from there he moved to White River, near Springfield, Missouri; and from there to Wyandotte, Kansas. My father, a three-quarter blood Delaware Indian, could talk very little English in his younger days, and talked brokenly up to the time of his death. I believe he was the greatest hunter and trapper that the United States has ever produced. He was very venturesome in his younger days and started out selling furs to the famous Choteau brothers at St. Louis when but a mere boy. He began learning the use of traps and guns early in the nineteenth century, and made it his life's study. His most valuable fur was the beaver, and he made a specialty of trapping beavers. The Choteaus later established a trading post at West Port, Missouri, about six miles south of the present site of Kansas City, but years before there was any town there, and later moved south to the present site of Salina, Oklahoma, where a stone marker was recently placed commemorating the establishment of the first trading post in the Indian Territory.

Nothing could suit my father more than the exploring of new territory and, all alone, he followed the trading posts down into the Indian Territory long before he came here to settle years afterward. Mustering a herd of five

---

1. On the Delaware Census, February 15, 1862, George Ketchum's age is listed as 75 years, and Lewis Ketchum's age is given as 50 years (Arellano, 1996, pp. 101–102).

pack ponies at Salina, he set out to the southwest, exploring all the small rivers and streams, and finally winding up at Fort Worth, Texas, but finding very few beaver. He had just about made up his mind that he was too far south for this kind of game, and was fixing to start back to Salina when the unexpected happened.

It was about 1848 and General Winfield Scott, with a large army of government soldiers, was marching from the north down the "Old Military Trail" into Mexico, where the United States was at war with Mexico. They captured my father and against his protest made a government scout of him and sent him on ahead of the army as one of the government scouts. He remained with them five days but, on the night of the fifth day out, he slipped away and came back to where the Grand River empties into the Arkansas. It was here he decided to find out where that big river went and he set out to the northwest, following the Arkansas River, and trapping as he went.

On his trip to the northwest my father encountered many wild tribes of Indians. He tried to evade them. They would take after him in great droves but, being armed with a good rifle, my father said they quit chasing him after he had shot one or two of them, as they were armed with only bows and arrows. Others of the tribes tried to be friendly but were very treacherous and mean. He stayed among them for nearly two years and learned to talk some of their languages. One tribe offered to bet him a pony that he could not throw their champion wrestler, whom they called the "devil." He bet them and threw the devil, and won their pony. Then they wanted to bet him three ponies he could not out-run their champion foot-runner. "How far?" asked Father. "Three miles," replied the Indians. "Horse can't run that far. I run two hundred yards—5 horses," my father told them, and they bet him and lost their five ponies.

This made them so mad that they tried to slip up on him that night and kill him, but he saw them and slipped away, and went to a government post several miles away and reported the loss of his guns, traps and furs. The soldiers went with him the next day and got his things, and told him he had better get out of there as those were bad Indians and would kill anyone not a member of their tribe. They sent soldiers to accompany my father out of the danger zone. He went back to Wyandotte, Kansas, where he organized a company of twenty Delaware Indians and went back to where he had been, thinking with twenty men armed with rifles, the whole Indian tribes could be whipped.

The Indians seemed to be friendly when they got back and my father and his party trapped for some time and entered into all kinds of jest with the Indian tribes. They measured their great men by acts of bravery, and it was possibly this that brought on more trouble with the Indians. To beat them at their own game my father slipped up on a buffalo while it was asleep, and cut the buffalo's tail off. He showed the Indians the tail as evidence that he had performed the feat. They seemed to be very jealous of this feat and that night they attacked my father's camp and bushwhacked and killed every man in his party. He escaped by crawling on his stomach until he was out of their reach and the next day made his way back to West Port, Kansas, where the Choteaus were still located, and retired to a farm in Wyandotte, Kansas, where he lived until 1880.

In 1880 he went before the National Council at Tahlequah and paid $287.00 per head for an equal right with the Cherokees, and the following year, in 1881, he settled on a farm ten miles south-east of Vinita, near the town of Ketchum, where two of his brothers were living. They were James and George Ketchum,[2] and it was from these three brothers that the town of Ketchum received its name.

When my father was hunting and trapping in the West he kept three buffalo robes with him, with which he made his bed at night. He said that no matter how cold the weather he could keep warm. When he settled in Craig county, the Delaware district, Indian Territory, there was plenty of game, and he kept right on hunting. His principal meat while hunting in the West was buffalo, but since moving to the Territory he had to content himself with deer, turkey, prairie chicken and the smaller game. However, he said that he had tasted every kind of meat there was, but the worst meat he ever tried was wolf.

As amusement for his old days he got himself a pack of fox hounds and chased deer, fox and wolves. He loved the music that a pack of dogs made and usually kept one small dog with a fine voice that, he said, was his "tenor" singer. To catch a deer quickly, he got himself two big wolf hounds (greyhounds). These two dogs would catch the deer on short run, and bay him until the old hunter and his fox hounds caught up, when the deer would either be shot or the dogs would kill him.

My father had an old mule that he rode during his last hunting days, that could swim any stream and if the deer plunged into the river and swam across, his dogs and the old mule with its rider would plunge right in after him. Like the hounds, he would run clean out of the country to get a deer and carry the deer back behind his saddle. On the day he died, he made a date with Dr. M. F. Fortmer of Vinita, to go squirrel hunting with him as soon as he got well. He is now sleeping in the happy hunting ground where

2. There is no record of Lewis having a brother named George Ketchum, so this must be an interview error. Sol Ketchum was probably referring to Lewis's brother, James, and to Lewis's father, George, who with Lewis were the three elder Ketchums in the area. See T. Wyman Thompson interview on page 36. The town of Ketchum was actually named for Elizabeth Ketchum, widow of James Ketchum, who was the oldest resident.

there is no wild tribe to disturb him. He is buried on the old homestead where he settled in 1881, ten miles southeast of Vinita.

When my father sold our homestead in Kansas and came to the Indian Territory, I was just 22 years old and decided I would sow a few wild oats before settling down in a new country. We got $50.00 per acre for our land in Wyandotte County, Kansas, and I took my part and went to Kansas City where I trained for a prize fighter. I got good enough that a promoter took me up, and after a little more training he became my manager and we began matching fights.

My manager's name was Billie Morris of Kansas City and he matched me first with John P. Clow of Pittsburgh, Pennsylvania. Our managers got into a squabble and this fight was called off. My next match was with Paddy Dunn, Champion heavyweight of Kansas. He weighed in at 185 pounds and I weighed in at 156, which put me in the middleweight class. The fight was staged at Vinita and I won in the eighth round and was declared the heavyweight champion of Kansas.

My next match was with Billy McCarty of Pittsburgh, Pennsylvania. This fight was staged at the old Fairgrounds in Vinita, and I won it in 15 rounds. My next match was with Ed Burk, champion middleweight of Arkansas. While in training for this fight, Burk married a rich woman at Fort Smith where the fight was to be staged and she induced him to call off the fight and retire from the ring. My manager then matched me with Billie Corn, the champion prize fighter of Old Mexico. We fought this battle at Choctaw Park, Fort Smith, Arkansas. It was the hardest fight I ever had in my life. That man nearly broke my neck before I got my Indian up enough to hold my own against him. He was a real fighter, and had set in to K. O. me in the first few rounds. I soon had both of his eyes bunged up [battered] so that he couldn't see very well, and in the sixth round I broke his nose and mashed his mouth so badly that he was a mass of blood at the end of the round. I knocked him out in the seventh round. A reporter for the St. Louis Republic was present and had me issue a challenge, through his paper, to any Indian in America, and when none appeared I was declared the champion Indian fighter of the world, and retired.

Cockie Brown, a Cherokee fighter from Pueblo, Colorado, and I decided to put on an exhibition fight at Muskogee, but as both of us were Indians we had to get the permission of Leo K. Bennett, then Indian Agent for the Five Civilized Tribes. Bennett told us we could fight all right, but if either of us got to hitting too hard, he was going to shoot us. We fought a few rounds and soon forgot all about Bennett's caution and were soon pecking away like a rivet welder, when Old Leo raised up from a ring side seat, drew a big old 45 from his holster, and I thought sure he was going to make his word good, but it was only a gentle reminder.

[Comments by J. R. Carselowry, field worker: When I called on this man, Sol C. Ketchum, now 76 years old, I found him plowing corn on the old homestead where his father settled in 1881. He is the only child left living out of five. He had two grown boys living with him. One was hoeing out in the orchard and the other was sitting around the house.

I asked his wife if this grown boy sitting in the house couldn't go and plow for him, and let him give me his story. She said that they couldn't plow to please him, and that he never let them plow corn for him; but he did, long enough to give me this story.

Sol Ketchum has been a powerful man, physically, all of his life, and in a way has kept up his athletics. I had a young man, who was very strong, and looked to be much of a man, tell me a short time ago that he would just as soon a mule would kick him as to have Sol Ketchum hit him one good lick.

His father lived to be 96 years old and died in 1926 near the town of Ketchum in Mayes County.[3]]

Sol C. Ketchum died in 1945.

Interview by J. R. (James R.) Caselowry. The original document appears on pages 12–23 in volume 61 of the Indian Pioneer History Project.

---

3. This is at odds with the statement by Sol C. Ketchum at the start of the interview.

Dee Ketchum and Ray Gonyea lead the procession for the 2005 dedication of the new wing of the Eiteljorg Museum of American Indians and Western Art in Indianapolis, Indiana. Mike Pace sings and plays the water drum. A blessing ceremony using smoke from burning red cedar rises from the pot Gonyea carries. The smoke purifies the new structure.

ELIZA JOURNEYCAKE MINSHALL

Born April 16, 1871, near Vinita, Oklahoma
Date of Interview: April 11, 1938, rural route 11 (Box 64),
Tulsa, Oklahoma
[The interviewer, Mary Dorward, created a narrative in her
own words from the words spoken by Mrs. Minshall.]

Eliza Journeycake Minshall is the daughter of Robert Jordan Journeycake and Mary E. Randall Journeycake, Delaware Indians, both of whom are now deceased. Eliza was born at the family home along Mustang Creek about ten miles east of Vinita, Oklahoma, where she passed her girlhood. She attended school at Car-le-owe along Mustang Creek, later at the Quapaw mission school near Miami, and at Bacone College at Muskogee at the time when Professor Bacone himself was in charge of the school.

Mrs. Minshall assisted in the enrolling of the Six Nations at Tulsa, Nowata, and Bartlesville, Oklahoma. She has a copy of the list of all members of the Nations who came from New York down to Kansas and then to Indian Territory. She also has a copy of her credentials entitling her to enrollment among the Six Nations, and to work on the enrolling, which began in 1828.

Mrs. Minshall was allotted land five miles northwest of Centralia, Oklahoma. She, with her family, had been living there previous to allotment and before Centralia had been established. She owned a mile square between Centralia and Mills but had to surrender all except eighty acres for herself and allotments for her children.

Mrs. Minshall's maternal grandmother, Eliza Sneed, married John Randall and had several children. John Randall served in the war with Mexico and in the Civil War, being enlisted with Company A, 12th Kansas Infantry, and serving as teamster for the Army. At one time Randall was en route to Fort Gibson with the rest of his company. He was driving a team of mules and in crossing a river at a ford one of the mules got down in the water. Randall got down from his wagon to see what was the matter with the mule when suddenly it got up and in doing so knocked Randall down into the water, injuring him severely. He contracted pneumonia from the exposure, went back to Kansas, and died. After Randall's death Mrs. Randall managed the farm herself, doing her plowing with oxen, and growing corn which she herself took to mill.

Prior to her marriage with John Randall, Eliza Sneed had been married to George W. Hendricks, but Hendricks had disappeared, and his wife, supposing him dead, had married Randall and reared a large family, in the meantime moving with the tribe from New York to Kansas. Her children were all in school at the Pratt mission in Kansas,[1] when one day, while out playing, they saw a strange man leading a horse past the school. He went up the road a short distance and stopped. The children paid no attention to the man but went on into school and after school went home. There to their surprise, they found the strange man whom they had seen passing the schoolhouse. It was George Hendricks who had returned to his wife.

Mrs. Randall had recognized her former husband instantly, greeting him with, "Well, George." Since Randall had already been dead for some years, Mrs. Randall remarried her first husband. During all the years he had been out in California prospecting for gold.

According to the records of the Six Nations Eliza Sneed Randall Hendricks in 1839 was thirty-five years old.

Mrs. Minshall tells of the marriage ceremony among the Delawares in the days before they came to Kansas. One mother would say to another mother, "I'll give you so much meat" (or so much calico, or some other commodity) for your girl for my boy," and that was all. If the offer was agreeable and accepted the two young people lived together from that time on.

Mrs. Minshall has a copy of the Will of Captain Ketchum, her great-grandfather. The original will has been sent to Washington, D.C. It is dated October 20, 1856, and on it Captain Ketchum, who was chief of the Delawares, names his nephew James Conner (Indian name Ah-lar-a-chech) to be his successor as chief.

Mrs. Minshall also has an old family Bible containing recorded dates as early as 1839. She has a quilt block pieced by her grandmother, Eliza Randall, about 1865. She has an old Seth Thomas clock which her uncle brought from Kansas when the Delawares migrated from there.

[Interviewer's note with the original interview: The Six Nations were the Mohawk, Oneida, Onondaga, Cayuga, and Seneca. The Oneida had adopted the Stockbridge and Munsee, who had, according to Mrs. Minshall, previously adopted the Delawares.]

Mrs. Minshall died in 1965.

Interview by Mary Dorward. The original document appears on pages 310–313 in volume 108 of the Indian Pioneer History Project.

---

1. Baptist Mission headed by Rev. John G. Pratt, west of present-day Kansas City, Kansas.

Isaac Secondine

Born 1874
Father: Fillmore Secondine, oldest son of James Secondine,
whose father was Sacondyan, a son of Chief William Anderson
Mother: Rachel Logan
Date of Interview: April 28, 1937, in Delaware, Oklahoma

DELAWARE INDIAN PAYMENTS IN INDIAN TERRITORY
AS TOLD BY ISAAC SECONDINE

These payments for the Cooweescoowee District were held at Vinita, Chelsea and Alluwe, Oklahoma. This was in the years of 1865 to 1887. They were held at first at Vinita and Chelsea until the Delaware decided that they could use the church house at Alluwe, Oklahoma, as a payment ground. This church house is located ½ mile north and ¼ mile east of Alluwe, Oklahoma; toward the last of these payments, this place was used altogether.

The amount each person received at these payments were from $30.00 to $40.00 dollars a head, and the payments were held every six months. It always took about a week to complete a payment. Hijacking in those days was an unknown thing. I remember one time there was about $150,000 in cash on the payment ground at one time. This money was hauled from Coffeyville, Kansas, in a buggy pulled by two horses, and there were only two men along with the money, and the distance was 35 miles.

One of these men was an Indian policeman by the name of Bill Foreman. Mr. Foreman always came to most of all the payments the Delawares had, and another man that I remember his name was Robert L. Owens, and he acted as a paymaster.

At any time a child was born and we wanted to get them on the payroll, there had to be as many as three old Indian men go to the home and certify the child's birth. Then every so often there would be a man come a round and register the new-born children. This man was sent out by the government, and people would take their babies to the place where he was and have them put on the [Delaware Indian] Roll. One thing about the enrollment was that if an Indian man married a white woman, the woman could not take the child and have it enrolled; the one of Indian descent had to take the child there.

This money that the Indians would receive at these payments was money that they had received from land they had sold up in Kansas. This was only the interest from the money. As near as I can remember, it was in the year of 1865 or 1864 [1868] that the Delawares came to the Indian Territory from up in Kansas. Isaac Secondine is a full-blood Delaware Indian.

How Indians Took Up Claims in the Indian Territory Days

Any Indian person could go out and find him a place he liked and put claim to the land and the land was his, only he had to come up to certain requirements. These requirements were: first, he would cut him a small tree down, smooth one side of it, write his name on it, also the date and the word "claim," drive it in the ground; then cut him four to six logs as though he was starting him a log house. This would hold the land thirty days. So at the end of thirty days he had to go back and do other improvements, such as putting on a few more logs or plowing up some of the land.

If a person plowed as much as one acre, that would hold the land six months, without doing anything more to it. The amount of one of these claims of land was ¼ mile north, ¼ mile south, ¼ mile west, and ¼ mile east; but if this land was fenced the owner would hold, in addition [to this] land, all land ¼ mile in all direction from the claim. Most of the fences in those days were made of rails and it was quite a job for a fellow to cut and make enough rails to fence in a quarter of a mile square of land.

Still, if a person could fence in 640 acres of land and start improvements on it, same was his, but it is easier to buy 640 acres of land now than it was to fence in 640 acres in those days.

I well remember my first claim I made. I was fourteen years old. I put up my stake and started my log cabin. I sold this claim soon after I made it, sold it to Mr. Frank Hicks, a father of the boy that is writing this story, and this is a true copy of the contract I signed. It is owned by Hicks.

Coody's Bluff, Cherokee Nation, Feb. 2, 1888
I have this day sold my claim to Frank Hicks for 15.00, the claim lays between the Elm Grove Farm and Fillmore Secondine Farm.
Signed: Isaac Scondine

Witness: James Chaney
Fillmore X. Secondine
His Mark

This was the only abstract we had in those days for land sales; also the only way we had in describing the location of land was by land marks of some kind.

The Elm Grove Farm mentioned in the above contract was just a few elm trees that had grown up close together near a claim that some one else had staked out.

A person could lose one of these claims if he did not do any improvements on it within thirty days from the time he made it, for another person could come along and look at the date on the stake and, if nothing had been done, all he would have to do would be to drive him a stake in the ground and date it, pile up a few logs as though he was starting him a log house, and then the claim was his. That is what we called jumping claims.

People were strict in their land deals; more so than they are today. I remember one time my father had his claim all under fence and he found an old Negro man by the name of John Freeman cutting his timber and making rails out of it. So Father told him he was cutting his timber. They went and stepped it off from Father's fence and found that the man was on my father's land, so the man asked Father what he wanted him to do. Father said, "Well just give me half of the rails and we will call it square," but not to cut any more timber on the land.

[Note by interviewer: Mr. Isaac Secondine lives 6 miles NE of Nowata, Oklahoma.]

Isaac Secondine died in 1963.

Interview by Alfred Hicks. The original document appears on pages 193–197 in volume 9 of the Indian Pioneer History Project.

FOLLOWING PAGE:

(Top) Mike and Ella Pace, Dee and Annette Ketchum and Don Secondine sing at the Anderson, Indiana Wigwam, the second largest high school basketball gym in the country. Their program teaches Delaware customs, language, songs and dances to Anderson fourth grade school children. They are singing the Lenni Lenape song to close their program. The city of Anderson, Indiana was named after Delaware Chief William Anderson. Mike Pace, Annette Ketchum and Don Secondine are all direct descendents of Chief Anderson. Dee Ketchum is a descendent of Chief Anderson's wife.

(Bottom) Ella and Mike Pace lead teachers and fourth grade students in the Two Step, an intertribal social dance. This is the only intertribal dance where men and women dance hand in hand and side by side.

T. WYMAN THOMPSON

Born March 20, 1862, Camden County, Missouri
Date of Interview: April 15, 1938, at Ketchum, Oklahoma

My name is T. Wyman Thompson. I live on my farm two miles north-west of Ketchum. I have been an adopted Citizen of the Cherokee Nation since April 25, 1888, at which time I married Jane Anna Ketchum, a part Delaware Indian. My wife's father was James Ketchum and her mother was Elizabeth Swannack [Swannuck] Conner Ketchum.

My wife's father died in 1880 on Christmas day and was laid to rest in a private cemetery on the place he bought when he arrived here from Kansas in 1867. His wife, Elizabeth, lived on a good many years and died about 1929 without having married again. [Some Old Delaware Obituaries (Cranor, p. 42) states "1925 at 109 years."] She was about ninety-three years old and was not buried beside her husband, but in the newer Ketchum Cemetery near the present town of Ketchum for the reason that the private cemetery estab-lished by James Ketchum will go under water when the Grand River Dam is built and will have to be removed. At that time we expect to have the famous old Chief placed beside his wife in the new cemetery.

We are the parents of Clara May, Gordon L., and James Corbett. My oldest son, Gordon L., was shot in the mouth while acting as a special of-ficer for the Frisco Railroad and carried a bullet in his neck for three years before it was removed. Several different doctors told him they had removed the bullet but three years later, Dr. Gorrell of Tulsa, whose son was killed by Judge Kennamer's son, found the bullet and removed it.

Reverend James Ketchum[1] was born in Indiana in the year 1819. He was a convert to the Methodist Episcopal faith in youth and preached in his own language at White Church on the Delaware reservation, Wyandotte County, Kansas, until his removal to his new home in the Indian Territory where he continued preaching until his death. He served as an Indian scout and interpreter for the United States government during the Civil War and served a number of years as chief of the Delaware tribe of Indians.

---

1. James Ketchum was elected acting chief of the tribe in 1872, following the death of John Conner in 1871. The election met with protests from various factions. In 1873 Ketchum was replaced by James Conner. John and James are the sons of Mekinges and William Conner, grandsons of Chief William Anderson.

When James Ketchum and his family arrived in the Indian Territory he had considerable money and purchased one of the famous old brick houses built before the Civil War, by Johnson Thompson on the north bank of Grand River, three miles south of the present town of Ketchum within a mile of the place where the $20,000,000.00 Grand River Dam will be built. Johnson Thompson was a large slave owner and built a fine two-story brick residence on Grand River, making the brick on the ground, all of which was done by the slaves.

The town of Ketchum was established after Reverend Ketchum's death and was named in honor of his wife, who was the oldest living citizen in that community at that time. Reverend James Ketchum was considered one of the most brilliant orators of his tribe. His brother, Lewis Ketchum, lived about three miles northwest of my place and was a famous Indian hunter. He died about 1905 and was one of the oldest members of his tribe at the time of his death. The two brothers talked several different languages and had acted as interpreters for their tribe on many occasions. Lewis Ketchum was buried in a private cemetery on his own place where many of his children were buried. James Ketchum was seventy-one years old at the time of his death, and Lewis was around ninety years of age.

I was born in Camden County, Missouri, March 20, 1862, ten miles east of Lynn Creek near the Bagnell Dam. I first came to the Indian Territory in 1881 and worked on a ranch in the Creek Nation near Wealaka Mission. This famous old Indian school was discontinued when the tribal governments were discontinued and was purchased by a son of Chief Pleasant Porter for a residence. It burned down in 1937.

I left the Creek Nation in 1883 and came to Delaware District, Cherokee Nation, and settled on a rented farm on Grand River near the present town of Ketchum. Five years later I married a Delaware Indian girl, Jane Anna Ketchum, and became an adopted citizen of the tribe. From the time I landed here in 1883, or until statehood, an adopted citizen could hold any office under the Cherokee law except that of principal chief.

There was another old two-story brick residence located across Grand River from the one purchased by my wife's father, James Ketchum. It was built at the same time the other one was built before the Civil War by slaves of Dr. Joe Thompson, a brother of Johnson Thompson, who built the other brick house. This second brick house, backed by a river bottom farm, had been purchased by Henry Tiblow [a Delaware Indian] in 1867, at the same time James Ketchum came down from Kansas.

We purchased this other brick residence shortly after our marriage and lived there for several years, finally trading it, for a farm joining the town of Big Cabin, to a man by the name of John Brown. Brown conducted the old ferryboat between his house and Ketchum for several years. The ferry is now doing land office business between the boom towns of Ketchum and Disney on account of the building of the Grand River Dam. There being no bridges near, it became necessary to enlarge the boat and, in 1938, a twelve-car boat was built and a motor installed. It now ferries twelve cars each way and is kept busy from early morning until late night.

After I had moved to Big Cabin, which was still in Delaware district, I held my first office under the Cherokee government. J. R. (Pete) Hastings, brother of ex-Congressman Hastings, appointed me as his deputy for the west side of Grand River. I issued marriage licenses, permits for white men to work for an Indian and performed all the duties of a full fledged Indian clerk. I only married one couple, Elmer Creek and Lillie Zane, both Delaware Indians.

In 1895 I was elected to serve as one of the regular councilmen from Delaware District as a member of the [Cherokee] national council, which met at Tahlequah in November of each year. Delaware elected six councilmen. The other five elected at the time I was were: Benjamin Franklin Lamar, William Henry Daugherty, John B. Martin, John M. Miller and William Stover. During my term of office we enacted many of the laws winding up the affairs of the Cherokee Nation preparatory to turning it over to the United States government on June 28, 1898, as provided by the Curtis Act.

In 1897, under McKinley's administration, Heck Bruner, Pleas Thompson, my brother, and myself were the first three deputy United States marshals to receive an appointment in the Northern District. Leo E. Bennett, head marshal at Muskogee, wired the court clerk to swear us in. There were over four hundred applications for three places. I served four years in this district, my brother served sixteen years, and Heck Bruner was drowned while attempting to swim Grand River while on duty.

When I first came to the Delaware District there was one of the oldest national schools, in the Cherokee Nation, located near a big spring on the place owned by ex-Senator William T. Davis, called the Contention School, about two miles southwest of Ketchum. It burned down in 1895.

After statehood I was a resident of Mayes County and was elected as county commissioner of that county for three and a half terms, serving six and one-half years, after which I served as under-sheriff, under Charles N. Kelley, for six years.

During this time I moved to the town of Salina, in 1921, and served three years as mayor of Salina. I then sold out and moved to a farm in Delaware County but only stayed there a few years and bought my sister-in-law's old settled place two miles northwest of the present town of Ketchum. She was Hester Ketchum and first married Walker Daniel and they settled on the place where I am now living immediately following the Civil War. The place is located at the head of Mustang Creek at the foot of a big hill and has a fine spring of water on it. Walker Daniel was killed by a run-away team and his widow [Hester] married John L. Hawkins, now deceased. His widow

[Hester] is still living and owns a home in the town of Ketchum. I live on the main highway between Vinita and Ketchum. Since the building of the Grand River Dam started, the traffic on this road has become unbelievable. There is a constant stream of cars passing up and down the road every day, coming from almost every state in the Union. During the past twenty days I have seen twenty oil rigs go by.

While drilling for water to supply the surging crews locating in Ketchum, oil was struck in a well within the city limits at a little less than three hundred feet. No less than thirty-six wells are rapidly making preparation to start drilling for oil. Today, April 15, 1938, I was in Ketchum and it was reported that lead and zinc had been struck in one of the wells in paying quantities. The town is running wild with excitement. Dam authorities are worried for fear this will make the land go so high that the money set aside to purchase the land may not hold out.

No death date found.

Interview by James R. Carselowry. The original document appears on pages 191–199 in volume 112 of the Indian Pioneer History Project.

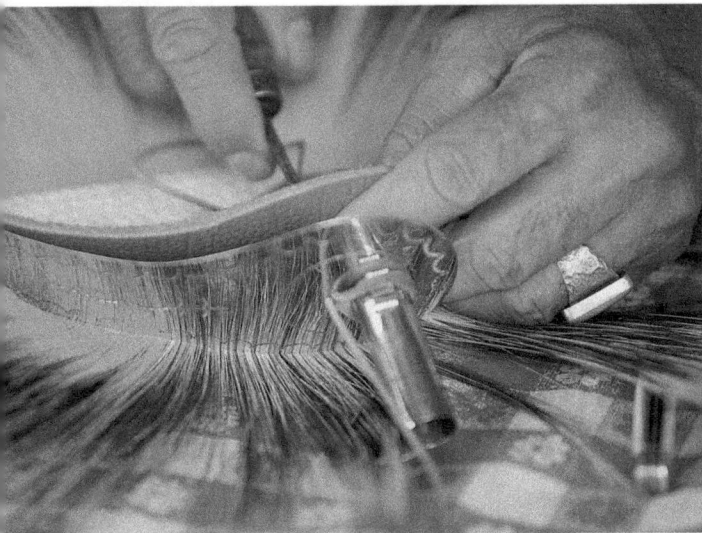

(Top) Dee Ketchum and grandson Jake Sears together prepare their
roaches for dancing. Lewis Ketchum reviews pictures in a family album.

(Bottom) Dee Ketchum adds leather to Jake Sears's roach.

Jake Sears tries on his roach as his grandfather Dee Ketchum assists. Jake was first "roached" when he was eight years old in a distinctive ceremony to introduce him into the dance circle. Leonard Thompson officiated for Jake. Dee Ketchum put an Eagle feather on Jake's roach and it was carried around the drum in the dance circle in a public ceremony. An honor dance was held on Jake's behalf. A "give away" is also part of the ceremony where Jake's family presents gifts to others.

CYRUS WASHINGTON

Dates of birth vary according to diverse sources, as around
1853, 1855, 1861, or 1863, the most plausible being May 1861
Date of Interview: April 28, 1937, on Packing House Road,
S.E. Miami, Oklahoma

My grandfather lived at Sandusky, Ohio, but I do not know his name.
I only know that he was in Washington, D.C., once and talking to President
Washington told him that he had a son and when being asked his name, he
told him that he did not have a name and Washington told him to name him
(the child) for him so he did and my father was named George Washington.[1]
Later, the president sent my father a small suit of clothes.

After my people's removal to Kansas [from Missouri] and from the
time that I can remember, we lived at Fort Leavenworth, where my father
owned and ran a big hotel. Many of the soldiers stayed with him. My father
was a government interpreter and spoke and understood all languages except the Cherokee, which he said was the hardest to learn. The government
paid him $200.00 per month in gold. In the Seminole War[2] in Florida he
was with General Taylor and the Indians would not shoot him for he wore a
shawl over his head. They could see him and knew that he was Indian.

He accompanied John C. Fremont on his exploration of California[3] in
1848 [1853]. Fremont had seventy-five Indians with him and they suffered
many hardships, lack of water, and at one time they were forced to kill their
horses and mules and eat them and were at the last forced to eat even the
leather skirts of their saddles. This hard trip, together with the strain on the
eyes, caused my father to go blind shortly after, so after his return to Leavenworth, he made no more long trips, but he had lots of money. He had a shot
sack full of gold pieces five, two and half, tens, twenties, fifties. It was heavy.

---

1. According to the Delaware census of February 15, 1862, George Washington was 43
years of age, making his actual year of birth around 1819 (Arellano, 1996, 115). For another
version of how George Washington obtained his name, see Julia Hall's interview on page 21.
2. In 1838, Delaware and Shawnee Indians were recruited by the U.S. government for the
second Seminole War in Florida (Weslager, 1996, 378–379).
3. According to Weslager (1996, 380), "Fremont made a fifth trip to California in 1853–54
as a private citizen. He arranged with James Secondine to engage ten Delaware hunters to
accompany him. . . . In 1886—more than thirty years later—one of the Delaware hunters
named George Washington was still trying to collect pay owed him and other members of
the party."

Also he had great stacks of greenbacks, tied in bundles so high (here Mr. Washington measured about three or four inches between his hands).

My father had two wives.[4] My mother was a full-blood and there were six of us children by her. My sister Sarah (married Rogers), Frank, John, Albert, Jim and myself. My mother's name was Quatundet. The children by the other were, Bill, Charley, Riley, Ed, and Julia. We all lived in the big hotel.

When I was little, the soldiers [at Fort Leavenworth, Kansas] used to put up nickels and dimes on weeds or sticks for me to shoot at with an arrow. The Fort was a big brick building surrounded by a high rock fence and four gates in the fence. Sometimes the soldiers would tie blankets together and help each other over the fence, get out and steal geese, turkeys, lambs and pigs. Sometimes when the soldiers' time had come to quit, the officers would set barrels of whiskey in the halls and let them have a lot to drink and while they were drunk get them to sign [up] again and in this way keep them.

Major Price was killed here.[5] They opened the gates and when they were close they shot from the fort and killed him and many of them with him. They just dug a big round hole and put all that were killed in it. They gave my father Major Price's horse. It was a big black with three white legs and was shot through the nose. Later you could hear him breathe as he made a noise because of this hole.

Mr. Pratt was the government agent and he gave my father much money. One day I saw him give him $400.00 in gold.

My father's hotel was where the hack started from, on its trip to Fort Gibson [Indian Territory]. The horses were kept at our place and I was always around, watching them get ready to start and watching to see them come in. They drove big mules to a long bodied hack rather than [to a] wagon, and two soldiers always went, one to drive and the other sat in the back with a musket and six-shooter. The mail was carried in big leather pouches with great locks and was just behind the driver. There were seats for passengers and they usually had some, seldom more than four.

I knew all the drivers and wanted to go with them, so one day, I got a chance; skipped away and went with them for one trip. We came across first to Fort Scott, Kansas, then to Baxter Springs. South of Baxter Springs we crossed Spring River and the Neosho, at the Mose Pooler Ford about two

---

4. The two wives of George Washington were Nancy and Quatundet, as listed on the Delaware census of February 15, 1862 (Arellano, 1996, 115).
5. This is an illustration of memory and fact diverging. In his Missouri expedition of 1864, the forces of Confederate Major General Sterling Price advanced toward Kansas City and Fort Leavenworth, Kansas. They were defeated at the Battle of Westport on October 23, 1864, and retreated. Price was not killed in this expedition.

miles mostly east and a little south of Miami. At the Trott Place, run by Bill and Harden, we changed horses again. In fact we changed at every stop. The horses were harnessed and ready for us and as soon as we drove up the men began to unhitch. The other horses were waiting and quickly hitched to our hack. While this was being done, the mail sack for that place was thrown out, more taken on, if any, and we were off on the run again. We drove all night. No stops to sleep. The Trott place was just a long shed of a place and east of Afton, six miles south and east on Horse Creek. From here to Fort Gibson, where our trip was ended, we rested and got the mail that had come in from Fort Smith and south, and started homeward. The hack had a top on it and curtains that could be let down.

One thing before I leave the old Fort life. We had blacksmith shops and I remember the blacksmith here. His name was Mundy.[6] I played around his shop. One day he was out hunting and he set his gun down, the trigger caught and it went off and shot his whole head off. Just nothing left of it.

I was ten or eleven years old when we started here [to Indian Territory]. We came in government wagons and brought lots of stock with us. My father gave, I remember, $400.00 for a big bay team before we started, paid for them in gold. We did not keep them long for after we settled on Grand River, they got into the lake and were both drowned. My father brought with him two yolks of steers, thirty-five horses and eighteen head of cattle. There were seventy-five of us and the agent, Mr. Pratt [the Reverend John G. Pratt], came with us. We had to stay at Humboldt, Kansas, a month because of the ice, which was breaking up, was dangerous to cross. So we came here to Miami in the early spring. I do not know why we were brought to Grand River to live as most of the Delawares were settled around Bartlesville and Caney.[7]

I am a registered Delaware, whatever that means, and I am told that a sister and myself and perhaps one other are all the registered Delawares that are still living [from those on the 1867 roll]. We brought stoves, things for the houses, and implements to farm with. My father bought, from Moses Alberty, land three miles south and four miles east of Fairland. There was an old field here, about one-hundred acres. The fence had been burned and

6. In 1858, Isaac Mundy died in a hunting accident while hunting with the Delaware Indians. He is buried at White Oak Church Cemetery, Kansas City, Kansas. This is another case where memory and fact diverge. According to the 1900 Census, Cherokee Nation, Indian Territory, Cyrus was born in May 1861 in Kansas. However, he mentions remembering Isaac Mundy, who died in 1858. Deborah Nichols-Ledermann offers, "I think he remembered the shop, but Mundy was already dead, and Cyrus heard about how he died."
7. See history, page xxv, for a possible explanation.

there were the skeletons of Negroes laying around over it that had been killed in the war [Civil War], I think by Stand Watie.[8]

The bones did not have any flesh but were all still together. There were a lot more in a cave nearby. Just a cave that forked this way (here he spread two fingers apart). We led my father around and he picked up the bones and, as he did not want the stock to get to them, he had a big hole dug and put all of the bones in and covered them up. My father built two log houses with fireplaces about four hundred yards apart for his families. The one where he lived had a large room, two side rooms and an attic. Ours had a large room, one side room and attic and a building in the yard that we used as a smoke-house and afterwards to cook in. I went to school very little, we did not think it necessary. Father had plenty of money, we did not think that it could ever give out. We began to farm raising corn, Indian corn, and wheat. The wheat was threshed by piling it out on sheets. (They were big government ones). Then we would ride the horses round and round over it. The white Indian corn was called "Flour Corn" and was ground into flour; also we would plait the stalks and leaves of this into great long strings. Ever see any? It also made fine roasting ears.

Having lots of horses and not much to do, we had a good time. We would go to, and have, races near home. We fished with a government seine [fishing net] given my father by Mr. Pratt. Sometimes we spiked them with an arrow. About four o'clock was the best time to fish as then you could see their backs in the water as they came up to feed. Later, we had fish traps. I have caught sturgeon fish that weighed 150 pounds, in traps.

At first, we would take a team and go to Baxter Springs and bring home a wagon load of food and supplies. We also got our mail there. Later, we sometimes went to Chetopa, Kansas, and afterwards to Seneca, Missouri. We had our wheat ground at the grist mill near by. We had government doctors when I was small. However, after we came here our mother made a part of our medicine from roots and herbs that she would gather and fix.

Having no churches, we went to Caney to our stomp dance [Big House Church], which was our way of worshipping. We danced around a big fire and had music made on drums and deer rattles around the legs, and sang. We had logs for seats. The first church built near us was the Baptist Church in Sulphur Bend.

There were five white men who came with our tribe but they had [Delaware] families and were settled near us. Mr. Pratt, the agent, often stayed with us for weeks at a time. Journeycake, who lived on Lightning Creek, was the first chief and my father was the second chief.

---

8. Stand Watie, 1806–1871, Cherokee Confederate brigadier general, was the highest ranking Native American soldier in the Civil War.

My mother, and father's other wife, died only about a year apart, so father moved us all to his house and got an Indian woman to keep house for us. We only had her a year when father married a white woman. She is still living or was a couple of years ago near Skiatook. I think she married a Mexican. My half-sister Julia [Hall, see page 19] I think is still living. She is 88 years old.

In the fall of 1880, I married Rachel Bowsman, a white woman who had come to Indian Territory when she was six years old, which would be in 1870. They had lived around Vinita and Afton. We were married by T. J. McGhee Sr., Clerk of the Cherokee Tribe, at his home on Cowskin Prairie at Dodge. His home burned before I got my marriage certificate so we have never had any. We went to live on a part of the old place on Grand River and had twelve children, eight of them grew up and seven are still living. We farmed and things went all right for a long time, then when I needed money, they told me to put a mortgage on my home, that it would not hurt. I did and lost it, so I moved to Miami about fifteen years ago.

When they were building the railroad from Miami to Afton in 1900, I had three big mule teams and hauled supplies from Miami to Afton for the men. They had two camps, one on Coal Creek and one at the Sulphur Spring on Horse Creek. I hauled potatoes, bacon, flour, etc. One day at Miami, the banks of the Neosho were slick, and as I had a load with bacon on top of the load, I had to give a man $5.00 to pull me up the bank.

My father died when he was 77 years old and is buried in a graveyard pasture known as the Washington Graveyard. He has a big stone and on it a picture of him driving a buffalo. The Alberty Graveyard near [?] has several soldier graves in it. Powell Black now lives on our old home place.

[Interviewer's comments: Mr. Washington still has a good memory and is very active for one of his age. He has a large and good garden, a nice flock of white leghorn chickens and a good Jersey cow and lives in a small very modest house which he owns. Thus, he and his wife are passing their days brightened by visits from some of their children each day.

His most prized possession is a very handsome beaded pouch that his mother made for his father. He wore it on his trip to California [with John C. Fremont]. It consists of a broad band eight or ten inches wide and reaches from the waist over the shoulder and down to the waist in front. The tobacco pouch is under the arm between the two ends. The work is beautiful and in excellent state of preservation. He also had a gourd rattle wrapped up with it.]

Death date not found.

Interview by Mannie Lee Burns. The original document appears on pages 239–249 of volume 11 in the Indian Pioneer History Project.

(Above) Mike Pace, a descendant of Chief Anderson after whom Anderson, Indiana, is named, joins Paige Perdasofpy and her father, Jerry, who served as head man dancer at the 2005 Andersontown Powwow. Paige, Commanche-Kiowa, has been dancing with the Delawares since she was a tiny tot.

(Right) Former chief Dee Ketchum is often a magnet for children. Here the cycle of generations continues.

REVEREND C. C. WILSON

Born 1875
Date of Interview: April 24, 1937, in Nowata County,
Oklahoma

The First Baptist Church was built soon after the Indians came to the Indian Territory (Delaware Indians that came here from up in Kansas). About one of the first things they did was to build a church house, and this church was built in the year of 1867, ½ mile north and ¼ mile east of Alluwe, Oklahoma, in Nowata County. It was built of walnut logs and the pews were all handmade, and they were of the very best that could be made. They were made by a [Delaware] man by the name of William Adams.

The plans for the building were also drawn up by the same man, Mr. Adams. There were three men who built the church; Mr. Adams, Thompson Smith and John Kenney were the carpenters that did all the work. Charles Journeycake was the first preacher that preached in the church. He would preach altogether in the Indian language but, as the white people got to coming out, he would have to have an interpreter. A man by the name of William Adams acted for him. It would take from two to two and a half hours to finish a sermon, for it would take Adams as long to interpret the sermon as it would take Rev. Journeycake to preach it. They would have some wonderful times at these meetings.

And every three months we would have a camp meeting and it would last for ten days at a time. People would come all the way from the Caney River and Bartlesville Districts, a distance of 40 to 50 miles, in wagons to these meetings. They would start a few days before the meeting was to start, and they would hunt on the way over and kill deer for meat that would be used during the meeting. The first thing they would do when they got to the camp grounds was to divide the deer meat up with all of those that did not have any meat. What they had left, they would cut it up in thin slices and hang it on poles to let the sun dry it out. By doing this, the meat would keep for a long time. As time went on and this church began to branch out, they built three more churches after this. The first one to be built was at Silver Lake, a place three miles southeast of what is now Bartlesville, Oklahoma; it was called the Silver Lake Church. The people in the district of Bartlesville and Caney River did not have so far to go to church and, when the people there had their camp meetings, the people from the Alluwe District would all go over there; also hunt on their way so that they could have plenty of deer meat to last through the meeting.

The next Church to be built was at Post Oak, a place two miles north of Dewey, Oklahoma. It was named the Post Oak Church. Now this church did not grow very fast due to the fact that the people in this district still wanted to worship God in their own way, by having stomp dances, and this church soon was abandoned.

Now the third church to be built was at a place called Koama Switch, 5 miles north of what is now Nowata, Oklahoma. It was just a switch on the MOP Railroad, but now the name has been changed to Delaware, Oklahoma, and this church is still active today. A man by the name of John Sarcoxie was called to preach at this place. He was a preacher that could preach in both English and the Delaware language. It always took him about two hours to [preach] the sermon. The people would all stay in the church house till he finished his sermons. I think I am safe in saying that is more than most of the people of today would do.

[The following is written by Alfred F. Hicks, the field worker conducting the interview:

While Reverend Sarcoxie was preaching at Delaware, there were three young men set aside for preachers, Jobe Thomas, C. C. Wilson and Rueben Sarcoxie. Rueben Sarcoxie was a son of Reverend Sarcoxie. Out of the three, C. C. Wilson was the only one that was ever made an ordained minister and, in fact, he is the only living Delaware Indian minister today. He lives at Nowata, Oklahoma, during the winter months and at his home in Colorado Springs, Colorado, in the summer months.

After Reverend Sarcoxie stopped preaching at the Delaware church, Reverend C. C. Wilson was called by the church to be their regular minister. This place he held for several years, and today he is a regular attendant at the church while he is in Nowata. The other two men that were set aside to preach, one of them is dead. Jobe Thomas is dead, but Rueben Sarcoxie still lives here in Nowata, Oklahoma.]

The Delaware Baptist Church and the Silver Lake Church are still in existence today, only they are within a mile and a half of the original site.

Charles Journeycake, our preacher, was also the last chief the Delaware Indians had. He was replaced by five men by the United States government. These men's names were John Sarcoxie, John Secondine, Henry Armstrong, John Young and George Bullette. They were appointed in the year of 1905. There are still a few Delaware up in the Dewey, Oklahoma, district that still have a chief, but he is not recognized by the [U.S.] government.

The Indians in those days had to have their fun. I well remember the joke a man by the name of Morman Everett played on a bunch of boys at one of our camp meetings. Mr. Everett lived in the Alluwe district. On one of his trips to a camp meeting he killed a deer, and when he had sliced some of the meat and put it out on the poles to dry some of the boys stole it. Mr. Everett did not say anything about it, but the next time he came over he killed a wolf on the trip. He skinned this wolf and cut it up just like he would a deer and hung the meat out, and that very night it was taken. The next morning the first thing he did was to hang the hide out on the poles where the meat was and then told some of the old men about someone taking his meat; then he told them it was wolf meat. There were several boys around there, and they all began to spit, and that was the way he had in finding out who had stolen his meat.

Death date not found.

Interview by Alfred F. Hicks. The original document appears on pages 454–457 in volume 11 of the Indian Pioneer History Project.

MOP Railroad is the Missouri Pacific Railroad. The original railroad was the St. Louis and Iron Mountain Railroad Company, later acquired by Missouri Pacific (Muskogee and Northeastern Oklahoma, vol. 1, by John D. Benedict, 1922, S.J. Clarke Publishing, Chicago. Chapter 36, Nowata County).

According to Ruby Cranor, Kik Tha We Nund, page 134, Cornelius Wilson was born in 1875 to Laura and James Pa mo wah Wilson. "Cornelius Wilson was a famous preacher. He made a tape of songs and sermons in the Delaware language." Laura was the daughter of Eliza Conner and Tom Wilson. Eliza was the youngest child of Mekinges and William Conner.

Reverend Cornelius Wilson married Arizona L. Zane (born 1881). Arizona is the daughter of Jefferson Zane (1844–1912) and Matilda Secondine (born 1855). Matilda is the sixth child of James Secondine and his first wife, Nancy.

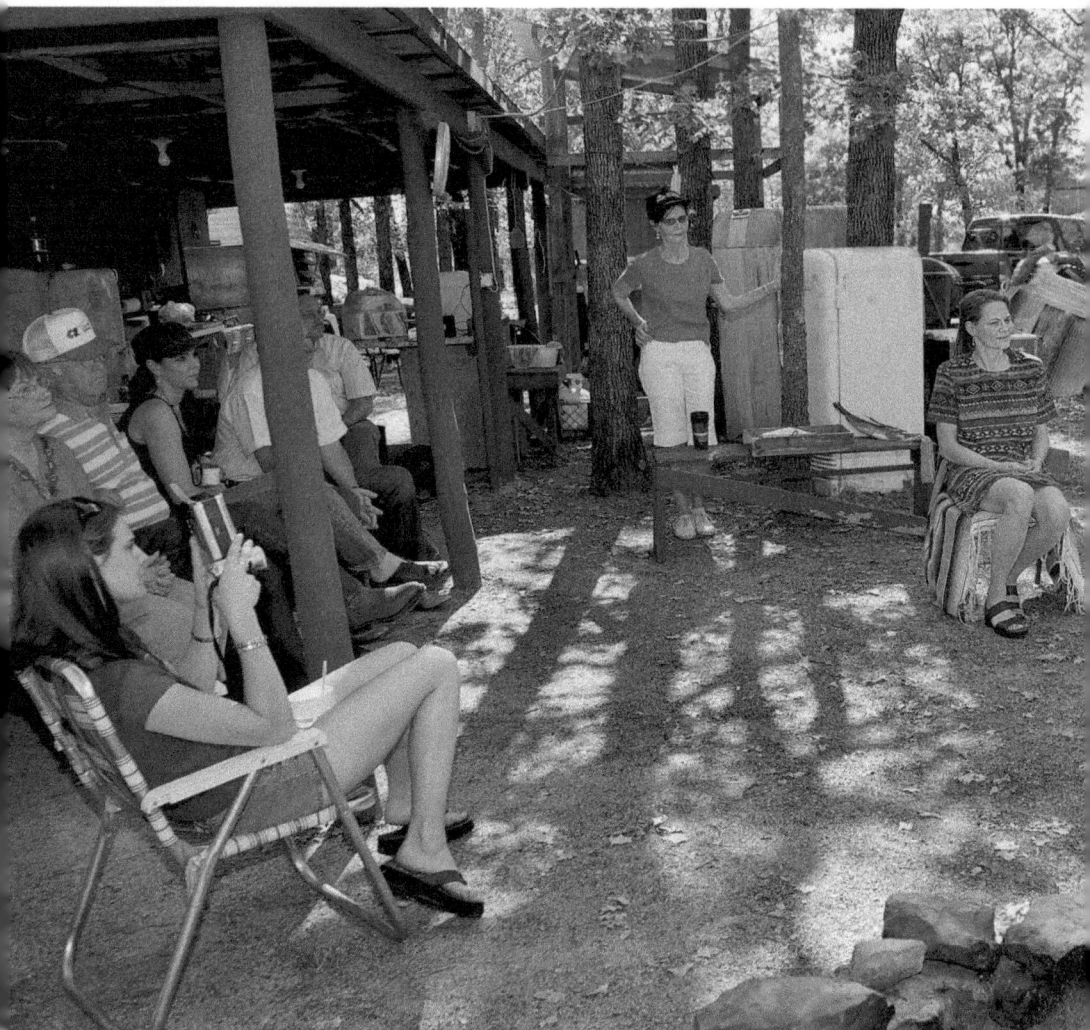

(Above) The Pechonick Camp is the setting for the naming ceremony of Kimberly Moore, M.D. Dr. Moore is the daughter of Paula Pechonick. The conferring of a name in the Delaware language follows a traditional ceremony taught over several years to Dee Ketchum by the late Leonard Thompson. Dee Ketchum asked his oldest grandson, Jake Sears, to assist.

(Right) Friends, family, and well-wishers fan red cedar smoke upward toward the honoree, Dr. Moore. Their good feelings rise up for the honoree as the smoke rises toward the sky. Lewis Ketchum, father of two chiefs, the late L. B. Ketchum and former chief Dee Ketchum, shares a tender moment with her.

(Above) Kimberly Moore, M.D., puffs the ceremonial pipe while facing east, south, west, and north.

(Right) Annette Ketchum lights the ceremonial pipe for Dee Ketchum. The pipe head was carved from jade and includes the Delaware clan symbols (wolf, turkey, turtle) and a Mësingw.

PART 2.
1968 INTERVIEWS

The following three interviews were conducted by Katherine Red Corn. They are presented here in an edited version from transcriptions supplied by Jim Rementer and verified by Mike Pace. These originals of these tapes are part of the University of Oklahoma Libraries Western History Collections.

An Anderson, Indiana, fourth grade girl follows Don Secondine's lead at a program at the Anderson Wigwam. The program teaches customs, language, songs, and dances to the children to help acquaint them with the history of the Delaware in Indiana. The children especially like the participatory dances. Secondine's moccasins are a typical Delaware design.

ANNA ANDERSON DAVIS

Born November 6, 1897
Died December 1979
Date of Interview: August 5, 1968; source: vol. 31, tape T-298

[Interviewer's note: Anna Anderson Davis was born in the area of Dewey, Delaware County, Oklahoma, and still lives in the same place at the present time.]

My mother's name was Josie Willett, and my father was Samuel Anderson. I'm the only child of my father. But I have several brothers and sisters on my mother's side. I grew up with my grandparents, and I went to school at Chilocco when I was six. My grandfather took me over there and left me the whole school term, and when I got ready to come home my grandfather came after me, and I discovered I couldn't talk Delaware. I couldn't speak it for two or three weeks. My grandmother'd speak Delaware to me, and I'd answer her in English. But it didn't take me long to get back to learning it, but I've never forgotten it since, up until now. And since I don't have anyone to talk to, I don't talk Delaware too much, and I'm just losing it. You know you've got to have someone that will talk back to you so that you can talk. Be like talking to yourself. But I have a little grandson that is learning to talk Delaware, wants to talk, and I have taught him to count and a few words, names of birds and animals. But as far as me going to school I just went helter-skelter lot of times.

If I didn't like to go to school some place I'd write home and tell Grandpa and Grandma that I was sick or I didn't feel good, and they'd come after me. I went to Haskell for two half terms when I was nine to eleven. Then I went to public school here in town pretty regular for about four years, and then the schoolhouse burned. It was during the Christmas vacation that the schoolhouse caught on fire. They found buildings for the children to go to school, and I lived out in the country so I didn't bother to come to school 'til my guardian come along and said, "You'd better go to school." He said, "You want the school authorities to get me?" He said, "You've got to go somewheres." So I went on to Pawhuska to St. Louis School for three years. Then I was married, and so, therefore, I just quit everything and went to raise my family.

I had several guardians. First it was Frank Phillips, then it was S. J. Combs, I believe was this man's name. And then Fred Woodard. He was my guardian up until I became of age. And, of course, I lived with my grandparents all my life, after I got two or three years old. So that way I just kind grew up all by myself, really, and I was always anxious to go to school, but that's what always happens whenever I got dissatisfied I'd just write to Grandpa, and he'd come after me. 'Course I insisted on my children not missing here and there all the time, and I made it my business to see that they went to school every day. They had to be just on the deathbed before I'd let them miss. So that way all my children graduated from high school, and college, and really trained themselves to do something worthwhile. Not like me, just fool around.

When I went to Lawrence, Kansas, and then went to Chilocco I'd go on a train, but when we lived out in the country we had horse and buggy. I boarded in town, Monday to Friday, then they [grandparents] come back for me on Friday, be home for Saturday and Sunday. I used to just get on the train and go back and forth to Pawhuska. I'd just go from here to Nelagoney. I'd go there on a little electric, I think it'd hold about ten or twelve passengers, train, bus, or cab, I don't know what you would call it, but it run on the railroad track and take us to Pawhuska.

After my children were pretty well along in school and I could go places, we organized an Indian Women's Demonstration club that functioned for seven years, up until the Depression. Bartlesville women and Copan women belonged. We'd meet at the fairgrounds once a month. But when the gasoline ration went on, some of the out-of-town women couldn't come to the meeting regularly, so we finally disbanded with the intention of reorganizing, but we never did. So I joined the Post Oak Club which had been functioning for years, and I belonged to it for several years. Then I joined Coon Creek Club for eight or ten years. In the meantime I belonged to the PTA. And then we organized a new club, and we called it the Dewey Club. I still belong to it, and at the present time I'm the president of the Dewey Club. But I have been with the PTA and president of the Coon Creek Club two terms. Then I belonged to the Indian Women's Club for the last twenty years or more.

It was during the war that I took a nutrition course, then the first-aid course, and took up home nursing. So for awhile I was quite active.

We have what we call the Doll Dance. That was the traditional ceremonial custom of the Delawares. It was usually put on in the summertime, most times in July. It was very ceremonial, and it was put on by this little old lady, she has passed away now. She had a little doll that was handed down from mother to daughter until she got it. It was always dressed in traditional Delaware costume, and when they'd dance, the leader would carry the doll. It was fastened on a little stick, a dowel, to carry it when you dance. Each song, when they quit singing, you hand it to the person behind you. And they would sing these songs over and over until everyone got to carry the doll. When the women finished, the last one then would take it to the men. So they carried the doll until everyone had carried it that was dancing, and then that would be the one to start the prayers, songs, I guess you would call them. I never really ever found out just how many times they did that, because they would quit at a certain time, you know. And then they would put the doll away, then they would have just social dancing until morning.

They used to make bread, pounded corn like Indians always make, made into little biscuits and dropped in ashes and baked in the ashes. Then in the morning, there would be, oh, two or three big old baskets full of this bread. And then there was one piece that was just a long piece. They always just called it a "bear." And 'round this bear was wrapped wampum beads about a yard long. Of course, everybody always wanted to get the bear to get the beads. They also used these beads at our Big House meetings in the fall. Just as the sun was coming up in the morning, there would be little ceremonial songs; they would clear the fire away and everything. Then they'd throw that bread up. It'd just be the family that would pick up hands full of this bread and throw it out there, and the bear would be thrown out. Some people would watch to be sure and get the bear.

I remember I was just a small child, and I wanted to get some of that bread so bad. And I wanted to go out there while they was throwing it out there. But Mother kept telling me, you better not because that bread is hard, and if it hits you it'd hurt. Well, anyway, I insisted on going. She said, "Well, all right, let's go." All Indian women wore aprons. She just gathered up her apron, just like this one, and go along and pick up as many little bread as she could. Well, I went with her, and I was picking up some, but I was holding two or three of them. And about the time one of them rolled rounds of bread hit me, and that was the end of my picking up bread, 'cause that hurt, and I remember I ran back to Grandmother. She was sitting in front of her tent, and I told her, "It hit me on the head." I remember I was just bawling my head off 'cause that bread hit me. And seemed like from then on I never was to one until I was about fifteen or sixteen years old.

We don't [have Doll Dances] because there isn't anyone who knows part of those songs. The men that did the singing and knew those songs, they've all passed away. The family that kept the doll finally just had to quit having it. But I know they used to always just have sort of a little feast to commemorate that day.

Mrs. Rosie Frenchman had the doll last.[1]

---

1. According to James Rementer, the only surviving doll from this group of Delawares is in the Nelson-Atkins Museum of Art, 4525 Oak Street, Kansas City, MO 64111-1873. Available information indicates the doll (a woman doll) was bought from Mrs. Frenchman by Charles Childers (a Lenape) of Fort Morgan, Colorado. He sold it to Dr. Ward Dunseth, M.D., of Jacksonville, Illinois. It is said each of these "owners" after Mrs. Frenchman had all kinds of bad luck befall them as long as they owned the doll. She was auctioned off for Dr. Dunseth by Four Winds Company of Chicago and bought by the Nelson Gallery of Art in Kansas City.

We used to have our Big House Meetings in late October or early November. This was more of Thanksgiving ceremonies and lasted twelve days. I don't exactly know the dimensions of it, but it was long and narrow. There were not supposed to be any nails used in building of it. It was made out of logs, and the roof, the shingles, just a regular log house. Where the logs meet there were two posts on the outside to hold it together, and then on the inside these four posts always had the face; traditional face on one side was red, and one side was black. And in the middle there was just one big square pole, it must have been say, two feet each way, four sides. And it had the two faces.

Three men would always sit on one side, and opposite them would be the singers. They were special songs. My father used to be one of the singers. He, [along with Jim Thompson, recorded] two or three songs. It was open to anybody that wanted to sing. I guess you'd call them prayer songs. Each song was their individual person's song.

They had turtle shells. They would pass it around, and whoever wanted to perform that night, when he come to him, he would pick it up and shake it. And then he would offer his prayer. When he'd sing, you might say the first verse, then the drummers would pick it up and repeat his song. And they would dance until he finished. You're supposed to do that twelve times 'til you get back to where it started. There was a period in my grandmother's time when for some reason they quit having them for several years. When I was a child about eight, nine years old, my grandfather invited them to come to our house and have a meeting.

So they had council, and they all agreed to clean up the building and repair it, and there was always six, three women and three men, and they call them Ashkasak, and that would be similar to ushers in a church. Everything was performed by these three women and three men. And they had to be chosen, you know, someone that was willing to do it, put in their time. And then they camped a week before or maybe two weeks probably, because I know it'd take quite a little while to clean this place up. I think there was supposed to be an acre of ground that this building was given to the Delawares by some family, but I don't know who they were now because they used to call everybody by their Indian names. But I know about where [the Big House Church] used to be. I attended maybe say five or six sessions, because I was about eighteen or nineteen when we went to the last one, and that was back in 1919.[2]

That building stood for years. Joe Washington volunteered to look after the building, but he got sick and wasn't able to do it. Then people began

---

2. The last session was held in 1924.

to go and tear those faces down. There's one in Tulsa. Mr. Endicott bought all that land out there. He has some of those faces that he salvaged from the building; it was pretty rotted down when he bought it. But he said that there was still two or four posts left with the faces on them. But the main pole, the big pole, it's in Tulsa [at Philbrook Museum]. You'll have to go down and see it sometime.

It was carried on as long as there was someone that knew the songs and the rituals, but it's a thing of the past now. Reuben Wilson made a little replica of the Big House. It looked quite real.[3]

One story is around the East Coast, but the little Indian version of the Delawares they were always along to coast, close to water and the ocean or sea. This one medicine man predicted there was somebody coming over from across the ocean. And they were coming on white birds, and he said that they would have white skins, red hair, hair on their faces, and foretold this coming.

He said they were supposed to come over on three white winged birds, and, of course, the white wings were just white sails of the boats, and he told just how many moons it would be before they would come. And so when they finally come it was these three boats and their sails and these people with the white skin and the red hairs, some of them, and the hair on their faces. Indians very seldom ever have a beard, you know, or whiskers. And, of course, it seemed like everybody was curious to see these people that grew hair on their faces and had red hair.

My grandfather [and] my grandmother used to tell me a lot of stories, little stories, Indian stories. But as a child I didn't have sense enough to write them down the way they would tell them. Now I just get to thinking about them, but I just don't remember lot of them, but that one I had always remembered so vividly.

One funny thing was that the rabbit was always the prankster. And he was always playing tricks on his cousin the bear. And he was always doing things to the bear. One of them was that he told him that he could catch fish if he'd stick his tail, dig a hole in the water and stick it down in there 'cause the bear used to have a long tail. So the bear went out and dug a hole and put his tail down in the water. And that's why the bear has a short tail—his tail froze off.

Interviewed by Katherine Red Corn.

Original oral history tape was transcribed by Cathy Griffin and proof-read by Nona Kerr.

---

3. This model is in the museum at Seton Hall University, South Orange, N.J. See Weslager, p. 419.

The Delaware Tribal Child Care Center in Bartlesville, Oklahoma, is a community facility providing educational and physical activity programs for pre-school children.

NORA THOMPSON DEAN

Born July 3, 1907
Died November 1984
Date of Interview: April 1968; source: vol. 31, tape T-296

My name is Nora Thompson Dean. I am a full-blood Delaware Indian. I was born east of Bartlesville, Oklahoma, about ten miles. I went to school first at a little country school called Midway School. Then I finished the eighth grade there at the age of twelve. Then I came here to Dewey and finished high school in 1925. Then after that, I took a little bit of nurses training at Tulsa, Oklahoma, at what was then called the Morningside Hospital.

My parents were full-blood Delawares, of course. My mother's name was Sarah Wilson Thompson. My father's name was James H. Thompson. And they were married in June 1900, near Vinita. They both spoke the Delaware language. So I grew up knowing the Delaware language. I grew up on a farm, and when I went to high school, I studied about animals so I was more able to help my people to raise good-blooded stock, horses, cattle, and hogs.

My mother's father's name was Billy Wilson, and his Delaware name was Kwĕtikapay. He had a half brother named John Wilson who, I understand, brought the peyote here in this area. And, my grandmother's name was Kweiti. My grandfather on my father's side was named Joseph Thompson. And my grandmother was named Welipahkineo. Grandfather Thompson was among the delegates who went to the Cherokee chief to file rights here in what it now Washington County from the Cherokee Indians. That's when they came from Kansas in 1867. My grandfather Joseph Thompson was one of these delegates who went there for this business. My father was raised by his aunt whose Delaware name was Kwetĕndĕt, and he was sent to the Quapaw Mission in those early days.

John Wilson was half Caddo and half Delaware. He was half brother to my grandfather Billy Wilson or Kwĕtikapay, and he brought the peyote here to the people here in this area; but right now I have forgotten the date, when this was all brought here. My mother's folks were all peyote people. We also had a religion, the Xingwikaon, in other words the Big House ceremonies. It went along as our religion about the same time we took with peyote religion, and some went to Xingwikaon services as well as to the peyote services. The Xingwikaon was about four miles northwest of Copan, Oklahoma. I attended all of these ceremonies that were held at this Xingwikaon from the time I was about four up until it ended in 1924. That was the last service that was held there at the Xingwikaon.

This Xingwikaon was a twelve-day prayer service. On the fourth day they sang special songs for the hunters that the Delawares called Alahoting Asuwakàna. That's what the Delawares called these hunters' songs that were sung for the hunters before they went out on their hunt.

No one was permitted to sing in this Xingwikaon unless they had had a vision, and that was where the songs stemmed from, the vision they had experienced in their youth. My mother was one of the women who performed Atehumwi, that is called the women's vision song. That was held on the ninth night of the services. A new fire was made before this service and the ashes all carried out the west door, and everyone was smoked with cedar. The Delaware people called this Pilhìksutin, and that's the "cleansing ritual." There were only about seven women in my day, as they were fast dying away, who could sing Atehumwi. My mother was one of those, and Lucy Willetts was one, and Rosie Frenchman, Eliza Falleaf, Paolinao whose English name was Pauline Blackwing.

The cedar purification ritual was held on this ninth night. The Delaware people always looked upon the cedar tree as being a clean tree. So, in nearly all of our rituals that we have ever held, somehow the cedar has always held an important part, especially in the Big House. And then, too, at the funerals when anyone passed away at a home there was always someone who burned cedar and took it all around inside and outside of the home. And also the clothing that was given away of the descendant, given to the workers that was appointed for the funeral. Before these clothes and personal effects were given to the workers, these clothes were purified or smoked with cedar. And if anyone was sick, someone always prayed for this sick person, and they used cedar, and they fanned this sick person with cedar smoke. So, as long as I can remember, the cedar played a very important part in the lives of the Lenape people.

When we held our feasts we always burned cedar after the feast to purify the house. To go into this word "feast," as to we Delaware people, when we hold a feast it is something in memory of the descendent. The food that's given to others in memory of the deceased one, different branches of the Lenape people had different styles of these feasts. For example, the Munsee people, their style of feasts was a little different from my folks. We always cooked our food the day before, before we had the feast, and we took it outside and covered this food where nothing could get to this food, and the next day we call different ones to come to eat this food. And anything that remained was to be taken by the people that came to eat this food.

Long years ago before many Europeans were here in this country the Delaware people had a special ceremony for weddings. The prospective groom's folks would go and take presents to the prospective bride, and if these presents were received that meant that the bride was willing to marry the young man. But if the prospective bride's parents refused the presents that meant that he was being refused.

The presents could be, oh, deer meat, bear meat, or kekok which is called wampum beads, something like that. Or in later years they brought materials, goods, for presents. This ceremony was held in a big congregation of all the Delaware people. One old man was called upon to tell the congregation what was going on, and after they used the white kekok, white wampum beads to put around the bride and the groom. After these beads were put around the bride and groom they were considered to be married. Then they went away to their own dwelling.

Sometimes they would live with the husband's folks until they could make their own dwelling place.

There are a lot of things that a Delaware young woman must go through when she reaches the age of puberty. I, myself, for instance, went through these old-time customs. I was hidden in a room. I was not permitted to see anyone, nor was anyone permitted to see me. My food was brought in to me, and my wash basin, soap, and wash rags was brought in to me, and I was given something to work on. In my case it was sewing. My mother said, "Whatever you do then that will be what you will like to do for the rest of your time." So she brought me lots of things to sew on. And I spent most of my time sewing. If a girl was hidden then, and after the required period of time was up, the girl was brought out of hiding, and again we used the cedar. She was smoked with cedar, and an entire new wardrobe was given to her by her mother. Even to new earrings, new moccasins, new dress, everything new was put on the girl, and then she was told, "You are a young lady now and from this day on you will act like one." All of her toys that she played with in childhood were put away. Dolls, toys, and everything. My mother said in the old days when she went through this custom she was taken down into the timber, and there was a bark house made for her, and they appointed an elderly lady of the tribe to stay with her all during this time of hiding. But that was years and years ago.

For about ten days a girl was not permitted to even touch her hair or her face. My hands in my case were wrapped, except for the time when I sewed and when I washed, of course, and to eat my meals. But during the sleeping time the hands were tied in order that you would not touch your face or your hair. And my mother combed my hair every morning. She said the reason for all that was because when I got to be an old lady, real old lady, she said that my hair would still be black if I went through all these customs that the old people went through.

I will talk a little bit on the birth of children. Years and years ago when a Delaware woman was to give birth to her child, a bark house was made for her, and a pit inside this bark house was dug, a shallow pit, and the mother then gave birth to the baby in a kneeling position. And this baby was not given a name right away, because they said the evil spirits might know this baby's name. They waited until this baby became stronger; then it was given a name by some old person who had received a vision. The people who received a vision are considered to be qualified name givers. My family, I had two brothers and have one living now. There were three of us. My mother named all three of her children because she was considered to be a qualified name giver since she had received her vision and was able to Atehumwi in the Big House services.

At this time I will explain about this vision. My mother received her vision through a frightening experience. It seems she was riding horseback with her mother, and her mother must have had a heart attack. But during those times years ago no one knew what a heart attack really was. So, while they were riding along it seems that her mother, my grandmother, had a heart attack and was just about to fall from the horse. My mother then tried to hold her mother on the horse, and finally she slipped out of her grasp and fell to the ground and my mother along with her. So my mother became so frightened, it must have been in the timber, she said that some of these trees around her turned into people. And these people, then, told her to not be afraid, that we will help you. And as she stood listening to these trees, they finally started singing a song to her. That is the song that she sang in the Big House. It was something like this; of course, the old people always said not to use these sacred songs carelessly. So I will now try to sing a part of her vision song. Of course, this is held in sacredness but, anyway, I'll try to sing part of it. [*She sings.*][1]

In our tribe of the Lenape people, otherwise known as Delaware Tribe, we have three clans. One of them is called the Tùkwsit, the Wolf Clan. The word "Tùkwsit" really means Round Foot. The next clan, Pùkuango, which is called the Turtle Clan, but "Pùkuango" really means, in the Delaware language, Hole in the Heel. And then we have the Pële clan which is the Fowl Clan. We observe these clans very strictly in the Big House ceremonies because each clan had a specified place to sit inside this Big House. The Tùkwsit women sat on the northwest corner of the Big House. The Tùkwsit men on the northwest. The Pùkuango, men and women, on the west. The Pële men on the southwest corner, and the Pële women on the southeast corner. This ceremony lasted for twelve nights, usually held in the month of October.

My mother's clan was the Tùkwsit, the Round Foot, the Wolf Clan people. My father was a Pëleìnu, that's a Fowl, Clan man. And I, myself, of course, belong to my mother's clan, Tùkwsit, because that is the way of the Delaware people. They take their mother's clan instead of their father's clan.

---

1. This tape is at the University of Oklahoma, Western History Collection.

There seems to have been a subdivision of these three clans. The Tùk-wsit clan was sometimes called Olàmàniyok, and the Pùkuango clan was sometimes referred to as Elipsit clan, and sometimes the Pële clan was referred to as the Wisawhìtkuk people. But the general and true name would be Tùkwsit, Pùkuango, and Pële clans.

About these clans, for example, as I've mentioned before, the child took the mother's clan, and it went to the other way for a chief. In the white people's point of view, for example, a man who was a chief in the Delaware tribe might have a daughter. She would not be considered a princess or any important figure. But this chief's sister who had a male child, he would be considered the chief. And that is one of the old laws and customs among the Lenapeyok, Delaware people.

Now I will go into some information about the mode of dress that the Delaware women wore. First I take up what I call the overlapping skirt. It was made of trade cloth, some say broadcloth. It was heavy woolen-type materials with a kind of rainbow border, and there was ribbon-work panel that went down the right side. Broadcloth must have come along in the 1600s, brought by the Europeans, I presume.

The bottom of this skirt was beaded with, usually, flowers or leaves because we were originally woodland people. And then we wore leggings with a strip of ribbon work down each side. And our moccasins were the one seam type, originally, with beaded toes and the ribbon-worked cuffs. And for our blouses, we wore a loose overlapping blouse, no belt, with a large Bertha-type collar it's called nowadays. And on our heads, we wore an hourglass shaped ornament. In our language, we call this Ansiptakàn, and it was usually decorated with silver spots and had a beaded edge and a long ribbon attached to the end that hung down the back about three or four feet. And this ribbon was also decorated with silver brooches, that we call Anixkàman. We usually decorated the ribbon with that and the little silver spots.

The Delaware women in the early days wore a lot of copper because I guess that was the ore that was in Pennsylvania and Ohio country where they formerly lived. Lately, they wore a lot of silver and used a lot of silver on their clothing for decorative purposes. These brooches are called Anixkà-mana. And I understand that the first type of cloth that was introduced here was called duffel cloth, a coarse, woolen type that came before the broad-cloth. Then there was another cloth called the Stroud cloth that was used before the broadcloth or trade cloth.

Before the Europeans came, the Delaware people decorated their clothing and hunting bags, smoke bags, and what the men carried, they were all decorated with quill work. And since the Delaware people no longer use the quills, I guess some of them do yet, they use the ribbon work for decorative purposes on their different items of clothing.

There were two types of Delaware moccasins. The old original type of moccasin only had the one seam. But later as the years went on they have another type with a narrow tongue in front, real narrow, I'd say about one-inch width for both men and women's moccasins. Of course, the men's moccasins were not as elaborately decorated as the women's moccasins, but they were both made on something of the same order.

When my ears were pierced when I was a small child, my mother and father pierced my ears. First they pressed my ears with thin strips of cork. Then they threaded a needle with white silk thread. They sterilized this needle, and they sewed through the cork, completely through the cork and through my ear and pulled it on through and tied the string. And each morning this string was to be worked in my ear until it was healed. And then I was able to put on my earrings, after this hole was healed. It took about, oh, maybe a week or so. I must have been around six or seven years old when they pierced my ears.

My father told me the story about the origin of the smokes between the Delawares and the Osage people. Long ago there was an elderly lady, and her name was Wahoney.[2] The tribe referred to her as "Old Lady Wahoney," who had one son. He was looking for his mother's horses out in the Osage Hills. And he was killed there in the hills, presumably by the Osages. So, when they found his body, there were two arrows on top of it, the young man's body. So, the chief of the tribe at that time, they wanted peace with all the neighboring tribes, so they went over to the Osage country and negotiated with them. So, they decided to have smokes between the two tribes. One year we went to the Osage people, and we smoked the pipe of peace with them and exchanged gifts, and the following year they would come over here and do the same. We had big dinners, smoked the pipe of peace, and exchanged gifts. This story was told to me by my late father as being the origin of the smokes. They held these smokes about once a year. And the last one, I was told, was held up here north of Dewey.

We all went over there to the Osage country. The whole band that was in this area at the time went over there to smoke the pipe of peace with the Osages and exchanged gifts and all eat together. I remember one time my father told me he was a young man, since this all happened before I was born, my father went over with the rest of the Delawares to attend one of these smokes, and he said that he was given a horse by some Osage man named Oluhomoi. And he became his great friend from that time on.

---

2. Weslager spells this name Wahooney.

Now then, I will tell about some the burial customs among the Delaware people. Take, for example, when a woman loses her husband; well, they appointed what they call four workers, two men and two women, and these workers would take care of all the necessary details. That was before the present-day undertakers. They washed and dressed the body and prepare it for burial, and they'd do all the cooking and prepare the food that was to be served during the time they stayed up with the deceased one, and he was taken to the place of burial.

An old man, any old man, was appointed in the tribe to talk to the deceased person. They would tell him, "You are now in another land or place, and you must no longer bother us or think of us. Go on in your world in your way." Then they would place the deceased one's clothing, some of them, inside the coffin. They would then bury the person, and the widow was led around the grave by some of her family. They went counter-clockwise when they took her around this grave; they led her towards the east. That was done by the members of his family instead of her family. And that was in the way of telling her that now this family is through with you. A sort of divorce, I guess it could be called. She was then told that you can get married to whom you wish to be married to from this time on.

Then a feast was held by the graveside. Long ago, they had two places to eat. One for the relatives and the other table was spread on the ground for the friends of the deceased. After they got home, of course, they then smoked themselves with cedar. And they smoked the entire house with cedar smoke. All the people who were there at the time the person passed away had their heads washed by the mourners on the third day after the burial. And as is the custom with my family, they had a feast in about seven days. But I believe with the Munsee's Clan it was twelve days. They had a feast for the deceased person at the home where he passed away, and no one was permitted to leave this home completely empty. Someone must be at this house at all times for one year. And whoever the mourner was, if it was a daughter, son, or wife, they were not permitted to indulge in any social dancing for one year. That was strictly against the rules, to dance before the year was up when a person lost a member of their family.

We consider twelve to be a good number because it represents the twelve months of the year. And red and black, too, are what we call Delaware colors, because we had this Mësingw in our Delaware Big House church. And this Mësingw's face was painted half red and half black, which, I was told by the old people, represented good and evil. And we had this Mësingw faces; we had twelve in all, but the center one was the main one. We considered this Mësingw face in the Big House as representation of the game spirit, the Mësinghòlikàn spirit, the Mësinghòlikàn himself. He was the guardian spirit of all the animals. Of course, in those days the Delawares had to depend on the wild meat before they could have meat. And this Mësinghòlikàn was the guardian spirit of all these wild animals. Deer, bears, so on like that. When we had the Big House, the Delaware people did not pray to this Mësingw image. We pray to the Kishelëmùkòng, which is God Himself. There had been a lot of misinformation that the Delaware people pray to this Mësingw face. But this is not true. We never prayed to this Mësingw face.

Interviewed by Katherine Red Corn.

Original oral history tape transcribed by Nona Kerr.

FRED FALLEAF

Note: Falleaf's birth date varies according to diverse obituaries, none of which match the date listed by the interviewer. Spelling is also at variance, with "Fall Leaf, Fred Leo" appearing in the obituary notice as re-printed by Cranor. For Fred Leo Fall Leaf, whose life events match those of the interview, the obituary states, "Mr. Fall Leaf was born on Cotton Creek, Indian Territory, March 30, 1900." The obituary date is May 14, 1971. See Cranor, *Some Old Delaware Obituaries*, p. 27. Weslager spells the name Falleaf. A problem with this transcription also exists with the interviewer stating "his mother was Emma Yellowjacket" in her notes, while Mr. Falleaf states in the interview his mother's name was Ida.
Date of Interview: August 15, 1968; source: vol. 31, tape 5-299

[Interviewer's Notes: Fred Falleaf was born in 1898, in Indian Territory near what is now Dewey, Oklahoma. He attended the local schools while in the grades and attended Haskell Institute in Lawrence; Kansas. Fred's father was John Falleaf, and his mother was Emma Yellowjacket. He is now retired and lives near Copan, Oklahoma, on his father's original land allotment.]

[My mother was a] Yellowjacket. Over west of Dewey, in there. 'Course at that time when I was born, it was Indian Territory them days. I was born over there close, but not right at Grandpa's house; we lived right there close. My mother, her name was Ida Yellowjacket. My father was John Falleaf. And let's see, my grandmother, I don't know what her name was. Never did find out. She died before I was big enough to even realize it, I guess. I don't even remember my grandfather. My grandmother I knew on my father's side. Her name was Falleaf. 'Course then she remarried again a man by the name of Jackson. Colonel Jackson. We lived over there on the river until I grew up about oh, I'd say, maybe six years old. But then they didn't have any schools around there so we had to move somewhere where there was schools. So we moved up pretty close to where we live now. Only about pretty near a half mile north and about a half mile west from here. So we lived there then until my mother died there. And then my father, he remarried again, and then we moved back across the river again, over on my father's place.

We stayed there until I come of age, and I got married in 1925, and we built our home up here, and our son was born up here. He's a deputy sheriff in Montgomery County, Kansas, at Coffeyville. That's all the family we've got here. Wife and I and son is all, but we've got a granddaughter. My father and I, his grandmother, his mother, my grandmother, we come up here and lived on her place. I bought the place from her afterwards, and we built our home on it. Then, in 1947, we sold it and moved to Caney. I worked for Cities Service Gas Company a long time up there. And then we went from there into Texas and California and Arizona and around different places. Come back to Oklahoma again. We couldn't stay away from home, you know, we had to come back. So after we stayed in Oklahoma awhile I went to work for a construction company, building houses, carpenter work. After we came back I went to Coffeyville. Went to work over there at Continental Can Company, but it wasn't cans then, it was aircraft. I worked over there in the carpenter shop about ten years. They finally went out of business. They just cut their contracting. So they laid off pretty near everybody.

So we went back over to Caney, and I got a contract of mail messenger over there, on the Santa Fe train to the post office. I worked at that, and we run a laundry. Fellow had his own laundry formed, and I worked on their machines every time anything went wrong. But I took the arthritis, and that fixed me. I got where I couldn't do anything then. So I just had to retire. But I worked up 'til I couldn't work.

I went first to country school, to Copan, church house, when I started school. Then they built a new building, and when we lived out here they put us in a different district. Built a new schoolhouse. I went to school there about two years, and I went to Bacone then, down by Muskogee. I believe it was two years; then I came back and went to Dewey public school about two years. When I left there I went to Chilocco Indian School out to Arkansas City two years, finishing high school.

Well, they finally made a white man outta me when they shipped me off to school, you see. But I did save my language. I managed to hang onto it. I lost a lot of it though. I been awful lucky. Now Nora Thompson Dean, she'll come up here, she'll ask me about somethin', and I been fortunate enough to think of it right when she asks me what something was, and I'll be able to tell her, see; so I been pretty fortunate that-a-way, but a lot of it I've forgotten. Oh, I don't talk enough. I just don't get 'round 'nough people talk it, and you just lose it that-a-way. Just like you would any language if you didn't talk it once in awhile, well, you get to where you wouldn't be able to.

Interview by Katherine Red Corn.

Original oral history tape transcribed by Blanche Hill and checked by Nona Kerr.

PART 3.
1995 INTERVIEWS

The following two interviews were conducted by Kay Wood during 1995. No specific dates are listed on the original transcriptions.

Kay Wood was an education specialist at Bartlesville, Oklahoma, schools for many years. Dr. Wood is part Prairie Band Potawatomi and part Peoria. She conducted these interviews for a paper she was writing while working on her doctorate, although these were not done for her dissertation. They are reprinted here in an edited version and with permission. These are in the James Rementer archive of oral histories.

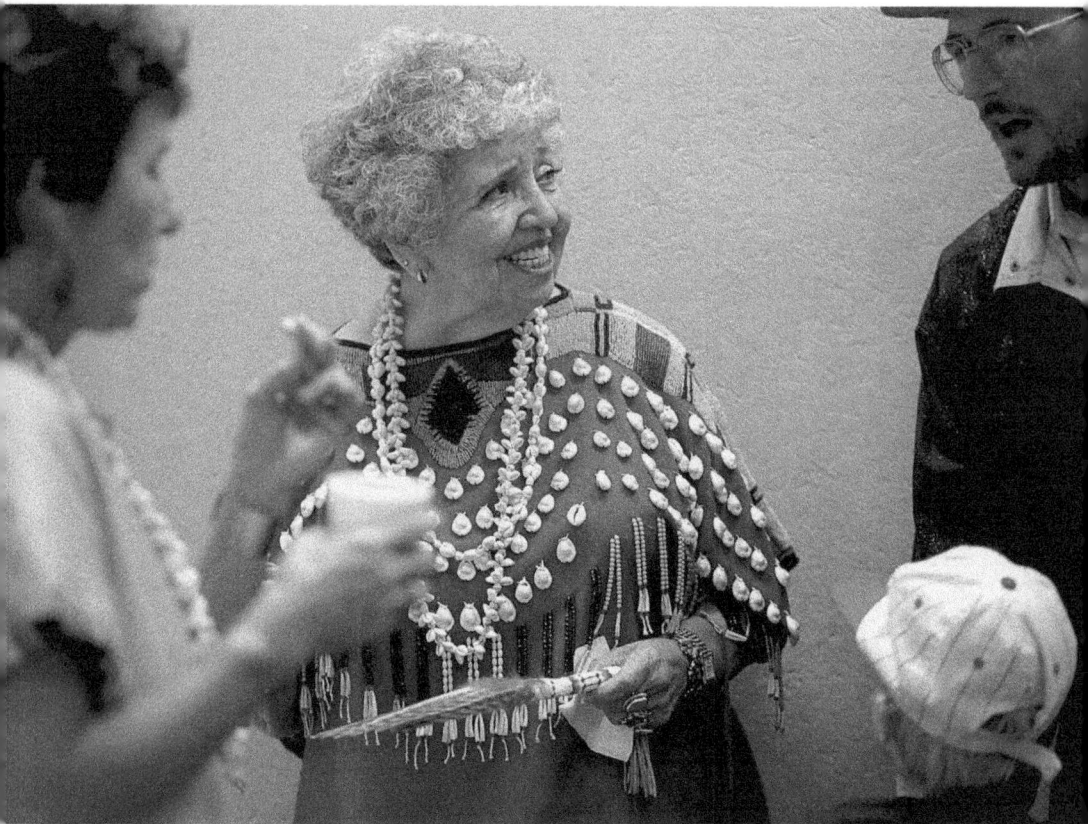

Mary Crow talks to admirers following a fashion show given by the Bartlesville Indian Women's Club in Peoria, Illinois, 1993. The women make Indian clothing representing many tribes and model the clothing to raise money for college scholarships. The club was founded in 1935. Mary Crow is wearing a Nez Perce dress decorated with cowrie shells.

MARY TOWNSEND CROW MILLIGAN

Born August 19, 1920
Died March 24, 1998
Date of Interview: 1995

I realized that after my last uncle passed away, I have no uncles or aunts now, and so I realize that I'm the elder of the family. I have three younger brothers. My father was half Cherokee and half English. He was Jess Townsend, and he was born in Cherokee country in Stilwell, Indian Territory. Yesterday would have been his birthday. He was born March 1, 1876, and he would have been 125 years old yesterday. Also it was my late uncle's, my mother's oldest brother's, birthday. He was born in 1885, I believe it was. My father had one full sister, and their father was killed, was waylaid. He was a merchant at Stilwell, and some robbers robbed his store, and they waylaid him on the way home and killed him.

The man that killed him was later found, and he was tried and was hanged. I did not know my grandfather. My father died when I was ten years old. My grandfather was killed when my father was still in a high chair. He was about two years old. My mother single-handedly reared us children. My uncles and aunts wanted to take one of us, but my mother wanted to keep her children together, and she fought like everything to keep them together. With some help from them she was able to take care of us, reared us by herself. My mother was Delaware-Shawnee.

My grandfather was Stephen A. Miller. See, he was a little bit of German in there where the Miller came in. My grandmother, my mother's mother, was an Armstrong. That's where the Shawnee came in. My mother's allotment was in Delaware, Oklahoma. Delaware, Indian Territory, just north between Nowata and Delaware. It was later sold. My grandparents' and parents', my mother and her brothers' and sisters' allotments were all in that same area, north of Nowata. Before Delaware was named, Nowata as we know was a Delaware name that was later mispronounced. No-we-tah is what was the name of it, which meant "Come here, little," "Come here," or "Welcome." Then north of Nowata, four or five miles north, was what is now called Delaware. Before it was called Delaware it was a railroad switch, and it was called "Chemamas Switch," and that "chemamas" means "rabbit" in Delaware. And then later the white people called it "Kah-mah-mus." They later called it Delaware.

Then about seven miles north of Delaware, is Lenapah, and that is "Lenape," which means "Delaware." So, there are two towns that were named that, one is in Delaware and one in English. That was written up at one time in Ripley's Believe It Or Not, that there were two towns that had the same name, only one was in English and one was in Delaware. Lenapah, which is north of Delaware, is "Delaware" in the Delaware language. It is pronounced *Len*-nuh-paw, but the real pronunciation of it is "Lun-*nah*-pay," the Delaware pronunciation.

We grew up on my father's allotment five miles east of Delaware. That's where all of us were born, at the farm place there where my father's allotment was. When my father passed away, we moved in with my grandparents about a year afterwards. When my father had a stroke, my uncle, my mother's brother, came and stayed with us, and my father was taken to the Claremore Indian Hospital. That's where he passed away.

I never had seen my father ill or anything like that ever. When we came home from school and we got off the school bus, I saw these cars there at the house, and one car I recognized as the doctor's car. We struck out running. When we got there, of course, they said that Daddy was sick. My father was a farmer and stockman. He raised cattle and horses and farmed. He didn't marry young. He was only fifty-five when he passed away. I was ten years old at that time. He and my mother were married in 1919, and I was born in 1920. So Daddy was, I think, fifty when he got married. My mother was born in 1889, and I was born in 1920, so my mother was nearly thirty.

He was quite a well-known bachelor, farmer, and stockman at that time. My mother said when they would go to the Fourth of July celebrations and the fairs and things like this, she said she knew who my father was. You kind of learn who people are. My great-aunt was teasing my mother and said, "Why don't you go get acquainted with Jess Townsend?" She said, "He's sure a nice-looking young man, and he's prominent there at the county, and he was superintendent of horses at the fair and was in charge of the horses at the fair." She said that she heard someone ask him, "Well, Townsend, how come you have this big badge on?" He said, "Well, of course, I'm the best man here." He was a Townsend. He had a lot of wit about him.

Somehow or another they got acquainted, and my great-aunt said next thing she knew here they were walking around at the fair together. It wasn't too long after then that they dated, and got married, and it all went from there then. It was a very happy childhood with my father and mother. I never heard them cross each other in any kind of confrontations or arguments or anything like that. If they ever argued it wasn't around we children.

Mother loved to cook. My grandmother, too, was a real good cook. I remember when I was a little child she was always able to cook anything. I remember my parents always liked to hunt. My father was a good hunter, likewise. My mother's father was too. They would have to turn him away from the turkey shoots because he'd win all of the turkeys. He'd come home from these turkey shoots, and all of these turkeys he had, and he'd be picking them up out of the wagon. They gave away real turkeys. They just put them in a sack. They'd just stick their heads out, and you'd come home from the fair with all these turkeys. They just finally allowed him so many. And he'd go squirrel hunting, rabbit hunting, and all that.

Talking about cooking, my grandmother would fix these squirrels a fantastic way. They would be cooked down in their own gravy or their own sauce. The way she'd cook, she could take that iron pot and just kind of flip it over some way, and these squirrels would be just turned over. She wouldn't even have to take a spoon or anything to turn them over with, but they sort of simmered down and cooked down in their own gravy. She had a wood stove.

My mother said there would be, a long time ago, a salesman or what they called in those days "drummers" come along. One time one came along, and he was selling cook stoves and things he had on his wagon. He went on, and they didn't buy one. After this guy was going on his way, my grandmother told my grandfather, "I sure would like to have that cook stove. That was sure a nice cook stove." He said, "Well, why didn't you speak up? You should have spoke up." He was already gone then, so grandpa jumped on his horse, and he took out and caught this drummer and had him to come back and bring that stove. My mother said that it was a Home Comfort cook stove. I still have the cookbooks that went with that stove. My mother would write up recipes in there. Like I say, my grandmother taught her all she knew about cooking. She could cook anything.

She liked to cook outside. I remember one time it was hot summertime, and there wasn't air conditioning and that sort of thing. You'd come down there, and my grandmother would be cooking outside, and she would make some fry bread. And she'd make some skillet bread, what she used to call it, sometimes on a Dutch oven, an iron Dutch oven. We kids would call [it] High Wind Bread because she could cook outside and wouldn't heat up the house. She'd make this homemade bread outside. I remember we'd have fried potatoes and bacon and sausage and pork chops, and she'd just cook everything outdoors like this. We'd have a picnic table area out there, and I remember when we were little kids we'd come down there, sometimes on Saturday evenings. We'd go to town on Saturday to take eggs and stuff to town and get our groceries. Sometimes we'd come down to Grandma's and Grandpa's and have supper, and oh, she'd fix up a good supper for us.

Altogether they had ten children, and six of them grew to adulthood. My mother was the third child, and between my mother and my Aunt Sadie Lookout (she married Chief Lookout's son, Charles Lookout) there were three children that died young. We'd tease my mother every time there'd be one of these little children that would pass away, it would revert that my mother would be the "baby" again, so she was kind of spoiled. So there were six children that grew to adulthood.

I have two brothers who died. Between myself and Jess there was a little baby boy that passed away. He died in infancy. And then my brother Blue Hill was a twin. His twin brother died when he was twenty-two months old, of diphtheria. We all had either diphtheria or measles. We were all vaccinated, but my brother Blue Hill also had the diphtheria. My daddy just happened into the room at the time he was choking up with this diphtheria, and he just grabbed him up by the heels and grabbed this phlegm out of his throat and got his breath, and he saved him. He really saved my brother Blue, but little Blueford he just didn't know at the time when he was choked up. So we lost my little Blue Hill's twin brother when he was twenty-two months old.

When Blue got well again, of course he missed his little brother. He'd just go from room to room looking for my little brother. That was a pitiful thing, and my mother grieved about that. She all of a sudden realized my daddy would take us all to town. He loved his family, and when he'd go to town for something he'd load us all up, we had a Model T Ford, and go to town. My mother would always before then buy us ice cream cones and things like this, and after little Blueford passed away she didn't do that. She always said that she just sort of woke up one morning and realized, "Why, I have these other children, they're my children, too." And then after that we'd go to town, she'd buy us all ice cream and candy and things like this. She realized then that she had the rest of her children, she still had a family, and so we fared real well. My little twin brother, the twenty-two months he lived, was a live wire. Blue and Blueford would provide for each other when they'd get into stuff.

I remember one time my mother started teaching me to cook when I was just real little. I was only about five years old when I made my first cake. I called it a Sunshine Cake. It was a yellow cake, and so I got that cake fixed, and I told her, "Now I want to ice that cake, and I don't want you to come in until I get it iced." I made a powder sugar icing you know, and so got that cake all fixed and got it all iced, and I went in and told my mother to come in and see my cake, I got it all finished. I went in there just in time; the twins were in the kitchen, and little Blueford had taken a big handful of the cake and had given Blue his handful.

One time they got into the ashes in the cook stove, and Blue was given his handful of ashes, but they always provided for each other like that. But then when little Blueford passed away, that's when Blue missed his twin so much. My grandmother said, "When a twin loses their twin they're just as satisfied to be by themselves as they are, because they'll always miss them." That's the way Blue is today. He's just as content to be by himself as he is to be with somebody else, and that's the way he always was. He'd go on vacations by himself and things like this.

He's made friends and acquaintances with people away. Just last week I had a phone call early in the morning. It was an acquaintance that Blue'd got acquainted with. Blue had a friend on location over in Pawhuska, Hugh O'Brien, [who] invited him to come out to Hollywood. So when Hugh O'Brien had this "Wyatt Earp," and he also had this TV series where he played, "Fury," there was a black horse that was named Fury; anyway, he invited Blue to come out there, so Blue would go to Hollywood and visit Hugh O'Brien. Then we had a friend who was reared over at Chelsea who was a movie double, Whitey Hughes was his name. He still doubled for a lot of movie stars, and we got acquainted with Whitey, and Blue did go over there. Anyway, Whitey hadn't been over here for a long while. The last time he was here was probably, I think it was before Joe passed away, so it was about fifteen years ago. Here the other morning Whitey called, and he had been living in Yuma, Arizona, now, so they're going to come out and visit us this spring.

In Alluwe they used to have Delaware payments and that sort of thing. My mother and grandmother, they would have the little cook tent. They'd fix chicken and dumplings and food stuff, and they'd sell it there. My mother was kind of little then, but she was learning how to cook and take care. My grandmother said, "Well, how did you secure your money you made?" She said when they'd go to sleep at night in the tent, she would dig a little hole under her pallet and she would put that money in a can and she'd go to sleep on it.

They used to like to sing, drum and sing, and that sort of thing. My grandfather he loved to sing. Sing Delaware songs and sing Church songs in the earlier days. And then later he became a Christian and learned all the Church songs, and then go to all the Churches, wherever he could sing. He always loved to sing and testify and preach and that sort of thing. He was quite a lay preacher. That was my Delaware grandfather. Grandpa Steven Miller. My mother said they'd go in later times to Coffeyville, which was about twenty miles north of Delaware, and they'd go up there to do their shopping. It would be an all-day trip because they would go early in the morning before daylight. They'd load up the wagon, and they would put comforters and things in there. Mama said she was the youngest one at that time when they'd go; there'd be my Uncle Ed, and my Aunt Eva and my mother, and they'd put them to bed. They'd put hay in there, and it'd be nice and warm. Mama said they'd be all cuddled together, she'd be in the middle, and the kids would get to scuffling, and the folks would make them behave.

They'd go up to Coffeyville, and they'd do their shopping and buy shoes, and clothes, and food, and things like this. Finally Grandpa would be missing, and they'd be looking around for him, and they're liable to find him there on the street corner singing with the Salvation Army people. He'd find something to entertain himself with, and he'd get with those Salvation Army people and sing with them.

Finally in later years he got involved in the Delaware tribal business. When Chief Charles Journeycake passed away, grandfather was then acting chief for a while. Then when they bought into the Cherokee Nation they always had a Delaware Business Committee, and my grandfather made many trips to Washington, D.C., in behalf of the Delaware tribe. I think on an occasion or two they recorded some of his Delaware singing. I think my brother has recordings of some of these Delaware songs that he recorded in Washington, D.C.

After my father passed away Chief Fred Lookout more or less adopted us into his family. "You're just like my children," so we'd go over there [Pawhuska] at Christmastime and holidays, that sort of thing. His daughter Mary Lookout, at that time her name was Standingbear, Nora Standingbear, and had a nice big home there just about a half a mile from Chief Lookout. She'd always have a big, huge Christmas party; I guess there'd be over one hundred people there. My uncle, Charles Lookout, was Mary's brother, and he'd go down there about every day. They were making big plans for the Christmas party. He came home one day and said that Mary said she was going to have her hired hands sing, and they were going to sing "Silent Night" and all these different songs. He said, "Those hired hands don't know much about 'Silent Night,' about all they know is Saturday Night."

So she lined up one of her friends who was going to be Santa Claus. I forget his last name, Pasetohpah, I believe; Mr. Pasetohpah was going to be Santa Claus. Of course, he had his Indian braids, and he always wore his hair long in braids. Well, Mary got a Santa Claus suit fixed up pretty, and we was all ready waiting for Santa Claus to come. Then finally we heard outside the jingle bells a-jingling and got to getting faster and louder and closer, and finally we got to hear the dogs a-barking and next, in through the window barged Santa Claus. I mean he was all out of breath because the dogs were after him, and he came just all out of breath. Here was Santa Claus, but he had these braids as I remembered it. He come out of there, and he was trying to grab his breath and sort things to say something, and he said, "I'm Santa, I'm Santa." He said, "I've come north," talking in his broken language, "I've come north. Here's Santa, I'm Santa." But it was so funny. But he made it in the house all right without the dogs getting him.

We started the wild onion dinners; they used to have these in Tulsa. My cousin, Marjory Newcomb Wheelock and I and Blue, we'd go down to these dinners, and I thought we could have these dinners, too; our Indian Women's Club could do that. So I came to the club and I told them we could have these Wild Onion Dinners. We had our first one at the YWCA, and we must have had over one hundred. Mama said we could clean these onions out to the house, and so we went out and dug our onions up here at Johnstone Park. We dug them ourselves, Galela Newman, and Anna Davis, and, I remember, Dorothy Bratcher, who was Sally Farley's aunt, and myself, and

Marge and several of us went out and we dug these onions. We brought them all over to the house, and Mama said, "Well, I'll fix dinner while you all cut the onions up and clean the onions." It was a big all-day job, you know.

So Mom got busy and cooked beans and fixed pork chops and corn-bread and cake. She'd make a big sheet cake and sometimes she'd fix cobbler, but she cooked for us, for the women when they were working getting onions ready. So then we'd have our onion dinner. My mother would fix cakes. I don't know how many cakes she fixed, and cobbler too. We had blackberry cobbler. She used to have to go and gather blackberries, too. We'd have it in about April. We had to jockey it around Eastertime depending upon when whenever Easter was that particular year. We'd have about the same menu as we do now, wild onions and scrambled eggs, then cobbler and sassafras tea. We serve six hundred now, limit it to six hundred.

A long time ago they used to have Sulaseekon, used to make it like stew meat from deer or elk or something like this. Chuck it up and boil it, or we used to grind it in later times. We just use ground beef now. Take your ground beef and sauté it, then put it in a pot and put a little water over it and simmer that. It doesn't take too long, fifteen or twenty minutes, and keep it covered with water, and put salt and pepper in there.

Then you make little finger dumplings. You just mix a little flour and water and you might want to put a little baking powder in there but hardly any, and you just take your fingers and just make little drop dumplings. You drop that into the meat, and it makes a gravy, and then you want to put a little bit of thickening in there. Then you put that over toast or just eat it with fry bread. Really, a good little one-dish thing. Just kind of like spaghetti and meat sauce, you know, but that's what you call Sulaseekon.

Well, we've always been pretty much not as traditional as we've been more or less just right in the middle of the affairs and things like that.

My grandparents were Christians when they came down from Kansas, but they just didn't have a particular church. The Delaware tribe was the nearest being like a Christian religion than most tribes. My mother used to go the Big House Church when she was little. She remembered going to it up here at Copan. They'd go in the fall. The twelve-day ceremony. She re-membered, when she was little, Mĕsingw used to keep them in order, keep the kids good. Momma remembered when she would get scared, she would run to her mother and hide under her apron. When she'd get scared, she'd go to her mother when she was a little girl. She said there was another little girl that she kind of played with, running around there, about her age; then come later it was that girl that married her brother, my Uncle Ed. It was Aunt Martha, and they realized that they played together when they were little girls.

My grandparents weren't as traditional Delawares as the Dewey Dela-wares. The Dewey Delawares, Dewey and Washington County Delawares, were the more traditional type of Delawares than the ones that had their allotments around Nowata County, Alluwe. The Nowata County Delawares went to the public schools, like my mother, but she did grow up talking Delaware, and so her first language was Delaware. She didn't speak English until she went to school.

Bessie and I were talking the other day about how far back we remembered people. I said I remember when my daddy had me in a little cage he built, a little pen I could walk around in when I couldn't walk too well. And I had a dog, a little baby like this. I remember when my brothers, the twins, were born because we were all born at home. I don't remember the time when Jess was born, but seems like he was always around, when he was a baby. Then all of this excitement about when the twins were born, and all these people were around the house and all this excitement, and I didn't know what was really going on, I had never even heard of twins, until these were born.

I was five years old. They said finally I became missing, and everybody around the farm was looking for me. They couldn't find out where I was. My daddy always called me "Dude," that was my nickname, and so they were all looking for me. Finally they said I dashed out from the closet, and I came running in there to Momma, and my grandmother then showed me the twins and said, "You got two little baby brothers." I looked and she showed me those baby brothers, and then is when I ran off. I didn't know what to do with two baby brothers. Then I finally bounded out from the closet, and I came running in there and I said, "Mama, Mama. How're we going to take care of these babies, two babies?" And I said, "I've got it figured out. You can take care of one, and I'll take care of one." So I got it all figured out, see. But I had to go into my closet and figure out how to do this. Then Momma said, "Well, you sure did do that, too," because we found out that's how we managed.

When I was growing up, I was very busy and had very much work that I had to do. I felt this great responsibility of helping my mother after my father passed. These younger ones, I worry about them because I hate this word that they use of being "bored." I think that's a terrible word that youngsters use these days of "being bored." They need to be entertained. They need to entertain themselves and be innovative. I think television is an affront to our mentality in a lot of ways, and I think it's taught a great dependency to the youngsters, and they don't need that. They need to learn. They've just now started opening up libraries to them. I think that something of very great importance is books and learning how to read. I worry that they can't do anything on their own. They've got to have some computers, and they've got to have entertainment facilities like cassettes and that sort of thing. They need to teach themselves how to do; they don't know anything about a lot of things.

I remember my mother used to tell her grandchildren about things that she used to do around the farm. My little grandniece, my mother was telling her about some things, how she used to help saddle the horses and help doctor the stock and help doctor this and that, and she just didn't even believe her. She'd just say, "Grandma, I believe you're just woofing me."

The very night that Joe passed away, my oldest nephew, Scott Townsend, Blue's oldest son, moved right in with me. He was a senior in high school at that time. He said, "Aunt Mary, I'll come in and stay with you and live with you and feed your cattle and horses for you," and he did that, and that was something that he taught himself. He knew because Joe had taken the kids and taught them how to do these things. So he stayed right with me until he went to college. Then his next brother moved in with me, and that's the way they did. I taught those kids how to carry on here at the ranch, and they knew how to feed cattle and horses, and they knew how to take care of them. They helped us in various gathering and roundups. They learned by just doing.

I graduated from Delaware High School in 1938. It was a good commercial school. I learned typing, shorthand. I was a whole year getting a loan from the BIA before I could go to business college. I lost a year there from the time I graduated in 1938, and I didn't get this loan approved from the BIA until 1939. So I didn't get to start Tulsa Business College until 1939. I went to Tulsa Business College for almost two years before I finished and was able to start to work at Phillips Petroleum Company. I had to pay it back. I sure did. Paid so much a month.

I didn't go to Indian school. My brothers did, to Haskell. Blue and Jess did, but Bruce did not. Bruce graduated from Bartlesville High School here, went to Tahlequah at Northeastern, graduated from there and then went to the service. When he got out of the service, he wanted to go on to study law, but he would need help. I said, "Well, I'll do all I can to help you." He enrolled for veterans help and went to law school and got his law degree from Oklahoma University.

I became state president and I've been on national committees of the General Federation of Women's Clubs. During the time I was state president, I hosted the International General Federation of Women's Clubs convention in Tulsa. The international people still talk about this great convention that we had in Oklahoma.

It was really, really great thanks to a lot of our Indian Women's Club members, Doris "Coke" Lane Meyer and Betty Shook. Peggy O'Neal was my convention chairman. She was a member of the Hugo Women's Club. We just moved in at the Williams Hotel in Tulsa and were there for about a week. I think we had about 1,200 delegates from all over the world.

I'm most proud of the representation of the Indian women. Betty Shook and I took a trip to the general headquarters of the Federation of Women's

Clubs in Washington, D.C. One of our Delaware Indian women became international president. It was Roberta Campbell Lawson, and her picture and write-up are now in the headquarters at Washington, D.C. That was one of my proud moments, to see her picture among the other international presidents in the gallery there. I knew her personally and knew when she was campaigning for international president. She was from Nowata and Tulsa, and she had a beautiful alto voice. I remember my mother taking me to a concert which she had in Nowata when I was probably just about ten years old at the time. She had a beautiful white buckskin dress, and she always wore her hair in a halo braid around her head, and she was always a nice gentle woman. She knew my people and my family real well. I went to the concert she had when she ran for president. Will Rogers was quite instrumental in her campaign, as was Doris "Coke" Lane Meyer's mother, who was a member of the Pocahontas Club at the time in Claremore. Mrs. Lawson was a member of the Nowata Women's Club. Some of the women from the east wondered about the feasibility of an Oklahoma Indian being international president. Will Rogers was quite instrumental in convincing them that she, in fact, was quite capable and was a brilliant and talented lady. She could sing, she was the wife of the president of the Nowata Bank and a Tulsa bank. In later years, when I became state president, the [outgoing] state president thought it would be nice to get Mrs. Lawson's portrait bust in the National Hall of Fame of American Indians at Anadarko. We started raising money to contract the sculptor to do this portrait of Mrs. Lawson. We were able to raise I think it was $42,000 to hire the sculptor to do this.

Leonard McMurray was the sculptor from Oklahoma City. To get her likeness we had only pictures of her. People who knew her personally said that I had more of the Delaware features akin to her features, so they had me be the model for the sculptor. I went down to Oklahoma City to this sculptor's studio on about five occasions to pose for the sculptor. We did all right except for the hair because my hair was different. We had a lady who was then the chief of the Choctaws, I believe it was, and she wore her hair in this halo braid, and he used her hair as the model. I, in fact, took the sculptor's knife and started modeling this hair, and he was surprised that I was able to get this hairdo started. Between the two of us, we got it. When we had the unveiling of it they had me to go down and do the unveiling of the bronze bust now in Anadarko. She was quite a famous lady, and she was always held high in the Nowata Club. She was Delaware.

Earlier they had a Lenape Club. Anna Davis was a member of that club, as was Thelma Pace. The Bartlesville Indian Women's Club was an organization when I moved to Bartlesville. Georgeanne Robinson was, I believe, president at the time. I'm not too sure, but she invited my mother and myself to join, and we joined the club just a year or so after I moved to Bartlesville in 1942. I know the very day that we joined the club they were talking about raising the dues, and so my mother spoke right up and said, "Well, I think that you ought to raise the dues," and this one lady, Mrs. Wheeler, said, "Well, you're not even a member yet." She said, "Well, yes, I am a member, here are my dues right now, and I vote to raise the dues as we need." So, as a result of my mother's nomination they raised the dues right at the time we joined. She was always quite vocal and quite active. At that time we didn't have a clubhouse. We met at women's homes, and we met at my mother's and my home quite frequently.

When we first moved here [Bartlesville] we lived at 611½ South Dewey. There was a little house in back of a big house. It was just across the alley from the then Civic Center. The Civic Center was there on Johnstone and went clear to the alley between Johnstone and Dewey. It was quite interesting, that little house where we lived. That was when my brother Jess went to the service, and Blue went to Haskell, and then he was drafted, so my two brothers went to the service. That left only my mother and younger brother Bruce at Delaware, so I rented this house at 611½ S. Dewey and moved my mother and brother Bruce over here with me. We didn't have a car and [the farm] was about a mile out of town. I remember my mother would carry groceries out there. We had a few chickens and some guineas and raised a garden not far from the house, and rabbits and varmints would get in the garden. We'd just take that gun we had by the door and shoot a rabbit if it got in the way out there.

My youngest brother Bruce made pets out of everything we had, chickens and all this and that. We had one little chicken that was sort of a runt, and he never did have very many feathers. He was a poor, little, naked chicken, but my brother made a pet out of him and called him "PQ." He was named after a little, runty guy that we knew of. One morning we were eating breakfast, and he looked up, and here a chicken hawk had grabbed little PQ and was flying off with PQ. He was a-crying and hollering, and Bruce looked up and said, "Oh, that chicken hawk's got PQ." He started crying, and I grabbed that gun and ran out there. I took a shot, and I killed the chicken hawk, PQ and all. So that took care of that situation.

My brother Jess, we learned, was either wounded or something happened in the service, but we couldn't find out what had happened.

My mother's sister, Aunt Eva, came and stayed with us, and we were trying to find out from the Red Cross and everywhere what might have happened to him. We got another telegram saying he was injured and was failing rapidly. And then my aunt woke up, and this is something about Indian intuition, both my aunt and myself we either had a dream or vision or something like this. Aunt Eva said, "Ida, I dreamed that Bugs (his nickname) landed on the West Coast." I said, "That's the very thing that I saw in my dream, and I saw him get off that ship." That very day he called from the West Coast in California and said he landed in the United States. And my aunt and I both had that vision or dream that morning we woke up that he'd got there. So then it wasn't too long that he was able to come home, and he said, "I've got all my arms and legs, I just had a hit in my shoulder." He's got permanent disability, but he got back all right. Blue was in the South Pacific, they were both in the South Pacific, and they both made it through. All my cousins that were in the service got back. I didn't have a fatality among all my Indian cousins. One cousin, he was a sailor, and he was able to get back.

I was married to Joe in 1967. He died in 1981. Then Damon and I were married two years ago on the 26th of February. We just celebrated our second anniversary, and so we've been having a good life together. He had his stroke three years ago, and I helped get him back in good shape. They said he'd never walk again, but he's doing everything, and he's doing great. I had my lung attack in 1986 when I had what they call a rare Sjogren's Disease, where your lungs don't give off enough carbon monoxide. I've been able to tolerate that and live with that. So between Damon and I we're able to help each other to where we make one pretty good complete couple.

You know, my mother was quite a remarkable person in the way she didn't hold back or step down on anything. When we were all working for Phillips here, my brother Blue was offered a transfer either to Illinois or to Texas. He chose to move to Texas, and he said, "Well, they want me to transfer to Texas." We were all single then, and I was working for the company. They had this solid fuels rocket plant for the government, Phillips did, at McGregor, Texas. My brother Jess had just got laid off, they closed the Continental Airlines where he was working here at Bartlesville. I told Phillips that if the company would transfer me also and hire Jess, we would all three go down there in a package deal. So we offered that to them on Friday, and Saturday they told us to come down there on Monday.

So, while our mouths were still open, we said Jess and Blue could go on down, and I would stay here and get the house rented. They could find a place for us to move to, and that's what we did. We asked my mother, "Since they offered this job for us down there, would you go with us?" She didn't hesitate one minute, "Wherever you children are going, I'm going, too." She'd never lived anywhere else besides Nowata and Washington counties, but she said, "I'll be glad to go with you," so she moved with us to Waco, Texas.

I was real busy in club work here, belonged to the Indian Women's Club, and the Cowbelles, and farm and ranch clubs, and a lot with the Historical Society, so I was very busy. I thought I'll go down there, and I'll just sneak in and just take it easy. We went down there, and Emil Malick was head of the plant in McGregor. He said, "Am I glad to see you and your family come down here, Mary, because we have just been called from the Chamber of Commerce at Waco, and their fair this year is going to be carried out in Indian style, and would you chair the plans for us? They called out here and knew that we had Indian employees, and so they met us with open arms." So there we were down there, and we just hit it just like that.

The Chamber of Commerce interviewed us, and so right then they called my mother an "Indian Princess," and so she got started with the churches and the clubs. They started calling my mother and asked her if she would speak to them. She said, "Well, yes, I'll speak about my people." I mean, she really opened their eyes, and one place especially she went and told them that, "Your sons, they fought for Texas, yes, but they also fought for Oklahoma and Kansas and all the states of the United States, and that you belong to the United States of America, just like my sons. They fought for the United States of America, and I'm proud of Texas and I'm also proud of all the other states." She got a standing ovation in some of the places, they told her, "You're a true American."

She just told them all about the Indian people and the United States and the Delawares and the Cherokees and all the tribes. We were in a big parade there, and my brothers led the parade riding white horses. The "Indian Princess," she was honored there, too. Ray McSpadden was at Texas at that time and Ophelia Overby, and there were several Indian employees that had been transferred from Bartlesville down there. We rode on convertibles and we dressed in our Indian regalia, and we had box seats every night. We were especially introduced at every performance of the rodeo. We just went in there and no chance of sneaking in and having any kind of relaxation. I mean we just hit it. Then my Aunt Sadie Lookout came down at that time, too, and they interviewed her and she rode in the parade, too. We were well known in Texas as soon as we got there. We were there about five years. They closed the plant down then, and so we moved back.

We enjoyed that time in Texas. It was more humid than this area, but it was quite a bit like this part of the country. Jess and Ramona were married the next February after we moved in August. They were already engaged, and we came back up to Kansas for the wedding. Then we were quite active in the Boston Avenue Methodist Church, and that's where Blue and Carolyn met. She graduated from Baylor University at Waco, Texas. Her father worked for the telephone company, and he was contracted to install the telephone system in Saudi Arabia, so they moved over there. She went to school in England some and different places in the world. She's been all around the world, so she and her mother were grand cooks. Her mother used to make fine cakes and did a lot of catering when she was over there for the Aramco Oil Company where Mr. Milam worked. That's where they lived when Carolyn and Blue were married. Her aunt lived in Dallas, and so they were married in Dallas and moved to Dallas.

Mother passed away when she was eighty-five years old in 1975. She was a very strong-willed person. It was a terrible thing when I was going to get married. She figured she was going to lose her daughter. She could think of what was wrong with Joe, but the very day we got married then—well boy, I mean, she'd fight wildcats for him, and nothing was wrong with Joe from then on. From the day we were married Joe was Number One. She thought that he hung the moon.

When she realized we were going to move her to the nursing home in Tulsa where my brother Bruce lived, since that was the place she needed to be, I mean that was terrible, like just throwing her away. Bruce just told me to go on out of there. He said as soon as I got out of earshot of where she was wailing and carrying on, she just took a big breath and said, "I wonder when they're going to serve supper?" The manager said usually it takes them five or six weeks to get adjusted. Land, you know, in two or three weeks you'd think she ran it. She just adjusted to the youngsters, they would have some high school kids come and visit with the patients. They would always love to go to my mother's room because she would tell them stories, Indian stories. And they would come there when they didn't need to, they'd come and visit my mother, and they would have her to tell them some stories. She was always ready to tell stories, and so she had quite a time in all of her life.

When she had this stroke she lived about eleven days. We stayed right with her night and day there. She was in the room with another lady, so my three brothers and I just stayed around the clock with her all the time. The other patient that was in that room said that it was remarkable the way we stayed with my mother. I know that she never spoke any more and she never said anything, but we could tell that she was rational and understood. We talked with her, and I know that she knew we were there and talked with her. I know she knew to the very end of her life. She was a very powerful individual. I'm proud of my parents the way they were, and my grandparents were quite great leaders. Funny thing about my grandfather, he was a leader in the area in Delaware. All the neighbors around there, most of them at that time were non-Indians, you know, white people. Most of them couldn't read or write very well. They'd come down there, and here my grandfather was a well-schooled individual. He even went to Bacone College and was a very smart, brilliant man, and they would come to him and have him read their letters when they'd get letters from people in different places. They said, "Mr. Miller, I got this letter from my nephew or from my grandson. Would you read it to me?" He'd read it to them and answer their letter for them. They'd dictate to him what they'd want him to write, and he did all or most all of the work for the community. It was funny to me that an Indian person like this would be the one to carry on, to do the work for all these white people around there, which you usually hear of the savage American, and here he was taking care of all the white people. He was quite a farmer and stockman himself. Raised all these animals like I say, helped a lot of people that were not as well off as he.

And my mother said at Christmastime and Thanksgiving time they never did invite a whole bunch of people, but people would start coming in wagons. They would have a big Christmastime. She would start cooking two or three weeks ahead of time, you know getting things ready. In the Delaware language there is no "R" sound in the Delaware language, and when you would see somebody coming you'd sort of hide behind the door, and when they'd come in you'd holler "Klishmish, Klishmish!" If you beat them to say "Klishmish" before they did they'd have to pay you a quarter or some money. So it was a real good fun time that they would always have at Christmastime. They always thought Thanksgiving time that they would have some Pilgrims around their table.

There would be salesmen and people coming through the country, just driving through the country. Mama said one time there was a Syrian peddler came through there, and Grandpa would visit with him, and he said, "You sing in your language and I'll sing to you in Delaware language." She'd hear them upstairs, they might stay all night, and he'd put them up upstairs. He'd go up there and visit with them, and they'd just be singing to each other and telling each other about their people.

My mother said one time some people came through there, and these ladies went up there in their room, and Momma said she and her brother had gone out and gathered some blackberries. Oh, they looked so good, and they said, "I believe I'll clean these blackberries and get them all fixed up and take a couple of dishes up there to these two ladies." So she went up there. She took these little berries up there, and the ladies thanked her. "Oh," they said, "honey, we're fasting but we thank you anyway. We can't eat, we're fasting right now. We can't eat these berries." So she said, "I took my little berries back downstairs."

Grandpa Miller befriended all the outlaws. They'd come by there. They lived just about a quarter of a mile from the railroad track. There'd be hoboes come by once in a while, and my grandmother would give them a meal. She'd set them out on the porch there and give them a good meal. One time, we had a pump right beside the porch there; she gave him a cup and told him to go pump him some water. She kept looking at him and said, "You've been here before, haven't you?" and he said, "No, I never was here before." So she got this meal fixed for him and gave him this stuff and told him to go pump him some water for him to drink. He went over to the pump, and he said, "Oh, you fixed your pump handle, didn't you?"

My grandmother said she had danced with Henry Starr [a noted outlaw, part Cherokee] at a dance one time. So they knew all them [outlaws]. Oh, another story—these outlaws, came in, and one of them was outside was kind of watching while the other one ate, and then the other one came in and he'd eat. My Uncle Ed was sitting under the table. He was a little kid about 6 or 8 years old fooling around there, and this outlaw had his gun on the floor under the table with him. Uncle Ed got to playing with that gun under there, and he got it all torn apart, and he couldn't get it back together. So he told this man, "I got your gun all separated, I can't put it back together." I tell you, Uncle Ed got it all torn apart, and he couldn't get it back together, but it didn't take this outlaw long to get it reassembled.

Sometimes they'd come through, and they'd be riding on the outside of their horses; they didn't want Grandpa to recognize them. Then he finally told them, "I can't help you folks any more. I'm a Christian and I belong to this Anti Horsethief Association. I'll have to turn you in if you come around," and so they quit coming.

Grandpa Miller died just a year after my father passed away. My grandfather and grandmother both died within about twenty days apart. Daddy died in 1931, and we moved down there and lived with my grandparents. Grandpa had asthma and got pneumonia. He just got real bad sick, and one morning they both became ill and didn't want to get up for breakfast. My uncle, Steve Miller Jr., was a single man, he never did get married, but he was a big league baseball player. He was a pitcher, and so off season he'd be at home. That one morning they both were sick, and my grandmother said, "We're sick. I've got something wrong with my arm." Grandpa he had this kind of pneumonia, or flu, or whatever. They stayed in bed, and Momma and Uncle Steve fixed their breakfast for them, and they took breakfast to them in bed. My grandmother's arm got worse and worse, and the doctor finally came to see about them. She had this, some kind of what they call "osteomyelitis" in her arm, and they had to lance that. She was getting better and she was coming along all right, and then my grandfather got worse and he passed away. They tried to keep that from my grandmother that he died, but she knew it, so she just lost her will to live. She was fifteen and he was sixteen when they got married, just real young; they just lived their whole life together. She just lost her will to live. My mother lost her husband and father and mother just in a year's time.

We walked to school everyday, and I remember Mother'd fix our lunches. Sometimes she wouldn't have meat that she could give us, so we'd go down to the grocery store. We'd have three pennies, and they'd give us three cents worth of lunch meat, three slices of lunch meat. That would be our sandwiches, and we'd go on to school. Mother would always make these cookies, and she didn't make them real rich the way you make cookies with a lot of oil. She made them more like sweet biscuits. One of Jess's buddies in school, one of his classmates, really liked those cookies, and Jess would sell him those cookies for a dime, and he'd go down there and buy cookies that he liked. I thought that was really funny. My mother really kept us together, and eventually she worked for this WPA sewing room that wasn't but just across the street about half a block from the school. They had a stove up there, and a lot of times she'd fix a lunch for us. We could go there and have lunch, and she'd bring us cooked beans. Sometimes she'd cook beans and sometimes potatoes and beef together.

I remember there were kids that didn't have everything they needed to eat and that sort of thing. I remember Mom really managed for us to have lunch, and when we still lived out in the country my daddy was still living, I didn't have any fears about being hungry or going hungry. I remember when I was about in the second grade the teacher said that they were wanting to have a Halloween party, and she sure wished we could have some pumpkin pie. I said, "Well, my parents could fix pumpkin pie for the class." There was about thirty of us in class, a whole bunch, so I went home that night and I told my folks, "I told the class I was going to bring pumpkin pies tomorrow." I mean she got busy. She made those pumpkin pies, and the next morning my daddy loaded those pies up in the Model T Ford, and away we went to school and took all those pies. Another time, it was my birthday, in August, and I wanted to have a birthday party. My aunt from over at Pawhuska came, and she made angel food cakes. I never will forget. I was eight years old. It was a three-tiered angel food cake, and I invited all my classmates.

We had a gallon freezer, and our neighbors had a gallon freezer. That just wasn't going to be enough for all the people that was going to be there, and Daddy took a gallon syrup bucket and he put that in a water bucket and put ice and salt around there, and he took a bail [a handle] and he made ice cream. He'd stir it up a while and then he'd make some more, and we had plenty of ice cream and cake and just had a big birthday party for me on my eighth birthday.

I was always in operettas and plays, school plays. My mother, when she went to Haskell, learned how to sew and how to do everything in a proper way. I don't remember the name of this particular play that we were going to do; anyway we had to have kind of little Japanese kimonos. None of those kids' mothers could sew, and so I said, "My mother will make the costumes," and so she made about ten kimonos for all of the girls in this play. Every one was a different color.

So I just grew up and I didn't have any fears about not being able do thus and so. Anytime anybody told me something can't happen is when I bow my neck and say, "It can happen." That's always been sort of my philosophy when anyone says something can't happen, that's just when I know it can. Mother was able to overcome all those hard times. I remember one time that some man from town brought us a big bushel basket of groceries. I think it had a turkey in it, but it was Thanksgiving time, and they brought that food basket out to us. That's the only time I remember that we ever received anything like this, but we did receive it.

My grandparents moved down here from Wyandotte County, Kansas. 1865. My grandfather was instrumental in starting the first school in the Delaware area, and he and my great-uncle, Simon Secondine I think was his name, half brother, they helped start the first school there. My mother said she remembers them making arrangements to start the school. My great-uncle had a sled, and she said one time there was snow, and he came there in this horse-drawn sleigh. He was quite a picturesque person. He made a gold-handled cane, and he was quite a picturesque person, as was my grandfather. They all took pride in their dress and they took pride in clothes. My grandmother would come to school, and she would bring my cousin Lena and I each a hat when she'd be in town in Delaware. Sometimes she'd buy us a pair of shoes each, and those shoes would just fit.

My mother and aunt and her mother would get to talking on the party line on the telephone, and they could hear different ones of the neighbors start to pick up the phone on the party line. Then my mother and aunt, they'd start talking Delaware, and phones started going down. Somebody finally told my mother, "Ida, just when you and Eva start talking interesting on the phone then you start talking Delaware, and we don't know what you're talking about then." When the phones started in over in the Osage village they started party lines. Henry Lookout was listening in on a party line when a couple of ladies was talking about they knew somebody that had some good eggs that they were going to sell. So they said, "Yeah, I sure would like to have some of those eggs," so Henry thought he'd sure like to have some. He said, "I'll take two dozen of those eggs." This little Osage lady, she recognized him. She said, "Eshe, Henry," that's Osage for "you know," that's an exclamation in the Osage. "Eshe, Henry, you're not supposed to listen, that's bad, that's bad, you're not supposed to listen," but he was wanting to get in on that egg deal.

My mother went to Haskell and I think she said when she was in the eighth or ninth grade she quit Haskell because it seems as though her mother was getting to where she felt like she needed her help at home. She helped do everything, cooking, and sewing. My mother used to do all the sewing for her mother and sisters. Aunt Eva, she had three daughters, one daughter passed away, had diphtheria, and so she had these two daughters, and Momma would sew for them. She sewed a lot for Aunt Sadie, too, when Aunt Sadie went to Haskell. That's where she met and then married Uncle Charlie Lookout. They had money to where they could hire their sewing done, but Aunt Sadie was a good seamstress, too. She learned how to sew and everything at Haskell.

My mother was talking about how she went to domestic arts and science, they called it then, and learned how to cook, the proper way to set the table, and proper way to do everything. She said different times they would be in charge of different tables. My mother was supposed to set the table and on each butter plate they'd have the butter balls. My mother said they were little butterballs, and so she made healthier ones. The teacher would critique the tables. They sat everybody down and they said, "Well, what does everybody think about Ida's table?" Everybody thought it was just fine, except, "Well, Ida was just a little bit too generous with her butterballs."

She said when they did their dishwashing and cooking they wore these long sleeves, and the long sleeves would go clear down past their wrists. They'd have to work and not get those cuffs wet or dirty in the least. They really had to do everything just very, very proper. When they went to school up there they were supposed to speak only English. She said there were some Chippewa girls that came from up north, and she said we could understand those Chippewa girls when they would speak when they'd sneak off around to where they could talk. They'd talk with those Chippewa girls that they could understand, and they could understand the Delaware girls.

After I belonged to the Indian Women's Club, which was in later years, I made [my Delaware clothes] on the occasion of the Bartlesville seventy-fifth anniversary. It was copied after my great-aunt, Mary Bezoin. A long time ago the Delawares would help sew and make clothes for the Osages. My mother recalls way back when she was young, they were friends of the Look-outs, and they would go on hunts over in the Osage country. They'd invite them to come to hunt for deer and elk. They'd camp together and visit each other. They'd invite them to dances, and they said, "Oh, those Osages would really dance, not like they dance now, just straight dances. They danced and they'd have this whip man, stripped from the waist up. They didn't have these fancy ribbon shirts back then. They just had roaches; all this regalia has been added since then." The Delawares had shirts, and the Osages sort of fashioned these Delaware shirts to their design. But to hear the Osages talk, the Delaware designs are like the Osages. But it's actually the other way around. It's Delawares that made these outfits and sold them to them. And that's the same way with the Osage women. They didn't have these big Bertha collars you know, like we've got. I fashioned my dress similar to my great-aunt's like she wore back in the late 1800s. I've got that picture of my great-aunt, Mary [Bezoin], and I designed, copied the skirt and blouse with a Bertha collar on it.

See Jess Townsend oral history (page 335).

Mary Watters and her great-granddaughter Skye Scimeca at the 2004 Delaware Powwow near Copan, Oklahoma.

MARY LOUISE SKYE WATTERS
AND
LAURA WATTERS MAYNOR

Mary Watters, born June 11, 1931
Laura Maynor, born 1958
Date of Interview: 1995 at the home of Mr. and Mrs. Watters

MARY:

My Delaware family is the Longbones and Wilsons. My grandfather was [Willie] Longbone[1] and my grandmother was [Anna] Wilson. From what I remember the Wilsons were a big family.

Grandmother didn't speak English. She died when I was nine, and whenever she talked to me it was mostly everyday things. It was in Delaware, and at the time I could understand. I knew what she was talking about, but I couldn't speak Delaware. The main thing that I remember is that I'd come home from school and tell her things that happened at school, and her comment was, "Gee whiz." That's what she always said. Her reply to anything was this, "Hmmm!" She didn't talk a lot, and she just refused to speak English. I think she could, but it was more of just an unwillingness to bend and to speak English. But my grandfather spoke English. He only went to the third grade in school [Quapaw Mission School], but he was real smart in common knowledge. He was born right after the Delawares moved into this area.

My mother's allotted land was down by Tahlequah. It's down in the hills where she never even saw it. She just knew that they had given her some acreage down there, but this was under the Cherokees. [Her mother was Elizabeth Longbone Skye.] I don't think she could even reach it. She's never done anything with it, and after she died we couldn't find her will; we couldn't find any legal document. She never tried to find out because she didn't ever want to live down there. To a lot of them the land itself didn't mean anything. The land they could live on, they could use, but they could never truly own because it belonged to God. That was the way I grew up thinking of land, is that this is God's, and man has a paper that says that he

---

1. Willie Longbone was born around 1868 and died in 1946 at age seventy-eight; Anna Wilson was born around 1877 and died in 1941 at age sixty-four.

can use or own that parcel. That that's marked off by numbers, but it ultimately belongs to God because that paper will go to another person. When that one dies and it just goes, so Indians say. My tribe or my family never placed much value in ownership because they enjoyed it. That's why they could sell their land, but they still felt like they could go there and hunt, or they could go there on that land because man could never really own it. So ownership of things was just something I had to learn the value of, and which I appreciate now.

I know when we bought this place here I remember walking across the barn lot, and Gilbert [Watters, her husband] was so excited about this acreage up here. Laura and Jim [their children], and Gilbert and I had walked all over, down in the creek bottom and up the hills and all around. When we came back we walked through there, and I was walking along by myself, and I said, "Well, God, if you'll help us, we could try to acquire this, we'll try to buy it," but I said, "But it'll have to be with your help, and we'll take care of it and we'll appreciate it, and ultimately we know that we can never completely own it forever and ever. When we're gone it will go to our kids, and then to their kids, but who knows down the line. Somebody's going to come that doesn't appreciate it, that wants to live in a condominium or something like that in a big city and won't want this." But I told God then that if He would help us acquire it that we would take care of it, we would be happy here, and we have been, and, of course, both my kids live here. It's like a little community, but Indians are noted for that, too.

When I became interested in the Indian Women's Club of Bartlesville, Galela Neumann was the president, and she invited my mother and I to a tea, an afternoon tea where W. W. Keeler was the keynote speaker. I was so impressed with him. I was so proud of him because he was on his way to being the president and CEO at Phillips. All the ladies were dressed up, and they had their silver service and everything out. I remember until then the connection that my mother had was working for the club. They had their wild onion dinners. At that time they were having them at St. John's School, and they hired Momma as cook, the club did, because it was the fancy, rich Indian women from Bartlesville. They were well off, and my mother never had any idea of belonging to that group of people. It's a very prestigious club, and it was then, and so she worked. Well, I remember going there and talking to her because she was in the kitchen. I think she was making bread, but anyway, it wasn't long after that that we were invited to this tea. We were so impressed with the speaker and the elegance of the day. It was just a short time later we were invited to join, and it was a big deal to us.

When Laura was a baby we had the Lenape Indian Club, and it was made up of Delaware families. At one time my mother served as president, and then at one time Nora Dean was president, and another time, Anna Davis. It was just kind of passed around. And Loyce Brown was president.

It was mostly run by the women, but it was families. Men could belong. We had a little powwow, a little dance, where the library is at Dewey, Don Tyler Library, and we danced there. Laura was a baby, and I had made her a little dress out of white batiste. I put that baby rickrack, rows and rows of that on, and it was a little three-tiered skirt, and a little plain top. She wore that, but she couldn't walk yet, but she could move with the drum. She was about two months old, and I took her up there in that little dress. Don Tyler was there, and he was one of our benefactors. He always really enjoyed the Delawares, and he was a good friend of Anna Davis, so whatever we were doing he was usually invited. We have a movie of it someplace, and he took her and danced with her in our round dance or whatever we had, the first dance. She'd just move her little body to that drum. She wanted to dance so bad, to be that little and hear the drum and everything. That was one of our club activities.

We put on several powwows at the football field. And whenever there was a parade or anything, we'd have an entry, and we usually won first. We had a real active group, but it seemed like after a while there was other things to do, and the interest lagged down. It just kind of died out. Then, about that time, right after that they started the Delaware powwows. That was a small group that started that. Numerous Falleaf and Don Wilson was in on it, and Nora Dean. But before that the Lenape Club was real active.

To me, tradition means keeping the old ways. The thing that I was taught and the thing that I've tried to teach my children is there are good things about our people, the good ways, good customs, and to try to keep those and not lose them. They can keep what worked. One of the things I like that my mother always did was to burn cedar when she prayed, and to use cedar as a cleansing, or purification. When anyone was sick my mother would burn a little bit of cedar. She called it "Smoking cedar," and that's hard to distinguish now because when you think "smoking cedar" you think "smoking pot" or something like that, something connected with dope or hallucinative stuff.

Mom had a little skillet that she used, and it was a little, long-handled skillet, and she heated that. Some people use coals, but Mom heated that skillet until it was red hot, and she sprinkled dried cedar sprigs, little needles, on that and that billowed in smoke, and then it would die down to a smoke. She'd call each one of us in to the kitchen, and as she stood there by her stove, she had an eagle feather or an eagle fan. I've seen her use one or the other, and she would take that fan and fan that smoke over to us, and she'd talk to us all the time that she was doing this. She'll say, "This will help you in whatever you need help and just give it to God and let God help." We stood like this, to receive this. When she was finished talking to us she took that all down our bodies, all down the front of our legs and the top of our heads. We turned our hands over and brought that smoke to us, put it here and on our heads, and then we could pray if we wanted to, to ourselves, or we didn't have to. Then we'd go, and the next one would come in, and she'd do that, personally talk to each. It wasn't a standard prayer or saying that she did for everybody in the room, but it was a personal thing. Each person that went in there she said something to, and that was one of the good things.

Her father had told her when she was little to keep the good things, to observe them, to remember them, to do them, and teach your children. And so he told her, but at the same time he was trying to teach her to go to school and to learn all she could at school. My mother was the first one in her family to graduate from high school. Once the other kids got to the eighth grade they weren't encouraged to go any further. She had two brothers and a sister, and she was the youngest, and she was her father's favorite. He had named her Elizabeth for the Queen of England. He thought that that was royalty, and he wanted her to have the royal name. She was always his favorite child. At the time I don't know where they got the money, but they did have money then. They lived with my uncle. That went along with the family that they lived with, the one that was the most prosperous. Then their mother and father might come and live with them, and then their brothers and sisters might come. I remember when my folks were divorced. Mom took us, my brother and me, and she was expecting my sister. She took us, and we went to live with them [her grandparents], and that's why I knew so much about them then. I was about nine, and that's why I was so close to my grandparents, but to me tradition is just keeping the old ways.

There are a lot of things that were lost. I would say in the twenties, in the 1920s, because people encouraged their children to go to school to learn the white man's way. At school the children were discouraged from speaking their language. They were kind of melted in with everybody else, and so a lot of things were lost. It's like when my father was young, athletics was his life. His mother was the medicine woman, and she tried to teach him what she knew of the medicine, and he said, "Oh, Mother, that's not important. We have doctors and we have hospitals, we have nurses, we have medical people that can take care of this need." He said, "That's not important anymore." But it is, because he was the eldest of her two children. He would have received this knowledge from her, and then he was obligated to pass it to his eldest child, which is me. But, he refused, so it ended there with him. I don't know that I could have learned or could have kept it up. I might have felt like him, that we have doctors, but there's a lot of good remedies and a lot of good ways that survived by using these things. There's a lot of medicines today that came from the Indians that doctors recognize and use.

I've seen a lot of changes. There was a time that Indians weren't well thought of. They were stereotyped, and I've seen changes in that way. I've seen the time when people were ashamed to be Indian, and they wouldn't claim it. If they didn't look the part, then they did not claim to be Indian.

Then I've seen it go just to the reverse. I've seen that everybody is claiming it. If they even have a little bit of Indian, then they're proud of it, and I've seen that. It's more the prideful thing. One thing that Mom always taught me is that she said, "You come from good people, you come from a good family." I was so happy one day I was sitting at the bank in Dewey. Gilbert had gone in the bank, and I was waiting on him. Sylvester Tinker, who at that time was chief of the Osages, came over, and he said, "Who are your people?" I said "Longbones and Wilsons," and he said, "I was friends with Willie and Anna," and he said, "I want you to know that your grandparents were the aristocrats of the Delaware tribe." He said, "They were very well thought of and they were fine people. Always be proud that you came from them." I was really happy. I was real pleased that he would take the time to tell me that.

This is another thing that this comes from my mother. Anytime anybody wanted to dress like a Delaware, learn more about the Delaware, she was happy. It was like a compliment to her, and she'd even help people who weren't Indian, weren't Delaware, she'd help them if they wanted to dress or if they wanted any kind of clothing she would help them. She considered it an honor that they thought that much of the Delaware people. I know there are a lot of tribes that are very protective of their tribe and their clothing and their ways and everything. They resent anyone wanting to simulate that tribe, but my mother wasn't like that. She wasn't selfish with her Indian-ness.

See, they adopted a lot of people. They took people in and made them their brother or their sister. They finally had to put a stop to it, especially when they started getting on rolls for payments because anybody who wanted to could come in and claim that they were of this family, so they had to stop doing that. Legally they can't do that any more. They can't make somebody their brother, or you can't adopt a child and say this is my child because of that. Many shared in that that weren't Delaware at all. That's changed in that respect.

I haven't really thought about what the future holds, other than I know that if Jeremy [her grandson] doesn't marry an Indian girl or somebody that's part Indian, then his children will have less Indian blood. Jeremy has a lot of feelings within himself that I recognize that stem from being Indian. I've always said that he is Indian, and I'm proud of him. I'm proud of his feelings, but it worries me because he likes to be alone, and to me that's an Indian trait when you like to be alone. In the future I see great things for Jeremy because he's very smart and he's a seeker. He seeks to know and to learn, and the future frightens me; when I think too far ahead it scares me. You want all good things. You want them to have a good life. You see them growing up, and they're soon going to go out, and you wonder if you taught them all the things you know. You wonder if they're being taught enough.

Jim [her son] was getting ready to go to college, and I was worried about him because he seems too trusting and so naive about things. I was talking to God one day, and I said, "You go with him and protect him, take care of him because he doesn't know how mean people can be. He doesn't know people that can lie and be mean." We try to hide from ourselves the bad things. We ignore or gloss over as long as maybe nobody else sees it, we think that it's not visible, but God sees it. Jim made it just fine, but I was just so worried about it. I worry about Jeremy. I don't know why I didn't worry about Jennifer [her granddaughter] as much. I guess because she wasn't going to be so far away. She was there in Kansas.

I've tried to teach Jim and Laura the things that my mother taught me, but at the same time I realize that they have to live in the world today. I've tried to think what I'm teaching them is the best of two cultures. I told myself they're lucky to know the best. It was just like when the boys were little I used to think, well, they go to dances with me, they have their Delaware straight dance clothing, they go and do whatever I require of them whenever I ask them. Even they've gone at times when the club has needed them and the church, whatever the church needed of them. Then Gilbert could come along, and they could saddle a horse, and they could go out and herd the cows in, and doctor them, and take them back across. So, I've seen them live in both worlds. And I've been glad.

I've been thankful for this, but there's just times that I think they're still babies. So I haven't thought ahead to what lies. I just hope and I pray every day for them that along the way they can make the right decisions. I've had to think on their lives because we're given them. They want to be named, and so we're having a naming ceremony in about two weeks, and Dee [Ketchum] and Leonard [Thompson] will do the ceremony, but Dee asked me to give the name, and then they would translate it into Delaware.

I had to do a lot of thinking about the kids, and Jeremy's name will be "He Who Speaks Wisdom," because he's always been like a little professor to me or to all of us, and he's going to go to school. He's getting ready, but it seems like all of his life he's getting prepared for this. Jimmy is "He Who Touches the Sky." I wanted a name with the English name of Skye, because that was my maiden name, that was my dad's name. Jimmy is a lot like I remember my dad. My dad was a tall man, Jimmy's tall, and my dad was an athlete and Jimmy's an athlete. Jimmy brings such light and brightness into our lives, he's not like Jeremy at all, and the days that are important to Jeremy aren't to Jimmy, but he just seems like he just lights up the room when he comes in. Sarah is "Little Girl in a Hurry," because she was born two months early, and ever since then she has been in a hurry. She just looks forward. She just is in a hurry to grow up. She'll be thirteen next month. Then Katie, she's the baby. Her name is "Little Sister, Little Friend" because she will always be the little sister, the baby sister, and she is a good friend to her friends, to her brothers.

It came to me, the names. I didn't just sit down and think, "This will fit." I had to think about it a long time and then be in a hurry. Dee wanted it done before the cold weather because it has to be done outside where they can build a fire. He'd say, "You know, we need to get this done." He said it's better from someone who knows them rather than him and Leonard. It's a lot how I see the kids and how I feel about them. Like I said, it frightens me, the future. Not so much for me. I never think about what lies in the future for my life or for me. I know that there's a lot of things that I thought I would do and wanted to accomplish, but it seems like it's not that important any more. But, I do worry about our young people. I want education and learning, but it seems like the more they're educated the farther away they go from you.

Note: Kay Wood, the interviewer, interjects her thoughts at this point. Ms. Wood states: "The options become more narrow and the more you're educated, the less choice you have about where you want to live, or do. I would've never left this area if I hadn't had to go on, and every day is kind of a [unclear] day because I don't have the support and the people I love around me."

MARY:

Well see, Kay, a long time ago when Jim was in high school, they had this Oklahomans for Indian Opportunity, and they were promoting programs for Indian kids. They were trying to get them to think about further education while they were in high school, and they had seminars for them and everything. I had taken the kids over to Miami to a seminar and took a carload of Dewey kids. The counselor told me that he had worked down in the south. I can't remember what tribe it was, but anyway, he had worked and worked with this young man and got him to go to school. He was brilliant. He said he was one of the smartest Indian men that he had ever known. He went to college and he achieved so much, and he went to this city and he wasn't able to study. He went back and he said that boy lives back with his people, back on this reservation or their family land. He was back there, and he said, he's not using what he is capable of. He's not using his learning because he couldn't stand to be away from his people. To that boy, it was being back home was most important, it was being with his people.

Kay: "That's a real problem, a problem we face every day."

MARY:

I saw a lot of children when my brother went to school. He went down to Okmulgee to tech school, and when we went down to visit him, they lived in these barracks. I saw a lot of old people. I saw some old grandpas, and I asked my brother, and he said, "Oh, that's so-and-so's grandpa." He said, "He's got better living conditions here with his kids than they did [at home]." He said, "A lot of these kids here, their relatives have moved in with them because they get things that they don't have at home so they moved in with them. Then when they got through with the school, they all moved back home." Well it's frightening.

Kay: "The saddening thing is that we force them to make a choice. Either you're going to choose to be an educated person and live in the middle of the city with nothing that you've ever known or no one you ever loved, or you live very poorly among your own people. Even today there's not a whole lot of choice. Those kind of jobs here because of the type of job he went after. But if you want to be an engineer or a scientist or business person, most often you're not going to find a job close to your people. It's a real problem. And I don't have an answer for it really. I guess our grandparents felt the same way about us."

Kay: Laura, I want to get you before you have to go home. Laura, tell me about when you joined the Indian Women's Club of Bartlesville.

LAURA:

I joined the club when I was eighteen because that was the youngest they would let you join it. I'm thirty-seven now, and it's been almost twenty years since I joined. I remember from the time I was little, Mom was always active in the club. She was always in the style shows, and Grandma was always cooking. I always had to tag along and do whatever. I think I was around twelve when I started dressing in the style shows with them. Whenever they'd have them when I wasn't in school then I'd go and help with that. I can remember always having to serve at the onion dinners. Sometimes I'd have to help cook because of Grandma.

I think after I had Jeremy I did less. I would help out when Mom would force me to. We've done a lot of style shows. My girls both have dressed, and the boys have dressed for the style shows. There were a lot of times that I couldn't work at the different things that they did because the kids would have something, their activities that they'd be in. But they've all four, when they've been needed, dressed and helped. The only office I've held has been the library chairman a couple of times in clubs, and that was interesting. We get to go buy lots of books to read and pick out which ones you want to purchase to send to the schools. I just remember the serving, the cooking and the serving.

Traditions to me are carrying on the ways that we've been taught. Part of our tradition was from the time I was able to walk. We didn't go to a lot of powwows. Some years we would only go to the Delaware powwow, but it was a yearlong process of getting ready for that one dance. My grandma was the one who taught me how to sew, how to make the blouses that we all wear now. There's been a few times back there that I've been told by Momma about how we are all dressed. We have on all the [Delaware] clothing, and that the reason you're there was because this was what my grandma enjoyed. You hear those drums and you start out. I told Momma, that's when I have felt like I was closest to God. Well we laughed, but I said, "It's okay if I die right now because at least I'd die happy." That to me, that's part of carrying on with the traditions that Grandma and Mom have instilled in me. I think my children all feel the same way. You know they may grumble and groan when I say we're going to go, I want you to dress. When they're there, and if they haven't dressed they wished they had of dressed. It's like it's there in them. Even if they say, "No, I don't want to." When they're there, especially Jeremy and Jimmy will go dance anyway, whether they have their dance clothes with them or not, because it's just, it's there, something that is in their heart. Those are the traditions to me. I guess [it was] drilled into me. I mean, I didn't like it sometimes. There were times when I wanted to get up and leave, but it seemed like this was really important that you stick with this and do this, and that's what we've done. And to mind, too. Whether they want it or not, they did. Daddy's included in everything that we tried to do.

What comes to my mind is the way we dress, our dance clothes, when we first started out to what we wear now. For instance, when I was little there would always be one or two buckskins. When you were little that's what you dreamed. That was the ultimate. That was what the rich Indians got to wear. We were always in the cloth, and now it's coming around where my whole family has buckskins, and you didn't see them like that when I was little. That was the ultimate, that was the best you could be. Mom has one, and I have one, and both the girls, and my niece. I mean it's pretty awesome when everybody gets together, and they're all in their dresses. Even getting my boys' things together took years. To get armbands, Mom and Dad would go looking for where we could find the best deal. It was just piece by piece from the time they were little bitty because when they were little they started out as feather dancers and then they went to straight [dancing].

When I was little it was a big deal to go to the western store to buy moccasins for that powwow because we didn't know at the time, Momma didn't know, how to make them for us. Now she makes all our moccasins, and I'll bead them. We did more study as the years went on; we studied tribal dress. We got pictures of the old dresses, and then we did more research on them. But all families went through this because Pat Donnell and I talked about it, and we laughed about how we thought we were just the ultimate, and now we look back. . . .

Kay: "I call it back to the future. You don't do things now that we used to do and have disappeared. My mom still does once and a while. At the first of the year we used to throw cornmeal over our shoulders for luck and protection. I didn't know the Delawares did that until I read about it. And yet now, no one does it."

Skye Scimeca, the baby held by Mary Watters in the picture on page 92, is now three years older and dances at the 2007 Delaware Powwow near Copan, Oklahoma.

MARY:

It's like a lot of customs though, because the people thought that that just wasn't necessary anymore, or they thought that was maybe a form of paganism. As they became educated they cut out a lot of those things, the old things, because the way they used to make you do when you lost a tooth, they don't do that anymore. I know they used to take your tooth and rub a piece of charcoal on it, and you had to go out in the yard and throw it over your shoulder, and hope that a dog didn't find it or you'd get a dog tooth.

Kay: "Well, why is that any different than a little kid custom of putting your tooth under the pillow?"

MARY:

I don't know, but that's what they do now. That's become pretty widespread with everybody.

Mrs. Watters was Head Woman Dancer at the September 2003 Delaware Days held in Bartlesville, Oklahoma. She continues to be an active participant in a range of community activities.

PART 4.
CONTEMPORARY
INTERVIEWS

The oral histories that follow were collected between 1998 and 2004 by Rita Kohn and James Brown, who also made still photographs along with videotaping each speaker. Speakers were designated by tribal leadership, initially by Chief Curtis Zunigha who, with James Brown, conducted the interviews with Joanna Nichol and Leonard Thompson, and then by Chief Dee Ketchum, who also personally interviewed Ed Wilson and Will Wilson.

The age range is from teen to elder. Generally, speakers were hesitant to state birth date, yet the content provides clues for their age at the time of the interview. In the interim between interview and manuscript preparation for publication, we tried to update positions held and life story, where applicable.

Delaware historian Deborah Nichols-Ledermann offers the following commentary:

> The reader can expect to see a wide variety of experiences in being Lenape as we are not all cookie-cutter Indians who grew up in the same circumstances. The interviews show the spectrum of influences on children of Lenape descent in modern times. Some will show people who have been involved with the tribe practically since birth. Others will show people who grew up under the influence of white culture, but have chosen to reconnect to their

Lenape roots. It also shows just how quickly those ties can be endangered. One generation, or two, is all that it takes. When I was on the Navajo reservation, I was talking to a girl about eighteen years old about the language and she made this statement, "I can understand Navajo, but I don't speak it. My mom can speak it and speak English. My grandmother speaks Navajo and really does not speak English." It was one of those moments of clarity for me, because my own mother had said the same thing about her father. She said her dad understood Delaware, but did not speak it. Her grandmother could speak both Lenape and English, though English was her primary language, and her great-grandmother spoke Lenape, with some English. I realized that in looking at the Navajo of today, I was looking at the Delaware of over a hundred years before. They were going through the same changes that we were in Kansas and early Oklahoma, and it was a weird deja-vu feeling. Like stepping into a time capsule, everything I had read in our old agency papers about life on the Kansas reservation suddenly came into focus for me in a new light as I observed the Navajo people.

The reader will, in many cases, recognize equally his or her own cultural or ethnic immigrant-family experience. The first generation speaks only its language or is multi-lingual. The second generation is pushed to assimilate. By the third generation much is lost. Around the sixth to seventh generation there is an active seeking to reconnect, and the language of origin must be re-learned, generally academically.

Family connections and recurring themes will become apparent, as will a unique rhythm or musicality of speech, the older the speaker. Younger speakers tend to come closer to mainstream usages and manners of expression.

The "roundtable conversation" encapsulates the meaning of "long journey home" and connects back to the overview history. This book, when read as a companion to viewing the documentary, becomes an important tool for grasping the deeper and wider American story as an oral legacy.

Don Secondine, an accomplished flute maker and musician, plays for Anderson, Indiana, fourth grade students. (Hear his music at http://brownimages.com.)

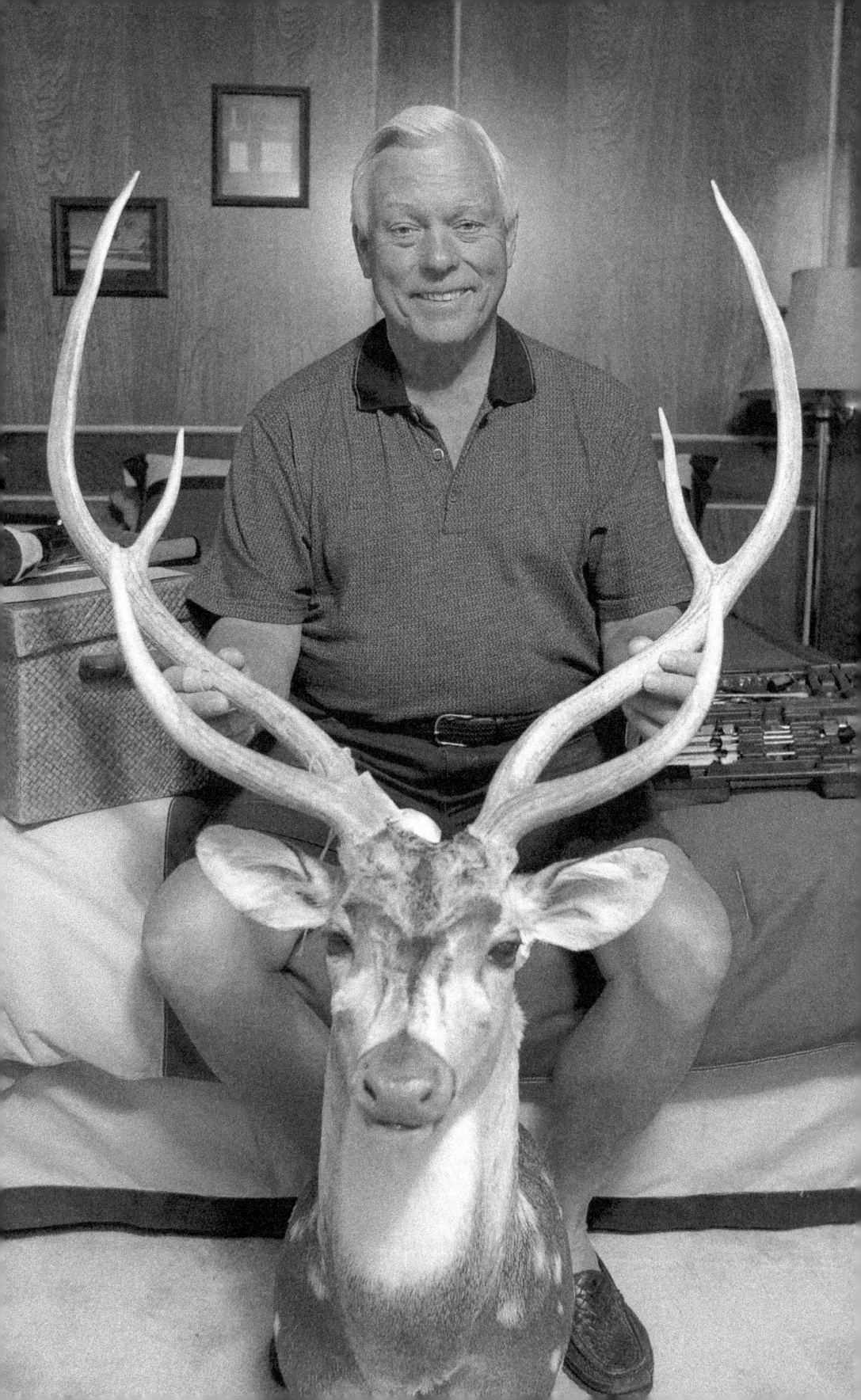

DAN ARNOLD

Former chairman of the Economic Development Committee
and member of the Reinvestment Committee, Delaware
Tribal Council
Born June 7, 1937, in Borger, Texas

Some of my early memories of growing up are the smell of the Phillips refinery oil. We lived right across the street in Phillips, Texas, which is very near Borger. My dad was killed when I was four years old, but I remember a little bit about my dad. But I mainly remember about the family here in Oklahoma. After he died we moved back to Nowata. I went all through school there and graduated from Nowata High School. But the early years, I knew that my uncle, Horace L. McCracken, was what we assumed was chief of the tribe, but actually at that time from 1951 to 1970 he was chairman of the Business Committee. At the time we did not have a tribal council, so he was the titular head for the tribe those nineteen years.

My Delaware heritage comes from my mother. Her name was Irene McCracken. My father's name was Algernon, or Al, Arnold. I have one brother, John McCracken Arnold. He's an attorney in Atlanta, Georgia. John was born in Nowata. I was born in Borger, Texas. Then after Dad died we all went back to Nowata and finished school there.

My grandfather, John McCracken, was vice-chief of the Delaware tribe back in the, I believe it was the late thirties and forties. Back in the thirties and forties, my mother and all my aunts and uncles were certainly discouraged from admitting that we were Indian at all. So during my childhood, I attended very few functions with the Delaware tribe. And even when my uncle was chairman of the Business Committee, I never attended anything at all. And I wasn't encouraged to. So, I always knew that I was Delaware, but we never participated and certainly weren't traditional Indians, especially traditional Delawares. I think during the thirty years when I was flying out of New York and Chicago, I became more aware of my Indian heritage than I have all during my childhood. Then, when I retired out of Chicago I came to Oklahoma and resolved to get more involved with the tribe. I started attending tribal council meetings and trust board meetings following my retirement. There became some vacancies, and Chief Dee Ketchum asked

OPPOSITE PAGE:

Dan Arnold holds his Axis deer trophy rated at 151.08 points (high Gold). Considered an exotic species in the United States, the animals were originally imported from India to a ranch in Texas in the 1930s. This trophy was taken near Kerrville, Texas. Arnold began quail, duck, rabbit, and squirrel hunting in Oklahoma when he was eight years old.

me if I would fill the position, and so I got on the tribal council. Then a little later I got on the trust board as an appointee. I'm on several committees. I'm the chairman of the Economic Development Committee and on the Reinvestment Committee. Before I returned to Oklahoma, there was just no involvement with the tribe at all, except reading the *Delaware Indian News.*

Joyce Williams, my cousin, and her husband did an extended family tree. And then I started reading some of the Delaware publications that were available to us. And that's the only way I found out [my connections with Mekinges[1] and William Conner] because I had no idea about my family history beyond my great-grandmothers and great-grandfathers.

On my grandfather's side, my great-grandmother was Sarah McCracken; her maiden name was Halfmoon. [On my maternal side] my great-grandfather was William McCracken. He was a U.S. deputy marshal in Indian Territory. They were parents of John W. McCracken.

[When I began to find this family tree,] it did change me. That's the reason I started attending the tribal council meetings and the trust board meetings, after I retired. I had felt that I had a responsibility to carry forward the family involvement with the tribe and try to help the tribe to the best of my ability. It's been quite a learning experience for me, and I hope that I've done a good job for the tribe.

I have one daughter of my own and two stepchildren, a daughter and a son. My daughter, Dana Arnold, would like to get involved with the tribe, but she's still in Chicago and is planning to move to Nowata in probably July or August [2000]. Then she would like to be involved with the tribe.

My stepdaughter is interested in the tribe and has some Cherokee Indian blood.

My stepson is in New Jersey, and he has some Cherokee blood.

I'm a pilot, and I was the director of flight operations for Abbott Laboratories in Chicago for the last fourteen years before I retired [1983–1997].

I graduated in Nowata and then I went into the service [the army] for a couple of years. I got out and went to Oklahoma University for a short time. Then after a short period I went to Northeastern State College in Tahlequah. That's where I found out that I wanted to start flying as a profession. I went to Spartan School of Aeronautics in Tulsa for two and a half years. After graduation, I just started flying and instructing in Fort Smith, Arkansas. Then I ended up in Connecticut flying jet planes. Shortly thereafter I got a job at Teterboro Airport in New Jersey. And I flew out of there for sixteen years. Flying for City Bank, Prudential, J.C. Penney, and some other large corporations. Then a headhunter came looking for me to interview for a job in Chicago for Abbott Laboratories. And that's where I retired from after fourteen years.

───────────────────────

1. Sometimes written as Me King Ees.

To prioritize [the basic needs now for the tribe], I think the number one thing is economic development for the tribe. We're looking at many industrial opportunities to be shared by our Delaware members for job training, and to participate in the profits. From monies generated, including casinos, we need to use proceeds to help the Delaware people including low-income housing, child care, elder care, medical prescription services for our people.

[The tribe is dispersed throughout continental United States.] Tribal members can use the health care services of any tribe throughout the U.S., but prescription services can be handled directly from here as long as we receive a certified prescription receipt. Other services for low-income families could be serviced from here. Hopefully each reasonable health care facility that's run by tribes throughout the United States would accept our tribal members into their health care facilities. Of course, we can better service the people that are in our area, if we have health care facilities in Nowata and expand to Bartlesville, and hopefully we can do something over in Chelsea. But we're limited in what we can do right now because of lack of funds.

When you were at work in one of your places away from here, you registered as a Delaware. If you had not had health insurance with your work, how would you have gone about getting health care if there's not a reservation where you were living?

I suppose I would have had to go onto welfare. But being a veteran I assume that I could have gone to any of the veteran's facilities, except for my family. But, for the general public, I guess they go without health care or welfare. In many cases in the past here, our tribal members would try to use the Cherokee facility in Claremore and were turned down because they didn't have the CDIB card that said you were Cherokee. Although they did have Delaware registration cards. That's a sore point with many of the Delaware Indians.

The land originally bought by the Delawares in the 1860s when they came here to Indian Territory [now Oklahoma] was taken away from the tribe by the federal government and was allotted to individual families based on the number of people in the family. What happened, taking this down to a personal level?

The allotments were given to my great-grandmother and my grandfather and my grandmother in Northern Craig County, right along the Verdigris River. And we had quite a lot of acreage. My Uncle Horace had land. My Aunt Lillian had land. My mother and Aunt Zona were too young. They were infants at the time so they didn't get any land. But my grandfather sold the land to the Todds; it became the Todd Ranch. And [my grandfather] started a grocery store in Watova, Oklahoma. I guess it was fairly successful. I can't tell you the year, but he was named postmaster to the city of Nowata by the president. He was there for about four years, I believe, and after that he became the county assessor. And he was in that job for about thirty years.

Allotment was gone long before I was around, [though] some people still have allotments. There's restricted allotted land that's still owned by some of the Delaware members. We hope to acquire some of that restricted land for the tribe itself, to run some businesses in the Washington County area. There are three individuals that we know of that have no relatives or relatives that qualify for half-blood or better for restricted land. We hope to acquire that land for benefits for the tribe. Other restricted land, or most of it, is located out in the country, and for economic purposes it's not very good. Anything that's along the highway or an interstate specifically is wonderful land that should be developed with the help of the tribe.

Allotment land means that it's supposed to stay in the family, not supposed to be sold out?

Not without tribal approval. But back in the early 1900s I guess it [permission] was given freely because people were so poor. It's a shame that it happened but it did.

Why did the government decide to break up the tribal holding?

Probably to take away the power of the tribe to be able to work as one entity for the benefit of the tribe. And to break it up, the land into allotments, in effect breaking up the power of the tribe. The individuals as individuals certainly didn't have the power of the whole group. I would think that was the purpose.

Now on the federal maps it's the Osage reservation which takes in this part of the area. The Delawares do not have an official reservation?

No, they do not. Which is too bad. It would make it much easier for us now to aid our tribe.

The land that you're now intending to purchase as a tribe, that becomes tribal land but cannot ever become a reservation land?

No, never a reservation. In Oklahoma, there cannot be reservation land.

There's federal recognition and state recognition. What's the difference?

Well, as to federal recognition, we are a nation and we deal with the government as a nation. With the state, we're just a tribe. They deal with us differently than the U.S. government does. With the U.S. government we deal with the highest level [the Bureau of Indian Affairs, through the secretary of the interior.] In Oklahoma we deal with the state Bureau of Indian Affairs.[2]

In Oklahoma, you have the Eastern Delawares and the Anadarko Delawares. The Anadarko Delawares never lost their recognition by the federal government.

---

2. During the years the Delaware lived in Indiana, before 1800–1821, Indian affairs were served in the Department of War.

Yes, the Western Delawares, as we call them, have now changed their name to the Delaware Nation, and we are the Delaware Tribe of Indians. We were known as the Eastern Delawares. This has just happened recently that the Western Delawares are the Delaware Nation.

We hold separate sovereignties. They've had theirs for quite a while, and I don't think they ever lost their sovereignty, but we did. In Missouri [around 1840] a band became disgruntled with how they were being treated by the federal government, and I guess they were unhappy with the chief [Chief Anderson] at the time for not requiring more of the government. And the band broke off and went to Texas and stayed there for a while, and then they ended up in Western Oklahoma. There are splinter groups still down in Texas though.

The Conner family has part of its history with what we call the Western Delawares. John C. Conner [oldest son of William and Mekinges] was a scout, served in New Mexico; land was promised but never given. What do you know about that?

Just what I've read. I thought that he was given some land personally in Texas. Originally, he thought it was for the tribe, but it ended up being a personal gift from the state of Texas. He roamed the country I guess for a couple of years, going out to Oregon and California and Indiana and Texas, came back to the tribe in Missouri. He ended up in Texas and became the head of the tribe of the few there. And then was called back to Kansas at that time to become chief [1857–1871].

I feel very fortunate to be related to both the Conners and the Andersons and the Ketchums and on down the line. But I guess in those times that Mekinges was the wife of Conner, there was no formal ceremony of marriage, and even though she had several children by William Conner, that the Indian ceremony was for life but that might be that there was no official ceremony. But I just think that in what I've read that she felt beholden to go with the tribe and move to Missouri and eventually to Kansas. And, of course, her father was a chief. But she was, I guess, well treated at the time before the separation. It's too bad the union didn't last between the two. I guess, after his death, there was a claim by some of the [Indian] family against the property that he had, and there was a private settlement.

The way that your family now has begun to reconnect, is this something that you're seeing more of in your generation with people who have moved away or not completely connected with their Delaware heritage, and there is a movement back to this?

In my case, yes. I've always been interested in the tribe and the heritage of the tribe and recently read everything that I could about the tribe, especially the quarterly *Delaware Indian News.* I read that cover to cover, and I knew that when I retired that I was coming back to Oklahoma and would eventually get involved with the tribe and try to do something; I didn't know what, but try to be of some help. I think my daughter feels the same way. I think what the economic development part of the tribe can do is to provide funds not only for health care, child care, elder care, and low-income housing, but also for the cultural part of the tribe. I believe that we could fund more studies, more cultural programs. We are not reaching out as much as we could, if we had more funds. We are having trouble getting funds for the language program. I believe that money generated by economic development can help fund more of those types of programs. And especially for our youth. We need to educate the youth and get them involved in the traditional part of tribal life. It's just not getting done enough. And hopefully the Indian children will have pride in themselves and their heritage. Maybe getting funding can help them get more involved in tribal activities and pro-grams. I wish I had that when I was growing up, but unfortunately I didn't.

I am still learning. I appreciate what our forefathers did to preserve the Delaware heritage the more I get involved in committees and with tribal members and the business of running a tribe. Hopefully, in the future, I can find a niche that I can help even more. Chief Dee Ketchum, the Council and the Trust Board, and I are working on the many problems confronting us for the betterment of the tribe, and that's the total focus, to help the Delaware tribe, that's all.

Total membership in the tribe is about 10,700 [as of May 2000]. In our service area, I believe [there are] 3,200. I think in the past, especially if you were a traditional Delaware youth, you didn't do very well in school and were limited in what you could do as an occupation. I feel that in the last few years or so, especially with computers and Internet, I think the youth are beginning to compete on a more equal footing than they had in the past. Hopefully the outlook for the Delaware youth is going to be very bright. But as a tribe, we should try to reinforce their learning, their heritage, and try to combine the two, but education is the most important. Hopefully we can encourage that and make it a tribal responsibility to encourage them.

Oral history interview on May 30, 2000, at Bartlesville, Oklahoma.

Dan Arnold savors a stogie between rounds of golf at his home in Shangri-La Resort, Monkey Island, Oklahoma.

Joe Baker, Delaware artist, at his office at the Heard Museum, Phoenix, Arizona.

JOE BAKER

Tribal member
Born 1946 in Bartlesville, Oklahoma

I am the son of Liberty Wright (known as Bea Baker in this community), the grandson of Stella Fugate, the great-grandson of Lillie Whiteturkey, the great-great grandson of Simon (Sion) Whiteturkey, who arrived in Oklahoma in 1867 from the last federal reserve of the Lenape people in and around the Lawrence, Kansas, area. I was born in 1946 in Bartlesville, Oklahoma, and grew up in Dewey, Oklahoma. I am proud that this is my community. Although I live at distance, Phoenix, Arizona, this community is my home and has very much shaped who I am today. As a child in Dewey, Oklahoma, we were related to everyone else—extended family. The freedom of this experience is a treasure. In a recent conversation with a dear friend, Marion West, we recounted some of our childhood experiences. Marion West, Mike Pace, and I were in the fifth grade when the three of us started seriously [tribal] dancing. We met each week at the home of Joe and Lucy Blalock and practiced. We were fancy dancers at that time. We danced competitively at powwows all over the state. Marion's mother, Lizzie Longbone West, carried us to the powwows. We would dress out of the trunk of the car. We also performed exhibition dancing for local and regional clubs, such as the Lions Club, the Rotary Club, Chamber of Commerce, etc. As adults, it is a pleasure for us to get together and remember that part of our childhood.

That's the wonderful thing about home and about this community. All things become available. They become available through aunts and uncles and cousins and friends and tribal members who support cultural expression and help young people participate. Mother made all my dance clothes; other people would pitch in, and suddenly you're ready for the dance arena.

How we learn is through observation. Being taken to the arena as a young person, dancing alongside experienced, mature dancers, is really how we learn. The fine points you develop through practice, observing movements and styles of dance. The powwow is a pan-Indian, intertribal, social gathering directed by innovation. New materials make themselves available over time and are incorporated in dress. The powwow culture is vibrant, alive! A culture marked by change and movement. Indian people are often viewed by mainstream audiences as people of the past. While we certainly embrace our history, our traditions, we live and work and are partners in the broad community that is today—a community that continuously changes and moves about.

Contesting at the powwow is an important part of the experience, as individual participants strive to be the best that they can be. Contesting is less important today for me personally. But for me, coming home every year for the Delaware [powwow] is more important than contesting. Our powwow is unique: it's one of the oldest organized powwows in Oklahoma. An old-style three-day encampment, individual families having established permanent camps. A great homecoming. And, for those who live at a distance, a chance to catch up on the events of the year and see everyone. This year was particularly exciting. I looked out at the dance arena, and there were many young people, more so than in the past. I find this inspiring, energetic, and hopeful. It's an honor to be part of this experience.

I have always been an active participant in the culture of our community. Key individuals within the community were important to me at an early age. I think children develop a certain way of seeing when it is shaped by tradition, and that way of seeing was, for me, expressed in my professional life—the arts. As a young person, I had a certain facility for drawing. Drawing and making things were more fun and fulfilling than academics. I never thought much about being an artist; I'm not sure I had heard the term "artist." I experienced the arts in terms of daily life—the way I saw the world. Individuals in our community encouraged me. Sometimes that is all that a child needs, "that's really good, keep up the work." There was never a conscious decision to become an artist; this seemed to me an appropriate path from the beginning. The art that I create as an adult is as much influenced by these early impressions and influences as it is from formal training. I think both are important. Primarily, I'm known as a contemporary Native American painter, whose early work was characterized by social satire and cynicism describing southwestern lifestyle. Today, my work is more related to abstract forms and patterns. Current painting describes my understanding of place and home and the land surrounding us. Alongside the painting is traditional beadwork. A process that I love, it's an art form that keeps me sane. I currently work at the Heard Museum, Phoenix, Arizona, and manage the Artist-in-Residence program [as of 2002]. Additionally, I coordinate outreach initiatives involving the twenty-one federally recognized tribes in Arizona. Two years ago, I brought to the museum a new program of which I am very proud. The Native American Seniors Association, a group of intertribal elders, meet regularly at the museum and work with the Native American Student Guides. My personal goal for the museum is to move the programming beyond objects. The creation of a program format that celebrates people and their communities as people gather, learn from one another, and interact. It is a pleasure to have the opportunity to learn about the tribes of the greater Southwest. While we are different, we are all much alike in many ways. Everyday I have the opportunity to learn more about other people, their ways, their thoughts. This is a great privilege.

My personal thoughts regarding contemporary Native American art, its past and its future, are directed by my experience in the field for well over twenty years. Native American contemporary art has never been, and continues to be, not that popular. Let me define what I mean by "popular." The art does not fit into any neat and defined category associated with mainstream contemporary art. I think this attitude needs to change, as there are great artists among us who happen to be Native American. However, Native American art is often stereotyped by mainstream thought. A young Native American artist who has the experience of two worlds—tradition and community, university and academic training—Western and non-Western. When this combination occurs the expressions through the arts are often significant. Work of content. Work that encompasses diverse formats, such as performance, crossover work combining elements of theater and performance, Native American composers, Native American writers, etc. The world of contemporary art is very exciting. And yet, Native American artists are still marginalized, categorized, labeled, and encouraged to work only in traditional formats by mainstream society. A few artists have been recognized in the mainstream art world, but fewer than we have hoped for. Education that demystifies the Indian and allows the public to come to know Indian people in the first-person voice is one solution. Our cultural institutions, museums, can create this educational opportunity for visitors. Change is not always fast enough, but things are changing. Humor continues to be a mechanism of coping with change. This has been an important aspect of our collective histories.

I am interested in working with youth today, largely as a result of the support that I felt as a young person. I was encouraged to experience the world and its possibilities. I feel I have a personal responsibility to give back today. I continue to teach, though no longer am I associated with a college or university. The Artist-in-Residence program allows me to participate in a cross-generational educational program, where the artist has just as much potential to learn as the student. Everyday is an opportunity to learn, and if you can share that knowledge with another person, then it is good. We have the responsibility as proud Indian people to be the very best that we can be and express that goodness in positive ways. Each day, the morning prayers are about being the best you can be in the day that you have. I learned that as a child through the example of others in my home community.

I attended the University of Tulsa. I hold a BFA degree in design and an MFA degree in painting and drawing from the University of Tulsa. I was interrupted in my education by the Vietnam War. I served in the United States Air Force for four years between undergraduate and graduate school. While at the university, I had the good fortune to study under Alexandre Hogue, an artist associated with the "Dallas Nine," a group of regionalist painters who gained national prominence. I was trained in a classical studio program. Other faculty members included Woody Cochran, Osage, and Brad and Gwen Place. Brad and Gwen made me a part of their family while a student at the University of Tulsa.

After graduation, I assumed that I would teach and proceeded to find a teaching position at a university. My first teaching assignment was in Farmington, New Mexico. San Juan College, located outside Shiprock, New Mexico, was my first introduction to Navajo culture. I returned to Oklahoma and taught as visiting faculty at Oklahoma State University, Stillwater, Oklahoma. I eventually left Oklahoma because I could find no full-time employment. I moved to Phoenix, Arizona, in 1981 and pursued full-time painting for thirteen years, represented by the Elaine Horwitch Galleries. In 1991, I found myself and my work changing. The commercial gallery world is an inflexible world, not allowing for individual differences and personal growth essential to an artist's creativity. I was committed to honor my own expression as an artist and continue this pursuit at all cost. I returned to teaching and held visiting faculty appointments at various colleges and universities across the United States for a period of six years. This experience was very expansive, and I appreciated the diversity of communities. I joined the Heard Museum on my return to Arizona and continue to work as a painter and traditional beadworker.

A bandolier bag is an important article of [the] Delaware man's dress. These are traditional designs and colors. The technique is two-needle appliqué, allowing for the creation of abstract floral motifs typical of Delaware style beadwork. My interest in beading is driven in part by the knowledge that we Delaware have always been recognized for our beautiful beadwork. This is how we are recognized. Bandolier bags were commonly seen in this community in the 1920s, they are not commonly seen today. I wanted to return the bandolier bag to this community. A beadwork project like the bandolier bag is an important project, often requiring a year's time to complete. I have completed two bags to date, and I am working on a third bandolier bag. Two years ago another member of our tribe completed a bandolier bag [Annette Ketchum]. There will be more in the future. This is another recent piece, a dance belt. I continue my beadwork, painting, and teaching.

Much of the research for design motifs for the bandolier bags was accomplished at cultural museums and libraries and archives of national museums. In 1998, I was Artist-in-Residence at the National Museum of the American Indian, the Heye Foundation in New York, and was privileged to examine Delaware cultural material collected in the early 1900s by Harrington, who was from the Bartlesville, Oklahoma, area.

As a tribal member, I am excited for the promise of our future. The possibility of a tribal museum is paramount for the future of our people. I would hope this might happen in the near future and that it will be properly considered. This requires careful and informed decisions regarding collection storage and conservation, so the art will be held for future generations. This is a significant part of who we are. The art is informed by tradition and comes to us through the people and as such has a life of its own. The art needs to be returned to the community from which it originated. I believe the art longs for this interaction of its community members. I would like to see an elders program as part of the new tribal complex, a community garden that provides for healthy alternatives to processed foods. I believe our responsibility to care for our elders is an important expression of who we are as people. We need to meet this challenge by increasing opportunities available to this population.

As a painter my work is non-political. I am formally interested in abstract forms, shapes, movements and rhythms, color systems that are reflective of place and land. My current work reflects back to the experiences of growing up in Oklahoma as a child and member of the Delaware Tribe of Indians, to autobiographical references of family and the Indian experience in Indian Territory. There are references to early ceremonies, some of which are no longer observed today. These hold my interest as an artist. They are non-political and non-humorous. I am interested in creating beautiful passages to describe a people and the land that is referred to as home.

Oral history interview on May 29, 2000, at Bartlesville, Oklahoma.

Eddie Barnes, 2005.

REVEREND EDDIE BARNES

Tribal member
Born September 16, 1923, south of Ramona, Oklahoma

There were five of us boys, two older and two younger than me. We had a sister. She was eighteen months old when she passed away. She was just older than me; about eighteen months older than me. We grew up not where a group of Indians [lived] at Ramona. Of course, after growing up and beginning to know most of the people, practically the biggest part of them had a little Indian in them. Always our family was a close family; a family that didn't do a lot of talking but, like of evenings or sometimes when we'd come back from school, we would get together and just sit. I guess let the spirit talk to us.

We hunted; it was during [the] Depression. We'd go rabbit hunting, squirrel hunting, and fishing. My mother canned. Now, she was full-blooded Delaware, and my dad was Cherokee. Of course, being during Depression time we grew [and hunted] whatever we had to eat. Survival. But I look back and I think I had one of the best childhood days. Now my brothers don't think that way, I guess. But I had really loving parents. They never went around always telling me that they love me, but I knew it, I felt it. It was just within them. We played ball together, usually on weekends. My mother would make us balls out of cloth, and she'd sew them up. We usually made our own bats and gloves. She'd take some old worn-out gloves, and she'd pad them up. My dad and mother played ball with us, and, of course, our friends would come, different ages would come, and we'd have ball games. I don't know what you call them—workup, softball. We played a lot. I remember especially my two younger brothers (my two older brothers weren't real sociable) [and I] were close together. The two younger brothers and [I] were just pretty close. We used to play with little cars; make our own roadways and things. Didn't have [store-bought] cars. We'd have to make our own toys to play with. We would have a tremendous time.

During the summer month when blackberries and things were ripe the whole family would go where the blackberries were. It weren't too far. We'd go pick blackberries, and my mother would can those blackberries and have them all fixed up for us. And come winter, I remember storing food; flour and sugar and a big lard can that you would buy in bulk and use all winter long. Usually lasts all winter long.

Summertime we would go to a stomp dance. Called it a Stomp Dance. We would go to Copan. We'd usually go to Copan about this time of year. I can't remember if we went to Copan or Quapaw first, but there were three that we usually attended during the summer months. We would stay there three or four days. The government would furnish the food or the meat or whatever, and the ladies would cook, and so we'd all eat together during those days that we were there. And, of course, evenings we'd get out and stomp dance usually up until twelve o'clock anyway. But you know I grew up in that, I say grew up in it just those weeks, those two or three weeks of the year that we went. The things that bothered me during those times was the drinking. We didn't have tents and things; we'd sleep under an old Model T Ford or if the weather was bad we had some quilts we'd spread out and sleep under. But the bad things that I remembered was the drinking and going on. And when I grew up I thought I'd never go back to that. It was no place to raise children. We started back just for the fellowship and the relationships. That's what I always looked to the stomp dances for, to bring your families together in relationship and having a good time with each other. But all of them didn't drink, just some of them. It's just some of the things that went on.

We went to Sunday school. All, especially my younger two brothers, but of course my two older brothers went with me. My mother and dad never went to church, they didn't participate, but my mother always had our clothes ready. She didn't force us, we weren't forced to go to Sunday school or church, but our clothes were always ready, and we usually went to every Sunday school and then to church.

In later years I was in the navy, which I was in for forty months. I was on a fleet mine sweeper [engaged in] sixteen invasions in the South Pacific. Usually we went in from four hours to two weeks before invasion. We were the first ships of [the] minesweepers division. Usually we lost the first mine sweepers that went in because they didn't know where the mines were even though we had sound gear and sonar on. But we were very fortunate, the ship that I was on; we never lost a man during all those operations only on the first trip, [when] one of our electricians was electrocuted. Of course, I had quite some experiences.

I always say I never bargained with God, but I guess maybe in a sense I did. I always said, "Now Lord if I ever get back home, I want to be helpful in some way. If I can be helpful to humanity in some way to make it a better humanity, that will help the people, that's what I want to be." When I got home after I was discharged, I ran, I drank. I tried to get away from all of it. I didn't want to think about it. God didn't keep me away. He always, in a way, kept me through that promise. Finally, I was able to humble myself before God and before man and say that I wasn't able to carry those burdens. The last five to six years I've been going to my ship's reunion. There were thirteen of us that went all the way, thirty months, on this minesweeper. It was such close quarters that I guess many of them couldn't stand it. It was just too close quarters. So we had just thirteen of us. We put it in commission. We put it out of commission. I don't know, I look back, and I don't know if it was because I was an Indian, the only Indian aboard ship, anytime there was a special assignment, I never volunteered for [a] special assignment, but usually I was on a special assignment.

I wasn't always a Christian. God revealed that to me when I was out there. I didn't know it. If someone had asked me if I was a Christian, I would have told them no. But I had a vision out at sea. I had this vision that became real. There was someone in white on a boat, motor whaleboat. There was one on the bow. He was shining and dressed in white, and one on the fantail. And I was in the middle; I was lying down. It was just calm and peaceful. I looked over at the shore, and our ship was beached. It wasn't sunk, but it was beached. I couldn't see light at all there. And it haunted me. It haunted me from that time until I surrendered to the will of the Lord. It was revealed to me that if my life was taken, my name was written in the Lamb's book of life. But there was nothing there to offer, there was no works that I had ever done. In my Christian life it was written down. After that, after I followed through and professed the faith through baptism, it just opened up to me and revealed to me, and life hasn't been the same since then. I'm just like everybody else. Jesus, when he walked on the face of this Earth, he told his disciples, "Now, I didn't offer to give you a rose garden, you know what I've gone through." You kind of expect to go through things. If your Master went through them, you can expect to go through the same thing. That helps me so much.

Every battle I was in, every invasion, there was sixteen of them; I started at Tarawa in Gilbert Islands. We went in four hours before ships went in. We went under eight-inch line of the coastal artillery of the Japanese. They would fire at us. I don't know how they missed us, but they did. The shrapnel hit our ship once. I had a life jacket on. We always dressed for battle. I had this kapok life jacket on. I was on special minesweeping. When we were minesweeping, that was my detail, special minesweeping. After we secured that I went back on the gun. But we'd just put out a minesweeping [operation], and we were sweeping. We had it all ready, all we had to do is sit and watch. So I was watching where these shells were hitting. One hit in front of our ship and another between us and shore. The next thing I knew, I turned a complete somersault. Backwards. I'd been hit with shrapnel. Mauled my arm like that. A piece of shrapnel just about that big around hit right here and just ripped the collar off of my life jacket. I had shrapnel in my helmet, just filled. My life jacket had helped me.

Then another time, this was before we were going to Okinawa, we were heading for Iwo Jima. We had already gone through several incidents, and I made seaman first class about six months after I got in the service, after boot training. That's pretty fast for the seaman first class, but I didn't want to advance. I had one of the officers ask me one day, "Say Eddie, would you like to go to officer's training school?" And I told them that really I don't have the education. And I don't want to anyway. But anyway, I went on, and one day we were in Mogmog in the Ulithi Islands before Iwo Jima, getting ready, and our executive officer called me up to his office and he said, "I have an important job that I want you to do. We've been selected to take seven officers to a designated ship for a meeting. We have to go by seven ships and pick them up." Then he said, "What I want you to do is go up on the flying bridge [highest navigational bridge on a ship] and read the compass, and I'm going to point these ships out to you. It's going to be dark." We didn't have lights at night because of the enemy. I was going to read the direction of these ships. The only training I had on compass was at boot camp. So, night came and we went. I still say, was that my imagination or did I just dream that, but we hit those ships right on the nose after dark. And that's the way God works, taught me, helps me now. I look back and I see that it was Him, it wasn't me. He chose me and He wanted to show me those things with what He was able to do, if I'd just do it. Of course, I came home and I tried to get away from my responsibilities. But finally, He gave me a wife that I'm just not deserving of. She's such a help. She's special.

My brother just younger than I; [Howard] and I were [school] drop-outs. We went to a school for aviation. He was going at a different time, but we were in the same place. I dropped out and went to New Mexico and worked on the Southern Pacific railroad before I went into the navy. As a gandy dancer [a railroad maintenance worker or section hand] we laid steel from El Paso, Texas, to Tucson, Arizona. After that I came back home and then I joined the navy. Anyway, Howard and I [had] dropped out [of aviation school]. When we got home after we were discharged we went to Chilocco Indian School under the GI Bill of Rights and got our high school diploma. A few years after my wife and I were married, we had three children and we had our mother with us. Seventeen years of her life, she was with us. We went to Oklahoma Baptist University. Graduated and got a degree. My wife taught. She got a major in English and Latin, and mine was mostly religious education. I was with the Home Mission Board of the Southern Baptist Convention for eight years. Training up, you know. I worked with all different tribes of Indians, most of them were Shawnee. I pastored a Mission church. Then in Lawton, [most] were Apache. Then on to four Texas churches, then back to Oklahoma. Usually, the churches I pastored couldn't pay full-time salary. So I supplemented; I worked and pastored two or three, just almost a full-time pastor. I had worked with the Willaroc Museum with [the] National Indian Guide Center. I was with the media [department] that showed the shows [and took care of] the projectors. It's out in the country. It's on Highway 123, about ten miles south of Bartlesville. It is 3,600 acres. It has wildlife, deer and buffalo and elk. It really is western. People from all over the world come to Willaroc. [I did] other work, too. I went to Fort Worth. Went down there to pastor a church then came back [to Oklahoma], and I became the Head Start director of Washington and Nowata counties. First Head Start director of Washington and Nowata Community Action Program. Eight or nine years I was with Community Action as the Head Start director. I had Head Start classes in Bartlesville, Dewey and Ramona, Ocheleta, Delaware and Nowata. I guess that was one of the richest programs ever. Many of [these students] have gone on to get a degree in college. The Head Start Program was for everyone, not just Indians.

When I was interviewed for Head Start director, the boss asked me, "Eddie, what in the world haven't you done?" And of course I said, "Well, there is a lot of things, and I never did become master [of] any of them." But, my life's been a rich experience. When I look back to the place where I grew up, in Ramona, that was the foundation. I had some of the greatest teachers that anyone could have. They were all Christian teachers. They never pushed their Christianity on me, as far as pious ladies, they were just good people. Not only that, they took everyone into consideration. When someone has come from a home that was unpleasant, well, they tried to make up for it. I remember my second-grade teacher; her name was Mrs. Bandel. And evidently I was needing milk because everyday she made sure that I had a little carton of milk.

I'll tell you when I went to Sunday school and church I had some friends that I sat with. And their mother and dad would always sit beside them, and then after Sunday school was over there was church. And they would go up, and they made sure they would sit beside them. And they made sure I always sat with them. And the thought never did leave me, and it never has. And I promised the good Lord, I said, "Lord, I guess I'd be the happiest boy in the world if my mother and dad were sitting beside me." And I said, "Lord, if I ever get married, if I can't offer my family anything else, I want to offer them a Christian home." And the Lord has been able to take care of that. We have three children, a boy that's a preacher in Kansas City, Missouri, and the youngest daughter lives here, and we have one in South Carolina. All Christians. Everything worked perfect. We just praise the Lord that we have three fine children.

I might say this about my brothers. When we were in the navy, when I'd go off with a girlfriend, when I'd talk with them, share with them, I'd say, "My brothers was the main center of my home." And I would tell them about my brothers and what we did and how much I cared for them. And I remember one girl saying, "Eddie, I don't care about your brothers. I want to know about you." *[Chuckles.]*

But it's been a rich time. My wife and I have a rich, rich time of it. My mother and dad, like I said, weren't Christians at the time as far as I know. That's between them and the good Lord. Eventually my dad was eighty years old, and he made a profession of the faith. I had the opportunity of baptizing him. My mother, she had been a Christian for several years, but she never [publicly professed the faith]. I used to talk to her, and she would promise me usually every week that she was going to make her profession public, but every Sunday she'd get sick. It took her a while but in time she did. She was so hard of hearing she couldn't even hear a freight train go by. She was hard of hearing when she was eighteen years old. She had pneumonia, and it was either that or death; they gave her quinine, and that made her hard of hearing. She always told me about her relatives, the Delaware Indians on her side, that there were preachers on her side of the family. I know you've heard of Charles Journeycake. He was related. And some of the others. My grandfather on my mother's side was the first mail carrier from Bartlesville to Nowata. He used to be the interpreter for the Delaware Indian tribe. He was over at Washington, D.C., as the interpreter of Delaware.

My dad's name was Harrison (Ham) Barnes. And my mother was Viola Marie, Willey was her maiden name, Barnes. My children's names are Eddie John Jr., we call him E.J., every since he been a little guy. The middle girl is Vinnie Teresa Barnes—well, it's Logan now. And then Mollie Rebecca Barnes Martin. My wife's name is Birga Leona Bennefield. She goes by Leona. She's a retired school teacher here in Bartlesville High School system.

[We participate in the powwow] as far as dancing. We enjoy it, we've enjoyed it, and we enjoy the fellowship. We get back with people and communicate with them.

[My mother] would tell us about the different things that they participated in. She had two younger sisters, and they went to the Catholic school at Pawhuska. I think my mother graduated from the eighth grade. And probably the other two did, too. But she would tell us different things. My mother was kind of superstitious in some things, too. She would tell us about how she'd cut our hair, and she would never sweep it outside when she cut it. She would pick it up because of bad luck. But she did have some superstitions that were passed on. Every way that she could she would try to help us in school. We never missed a vaccination or anything, for like small pox and yearly things. They took real good care of us. Well, that's possible, you know, in that day and time. I'm just thankful for it.

I retired last May 16.

Oral history on May 28, 2000, at Bartlesville, Oklahoma.

Clayton Sears inserts an Eagle feather in his roach in preparation for dancing at the 2007 Delaware Powwow near Copan, Oklahoma. He received his roach when he was eight years old.

Howard Barnes, 2005.

HOWARD BARNES

Tribal member
Born August 17, 1925, in Plain Oaks, Oklahoma

I've always said I was born in Ramona. I was raised in Ramona. That is when I first remember anything. I was about four years old, and I remember things that happened, snowstorms and going to school. Actually, in my class there was only one other Indian. Everyone else was white. I was treated just like one of them. There weren't any problems. I left school when I was a sophomore and went up to the Indian School, Chilocco. Me and my cousin got too smart for that so we left there and went to Wichita, Kansas. My dad was up there at the time. I stayed there probably six or eight months. And the war was going on, and I went into the service on April 7, 1943. I was in the U.S. Navy. I took my training in the navy in Idaho. Out there in those mountains. After I graduated out of there and went to Maryland, I was in the amphibian navy. I went to Evansville and picked up my ship. It was an LST. And we went down the Mississippi River and went down to New Orleans. It took us seven days. And went from there back to Mobile, Alabama, and put on some guns and went up to New York City. Then we went to Boston Lake, Boston. Biggest amphibian force I've ever seen. And each one of us on that ship, it was 325 feet long, and we had 900 and some odd soldiers and I think 36 jeeps and armored tanks plus 400,000 gallons of fuel on each one of them. And we went across this lake. Then we'd run up and down the coast of England. We couldn't stay in one place with those Germans bombing. Until June 6th, then we made that invasion. We went in and out of there eight different times. The first time we came out we had about 1,000 German prisoners that came back to England with us.

And then the next trips we made, we'd go back and forth and carry troops in and carry prisoners back, and we'd bring back the wounded, too. Then we went on down to Africa. And then back over to Corsica and picked up a bunch of these African troops, the Singhalese troops. We'd pick them up and made the invasion of southern France with these Singhalese troops, that was quite an experience. Then we made that invasion, and I left. Our ship came back to the United States. And then they put me on another ship and went to the South Pacific. We went down to Norfolk, Virginia, and went down through the Panama Canal, stayed about six hours in Hawaii. This was during fifty-two days that we were on the ship. *The Indianapolis* got sunk, we were about sixty miles from that. Our skipper, he had a log that the [Japanese] submarine actually came up and looked us over. But they knew our ship was too small. That wasn't what they were after. They knew what they were after, you see. So we got in to the Philippines and we stayed there until we invaded Japan. While I was there the Japanese had given up, you know, they had bombed them.

So they sent us into Okinawa and told us to go there for cover, and then a typhoon came up. The navy said they couldn't go in there, so we had to go on into Japan. We were the first ship into Japan after the war was over. And we stayed in there. We were there eleven days, in Sasebo, Japan. And then they told us we'd have to wait there for the marines to come in where they take pictures of things. Then we went out and then went back in there, and we tied up this buoy again and circled that thing about six months. But we'd get off every afternoon and drink beer, play softball or something. Then we got started home. The ship I was on was a diesel-powered ship; they built only three of them. Two of them was out of commission, and this one we had was the last one. So we got just outside of Yokohama, and the water pump went out of it, so we had to go back into Yokohama and stay there. I think we were about fifteen days late in getting home.

And as far as leadership in the tribe, I got started by Henry Secondine and Bruce Townsend, that was in 1954 when the government said that they could form their own tribe. There wasn't any money or anything for the tribe, so we all just kept meeting and kept it going and finally got a smoke shop going out there. We had all went together and found a note for the building, the original building down there, to get it paid off. And after we got our smoke shop going we finally got the money to pay it off. Henry and I got the housing authority started. I ran for office two or three times. I forgot how many years that I was on the tribal council. A younger bunch came in, and they can run it awhile. They started getting money, grants and everything. Then everybody wanted to be a Delaware. I was out of the Delaware business for I don't know how long, but anyway, Chief called me about economic development now.

See they was having problems with the BIA [Bureau of Indian Affairs]. They had people in there, and those people didn't want anything to do with the Delawares. So it's just been a fight all this time, and we were meeting down in Tulsa at the time when they brought a letter in. I forget what his name was, but there was a guy in BIA was fighting against us. He had wrote the letter himself, I know he did, telling us there wasn't any more recognition for Delawares. But the Housing Authority got started on that when it came out that any tribe could be recognized and form your own housing authority. So we got it, but the Cherokees wanted it. They didn't want us to have it. We went to Oklahoma City and met with the board down there, HUD, and they said, "Yeah. Delawares can do that." It's getting stronger all the time now. It's getting a lot of houses built. But our first houses we built down in Chelsea, and we got another grant to build somewhere there in Nowata. They are just Indian housing. But there is a preference for Delaware if they can do that.

At that time I was on there, [I was] called the executive officer. But the tribe ran it. The Delaware Tribe. You couldn't use that housing money for nothing other than housing. Only source of income at that time was mostly from Smoke Shop. It was out on Madison Street. Well, we ain't got none right now.

[We ran that from the 1960s until] probably '80s. Well it is like this. In any other tribe someone is going to get their hand upon it. But it finally went by the wayside. They were supposed to have sold it for about a thousand dollars, but it never did show up. Then the Cherokees came back and told us that they were going to charge taxes on these smoke shops, and they were getting tax money off of them. And they told us that all the smoke shops in our area that we had been collecting taxes off of, that we could have that. Plus, they would give us five thousand dollars a month. Just give it to us, but they [Delaware Tribal Council] wouldn't accept it because they didn't want anything to do with the Cherokees.

I am not on the council. [The Housing Authority] is still growing, I think. They just recently built some kind of center for the kids and maybe the town to use. I don't know what all is down there. I haven't been down there in years. But they have got a lot of money.

Delaware wasn't spoken, but my mother, she grew up in that environment. I don't know why, but she could understand it. They shipped her off to girls' schools. Anyway we went to all the powwows when we were kids. We had to go back during the Depression time. We would go to Sperry. They had a three-day event down there every year. Where you go down there and spend three days with them. Sleep under the cars. Anywhere you could sleep. Then we had one over at the Quapaw. We would go to spend three days. They fed us and everything. There is one at Copan. We always went to that one. Back then you get something to eat so we would go. It was all tribes.

Sperry was Creek and Cherokee. I think that they are all down in there.

Well, Delawares weren't only Delawares. When we went to school, Chilocco, we had to go under Cherokee. What happened in 1876 when that treaty was signed, Cherokees and Delawares would be known as Cherokees. But I always said that I was Delaware 'cause you couldn't change your blood.

My mother was full-blood Delaware. But the time she was enrolled they put her down as three-quarters because back then it wasn't good to be an Indian. And they thought maybe leave a quarter off. That way if anything came up she would be entitled to it. Yeah. Back then, my brother married a lady who was full-blooded Delaware, and she said I wish I was never an Indian. It's tough, but we never had any trouble with it. I guess because we were able to take care of ourselves.

[My father] never was on the rolls, but he was Cherokee. But, he never could prove it. He said at the time that they didn't want to be known as Indians. His folks didn't. So, they never did get registered.

[My mother's maiden name was Willey,[1] and] all I know is that they have their own cemetery over there. My grandpa and grandma are all buried over there. But my mother never did tell too much. I guess because we didn't ask her. That's the same way with our dad. We never did talk that much. We weren't that close of a family. We just come and go ever since we were kids. We did anything we wanted to do. My grandpa, his name was John Willey. But he got that last name, Willey, when the teacher asked him one day what his last name was, and he said Willey, and the teacher put him down as John Willey. He just pulled it out of the clear blue sky. Back then I guess you could just call him anything, and they would just write it down.

[My mother inherited] eighty acres. Her and her sister and brothers over at Glen Oak, where the cemetery is, she had eighty acres in there. Well, after she passed on we sold it.

Just went ahead and sold it. Took it off the rolls down there. See the BIA had control of it when she was living. They ran it for her and everything. And they would send her a check. She had eighty acres over there, and I think she was getting eighty dollars a year for eighty acres. I think forty some acres was hay meadow. Which was making some pretty good money.

They're still hollering about that throughout the country. The BIA had to explain all these years, and now they can't account for all of it. There is the Osages. They beat them out of millions of dollars. They had figured out something on the oil. It wasn't put down the type of oil that it really was or something. I don't know the story on that. They've had quite a shake-up in the BIA about controlling Indian's money.[2]

[My mother] couldn't rent [her allotment]. It all had to go through the BIA. To sell it I don't remember whether we had to go back through the BIA or not. But I don't think so. There was oil and hay meadows.

It was pretty well expected [to attend powwows]. It's about the only place I had to go back then.

[My mother] made quilts and stuff like that. We didn't have any money. We were poor people.

[After coming back from service], I went to work. I retired from Reda Pump Company. I spent thirty-five years there. But before there, I worked at a plumbing shop for four years. Then I went to Texas and worked for El Paso Natural Gas and then came back to work for Reda Pump. Only submersible pump there was at that time. The pump itself was put down in the well, and it would pump up instead of putting it on top and sucking it up. You would set it down in there, and it would pump it up. Mr. Arutunoff invented it.

---

1. Spelling according to Ruby Cranor, *Kik Tha We Nund*, p. 23.
2. On January 7, 2003, the *New York Times* reported that more than 300,000 Indians gave a federal judge documents claiming the government had cheated them out of as much as $137.2 billion over the last 115 years.

Howard, Ray, and Eddie Barnes regularly play a game of pool at the senior center in Nowata, Oklahoma.

He's a Russian. They ran him out of there [Russia] when he was a kid, and he brought the invention. And I think Frank Phillips was the one that got him started there. And he got started in 1933 or somewhere in there [Reda Pump in 1930].

I never had any prejudice. That's one good thing about being Indian. You can go anywhere, and they don't know what you are. You just fit in.

I never had any trouble getting jobs, but there really wasn't that many jobs around back then. Back in the late forties. But when I found a job I had two or three offered to me then. So I took the one that I thought was the best. I never did have any trouble. Just like the thirty-five years spent down there. Had my boys working down there [at Reda Pump].

I've got a son in Lake Charles, Louisiana. My older son works for Ford Motor Company in Dallas, Texas. He's been with them about twenty-five years. He's a Vietnam veteran.

One boy, he's a contractor and he lives up in Copan. I got three boys.

The oldest is Rick Lynn. Then Lindsay, he's the middle one. And the youngest one is Sydney. The middle one, his real name was Howard, too. Howard Lindsay. But he goes by Lindsay.

My oldest boy is really interested in [Delaware culture]. He tried to get them set up on his land on the Copan Lake where the old tribal house was, he worked on that. He never did get too much started. Yeah, he's really interested in it. But the other two boys are just trying to make a living and going on. As of now, I have one granddaughter; she's twenty. She's won a lot of pageants for beauty queen. And the boy, he's seventeen. That's my middle boy's kids. Lindsay's kids. He goes to school, and I think he's the only Indian boy in there. But he seems like he gets along with them.

Oral history on May 30, 2000, at Bartlesville, Oklahoma.

Ray Barnes, 2005.

RAY BARNES

Tribal member
Born December 27, 1927, in Ramona, Oklahoma

It was hard times back in those days. But my dad, he was a good dad, and he worked hard. Did the best he could for us. My mother was the same way. I was born and raised in Ramona. My brothers and I think there was one other Indian family in Ramona. They were all girls, and we weren't all that well acquainted with them. So, we, me and my brothers, grew up like other kids. We were Indian and didn't deny it, but there wasn't any distinction. We enjoyed going to school there. My mother, she was hard of hearing, and it was hard to talk to her. She was full-blooded Delaware, and my dad was half Cherokee and half English. So we didn't get to keep up with a lot of the old Indian customs because we weren't around it. We did, once or twice a year, go to the powwows and things like that. But that's about the only connection we had with other Indians. And still today I'm not too familiar with the other Indians around here because I never was integrated with them. But I am always Indian.

My Dad had kinfolks around Ramona, and my mother was raised over in her family's allotment over in Nowata County, north of the old Glen Oak store. My dad's uncle, my great-grandmother's husband, died, John R. Willey,[1] and my Dad's uncle, after a while I don't know how long, married my great-grandmother, and they lived on the place up there, and my dad stayed with them. That's how he and my mother got acquainted, and after they were married they moved to Ramona.

I went to Chilocco Indian School during my sophomore year. I went there one year. My dad was working in Wichita, but we still had our home in Ramona, but there wasn't anybody there. I wanted to come back to Ramona, so I came back to Ramona and enrolled in Ramona for the eleventh grade. And it just turned out to be too much, and I had to drop out. Sometime later I joined the Merchant Marines, I came home from the Merchant Marines, then I was drafted into the army. Being a draftee I only spent eighteen months in the army. I was discharged from the army. Then I got married and I went to night school at Bartlesville Business College and studied accounting. That's how I went to work for Phillips Petroleum Company. I worked for Phillips for thirty-five years. I took the early retirement program.

The Anna Davis allotment was the first well that was built in this area [what is now] down on Johnston Park. The drilling well is still down there. The city refurbished it. I really don't remember whether Frank Phillips was in on

---

1. Spelling according to Ruby Cranor, *Kik Tha We Nund*, p. 23.

that or not. What really kicked them off was the fuel in Oklahoma City and the fuel over in the Burbank area. That's what made them into a major oil company.

[My mother's] allotment was over in Nowata County, the whole family allotment. There was my mother, two sisters, and one brother, they all had allotments and of course the original allotment to my mother's folks. Later on, on my mother's allotment, we leased it out, and there were two small wells we drilled on it.

One of the sisters, her son has still got her allotment, and he lives on it. He built a new home. My mother's allotment was kind of isolated eighty acres, and it didn't have a road in it, and it just wasn't much. It was just pasture land. We kept it leased out to a local farmer for pasture land. It wasn't any farm land on it; it was just rocks and grass. But we—me, Howard, and Eddie—finally decided it just wasn't worth it to keep it up, so we sold it.

We keep up [with cousins]. One of the sons has kept their aunt's allotment, and there was kind of a large family, there was about five in that family. We keep up; they're scattered, but we keep up with them through the son on the farm out here. And one of the other aunts, she only had one daughter, and we keep up with her through visitation and through the other relatives.

I've got four [grandchildren], two girls and two boys. They're not real active in Delaware business or Delaware tribe, but they all still are Delaware. They're Indian and they're Delaware even though they're not real active in everything.

My oldest daughter lives in Marietta, Georgia. My oldest son lives over on Grand Lake in Oklahoma. My next son lives here in Bartlesville. My youngest daughter, she's not young anymore, she is in her thirties; she and her family live here in Bartlesville, too.

They didn't [come to the powwow] this year, but they have in the past. You know how things are today, specially if they live off, they've got things to do which they think are important, and they just didn't get to come.

I'm sorry to say that I really haven't been doing a very good job [of passing on Delaware heritage to my grandchildren]. After they get a little older I probably will, but right now, I don't really know what to do. But they all know that they are Delaware, they all know that.

That's why I'm concerned about the Delaware tribe now. We're getting into a lot of things, and I'm wondering about the younger generation coming up. We're all getting old. And our younger ones, only a few of them come to the meetings. And I'm wondering if there will be enough interested younger people to carry it on. I really don't worry about it, but I think about it.

[My children] keep up through me, what's going on. My youngest daughter's kids are active with all the little children's programs here in Bartlesville. I can't even remember what it's called now.

Several years ago, when we were down at the other building, more or less getting started out, while we had the Delaware language programs, I tried it for a while, but I couldn't. I finally had to give up. I'm very proud and appreciative of the ones like Dee Ketchum. I'm very proud of him because he's really carrying on the traditions with the language and everything. But like I said, we just weren't raised around other Indians, and my mother being hard of hearing, she could speak Delaware, but she didn't do it around us.

I was on three different ships [in the Merchant Marines], and I think maybe I might have been the only Indian on the ship. But there wasn't any discrimination or distinction; in fact, all of my friends were white boys. Of course, it had to be that way because there weren't any other Indians on there. But I never have run into any racial things in my life.

[With the army] I took my basic training in Camp Polk, Louisiana. And then after I finished boot camp, basic training, I was sent to Camp Stoneman, California, and I spent the remainder of my time, sixteen months, there. I was on a shipping list to go to Japan, but I had a little accident previously and I had a bad knee and I was in the hospital, and the shipping list was sent so I was scratched. Spent the rest of my time in Camp Stoneman, until I was discharged.

I was drafted in April of '46. And I got out in October.

In the Merchant Marines off of West Coast from San Pedro, California, [we were] taking things up the coast on tankers, to Portland, and then going overseas to New Guinea, but it was right at the end. At my age, I was only sixteen. We stayed on our way to New Guinea, but all the way over we had to zigzag all the way across.

When I got out of the army, I came back to Ramona; I wasn't really sure what I wanted to do. There wasn't much work available. Things hadn't started picking up yet from the end of WWII. So being young, too, I just didn't think that much about it. I didn't think that far ahead until I started thinking about getting married that I'd better kind of settle on something. So, I went to a plumbing school in Kansas City, but I saw that wasn't going to work out, so I didn't last long there. I just gave up. At that time, Phillips Petroleum was really growing, and I just said to myself, they're going to need some help up there. Because they are expanding and hiring, and I better equip myself to be able to get a job. And at that time if you got a job at Phillips, you were set for your life if you made them a good hand. And that's what I intended to do. So I spent thirty-five years up there.

Phillips is a pretty large company, and there were a few Delawares there, but none where I work. I've always just seemed to fit right in, and I'm still Indian but that was it. I was just one of the boys. One of the workers, no distinction. But there were several Delawares working for Phillips. Mary Crow was.

My oldest son graduated from Northeastern University down in Tahlequah. And he went to work for the Grand Lake Association after he graduated, and then he went to an insurance company in Oklahoma.

[My youngest son] lives here in Bartlesville, and he was a type that didn't want to work inside. He's got his own tree business.

My oldest daughter lives in Marietta, Georgia. She went onto college and got her degree at Tulsa University, and then she went on and got her CPA. So she went to work at a book company in Tulsa. And another company offered her a better job in Atlanta, Georgia, so she moved to Atlanta, Georgia. She works for a major company in insurance and finance. She's doing very well. And my youngest daughter, after she graduated, she didn't want to go to college, but she wanted to go into travel, so she went to school down in Atlanta, Florida, and got her training there, and then she came back to Bartlesville and went to work for Spears Travel agency in Bartlesville, and she still works there today.

I liked Chilocco and regret that I didn't stay up there for my last two years. But the reason why I didn't, when WWII was starting—well, it had already started—a lot of my friends up there were older than I was and were being drafted, and I thought, well, if I go back, I'll have to make new friends, and being a kid I just didn't. Of course, it was kind of silly, but that was my reason.

One of my brothers, Howard, was there. But Eddie and Howard went back to Chilocco and finished high school after they were discharged from the navy. I got my GED in the army before I got discharged from the army.

My parents impressed on us that we needed to get an education, Howard, Eddie, and I, but my two older brothers felt like they needed to get out and work. But we always liked school. But our family had problems. My mother got sick and she was in the hospital, and my dad was having a hard time finding work, so Eddie and Howard dropped out, and then they went back after they were discharged. And Eddie, of course, he probably already told you, he went on ahead to college later. And Howard also, he didn't go to college, but he went to business school. But yeah, my parents, they impressed on us that we needed to go to school. It wasn't any fault of theirs, it's just things that happen, we just had to do the things like the laundry and the cooking and just trying to stay in school. But it is finally working out.

Howard, Eddie, and I, we try to keep close contact, and we enjoy being with each other. And I am kind of concerned about the younger generation, whether they will carry on like this generation is doing. I have great respect for Mary Crow [secretary-treasurer of the Delaware Tribal Business Committee during the 1960s] and Bruce Townsend, he used to be the chairman of the business committee; they didn't call it chief back in those days [1950s to 1980s]; before Bruce was chairman, it was Horace L. McCracken. He had a big job at Phillips. For several years, there was just a few of us to carry things on. And it's a wonder that things didn't kind of die out really. But Mary Townsend Crow and Bruce Miller Townsend, they went on a mortgage to buy the building down on Shawnee, just to have a place to meet and have a little office down there. But I do give them a lot of credit for keeping things going. Now, Dee [Ketchum], I think, is doing an excellent job of keeping things going. But I am concerned after when this generation's gone on whether the other kids will keep it going.

I was on a Grievance Committee, in case things came up that need to be settled. We talked about a lot of things that are still getting talked about today. About getting the tribe recognized. At that time the government owed the Delaware Indians some money for all the movements that were made, and we were working on that and trying to get that settled. And finally did get it settled. And the remainder they held out, I think it was 10 percent of the pay out, to preserve the tribe, and that's really what the tribe's been operating with, for quite some time.

If I remember right, it was quite a few years ago, but I don't know how they proportioned it out, but it all came out to a little over 1,700 dollars apiece to the kids; my four kids got it. I don't know how they arrived at that.

I was appointed [to the Grievance Committee] by Bruce and Mary and [Horace L. McCracken]. I lived in Ocheleta at that time, and they came to my house and asked me if I would be on the committee.

We had things people had a concern about. We would bring it to the business committee and try to hash it out. [I served] fifteen, sixteen years, something like that.

We were down there at the building on Shawnee, and they were starting to begin a little rivalry or whatever in the tribe. There was a lot of arguing. And that was about the time for me to give it up and let someone else carry it on. Bruce got voted out. There was a rivalry there between him and the person that beat him.

My dad was never involved in Cherokee business. His family just wasn't interested. He liked to go to the powwows and things like that, but that was about as far as the Indian activity.

I have admiration for the ones that did start the Delaware powwow and kept it going, because it was a very small thing when it first started. And it just kept getting bigger, and it is one of the biggest now. But I wasn't in on that. It was mostly the Falleaf family and their circle of friends that got that started.

When I was a kid I'd dance some, but I just went mostly to participate. But I admired the ones that were participating. Most of those in dancing have been raised up in the customs, and that's their life. Our family wasn't raised like that.

I've encouraged my kids to indicate [on the 2000 census] that they're American Indian. Because that's the only way that they're going to be able to keep track of how many Indians there are. Also, give them a good part of the tax money that they paid into. We're concerned about the money too, but mostly to keep an accurate count of American Indians, that we haven't disappeared.

Oral history interview on May 30, 2000, at Bartlesville, Oklahoma.

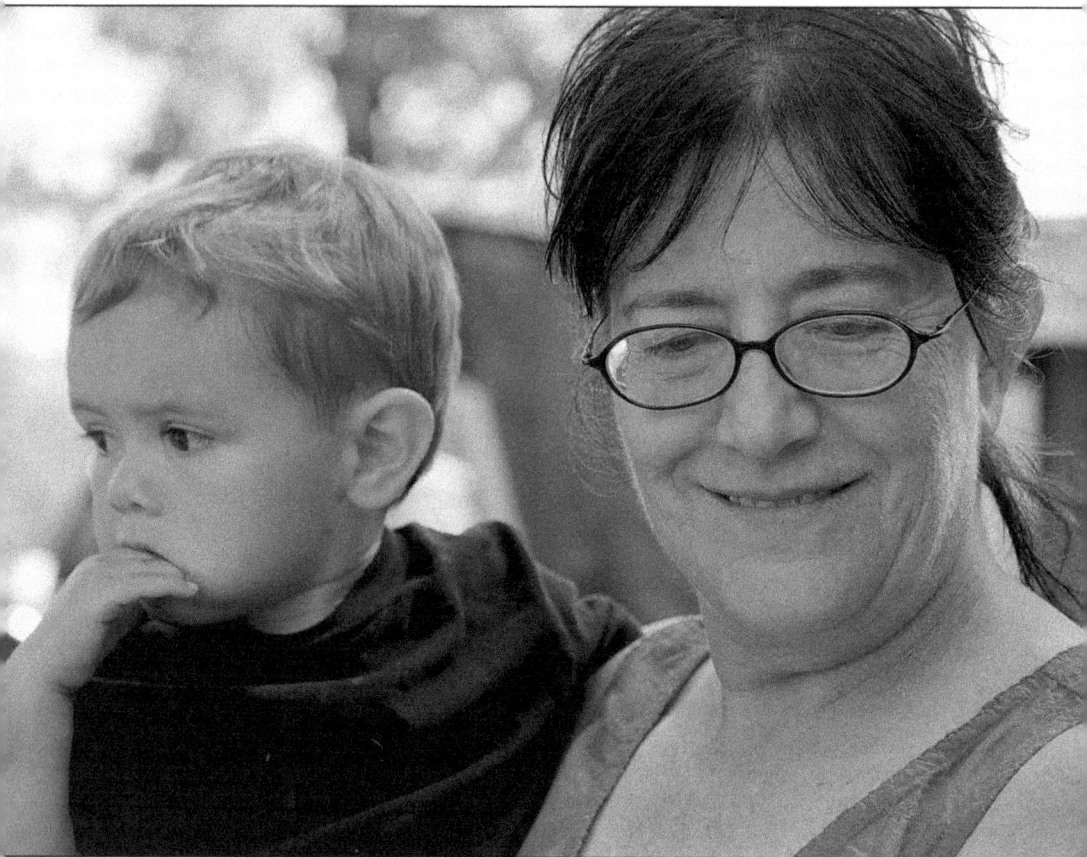

Jan Brown with her grandson Tyler at the 2006 Copan Powwow
near Copan, Oklahoma.

Janifer Brown

Former head judge, currently language assistant
Born August 23, 1946, in Elk City, Oklahoma

Since I was raised by my mother, who was the white part of the family, I didn't even know I was Delaware until I was in my early twenties. I discovered this when I met my dad; he also got to meet his first grandchild. I knew that something was different in the way that I felt about things, about what was going on in the world. I didn't realize that I was Indian. I just knew something was missing. And when I discovered not only my tribe but also that they were teaching language, I came over and met a lot of the tribal members, and they just welcomed me with open arms, and that started my learning of exactly who I was. And because I know what it's like to want to know and not to know where to go to get it or how to learn about it, I love to teach others that are in the same place. So I try to share what I've been taught with them and try to help them find their place. I'm turning into an elder before I want to be, just like everyone else.

My father's name is James William Allen. His father was Rufus Allen, which was from the alliant doctors.[1] He married a Joneycake, which came from the Isaac Joneycakes. Isaac was a translator. He knew many languages. Maybe that's where I got my hunger for language. His father was Solomon Journeycake [spelled Journeycake on the government roll], who in the 1800s was chief of the [Sandusky River, Ohio] tribe.

When I met my father I lived in Stillwater, Oklahoma. I started coming to the yearly powwow that's on Memorial Weekend; it's held in Copan, Oklahoma. I didn't move to Washington County until early 1994. I'm married to a Choctaw man, Thomas Brown. We would go to his festival once a year, and we would come to my powwow, and we were actually more comfortable with the Delawares; even he was. So when he retired, it made us able that we could move. We were coming here twice a week, sometimes three times a week, which was like two and a half hours from Stillwater. And he said, "Dear, I really think that we should move there." Because it was kind of tiring, he so nicely moved over here so I could be with the tribe. And after I was over here a year, I felt like I needed to contribute a little more than

---

1. Alliant doctors were part of the Bureau of Indian Affairs Health Service.

I was. So that's when I ran for the judgeship and got elected to be a tribal judge. And since the chief justice position was vacant, I was appointed to that, which was very interesting. There weren't a lot of cases to be heard. We were gaining more cases as the years went along. It's basically just deciding which person is actually following our Delaware constitution. If there is someone in disagreement, saying that they are not abiding by it, it's actually reading the constitution or trust document and deciding which person is the accurate person, if there is one that you can actually say this or that to. I had a little bit of law in college, but I'm definitely not a lawyer. I was a housewife. I didn't really have any training in that, but you don't need it, to know right from wrong, you just do it.

In the [Delaware] judicial courts, our system is much more informal than a state court. The cases are usually between Delaware people about Delaware problems. Also, the way we run our courts, they are more relaxed. Everyone has a chance whether you were actually involved in the event or you just have an opinion, which I don't think is the case in state courts, where, if you were not directly involved, you are not allowed to talk. And that's not the way the Indians [handle] their disagreements. Everyone can voice their opinion, everyone can contribute something. If I know my history right, which I'm not promising I do, the Delaware women actually were the ones that decided. It's kind of strange, at one time we had four women judges and one man; he felt a little intimidated occasionally, but we tried not to.

The Delaware Constitution is created to show what power the tribal council has, how they are allowed to run our tribal businesses so that we do not need to have a group of voting members at every month. We meet once a year as a tribe. The council meets every month to help run the tribe. [The Delaware Constitution] states the rights of the people as far as who can be a Delaware. It sounds kind of funny to say that, because it's in the blood. But you've got to prove it. But that was more because of the United States government. You have to be able to prove your lineage back to a tribal member that was on the official roll [compiled in 1906] representing blood kin enrolled in 1867 on some roll. I'm not exactly sure which one. [The Delaware Constitution] is basically how to keep the tribe going, when to meet, how to run an election, things along that line.

I've always considered myself to not be a very strong person in English language. I was a slow learner. I had to have a lot of help. When they taught foreign language, I did not take it because I thought if I couldn't learn English, I sure couldn't learn this. But when I noticed in the tribal paper that I was receiving that they were teaching the [Lenape] language here in Bartlesville, I wanted to learn who I am. And the Delaware tribe, they were not only teaching language, they were also learning their social songs. And, of course, I love to sing. And when they said singing, I'm going to show up if I could. You do realize that the women do not play the drum; they are not allowed to play the drum, it is a social taboo. We can mess around with it, it's not like we can't touch it, but you do not get out and perform in front of people playing the drum if you're female. But you can sing and you can dance. So I found out that yes, the women do sing these songs. They do learn these songs. There are some that the women do not sing, and so I asked them, "Do I learn the woman dance? I'm dancing. Do I sing it? I don't sing it while I'm dancing." They said, you learn it anyway. Who's going to teach your son, or your grandson, if you don't learn it? So these are things that you have to, if you want to continue the line, you have to learn this. That's why I was coming two and three times a week. I'd come over and take language class, and then I would come over and do a drum class. And then we had the fourth Monday where you had to learn how to dance. I was just wearing the roads out.

At one time I ran a business. During this business I taught class to people. I taught sewing. I discovered that teaching teaches you. And it also gives you a thrill when the person that you're teaching discovers—oh, their face lights up when they actually comprehend what you're doing. So it was kind of a thrill. As well as learning, you got a thrill from teaching someone that didn't know. So when the language class was going on, I wasn't learning everything that I wanted to learn quickly enough. I wanted more of it, and I wanted it faster, and I wanted to tear it down into little pieces and put it together for myself. Not to just learn a phrase, "How are you?" or "What are you doing?" I wanted to know how to say, "Get me that knife over there off the table." Or "Hand me a glass of milk." I wanted to do it quicker. So when we moved here, the opportunity was there because Jim Rementer was seeing Lucy Blalock, our Native speaker, who lives about an hour and a half away. Jim would try to go once a week. So I said, "Jim I want to go. I want to go with you." And he thought that I would interfere. But I kept pounding him, and he was kind enough to let me ride with him one time, and he discovered that I didn't interfere, I helped. So then it became every week we would go and see Lucy. We would ask her to say phrases, and I could ask her what I wanted. So it increased what I was learning as well as getting more information that we could record and keep and analyze to somehow offer it to the other tribal members. I just kind of got hooked on it. I really enjoy learning that language. I would say I was going to learn this certain word. For example, there is bean bread, which Jim immediately said is the hardest word to say, and I told him that I wanted to learn that word. There was one song that I wanted to learn how to do. Whenever you go to a powwow, you see the ladies in their buckskin dresses get up, and they turn the tape on, and the guy sings the "Lord's Prayer." And they're out there doing Indian sign language. I was wondering why they weren't singing it in Delaware. Jim had worked on the song at one time and had it, but he said the words were too long. They're huge words. And I told him that if he would give them to me, I would learn it. For three days I said I would learn it. But, oh my gosh, it took me three weeks. It was a lot more complicated than I thought. And I was working on it everyday for probably three or four hours a day trying to learn those words. But I did get it in there, and I learned those words. It's fun to do. I love singing that song.

To be able to do that sign language with the way I sing the "Lord's Prayer," you have to know the "Lord's Prayer" in your mind, unless you know Delaware. You have to listen to the melody and know which movement at what time, because you won't know what I'm saying. I don't actually know the sign language myself, but I have watched them doing it the last five years, and it's really a beautiful language. I was told by one of the girls that has done the language that it's actually an Indian sign language that they used to do when they traded into tribe to tribe; they did this hand motion that would mean words. We had a deaf girl that came up and mentioned that there are many of the signs of that poem that are the same in her sign language that she learned. So there are a lot of similarities; of course there's not the A, B, C part; it's like the sky's up, and some of them are obvious when you watch them, what they mean. I was told later that the sign language that the deaf use actually started from Indian sign language, if I'm not getting my history mixed up.

I personally don't own any of the prayer books that are in Delaware [printed by nineteenth-century missionaries]. I have been given some that have some of the songs like "Amazing Grace" written in Delaware. It's not actually word for word. The "Lord's Prayer" that I know is almost a verbatim word-for-word translation. It's not actually how a Delaware would say these things. We have translated it again in how a Delaware would have said, "Our Father in Heaven." It's in much shorter words, but I have not taken the time to learn it. Actually I don't know if I could learn two different methods. I'll probably get them messed up. But one of these days I might. I do have "Amazing Grace" that has four or five lines of Delaware singing praises to the Creator. It's not word for word, it's not even close in that issue. It's just words that fit into that theme of music. We also have "Silent Night" and "God Bless America." Many of the Delaware became very religious as far as taking on the Christianity because it went right along with what they believed all along. There was a Creator, and there was right and wrong, and you behaved all the time. You didn't wait till Sunday to act like you were a good person. You lived it, you didn't talk about it, you just lived it. So I can see how they can be moved over very easily. And because of that we have actually lost a lot of our tribal religious ceremonies. I remember [hearing about] the [Delawares'] twelve steps to heaven, and we don't know what those steps are now. I don't know if someone out there has copies of the twelve steps or not. I've heard about them. I know that they did exist. But that's all I know.

I guess the part that amazed me the most [when I went to Conner Prairie in 1992] was the way they helped us. Like we were somebody really special, whereas in Oklahoma there are so many Indian tribes we're just another person. Oklahoma has not learned how to embrace its Indian heritage as well as Indiana is trying to. But yet, we're still living it here, whereas Indiana lost their Indians, so they're searching. And it was very exciting. The children were very impressed. Of course, they asked some of the questions they would ask. If I hadn't been warned about what they were going to ask, I don't know if I could have kept a straight face on some of them, because they asked if we rode a horse all the way from Oklahoma there [to Fishers, Indiana], like we didn't have a car. Why? I don't know. But they're still thinking that anybody still in Oklahoma is still living in tipis and wearing our buckskins everyday and having war parties and raiding people. They don't realize that we live like everybody else does. It was kind of cute. I thought they were sweet. It made me feel good, it made more proud of who I am. Because they wouldn't let you not be, I loved it.

Since the first time that I arrived at Conner Prairie and the last time, which was last year (1999), it seems that the teachers are preparing the children for coming to see us, encouraging questions that are more knowledgeable than silly. They seem to emphasize the Indian part more at the school because they realize what they're going to get when they come to Conner Prairie, that it's going to make it more real to the children. I had one child that asked if I was really an Indian. Well, I'm not full-blood; I guess that they see so many people that act like they're Indians in these re-enactment places that they don't know who to trust on who's real and who isn't. That was strange when I got asked that. I honestly didn't know what to say. I think that's the main thing though, that the teachers are more prepared now than what they were in the beginning.

I learned my history of my family three different ways. I didn't learn that much from my father. Even though I asked him a lot of questions, he talked in parables and riddles, and I couldn't comprehend what he was trying to tell me. But there is a Delaware history book that has the story of my ancestry in it. That's where I got the fine-print part. The tribal history I actually learned while I was in Conner Prairie. I know this sounds crazy, but as far as some of the clothing particulars, I was told what I was supposed to wear, but I didn't realize how specific it was Delaware and how much of it was Indian in general. While the [other Delaware] presenters were presenting to the children, I learned. I enjoyed that a lot.

[Concerning my personal feelings], well, Conner Prairie was created almost the same way Bartlesville, Oklahoma, was. White man comes and marries an Indian woman so he can get land. And he makes all this money and sends the little Indian lady off on her own. Now, of course, with Bartlesville, they stayed. But if we would have been moved to another area, I imagine that it would've happened again. And so how many other times has that happened? They saw a lady get land, Indian land that they were not actually allowed to have, so they married in. I think it happened in a lot of tribes. And I was a little bit angry about that. But it's history; there's nothing that I can do about. They [Conner Prairie] do acknowledge it, which I think that helps. It helps to know that they do at least realize where it came from.

One of [the Conner Prairie staff members] is my best friend. We write each other all the time. So I think it's thrilling for them to come [to the Delaware powwow in Bartlesville]. I enjoy it. I like anybody to come to the powwow. It helps eliminate misconceptions. There are still people in Oklahoma that don't understand what a powwow is and what actually happens. My son was dating a girl in Stillwater, and he wanted to bring her over to the powwow. And she was afraid to come, she was afraid that she'd be attacked. But it's just one person here and there, people that are ignorant on things that actually go on in Indian life. So I'm of the opinion that the more people that we can bring in to see or more people that we can go out to visit, then so much the better.

[My son's Delaware] connection isn't that strong at the moment. It's through me at the present. He does come to the powwow every year. He does not participate in a lot of the other things that are going on, but when he wanted to learn when he was young, I didn't know who to get to teach him. Of course, now I have many people that could teach him, and he's a lot older and he doesn't want to now. I may not get him directly connected, but I figure that once he does get married and has children, we will probably get a strong connection through him, because I already am through the older boys [who have children]. They were with me all weekend, and they were right out in the middle of it. And they come over for a lot of some of the other things like the Delaware Days that we have. It's the twenty- to thirty-year-old people that will come around later, when we get the children hooked or when they get just a little bit older. They'll start wanting to know. It's happened. We have people all the time come up and tell us that something is missing in their lives. I met a young lady at a camp day a couple weeks before powwow to clean camps, and we did a potluck supper and dancing afterwards, like we do on "Fourth," and she came with her children. She knew something was missing so she showed up. We tried everything we could to hook her, to come back, because she was a wonderful girl. And I think a lot of people that are in their twenties and thirties are looking for something, and they don't realize what it is. It's right here. It's in their heritage, who they are and the community comes with it. Every month we have "Fourth Monday." It started out with the culture committee, when we were trying to learn the social songs, and we wanted to learn social dance. And the best way to teach it is to do it. We created "Fourth Monday" because the other three Mondays of the month are busy. We have meetings those Mondays. So nothing was going on the fourth Monday of the month, so we said that we would meet then and have a potluck and after we eat we would dance. You might go, and there might be six people show up at first. But after a while it's become a pretty consistent fifty, and sometimes it's a hundred. We have that time stopped in the summer because we didn't have a place to meet. But I don't think we'll do that this year. The elders love it because they get to visit and see the kids. We're going to try to keep it going for everybody.

I actually have one Choctaw son and one Delaware son. My Choctaw son my husband had before we were married. He has five children. We also have two girls, one each. In fact my daughter could not come to powwow this year and called me Sunday and said, "Happy powwow!" like it was Mother's Day or something. So it's definitely in the family, but they live too far away to get them too involved.

Oral history interview on May 30, 2000, at Bartlesville, Oklahoma.

Connie Collier at the 2006 Delaware Powwow near Copan, Oklahoma.

CONNIE COLLIER

Tribal gift shop
Born in Bartlesville, Oklahoma

I grew up by the cement plant in Dewey, Oklahoma. All of my memories are related to this area because I always lived here, nowhere else, other than Wann, Oklahoma, where the Delawares lived in early years. Wann is where I was raised in the first years of my life and came to Dewey when I was about the third or fourth grade. I've just always lived around here, never have been anyplace else. I went to school with Mike Pace. We were in the same grade with Louise Dean, David Whiteturkey. Mike has a lot more vivid memory of all the people that was there than I do, and a lot of them I didn't know they were Indian; you didn't know that. They were just like any other kids. I did know who Louise Dean was. She had some problems. She was a little bit slower than some of the other kids, and they would pick on her. I'd walk her home or ride the bus with her and see that she wasn't picked on. So, those are my real strong memories of the Delaware Indians.

My ancestors have followed the Delawares all the way through. I have not been able to really connect. I haven't got proof that they are Delaware, but they have followed them all the way through. They started out in Pennsylvania and onto Ohio, Indiana. I've gone out to Indiana and found them. And, you know Hugh Harrison at Conner Prairie, well I just found out [September 1999] that we are related. He's related to my family that was [in Indiana]. He took me to the old farmhouse [where my family lived]. The old farm is still there. Then they came on in through Missouri and Arkansas into Kansas. But, my family didn't sign up to come on in to Oklahoma. They stayed in Kansas. So, I don't have any proof of [Delaware ancestry].

I've always wanted to go [to Anderson, Indiana], because we don't know too much about that side of the family, and so I had the chance to go [to Conner Prairie fall of 1999] with the Delawares' gift shop, and Anderson is about thirty minutes away, so we went on. I went to Anderson and went to the library, and they told me where Beech Grove was and how to get there. And we went there and found their graves, and they were buried there in 1877, and we took pictures. It was kind of a real exciting weird experience, the running into all of that. And then when I got home [Bartlesville, Oklahoma], we had ordered a new computer; first thing I did was put in Parsons and Pettigrew. I got into the registry, and someone had written that they wanted information on anyone with a Parsons/Pettigrew line. So I went and wrote in on the computer to them, and it's still strange, all their family, all the Pettigrew, they had been able to trace them down; everyone but my great-great-grandmother, and she came back into Kansas. And, so I have all the information on her, that she [the other person tracing lineage] doesn't have on Pettigrew. It was really exciting. And then I was telling Hugh about it and come to find out he's related.

I think it was about four or five [in the burial grounds]. I didn't know any of the others. I was just looking for the particulars. I didn't know these other names.

It's just kind of like finding missing pieces. And every part I've ever traced them down, it's just like I've known the area because there's a piece of me that knows, that has the same feeling of the land and the country. They were farmers, and I've always lived in the country, so I just kind of related to them.

I never got to share any stories like that because I never really knew that side of my family. My mother divorced that family when I was an infant. And she remarried later, and I never did meet them until I was seven, and my dad died when I was twelve. So I never got to go around any of them much. But my grandmother [on my father's side], I did know that she was Indian. When you're young you don't start asking questions like that; it'd be nice if you'd do it when you were young and not wait until they're gone; get interested.

I found out since that [my mother's] Indian, but I don't know of what tribe. I haven't got to look into that yet.

It was just something I knew. Well, even when I was a little girl I lived way out in the country, and I always lived on the creek. And always since then, I always had that sense of connection to Mother Earth and to the surroundings, and I was that kind of a person. I've always known; it's just something that's inside of you that you don't have to be told.

I guess I started sewing when I was about seven. I used to mend all of the grandparents' and all of the boys' overalls on a treadle machine. My grandmother on my father's side, she was very craft-oriented. And she could build anything, do anything, and I just was one of the fortunate ones to get it from her.

The men's [clothing] are pretty well the same in the straight dancing. The women's clothes, their jewelry is pretty well the same. But, the Delaware have a cape that goes around what's called a Bertha collar, where the Osages is just straight, plain. And the Cherokee, they're not near as fancy as the Osage and the Delawares.

The Osage wear a wrap-around skirt with the ribbon work. And the ribbon work is fairly the same. Of course, nowadays, people pick up different things, whatever they want to do, it pretty well goes. Well, I found out that most tribes, when you ask them their colors, they'll say red and black. I worked for a full-blood Delaware in his smoke shop, and I asked him that question, because I did crafts out there, and he said that the Delawares wear darker colors like maroon and green and those kind of colors. But I found that a lot of the Osage, they wear a lot of bright colors; I think their colors are purple and gold, and I've seen a lot of orange, too.

[I learn by] observing. My favorite people are elders, so you learn. You're going to learn no matter what you do.

[In the tribal gift shop], it's been to have different kinds of clothing and things that has their [Delaware] name and their seal. We're hoping to, in the near future, to get supplies, like fringe and beads and ribbon and that kind of thing, so that they [the Delawares in Bartlesville] won't have to go to other tribes or other towns to get their supplies. So, it's going to be even more for them later on. But, in the past it's supposed to have been to have gifts [to purchase] to give to other people that's [made by Delawares], some kind of significance of the Delaware. And we plan on having other tribes' things in there before long because there is a lot of people that will be coming to see what we have that aren't just Delaware. So we're hoping to have some of the surrounding tribes' stuff in it. We have a committee, and we don't put anything in [the gift shop] until we have a meeting and we can discuss it, whether we want it in there or not, that we think it will please everybody; we don't want to offend anyone. We have a committee; we don't have just one person's ideas.

A lot happens at the Delaware powwow because there is so many people that comes from all over the United States. That's a gathering time for them, a time to come home and be with their People. And so they want to take something back that's a souvenir that's from their People. So, they buy the T-shirts and the hats with the Delaware seals on them, anything to do with the seals. Then we have other things there that doesn't specifically say Delaware.

We have people that come in here that sometimes they have business with the tribe, and they want to take their children or grandchildren something home as a souvenir or a remembrance of their trip; something to attach to their clothes, like a pin or a patch, that shows the public that "I'm Delaware." And that's the main thing, for those kind of people that come to visit or has business here.

It's not an enormous amount [of income] because they'll give discounts to the Delawares, or they don't have that big of a percentage [retail markup price] so it's not to make any large income for the Delawares. It's just something that's a nice thing for them to have, a convenience and complimentary thing, and to spread who they are.

[When I went to Conner Prairie in 1999,] everybody was friendly and inquisitive. They wanted to know about the Indians. I think they think in Oklahoma that we still wear headbands and feathers, because all they know is from the history. But, everybody wanted to know about how the Indians live. They were real inquisitive. And a lot of them are sensing now that they are Indian, too, and they want to learn more about [their background]. That's what a lot of the people back East is realizing. And there was a lot of Indians that stayed back there. I think that they're just realizing that they are a part of this. They were very very inquisitive about it, and informative, too, about a lot of things.

The schoolchildren would ask questions from the difference of what they've read in their history books and what they learned in school. But the adults, they would ask questions from things they've heard from their ancestors or their parents. They would ask questions like that. And I've had several of them say that, "We know we're Indian, but we don't know how to go about finding it." I try to share my experiences, and they would share their stories, and we had a lot of talks like that on sharing our stories.

One lady, she has family here [in Oklahoma], and she [wanted] to come [to Oklahoma] and meet them, but she never realized that she was [Indian]. She wasn't raised to be Indian, and she was wanting to come back [to Oklahoma]. [Her family] lived not too far from [Bartlesville], probably an hour away. It was kind of strange that her family was here. You see, I was the other way around, I was here [Oklahoma], and mine was there [Indiana], and I was trying to research that. That was kind of a neat thing that our stories were opposite directions.

I've just always felt like I was Delaware because I've always been around them all my life. I've never felt any different. And it's just kind of strange that I'm finding more and more that I probably am. As I get older I find that life is pretty strange in ways like that.

Oral history on May 29, 2000, at Bartlesville, Oklahoma.

Mike Pace wears replicas of his great-grandmother's brooch. Pace wears the original brooch on his otter hide turban. He wears the small wampum bead necklace in honor of the late Louise Dean. The replicas were made by Don Secondine.

Don Collier at the 2006 Delaware Powwow near Copan, Oklahoma.

DON COLLIER

Delaware gift shop manager

We just feel a kinship. So, we kind of volunteered to help with the gift shop to help Delaware people. I see a need there and a possible chance of making that a very large economic development for the Delaware. That's why we went and did that. It's not for the money, but we enjoy it. We did real good this weekend; they were really happy.

We had never been [to Conner Prairie in Fishers, Indiana]. When I was young, I did drag racing. And [Indiana] is where we went every year for the nationals to drag races. That was my experience with Indiana and Indianapolis. Of course, it had been several years since I have been there even doing that. And things change quite a bit, and it's big. I didn't know what to think, but I tell you what, your people opened their arms to us. They treated us like family. They are tooting the horn for the Delaware people, absolutely. And I wish more would do that, in the sincerity that they are doing it [at Conner Prairie]. The banquet we went to on the Saturday night and the reception and everything, they have opened their arms to Delawares. Of course, that's where the Delawares were. I think it's great. And I think the people up there are great, and we can't wait to get back. We're going again in October [2000].

This year [2000] my grandson is six years old. Last year he was five. The year before, our friends had given him an eagle claw staff to dance with, with five eagle feathers on it. It was beautiful. He had the blessings of Ed RedEagle to carry that and to have his eagle feather. In 1999, during the grand entry of the Round Dance, he dropped that stick. Five years old, he did not know. He did know what he had done; he knew that he had to pick that stick up and finish the Round Dance and leave the arena. And he did that, and he said nothing to us until the next morning after the powwow. And he said, "Grandma, I dropped my stick, and Levi knows I did because he was right beside me. I just wanted you to know." So we thought, "Well, something's got to be done. You drop a feather now, it's gotta be blessed." So, we asked what we had to do to bless that feather, that stick. So, I went to Mike Pace, and he and Bucky Buck volunteered to be with Brody to go have his stick and eagle feathers blessed. We got Tony Arkaketa to speak for Brody. He's a Ponca Indian. Most all his life he was a dancer and everything, and he knew the right thing to do. And we had Charlie Chibitty bless the eagle feathers and the stick. He is last of the Apache code talkers. It meant a lot to be out there with him, with our grandson, his father, Mike Pace, and

Bucky Buck.[1] The ceremony was to bless that staff and the feathers again, so he could use it again. It couldn't be used until that was done. The people that was involved in it, that's why it meant so much. And for a six-year-old child, how long do you think it will be before he forgets that? While that was going on, at the end when Charlie Chibitty did the ceremony for the feathers, he said, "Okay Brody, from this day on, I'm your grandfather, and Mike Pace is your uncle now. Bucky Buck is your uncle." So, we got that done and when it was over, I went around to Mike Pace to thank and then to Bucky Buck. And now my grandson has two great uncles that he can call on anytime he needs them. It's like Bucky Buck said, "Tell Brody not to be afraid of us. We are his uncles now. If he needs something, wherever, if he's out of town and he's got a problem and he needs us. We're his uncles." They're real serious about that. It's now a grandpa, grandfather, and grandmother. It makes him feel real good when you have something like that happen. It's just a great feeling. That's why it had to be done. That stick and the feathers had to be blessed.

My grandson's name is Brody Blackbear Gay. And his father is George Gay. [His] mother, our daughter, is Christy. George's mother is a full sister to Ed RedEagle, who was Osage. He was an assistant chief and on the council, and the RedEagles are well-thought-of Osage people. They call him Uncle Eddie, everybody does. He recently died, about a year and a half ago. And Ed, his great-uncle, named Brody, gave his baby name and his adult name. We've had a cradleboard ceremony for him and everything. He has been raised the Indian way. We had him in a buckskin outfit when he was two days old, at a powwow. He's a real good little straight dancer now, at six. But, he's a good boy, too. He's learning the Indian way, and his grandmother is responsible for that, Connie is responsible for that.

Basically young kids learn just by going out there and doing it. For a long time he walked around the [dancers], and last year, we looked out there, and he was dancing. And I said, "Brody, where did you learn that?" He said, "I've been watching the other guys, Grandpa." They learn, and the older guys will take it upon themselves to teach the [younger] guys. But you're not supposed to wear an eagle feather until you're roached. The Osage believe a little bit different than the Delawares and the Cherokees and everyone else. His great-uncle, Eddie, we went to him and asked him if we can do this. He told us we could and did his ceremony and smoked the feather, and that's how he was able to wear that feather and any other eagle feather. Otherwise, we would have had to wait. You see, they have a ceremonial dance, the Osage do, every year. And we would have had to wait until Ed-

---

1. Bucky Buck was chairman of the Delaware Culture Committee, succeeding Mike Pace.

die would have roached him in the Osage arena before he could have ever worn a feather. And we were going to do that this year, but his great-uncle just died. So, we're going to have to wait now. The year of mourning is over, but we have to choose now, in the RedEagle family, who we want to take on what Eddie was going to do. But the teaching of the dancing is usually done by the older people. Mike Pace has even helped Brody, because Mike Pace is a good straight dancer. Everyone has helped. We've been around everyone, more Delaware help us than anyone, because we are around the Delawares all the time. We were raised with them. They are kind of like family.

Most Delawares are straight dancers. And most, 95 percent of the Osage, are all straight dancers. Now, to get him started, we went to a very close friend, which is Osage, Margaret Bird. She helped us with Brody, and she still is. We would have been lost without her. She has powwow danced and ceremonial danced all of her life; she was born dancing. She's good, she's always been a champion dancer. Of course, we had to have someone who knew the Osage way. That meant that she was responsible for that. But she has said right up front that he will be a straight dancer. Until he becomes to the age where he comes to us and tells us that he wants to be a grass dancer or anything else, that's up to him. In our hopes we would like for him to stay a straight dancer, because that's his lineage and that's his heritage as a straight dancer. But if he wants to change, that's up to him. But we will do it, whatever it takes.

Margaret Bird lives in Caney. She has enough old authentic Indian clothes that she puts on complete style shows of all kinds of dance clothes, all kinds of women's clothes, men's clothes, Osage, Delaware, Cherokee, everything. She will do a three-day seminar and put on all these style shows and everything; she teaches them how to bead and how to do ribbon work, because she does it all. She makes moccasins. Between her and my wife, no one else has made anything for Brody but them. I don't know whether Connie [my wife] has told you, but there was seven people that had come up to the Delaware booth last night, and all seven of them were dressed in her clothes that she had made for them. She makes a lot of dance clothes. But that's really neat to see that. The reason they came over here, was like, "Here, here we are, we got your clothes on." It's nice to see that.

There are a lot of gift shops in Oklahoma—Lyon's Indian Store, for instance, it's big. If you want something, you go to Lyon's; they have expensive art, anything you want. It's something. If you do beadwork, they have beads, they have everything that you could possibly need if you need something for an Indian purpose. The Delaware gift shop I see is an economic development for the Delaware people, to employ people. That was my goal when they first called me and said, "Would you come and fill out an application to help us and tell us in writing what you would like us to do?" And I said, "Well, number one, it's a Delaware gift shop. Delaware people should have first chance at making something to sell at that gift shop. Let's make it something that the Delaware people can make money with. And then when they sell it, they're going to make money again because all of the proceeds are going to the tribe. Let's teach Delaware people how to sew their own clothes. My wife knows how to sew, and she's ready to teach them. Right now the gift shop is downstairs in the Delaware Center; she could teach them down there. Then we could hire those people later if we need to make some clothes to sell. Hire them, put them to work. Let's get a big gift shop, let's have everything we need, and stock it with an inventory [for all the craft needs]. Put Delaware people to work in that gift shop." I see that for them, and I think it will work. But it is something that they are going to have to dedicate to and do it. This weekend we did a tremendous amount of business, [more than] has ever been done since they had a booth at powwow. We took our gift shop to Indiana; we didn't have much but we sold a lot of stuff quick. So I think it can be a success; we just have to build an inventory, get more people interested. In the past, [people said,] "Ah, they don't have nothing, why even go down there?" Now, they see it as something that can be economically valuable, too. So they want to do something, too. They possibly have the same vision that I do for the Delaware people. I hope we can do that.

I think [language is] very important. Matter of fact, our grandson is Osage-Cherokee, and we bought him tapes, everything now. And he's wanting to learn Delaware, and I think it would be so neat. You'd be surprised at people that don't realize that the gift shop has this stuff. They just never come to the gift shop. I think we need to tell more people that they can get these things and to teach their children. Indian people have no future without our grandkids, and the kids, they have nothing. We need to get [them] these tapes. The CD that's out, is the greatest thing that has ever happened. I hope Jim [Rementer] can take that and make volume two to ten thousand and just keep going and teach the young people because we are going to lose it if we don't start teaching it. I think it's a good teaching thing, and I think if the Delaware people or anyone else is interested in it, we have got to start advertising and letting the people know that it is there and they can learn. If they don't want to come to the language classes, take that and learn.

Years ago when I was young when we would go to powwows, the powwows weren't serious like they are today. They were more happy-go-lucky, good time, go out there and dance and have a good time. Get through and have a big meal. Sit around and talk and then go dance again. They're more serious than they used to be. I can remember when I went as a kid, they used to have clowns that were dressed up. They would have faces painted funny, but they don't have that any more, but when I was young I remember that. And they are more serious. I guess that's okay, but I think ceremonial dances, that's when they get serious. Powwow is to have a good time. Part of the serious is okay, but it's not what I remember when I was young.

When I was young, there was no contest really. It was just everyone got out there and had a good time. There were straight dancers and fancy dancers, but today sometime it becomes a race to see who wins the most money at a powwow. And that's okay because times do change, and you have to change with them. But the Indian needs to never forget the ceremonial stuff, too. I have a lot of friends that are good dancers. They will not dance for money anymore. They will dress, put a number on, but when it comes to the final, they're out because they looked up and said, "Hmm. I'm dancing because I'm Indian, but I'm really out here for the money." So they quit.

There are not enough younger people out there now. There are several, but I feel that there needs to be more. I did notice more this weekend, but like last year, the junior boy's straight had five people in it. [This] Friday night, there were eleven or twelve, so there is more starting to get interested. I'm glad to see that because, as I said a while ago, we have no future without the kids, and to teach them, kids, and to take them to the powwow. And, like, times are changing; if they want to be serious, that's fine. I can remember, like, the ceremony that we were talking about with the eagle feather; many years ago if you dropped the eagle feather they didn't ever stop the dance to bless that feather; they just picked it up and went. But the Indian people are very serious about their eagle feathers, and now they do that. And that's good because, especially for a young person, it teaches the importance of the reverence of that feather.

I've been taught all my life that the eagle feather is a fallen comrade, and that's why it's so important when you have the Veteran's Dance and the Memorial Dance. That's what the eagle feather stands for, a fallen comrade. To me, that's why it's important. I've heard other people say other things too, but that is what I've always been taught. That's what my mother taught me. So that's important.

The federal government has eagles. There is a form that you fill out; you put your roll number, name, address. It takes a while. We're in the process of that for Brody. They will send you, most times, a full eagle, both wings, and the head and feet; that's what you usually get. It takes a month, sometimes three months, but you can do that.

My wife's son runs a big ranch over here that they call Four Acres, and he's got three or four of them that have been in fences that he's found and he's turned them in, and that's where they've wound up. And I think, I can't remember, but I think you send off to, like, Utah is where they are all lined up. But he called the game warden, and that's how it all happens. I think they're off endangered, but they're still protected. But that's what happens, and they all go to the same place. He's very fortunate up there at the ranch. They probably have three, four, or five hundred eagles that stay up there all the time. They are beautiful; we go up there every now and then and just sit and look with binoculars. I have a Bronco that's pretty big, and we saw some eagles off over by the tree; I just drove over and looked, and one flew right over the windshield. It completely covered the front of the Ford. It's a beautiful bird. It's something that you might want to do sometime.

There were a lot of things said in Indiana that I listened to that was great, at the dinner and everything, what Dee [Ketchum] had to say at the dedication [of the Lenape Village and Trading Post]. It's a beautiful place they've got, and they just keep adding to it. The people from Conner Prairie, there are some here at the powwow, and I suspect that they will all want to come back.

Oral history interview conducted on May 29, 2000,
at Bartlesville, Oklahoma.

Bucky Buck dances as Head Man Dancer at the 2004 Delaware Powwow. Annette Ketchum and Paula Pechonick made his leggings and Pechonick made his moccasins. The ribbon work on the flaps represent the color scheme of his navy Vietnam service ribbon. This scheme was derived from the colors of the South Vietnam flag.

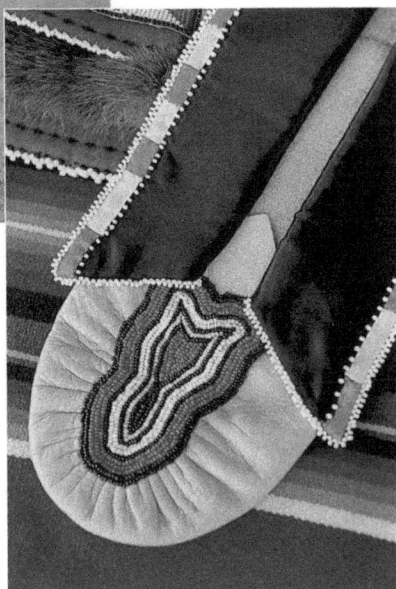

Doug Donnell sings as head man singer at the 2006 Delaware Powwow
near Copan, Oklahoma.

DOUG DONNELL

Main singer, drum keeper
Born in Bartlesville, Oklahoma

I was born in Bartlesville, and I was raised in Copan most of my life, most of my younger years, up until I graduated high school. My memories of growing up as a child was just going to school there and with the kids. We lived in town in Copan. I remember when, as kids, we'd go to the dance at Copan, the powwow. I was probably maybe twelve or fourteen. And we were just on our own. We would go up and camp. Our parents, that I recall, weren't going, it was just the kids. We would go up there and camp out and watch as they danced. So I don't remember a lot about the dancing as much as I just remember camping out and just being around those people late at night when they were doing the stomp dancing and stuff like that. I just wasn't really quite involved in the cultural thing, which wasn't much going on at that time, and I can recall the powwow every year. That's pretty much all I remember, in that part of it.

My parents, we were raised in a tradition-type atmosphere. My dad worked on a ranch for a while up around there for the Mellondorfs that was a huge ranch around Copan. I remember growing up just a little south of the Kansas line. We had a ranch house there that we took care of, and the Mellondorfs was the owner of all that land. They actually had a lot of land. Miss Mellondorf was Osage, and she had a lot of trust land. Anyway, I remember growing up there actually as riding horses and wrestling cattle a lot. My dad and I, when I was real small, we'd get up way before the sun came up, and we would go get the horses. We'd load them up, and we'd go to the Foreman's house, that's his name, he had lots of kids, he was Cherokee, his whole family. And he was the foreman of the Mellondorf ranch. And I grew up with those kids. They had some nicknames: one boy was Shorty, and the other was Tarzan, and Boge was the other one. I think they had nine or ten kids. Anyway, that's what I did.

We'd get there, and there was about seven or eight ranches that they owned, and the heads of each ranch would come together at the Foreman's house, and then all the men would go together to move cattle somewhere, and all of us kids would either go with them sometimes, or we would stay at the house and we'd play and rope. We did everything. We roped chickens; we roped everything that moved. As kids that's all we did. We had little ropes, and we would rope anything that would move. That's what we did, and it was fun. We roped pigs and goats. We would rope goats and tie wagons on the back and let them pull us around and that kind of deal. We had a lot of horses, lots of horses. Some were called Galicenos, they were in between Shetland and a full-grown horse, and us kids would have those Galicenos. We had a couple that we would pretend that we were in rodeos, and we'd buck them out. You put a flank rope on them, and they will buck then. We called this one horse Oklahoma Silvers, and it was a little Shetland, and we took them in the hay barn, and it was fenced in. And about a fourth of it had hay in it, the rest of the hay was on the bottom. And we'd get that horse in there, and we'd just ride him until he couldn't move anymore. He'd throw us off numerous times. Those are really vivid memories for me because I enjoyed myself so much as a kid doing that. And that's where I guess my dad and I evolved into rodeo together, and we team roped; my brother rode bareback horses. And I was kind of in the family. My cousin Ace Berry was a world champion bareback rider and team roper. He has a school in California. I think he's retired in a ranch now. I knew of him when I was younger because of how successful he was, and I'd seen him on TV at Calgary when he rode up there. And he was the youngest ever to win a world champion, at the time. And it was really something. He was really good. A guy at work said he had a book about the history [of rodeo], and he was in there. We talked about what it was like back in those days. They were pretty tough guys.

Well, how I got involved in the cultural things was that when I got older, in high school, my senior year, my grandmother Lillian Hadfield expressed to my mother what she wanted. And my mother told me that she always liked going up to the Copan dance, powwow, and she wanted her kids to get involved in that. And so I think it was my nephews Shawn and Stuart, my sister's kids, they were going to Operation Eagle, an Indian education program in Bartlesville, and Evan Ray Satepauhoodle [Kiowa powwow singer and language preservation activist] who was teaching them how to dance. That's kind of how I first got started into getting involved into the culture in the powwow end of it. Which is completely different from our [Delaware] culture, but it was at Copan, where all our people were going and dancing. So those kids, they set up a little camp at Copan, and I seen them dance, and I really got interested when my grandmother and my mother were involved, so I started. They bought me clothes and made me clothes, and I started to dance, too. I can't remember exactly, I think I was a junior or senior in high school when I started to dance. Just by watching other dancers I got involved. My Uncle Dee [Ketchum], who is the chief now [1998–2002], was living in Dallas at the time, and he came up for Copan powwow seeing that we were involved in that, and he started to dance, too. He got his clothes. And then we really got involved and decided that we wanted to go to some other dances. And we traveled around Oklahoma. We'd go down to Texas and Missouri and just go to dances and compete.

Most of it was just that Grandmother was really proud of us for being involved, and so she would go with us. That kind of progressed; then my Uncle Lew Ketchum, we heard that he was trying to run for chief of the tribe. Then, when he won [served 1985–1994], we really got involved into the culture. He would ask us to come and put on exhibitions for him and his business. They would have a show, and he would call his family to come down and put on an exhibition. And about that time they had quite a bit of money in the tribe that they wanted to put into preserving the culture because there wasn't anything going on. There wasn't any singing, other than the Copan. There wasn't many Delawares that were doing that. It was mainly outside, the Shawnees and so on. Of course, they had the ceremonies over at White Oak with the Shawnees that a lot of Delawares went to. So they set up a trust and had little committees set up to preserve the culture. My Uncle Dee was chairman. He was, I think, trying to get involved. He moved back to Bartlesville, and he was getting involved. I think his brother asked him to get involved in that area. I had since moved back; I moved away and came back. Lew asked his brother Dee to help him to try and get something started. I think Rosetta Coffee was actually our first chairperson. It was an election. And she was actually voted in as the chairman of the cultural preservation. They asked me if I wanted to sit in on the committee because they needed some people that have been instrumental in some dancing and so on. And being that my uncle was the chief and so on I felt obligated to get involved being as I was here. We'd have meetings about certain things about preserving our language, and Jim [Rementer] being there really helped a lot and expressed that they would like to try to see if we can bring some of our dances back that we used to do, our social dances. Several people on the committee said that they needed someone that would try to sing and try to learn some of the songs, because if they do that first, then they can teach the dancing and maybe get a dance started and kind of progress from there. Everybody else had picked something up, and I said I would try, too. Jim told me that there wasn't really any singers left, but they had numerous recordings of those singers, our ancestors singing. He said he would get me some of the recordings, and then I could work on them and do them. So I took it. The rest of the story is that I've just been learning those songs. We came out, and I had a couple of songs from one dance cycle, and we would kind of put on a little exhibition to demonstrate, this is what the dance is like. We couldn't go through the whole thing because I didn't know all the songs. There's so many songs to a dance, and I've learned maybe one or two of a few. We would kind of show people and try to get them interested in coming in to get involved into the dancing. So we set up a dance class the fourth Monday of every month. To attract Indian people, we thought that if we offered food, they would come. That was the key. It got people in. A lot of the ones that are gone now, Lucy Blaylock, really helped. Jim and Mike

Pace had started language class, and Lucy was the teacher. She was the fluent speaker, and she actually inspired me to sing and learn those songs. She was my critic. We would do a little exhibition, and she would watch and listen and tell us what we were doing wrong. Her and I would get together, and she would tell me about this and that, what they used to do a long time ago, so forth. So that's how I got involved in the singing and learning of the songs. It just progressed. I learned two songs, then four, then six. I learned a complete dance.

At that time I wanted to be a singer. The term "singer" in this time is a really gifted person. I'm familiar with and I know and meet a lot of singers with other tribes, and they share a lot of things with me. The first thing they told me was that if I wanted to be a singer, I would have to commit my life to it because you can't do it halfway. You can't just learn a song or two and sing it and then go back to your life and then try and come back and sing those two songs maybe once a year or whatever. If you were going to do it, you need to do it all the way. Commit your life to it. So that was a big moment in my life because I decided that I was here to stay and that I wasn't going to go anywhere. I wanted to be fully involved with the tribe because of my uncle. I could see that the tribe was coming back stronger with the things they were trying to do. So I made a decision to commit my life to it, and Lucy helped me a lot. She would tell me about the Delaware singers and how well I was doing. I just got so much praise with people telling me that it was good and right and that it sounded good. We started getting people more involved. It was good to see the elders come and smile, because they knew that at least part of this was coming back. There were some discrepancies; there were some young guys that wanted to do Big House ceremonial things, and that was a big no-no. The elders said, "no." That particular ceremony had its time. With the way society now is, it couldn't happen the way it used to happen. They wanted it to go back to the Earth the way it came to us. And as soon as people, young guys, would talk about that, the elder people would just get infuriated and tell them that they were not going to do that, that they were not going to attempt to bring that back. So, Lucy and I talked, and she said that we could do social dance songs, which is something that we did afterwards and at night when they did the lead dance, which is that stomp dance. You can do those dances, because those were for fun, those dances were actually opened to anybody that wanted to come. She said, at Copan, where the Big House used to be, they actually at times would invite the people in town to come to the social dance, not to the Big House ceremony, but to the social dance. So she said that those songs, there are a lot of them, that's what they were for, to bring our people together and have fun and enjoy one another and meet one another. It was just a social time. She told me that I could learn all those songs and sing them. I think that's what we need to do.

Well, as far as tying and the knowledge that I have of the drum, I'm still learning. I'm involved in singing at powwows, hand games, and our cultural dances. The Native American Indian Church and our social dances have our water drum. The hand games that we play are with a hand drum that you hold. The powwow has the big Plains Indian drum, as they call the skin drum. Those are the different kinds. I'm involved in all of those. When you become a singer, you become active in all of those things, and you get a tie with all those singers around. So all of them help me, and I help them. That's the difference that I found out being a singer. The water drum, history-wise, came from the East all along the coast. From what I understand those tribes had wooden, either cyprus tubs, they started with that, or a keg. They stretched a hide over it and tied the stones together to pull the hide tight with a particular type of rope. Actually it was Jim and Charlie Dean [who] helped me tie the first one that I've ever tied. They showed me how to do that. Then Leonard [Thompson] gave me a crock; it was big, it was about a four-gallon crock. He said that they used to use those a lot, too. So I learned to tie the water drum on this crock to begin with, and I used it a couple of times. It's a big heavy thing, but it has a great sound to it. Nowadays they use a small iron kettle with the three legs; there's no handle on it. Usually a size six is the best; seven is a little bigger. All of them have a different tone to them. It's hardly ever the same because you never really get the same tension on it. The hides may be thin or thick and the water and the size of the kettle or whatever, big or small. Tynor, who is instrumental in Native American Church, asked me to come out. They showed me another, different tie, tying the drum, the water drum. So I've got several ways of tying the water drum. Charlie showed me a way, and so did Leonard, which was an old traditional way where, when you turn it upside down, there's a star on the bottom made by the ropes. And they said, whenever you do it perfect, you'll flip it up and see a star on the bottom. That's the old kind of traditional way. Now, the Native American Church created a tie that used the legs of the kettle, and you go around those. You don't see the star as well, but it still has the little points. But with the traditional way the rope got bunched up on the bottom, and when you tried to sit it down, it would kind of rock, so the church created a tie with the legs. That's the other style of tie that I'm familiar with, and it's a lot better. The amount of water, when they're talking about the small kettle, the number six, I want to say close to probably two to three inches of water in the bottom. The hide that you stretch over is either deerskin or elk. The best is brain tanned because it's kind of sticky. When you pull it, it stays, even when you pull it down with your hands. I was given some rope that's like what all the churches around here use; also the Osage use. Charlie Dean gave me some. He said that you get it over at Homony. It has the little red dots in it. And it's solid cotton; there's no cord in the middle. When you pull it down, when it comes back it kind of swells, so it holds. With a cord in it, it doesn't hold as well. It slips back through. I would say sixteen to eighteen feet of rope is what you use, and you use it all up from one end to the other. On that small drum, I would say probably close to thirteen. On the big crock, we're going to use at least eighteen feet or so.

The water drum [is used for] the social dances of our tribe. The water drum for the Native American Indian Church is ceremonial. The other drums are for intertribal. The big drum that is now introduced into the powwows is all intertribal; all tribes can come together and do that. That's where I get the distinction. When I talk to young kids, I explain to them that when I do the water drum, it's kind of a rare thing that Delaware people do as a tribe. So that's the distinction of the water drum and the big drum. Big drum is intertribal, and the water drum is specific to whatever tribe it is, on their own.

Taking care of the water drum, when I set out to do that, people gave me things to keep the drums in. I have a place at my house that I keep all of it together. I have a cedar box that I put all of my small things in, which is the stones that I collect. I go around, and the places that I go, or have been invited to, I try to find stones that would be good for our drum. So I collect them. I keep those in a pouch that people gave me. I've had beaded pouches that I use to put my stones in, and I've got stones from all over. I've got some from Sandy Hook up in New Jersey. They say that our people were there, and we do that exhibition up there, and I went to the beach there and found some real nice creek, smooth, round stones there. And when I came back, I tied the drum with that. It was kind of a special occasion because it's the first time that I've used something from our home ground like that on a drum and used it and made a drum with it.

Well, how I use the stones is, when you stretch the hide over the kettle, and it's wet and you pull it down, you measure out, and there's a particular point to start when you use the leg. You try to start with one stone on both sides of one leg. So I start with one stone and I go around clockwise. I start and I wrap, the stone goes underneath the hide and I wrap the rope around the stone so the stone sticks out of the hide with the rope around it. Then I go around in particular, and I measure with my fingers to measure in between the stones. And I like all those stones together. Seven stones.

I've been asked many times about seven. Why seven stones? Still even talking with the Native American Indian Church, the elders there, they really don't have a reason why, other than people say that seven is supposed to be a perfect number. So honestly I don't really know. It works out perfect. Maybe it was that they just experimented with a lot of things and just decided that it was the best number to use, and that's what they did. And it so happens even with Native American Church, they say with the Bible and Christian religion, they say the seven was the perfect number, so that was it. That's all I know about the numbers, and that's what I tell them. I don't want to make up anything or say anything like that because it wouldn't be right.

With the big drum, once it's tied, it stays tied. I've made several drums, big drums. I had a drum group that we had started. And I even tanned my own hide and everything. It's a lot of work, with the rawhide, the cowhide. It's a lot of work. You cut it all out. You measure it all. The lacing is tedious. Rawhide's hard to cut. You've got one hundred feet of lacing you use on some of those drums. And you lace it all up wet. You make sure you ran this good and sturdy and strong. Make sure that it's going to last for a long time. And then you get all your hide cut out, get all your lacing ready, and then you tie it. You pull it tight, and then you sit it out in the sun for at least three days before it completely draws out to get hard and tight.

Those drums, there's a lot of them. People have lots of drums. Keep them in cases that were made for drums; we had a canvas bag that we put one of our drums in. As long as you keep it inside the house out of the weather, best if it's in kind of a dry place, because they get flat, as they call it, it's not a big deal. When you get ready to sing, you just set it out in the sun or put it in your car out in the sun, and it will heat up and get tight. But I use a preservative a lot of times, because rawhide will rot just like anything else. If you don't put something on it to try and preserve it a little bit, it will rot and crack and split. They've got stuff out on the market that's like an oil. It's not real heavy; it's enough to where it won't rot. So we use that and keep it covered.

The striking instrument for the kettle drum is usually from eight to twelve inches long. It depends on what kind of sound you want. A lot of them have smooth heads. They're a little bigger round and probably twice the size of a pencil. A lot of them are made with ridges cut in the handle part so they don't slip. Some of them have little grooves cut in them so they won't slip out of your fingers. On the water drum they use a striking instrument with a head on it that's round like a marble. Most common is a teardrop shape on the end of the drumstick as the best for the water drum.

It's just straight wood. I've seen lots of different kinds. My dad, he has lots and lots of those drumsticks that are just gorgeous; they have intricate detailed carvings in them. Some of them he doesn't use that his grandparents passed down to him. He's the one that's helped me in really getting involved with the water drum and the singing with that. I have a drumstick that is cherry wood. Charlie Dean is the one that gave it to me. I'm not sure, but I think it was given to him. But he said it was made out of cherry wood. It's just smooth, there's no carving on it or anything. Both ends of the stick are almost the same, one's a little bit larger than the other, so you can flip it over and use one end to get a little different sound out. The sticks for the big drum, though, are quite a bit longer. They're about two foot in length. They have a larger handle made on them for gripping like a golf club, so to speak. Singers, depending on how loud they are, is how they want to drum. I was told, when I was starting to sing, that you drum as loud as you sing. If you don't sing very loud, then you don't drum very loud. A lot of singers that are real loud have a real heavy stick because it's louder. So the end of it is hard and heavy. Some of the singers that sing real soft, they have a real soft end and a real light end. So that's the differences of the heads. A lot of the sticks average around an inch diameter and about four to five inches long on the end. Most of them have like a teardrop shape to it. Nowadays they use a bit different things to cover it with. Usually just regular tanned hide. Or they use like a carpet thing they put on the ends of them. Harrison Hunter was a singer, he's deceased now, but he used to make drumsticks that were well known. If you have a Harrison Hunter stick, you got something. He was well known in the powwow world. He started a drum group that was real successful and traveled all over the world. I got to meet him one time, and I told him that I was singing for my tribe, and he said, "Well, you learn all those songs for your tribe. Someday you can sing for them at your dance, at your powwow." That's always lasted with me, and I've always respected him for sitting down and talking to me. He was a busy guy; he was demanded. People wanted him to sing for them a lot. And he sat down with me, just him and I, and we talked. It felt really good. But his drumsticks are unique. They're all the same, they look the same, and you can identify one right off the bat when you see one. For some reason he just had good drumsticks that he made. A lot of people wanted them. I don't have one, unfortunately. I'd like to have one. They're nice. I've made my own and tried to replicate his the best I could. A lot of the drumsticks that people use today are kind of an offspring of what his is.

There are different kinds of songs sung that everyone gets into the arena for; some are special for honor songs, some are social songs. How do you decide, at a powwow, what you're going to sing? I probably need to explain; like at Copan, there's other dances that don't have a center drum. You have northern style dances where the drums are on the outside [of the dance ring], not on the inside. The inside, with the center drum, is from Oklahoma. That's where it started from. The other dances that you may go to, have a northern style, they don't have a center drum. The style that is at Copan is Oklahoma-style powwow, with a center drum, and you always have a head singer that the committee of the powwow elects or asks a singer that is well known. Most of the times though, those head singers are just well versed in all songs. And they can sing every song, even from other tribes. For instance, if there's the head man dancer, the head lady dancer, he will know probably a song from their tribe. If they have a special, if they want to have a "give-a-way," he will sing a song from their tribe for them. So he has to be well versed. The songs that he sings out there most of the time are of his tribe. The flag song that's sang we usually beat from his drum. And he will bring mostly singers that are from his tribe. But the drum is open to anyone to come out and sing, to help him sing. He will rely on those other singers to help him sing. For instance, if there was a head man dancer that's

Delaware, and he doesn't know any songs from that tribe, he will hopefully have someone in that circle sing a song of Delaware. But if not, he'll sing a song that's appropriate, which is just a good war dance song for that person. And a lot of them will ask just for that.

The head staff of the powwow sets up the events, the order of things. They may get that from either experience of what they've done over the years or from some other people that are knowledgeable in Oklahoma powwows, who know how it's supposed to be ran. In Copan, they've got a guy there that's Lakota Sioux. He had put in some of his ways that they have up north in that dance. There's kind of a mixture of a lot of different tribes and some of the order of things out there, taking the flags down and taking the flags out of the arena and victory dances and so on like that. It can get complicated because it's just a mix. Like, well, whatever works best we're going to do. Things have changed a little bit up there, but it's still, when you have the drum in the middle, it's Oklahoma powwow. The head singer decides what songs to be sang. For instance, if the head man dancer, depending on what he is, if he's a traditional, a fancy dancer, a straight dancer, when he has a special, he will sing that type of song. It could be that type of song from his tribe. And so as an instance, a straight dancer, those are usually just a normal war dance song that they all try to sing. If it's traditional, those normally came from the north, so you'll sing a northern war dance song. And that's the song he'll pick. If it's buckskin, depending on if it's a southern style buckskin or a northern style, they'll sing a war dance song that's of the southern style, which means, southern is Oklahoma singing; it's a lower pitch. Northern is the real high-pitched singing that all came from up north. So that's how you divide up the categories, northern and southern. And that's the type of songs he'll sing. If it's jingle dress, that came from the north. They'll sing a northern song, southern style, too. That gets kind of complicated. Many times Oklahoma southern singing songs come from the north. They'll take those songs and change them to a southern style and sing those. So if I was singing on a drum as head singer, and a northern shawl [dancer] is going to have a special, I would want to sing a northern song; but I'm a southern style singer, I would have to sing it southern style. I wouldn't sing it high pitched like on a northern drum because I can't sing that way. Or, I would turn it over to a northern drum to sing for her. The head singer has that power. He controls all of the singing and drumming; all the decisions that are made as far as songs, that's his, he can do whatever he wants. They give that all up to him.

[While dancers wear clothing specific to their tribe and type of dancer, singers and drummers do not dress as spectacularly.] No, none at all. Even on drum groups, I never even see them. The only thing that they have in common together as a group, they'll get jackets or something all the same. Other than that, they wear whatever they want to wear. Traditionally, when we sing in our social dance songs, we all try to wear ribbon shirts of our tribe. That's the only thing I feel is appropriate to wear. Even back in the older days, other than ribbon shirts, from what I understand, is all they wore. They would wear a ribbon shirt with jeans, and that's when they go into ceremonies, and the singers would always wear a ribbon shirt. When I go to White Oak to their ceremonies over there, they'll wear a ribbon shirt.

The way that is in the passing on, it's kind of strange. There was a well-known singer that sang both Delaware and Shawnee. But he ran into that problem with passing on the songs. He, at one point, tried to teach songs to young people, but they weren't interested. He got to the point where he said that if anyone wanted to learn these, they come to me, and I will teach them. Other than that he wasn't going to teach them. He was very afraid when he was older that those songs weren't going to be passed on. And he was failing in health. There were a group of young men my age that came to him and expressed that they wanted to learn. And he taught them everything he knew. To this day, they're the ones carrying it on. Once they got older, enough to understand the importance, they got involved and had to learn. When he passed away he was satisfied that those dances were going to carry on and that he passed it on to the right people. And I feel that probably unless something happens, there's going to be some young guys that are going to come up and want to learn. And they're going to have to commit their life to singing in order for it to carry on. You can't do it on your spare time like that. It just won't work. And the more I sing, the more I realize how you have got to commit your life to it, or it just won't happen. And the reason why I say that is because you have to sing a lot in order to develop the sense of the way the songs are and the way the vocals are sang. It's just a way of life that you get through experience. I can sing any songs now, whereas when I first started, I could sing only our social dance songs; that's all my range would go. Now that I sing a lot of other different songs, I can sing pretty much anything, and I can learn pretty much anything, any song. Now that I've got all that with me, it's a lot easier for me. When I get old, if someone comes to me, if they decide to commit their life to singing and to carry it on, they really need to commit to singing all the way [I'll teach]. I met one well-known singer, well respected, who told me that he sang 365 days a year—365 days a year he sings something. Somewhere, whether its sitting home and singing, he sings everyday. I want to be like that when I get old. I want to be where I can sing anything for anybody at anytime. And hopefully our social dances will get stronger and build up and get more versed in dancing. Add more dances to our repertoire. It's a slow process. I keep telling those people before, our people say we need more dances. It took a long time to lose this; it's going to take a long time to gain it back. And so you don't get it back that quick. So, I'm just taking my time and learning all facets about singing.

[When I traveled from Oklahoma to Conner Prairie in Indiana] I carried [a drum] with me.

[Growing up], I didn't hear much of those stories about [removal from ancestral places]. I had my own thoughts about it. I don't think a lot of those things were talked about. It was probably a bad time in their lives so it was pretty much not talked about. That's my feeling about it. I just don't think those things were even thought of. Now I have heard people say, "That's where we used to be, or we have been there." And they felt good that we got to go back and visit some of those places. They were excited that we got a chance to go back. A lot of them have never and probably were never able to get to go back there as far as expense wise. When they arrived here [Oklahoma] they stayed here and didn't get to go anywhere. So as far as stories, I haven't heard of any other than some experiences of some elders that went back and what they felt. One in particular was when Nora Dean went back and then told me those stories of when she went back with her ancestors. That she had some kind of feeling of that's where she belonged was back there. It was like home. That's what she felt. And I've had that; it's kind of strange to say that, but when you're there [ancestral places] . . . you know the history. That bloodline is in my veins, and I know that some of my ancestors had been there. And it felt, like we say, that that spirit is still there. We can still feel that going back there. And I have felt something when I was there, some connection. It's hard to explain, but I could feel it there. It's peaceful. When you're there by yourself, and no one is around in the woods, you have that feeling.

[At Conner Prairie in 1991] I was kind of amazed at the questions they would ask: how'd we get there? Do we ride a horse? Do we still live in tipis? How long have you been Indian? Those kind of things, they make you laugh. It sticks in my mind now when you think about what it was back then. The first time I've been [to Conner Prairie] and got a reaction from the young people that had studied our culture, I didn't realize that's what they did. They treated us like we were kings or something; we were really special to them. And it amazed me that they had that kind of outlook towards us. I learned later on that they study our tribe, our people, in their history. It made me feel good that they did that. I think they honestly didn't think that there was any of us left. And it kind of goes with the amazement. When we were there [at Conner Prairie], they couldn't believe that we still existed. And that's why they were kind of in awe at us. And it makes me feel good to know that our bloodline is still around. And for those kids to see that, that I could bring something to them and share it with them, that we're still around. It amazed me that they didn't realize that there are still some of our people around. I felt good with those kids. They treated us well. They respected us, a lot of them did. I was amazed at some of the questions. They don't know what we're doing currently and what's going on. And it made me feel good to teach them, this is what we're doing now. Things change, we're not like what's in the book that you may read. We're just like they are. We've blended in with society. We're no different.

Our tribe is Woodlands. I don't know how this is and why, but I love trees. I love to be surrounded by trees. For some reason I can't stand to be out in the open prairie. I don't like that at all. And when I went back and seen how huge and how big the trees were, I was in awe. And I was, like, this is incredible, our people lived here. It was just fascinating to see those huge trees, I loved it. That's my response to being back there. It was incredible. I thought that I would love to live there and be there among those big trees. Even here [in Oklahoma] we have little small blackjacks, but that's where we live. And that's where I live among the trees. But for some reason why I feel that way other than that it's just in my blood. There's just some attachment to those trees. That's where my ancestors are from, and that's the connection. When I went back, the thing that lasted to me in my mind and in my heart was that the trees were incredible. I just couldn't believe that we couldn't stay there, that our ancestors couldn't still be there. Because that was really nice, to be amongst them big trees like that. I like those. If there's anything that I could have, I'd want some of them down here, some of those big trees. I grew up on the Cheyenne River down in Copan in the river bottom, and those were some big trees down there. That's where I ran when I was little. That was my stomping ground, so to speak. And we had trees; we had one tree that four of us hand-to-hand couldn't touch. And it was the largest one that we'd ever seen. We always played around those big trees like that. Of course, the lake's got it all now, but my dad told me that it was one of the biggest trees in the river bottom. It was a cottonwood tree. But four of us kids hand-to-hand couldn't reach around it. That was my part here. We'd play around those big trees like that, where we could find them.

Oral history conducted on May 29, 2000, at Bartlesville, Oklahoma.

Don Secondine holds a trailer of silver hairplates that he made. A trailer is a part of dancing regalia that extends from a Delaware man's collar down the back to just above the ground when standing.

Pam Elvington in her office at the Southtowne Branch of the Home National Bank. (2007, Bartlesville, Oklahoma)

PAMELA DIANE ELVINGTON

Tribal member
Born August 23, 1961, in Nowata, Oklahoma

I was born to James Wayne Barnes Sr. and Mary Lou Barnes (Beumeler). Both of my parents were born in the Nowata area. My Delaware heritage comes from the paternal side of my family. My paternal grandmother's name was Margarieta Moore Barnes; her mother was Lucinda Secondine Moore. My paternal great-great-grandfather was Fillmore Secondine. [Fillmore's father was James Second Eye, the son of Sacondyan, the son of Chief Anderson.] My family moved from Nowata to Bartlesville in 1963.

I am married and have two sons. I have one younger sister and two younger brothers, all of which are married with children and live in Bartlesville.

My family was not very involved with the Delaware culture so I don't have the knowledge that some do regarding the customs of our people. My grandmother, Margarieta, lived in Nowata; she was raised with the Delaware traditions, but she did not speak often of it. She was a very stern woman who seldom laughed, always very serious. I'm not sure if that had to do with her upbringing. Margarieta was a registered nurse and worked at the Nowata Hospital and at the Hayes House (home for the mentally handicapped). I don't know the obstacles that she had to overcome to get her nursing license, but I am sure there were plenty. She never talked of her childhood, so there is a lot I do not know about my family's history. I remember only once seeing my great-grandmother Lucinda before she died. She was in a nursing home. I remember her being pleased to see me. I remember her reaching out and taking my hand and smiling. She would have been around eighty-five years old at that time, and I was around seven. I was not sure what to say or do, so I just smiled at her and said hello. I would love to have had the opportunity to visit with her when I got older so I could have learned more about her and how she grew up.

I attended Bartlesville schools and graduated from College High School in 1980. I got married and started my family right out of high school. I worked as a cashier while my boys were little. When my oldest one was five I decided to further my education. I enrolled at the local vocational school in the electronics program. I finished the program and then enrolled in Coffeyville Community College in Coffeyville, Kansas. I graduated with an associate of applied science in 1989. The job opportunities in this area in the electronics field were limited, so I continued to work as a cashier until I got a job at the local credit union in late 1989. This was my first professional job, and it lasted until 1998. At that time I decided to go back to college full-time and pursue a business degree. In my search for financial assistance I happened into the job that I currently hold with the Delaware Tribe in January of 1999. Since that time I have had to discontinue attending school full-time and am currently taking classes as I can. I anticipate graduating in May of 2002, after which I will continue towards my bachelor's degree.

Various assistance programs are offered to Delaware tribal members who live in all parts of the Nation, with the highest concentration in Northeast Oklahoma. A trust fund was established in the late 1970s, and various assistance programs operate off the annual interest of these funds. Programs operating from the trust monies are available to all tribal members regardless of place of residence. Programs that are federally funded are offered to tribal members who live in a specific service area, which includes Washington, Nowata, Craig, Rogers and North Tulsa counties of northeast Oklahoma.

When the tribal headquarters moved from its former location to the current location the tribal council saw an immediate need to centralize a point of contact for tribal members seeking assistance from the various programs that are available to them, so they developed a "One Stop Shop" which is a combination office and classroom for tribal members. This office has computers with Internet access available, adult basic education classes are held twice a week, and a staff person to assess needs and offer the proper applications for programs that can address those needs.

I currently hold the staff position that assists tribal members in the One Stop Shop; this position involves working with people who are seeking job training or higher education. The tribe offers financial assistance for job training to tribal members who qualify by meeting income criteria. Those who qualify can obtain training through vocational or on-the-job training. They can earn a wage (paid out of government program funds) while on-the-job. If they choose vocational training, the program can help offset the cost of tuition and books required for the training. Once training is complete, then the tribe will assist them with job placement.

Those seeking higher education through colleges, universities, or vocational schools are also eligible to apply for a one-time scholarship that is provided through the Delaware Tribe Education Committee. This committee is responsible for oversight of interest monies received from the Delaware Tribe Trust account. This committee also offers assistance to tribal families with children in kindergarten through fifth grade with the cost of school supplies. There is education/athletic assistance available to tribal families to assist with those type of expenses. The committee also awards monies to tribal members who demonstrate exceptional academic ability.

My responsibilities include the outreach of these programs by letting tribal members know what is available to them, the intake of the applications, and the processing of the applications after they have been approved. The primary source of outreach is the quarterly tribal newspaper, the Delaware Indian News. I also attend job fairs and other community events and hand out informational material. I participate in local workforce council meetings in which the area workforce needs are addressed. These meetings give agencies a better understanding of what employers want and need in their employees. The agencies can then better assist the program participants by counseling them and directing them to obtain training in the areas that are suggested by the employers.

I have had the opportunity to work with tribal teenagers through a summer youth work program that the tribe offers. I enjoy this part of the job most of all. It is encouraging meeting the youth and seeing them have a desire to work, go to college, and go into careers that interest them. The summer of 1999 I worked with a group of seven teens; of the seven, six planned to go to college and one planned to join the armed forces. All of these youth come from economically disadvantaged families, so they know they must work hard to reach their goals.

I am proud to be working for the Delaware Tribe. It is challenging and rewarding at the same time. I enjoy working with and assisting tribal members.

Oral history interview on May 30, 2000, at Bartlesville, Oklahoma.

Annette Ketchum dances at the 2005 Delaware Days at Conner Prairie
Living History Museum, Fishers, Indiana.

ANNETTE KETCHUM

I was born up at Dewey, Oklahoma, northeast of Dewey, up on my grandmother's allotment. My grandmother, Minnie Willits, delivered me actually because the doctor never did get out there. Not everyone knew mother was pregnant, I don't think, 'cause she was real little. So I came into the world as a big surprise to all the other people. I think she won a case of beer for it. [Mother: Violet Jean Woody. Father: Frank E. Martin]

Living on an allotment means that it was land that was given to each Indian that was born before Oklahoma's statehood. My grandmother was born in 1900 or 1901, and so she got the allotment. In Oklahoma they broke up land differently; they didn't really have a reservation. It's not a reservation. Sometimes we talk about the Copan Res or the Dewey Res because that's where most of our people were congregated. It's a land base, and people were on allotments. But most of the people have either sold their allotments already or they lost them to settle debts or other ways.

Allotments were given to Indians by U.S. government: 160 acres for full-bloods and 80 acres for mixed bloods. So that's how they gave them to each person because it made up for the fact that they were taken from their land in Kansas at the time. So all our ancestors got allotments. But it wasn't when they first got down there. There were almost one thousand who came [to Oklahoma from Kansas], and [the tribe] got the land base. But later on the government decided to break up everything into [individual] allotments, and at that time they gave everybody a piece of land.

One of the earliest memories I have is when we lived with my Mother Toots [her mother's first cousin, Pauline Morrison]. My Mother Toots was Delaware and Pawnee. My father and mother lived with her in town, Dewey. I was about two years old, I think. My father went to work for his father-in-law, Art Woody, in the oil patch. The oil-drilling business. It's probably called a "patch" because some times there is oil in the ground where they drilled and sometimes not; thus oil here, oil there, oil over there—like patchwork. In fact, that was when there was a booming time because of the oil. Grandmother Minnie probably lived at the farm, at her allotment. But my folks were living in town with Mother Toots. You know it was a bad time, right after the Depression [and then] during the war [WWII], and [the government] was calling for people to live together, more than one family in a house. Mother Toots had two older kids at home. Jimmy was a few years older than me, and he would tease me, so I told on him. And he said, "Well, I didn't know she could talk." But I told on him. And I don't know whether I heard it or I remember it. But I can remember that we were just little brown kids out in the dust all the time. I guess that's the earliest remembrance I have.

When I was a child, we were pretty happy. I have a sister [Paula Pechonick] a little younger than I, just the two children. My father went away for a while to work in Alaska. So my mother, my aunt, her son, and my sister and I all lived together. When I got married, I tried to raise my kids the way I was raised. We lived like my people lived before me. I didn't think things changed a lot, except when my papa went away to be cured of tuberculosis.

When I was a young girl, my mother and aunts took all of us kids to a Delaware General Council meeting. It was at the courthouse in Bartlesville. I was young. I can remember all of our relatives, and mother introduced us to all these people. In fact, that's one of the things they always did, take you around, introduce you to the old people, and shake their hand. We did that to show courtesy toward the old people, to introduce all your kids to them. But we never acted rude or disrespectful even if we were bored. The only thing I remember about the tribal government at that time was that the tribe was having a big fight over something. And finally they took us kids out of there. At that time, in Oklahoma, we weren't under any kind of tribal rule. The families got together, like if you have a lot of cousins and relatives, everyone got together on Sunday. The men sat out in the backyard, and the kids played. We stayed out on the creek and played and had fun, and the women sat up in the house and they cooked. We did probably pretty much what the non-Indian families were doing at that time. Except where I grew up everybody I knew was Indian. There were some white people around, but everybody that surrounded us were all Indian people. It seemed like our friends were Indian people and all of our relatives and everybody mixed together. And we had fun. I just remember fun times.

When I was a girl, we went to Bartlesville every weekend, to go to the movies and go do things that other people did. Bartlesville was a real bustling town. It was exciting to go down to Bartlesville on Saturday. There'd be lots of cars down in Bartlesville. And lots of people on Third Street, now it's Frank Phillips Boulevard, and in the dime stores, walking down the streets and in the restaurants; there were people everywhere. Today in Bartlesville it's kind of dead downtown. The people aren't out in the place; they're not out doing things on Saturday. They don't go to town like that. They go to the Wal-Mart store. Saturday was like a festival. Compared to what it is today, you go downtown on Saturday, and you wouldn't see anybody. No cars or anyone. Same way with Dewey. I can remember when we were kids, on Saturday night, we put on roller skates and skated down the street. Ordinances prohibit it now. People would park on Main Street just to watch people walk by. But you don't see a lot of Indians walking around Bartlesville or Dewey anymore either.

Back then, you went to the store one time a week. You got everything done on Saturday. Now, I can go anytime. I get in my car, I go all over town everyday and run my errands and do all the things, just like everybody else does today.

The automobile changed our lives. Between my children and me, there's a bigger difference than between me and my mother or my grandmother. It's the automobile, the fast foods; it's been the way people move around, doing their jobs. They don't stay in one place. They move all the time. It's the television, too. We didn't have television when I grew up. We had no exposure to TV. We never had a TV in our home until I got married. Our neighbors had a TV, and we'd walk up there because they grazed their cows on Grandmother's allotment, and they gave us milk. And that was our job to walk up the road every night and get the milk. They had TV, so we would hang out at their living room. We didn't drink pop or eat candy and all that sugar. At Christmas, we got candy. Grandmother baked. And we had fry bread every night. I thought fry bread was the most boring thing in the world, and people make a fuss over it now. I don't even eat fry bread today because it was so commonplace then. Everybody thinks it is such a delicacy, and it is, it's great. But I always wanted somebody to give me things like cookies from the grocery store.

In Delaware way and most all Indians' way, the extended family plays a much bigger part than just your little family unit, like the four people in our family. I don't ever remember a time when there was just four of us. My parents always had somebody else's kids in the home or adults that had some domestic difficulty. I didn't know why we had the kids there sometimes, but since my father and mother stayed married people viewed them as stable. My father is white and my mother's Indian, Delaware. So if somebody is having a problem, they'd come to our house and stay with us. If somebody's husband was gone, then the wife would come to our house. We always had extra people at our house. And my Grandmother Minnie lived with us, too. Her last husband was a Cherokee man, Lawrence Fields. And he had land down around Tenkiller (Tenkiller Ferry Reservoir), down by Tahlequah. He had gone to the civilian military service in the Philippines, and he married another woman over there, while he was still married to Grandmother. My grandmother got his land [around Tenkiller], and when the Corps of Engineers came through, some shysters came through ahead of the Corps and bought the land up, and Grandmother sold the land to somebody and didn't hardly get any money for it, and it was his land. Well, Grandfather Fields wasn't too happy about that. I was born on Grandmother's allotment. While Papa was up in Alaska we lived in Bartlesville. We moved back to the farm when I was in the second grade.

Grandmother came to live with us when I was about in the sixth [grade]. She was a very traditional woman. She planted two big gardens every year—as big as one person could ever take care of, so it was our job to help her. Each morning, we had to get up, go out, and help her dig potatoes or snap beans or gather something. We'd do that from about six A.M. till mid-morning. We'd take a break, and she'd get her fishing pole, and off we'd head for the creek, my sister and I. She'd give us a little jar, and we'd catch grass-hoppers off the tall Johnson grass. Johnson grass was taller than we were. And we'd get grasshoppers and put them in the jar, and that's what she used for bait. She'd stand on the creek bank and fish while my sister and I would go up the creek from her and swing on the grape vines and play in the water. And she called us "fellars." "You fellars," that's what she'd always said to us. So we would play in the water, and she would fish a couple of hours. We would go back to the house where Grandmother cleaned and cooked the fish and we ate them. And then in the afternoon, we would rest a little bit, and then we'd go back, and she'd fish again; maybe she'd get a turtle or get some other kind of bigger fish. She'd take them home and cook up everything. She was a great cook. We would have supper. If Mother or Father wanted something else to eat, they did, but my sister and I ate what Grandmother ate. That was one of my memories. Every day we'd go down to the creek to fish and swim and play, and Grandmother would be right with us. One of the stories I like to tell is when one day she had a big turtle that she caught. She'd always clean them, to cook. First of all, she stuck a stick in the turtle's mouth to pull its head out and chopped its head off. That's the first thing that you do. Then she laid the turtle on its back and cut around the skin that's connected to the shell. That day when she cut that turtle, eggs rolled out. So it was a female. And when that happened, I screamed, I said "Ohh-hh!" And when I did it, she said, "Oh, quit screaming like a white woman." And I was a young child, and I didn't know what she meant; I'd never been scolded like that. It was sort of surprising to me. She hurt my feelings. So I went in and told my mother, "What did Grandmother mean?" She said, "I'm screaming like a white woman?" Mother said, "Oh, don't pay any atten-tion to your grandmother, she's just in a bad mood today." And I just went back outside and watched her finish cleaning the turtle, like she always did. Grandmother went in and cooked it, and we ate it. But that is probably my earliest memory of Indians being prejudiced against Caucasians—although I didn't understand it as such. Finally, we got older, and probably by the time we were teenagers, Grandmother didn't take us to fish anymore because we didn't want to go. And we didn't want to do the same things we always did; we wanted to get in the car and go to town. And so that's kind of when the change came. But before that we did what our parents told us to do. We were obedient children, and we could do anything but tell a lie or steal. They didn't have a lot of rules. We could go bare if we wanted to, swim naked, go in the creek. We just did what we pleased. We lived way out in the country. But by the time we were teenagers, we started having to wear a bathing suit if we went swimming. I went to school, about eighth grade, and heard the boys talking about those girls out there skinny-dipping. And my neighbor's mom got so upset when she discovered her girls skinny-dipped, too. She followed us one day. They got in trouble, but my sister and I didn't. We didn't ever do that anymore.

In our home, Grandmother would not talk Delaware to us, and mother wouldn't either. The thing was, they didn't want the kids to talk Indian. And we would ask them, "Tell us some Indian words." Sometimes we would get Grandmother to say something in Delaware. My grandmother's last husband (I think) would teach us some Cherokee words. And we learned those words when we were kids. But Grandmother did not want to talk about anything about Indians because she had very bad experiences, and my mother had worse experiences because she was mixed blood. It was like they were bitter and angry about things that happened in their lives. We didn't go to church; we didn't do anything like that. There wasn't any kind of religious training in our life. Mother didn't make us prejudiced or hateful toward other people; she was very good about keeping us from growing up angry and bitter like she did. Grandmother had been a semi-orphan. My mother wasn't an orphan, but they had a hellacious fight over her when she was a child. And because her dad was white, Grandmother could not win in court. They have laws against that now. The Indian child has to go with its Indian parent. Mother got to go with her aunt, too. And she got to spend time with her mother. But she had to live with her father to go to school. So she didn't board. And it was a sad time for her because her Caucasian grandmother thought that a "breed" was the worst kind of Indian there was because you couldn't trust them. It was sad for her. She had a sad life. (Mother died in 1996.)

Our people left [the Muskingum lands in Ohio] and came into Indiana. I'm a descendent of Chief Anderson, so I know that they came this way. We can trace our family back to Kik Tha We Nund,[1] who was Chief Anderson. Sa-cox-ie was one of Chief Anderson's sons. Sa-cox-ie, later known as Anderson Sarcoxie, had children. It was Chief Anderson's granddaughter that was our ancestor that came from that group that came through Indiana that we know for sure. And her name was Jane Sarcoxie. Then Grandma Brown and Grandma Josie. Grandma Brown, her name was Mary Brown. She was Grandma Josie's mother. And then Grandma Josie was my grandmother's mother. And that's how we know our line back to there. So we know they came through Indiana.

---

1. The Crossroads of America Council, Boy Scouts of America, maintains a camp near Anderson, Indiana, named after Chief Kik Tha We Nund. Order of the Arrow, a national Boy Scout honorary camping group, bases its ceremonies after Delaware culture.

When I went to elementary school, it was fun. I changed schools. We were staying down at Bartlesville. Father came back from Alaska. And when he came back, we all moved back up to the farm. Up to where my grandmother's allotment was. We moved up there, and I had a new experience. I'd ride the school bus to school. We were about five and half miles out of town. I was pretty active in school. I had a normal childhood and normal experience. My papa worked down in Bartlesville. My mother stayed at home for some of the times. Some of the time she worked; we'd go with her. But when we were young we learned how to sew and how to do bead work and do a lot of things like that. That has served me well, to learn sewing, so I could make traditional clothes. After I got out of school, I got married to Dee Ketchum. When I grew up, there was no running water, there was no electricity, it was way out in the woods. I raised my kids like contemporary kids, to a certain extent. And I even notice that my own daughter raises her kids as contemporary kids to an extent because they have a lot of different exposures. Dee and I took our girls back to the powwows in Oklahoma. We lived in Kansas; Dee was a basketball coach. So every year we'd go back; we'd go to the dances, and we would take our children, and they always knew from their earliest age that they were Indian kids. I was afraid that they would grow up not knowing because they weren't living in Oklahoma. So our children were always proud of their heritage, just like we were proud of it, but it wasn't really popular when we were kids. It became very popular but not where they lived. In Kansas, it was like "Oh, you're Indians." But the girls, they always identified with their culture. And now they're raising their kids that way. We encourage that now. We'd dress the girls in their Indian clothes. We dress our grandchildren in their Indian clothes. We hope to keep passing it on down.

Dee and I moved back to Oklahoma in 1984 to live full-time. We came back at the right time because as the old people start dying off, we were there to replace them. And we are there to carry on the ways because we listened to our ancestors. After we got to be young adults, we were always trying to soak up everything we could because Grandmother died, but Aunt Anna Anderson Davis was still alive. And Aunt Anna taught us how to make fry bread, taught us how to make clothes, taught us how to do a lot of things and told us a lot of stories that we wouldn't have known if it hadn't been for moving back to Oklahoma and being around at that time. We've always danced and taken a part in our tribe's activities. But since the Delawares don't live in just one community, we live all over the county, we live in our own houses; we get together for special occasions. After our federal funds were released in 1990, we started having funds to begin to restore a lot of our culture. That's when we started having our language restored, our dances restored, and Dee and I were right there for that. We made that commitment to our people and our tribe to learn all these things. Some of the people had gotten too old to do it any longer, so we stepped in, and we learned the dances, we learned the songs, we're learning the language. We're always learning. We're passing it on, it just keeps on going, [even] if somebody drops the ball like back in the generation of our parents where they had been told, "Don't do those things. Learn to fit into white society." It wasn't necessary to tell us that because the white society was all around us anyway. It wasn't lost for us, and I think that it won't be lost for our children. I don't know about the grandchildren yet. It's too soon to tell. But the grandchildren have a real interest. We had our grandson up here in Oklahoma during July 1998. [Jake Sears turned fourteen in August 1998.] He stayed with us, and he went to a basketball camp. He is so proud of his heritage, and he wants to sit around the drum. Dee will teach him songs and things. He is saying, "Well, you know, I'm an Indian, and I'm proud of it." He lives in Dallas; there's lots of black kids, Hispanic kids, kids from Asia, Oriental kids. And he fits in; they don't know what he is because they don't know what an Indian is down in Texas. But he is proud of his heritage.

My Aunt Anna is one of my favorite people. She is my grandmother's sister. She outlived my grandmother by twenty-five years. When we were growing up we were close to Aunt Anna because Annette Reeve was Aunt Anna's daughter, and she and my mother were like sisters in the Indian way. They were first cousins, only daughters of their parents at the time, but Aunt Anna eventually had a daughter that was my age. And when we were growing up, Mike Pace was a little kid. He's been one of the presenters at Conner Prairie in the last few years. He was younger than me. He says he remembers my sister and me, that we were always out doing cartwheels and flip-overs and giggling. He was just a little boy. We called him Mikey. But Aunt Anna treated all kids special. Aunt Anna was his aunt, and she was our great-aunt because the generations overlapped each other. His mother and my mother were niece and aunt. So I'm really in a different generation than Mike. If he had any children, they'd be my second cousins. Mike is first cousin to my mother actually. But his mother is a little younger than my mother. That's the way a lot of the Indian families are. They just overlapped the generation. If you had enough husbands or enough wives, pretty soon you're having kids that are the same age as their aunt and uncle. And that's what happened in our family. Aunt Anna was always a very benevolent woman in the community. She was a little different than my grandmother because my grandmother did not take to the white world at all. She always wanted to stay in the background, stay out in the country, do her farming, her gardening, do her fishing, and she liked that. But Aunt Anna, she liked to go to clubs, meetings, and she dressed up really nice, and she was such a wonderful lady. Aunt Anna was maybe five years older than Grandmother. But they did go to Indian school together at one time. They had guardians when they were young because they were considered incompetent as Indians. And these guardians, one of them married Grandmother off to a white man. Aunt Anna married a white man, too. But that was very fashionable in those days. If you were an Indian woman, a white man wanted to marry you. If you were an Indian man, then you usually married an Indian woman if you could find one that wanted you. It was different then, I think because they always told their girls to be careful who you marry. They always wanted their girls to marry up. Of course, everybody wanted a Delaware woman. There was this thing to really give your kids a leg up by having an advantage, maybe, of a white father that worked every day. You know, that was part of it. There was a mentality about that. And it made a lot of people ashamed of being Indian because we were poor, we weren't rich. It was hard. But you know what? When you're with everybody that is in the same boat, you don't know that you're different. Or you don't know that there's any better way or anything. And when Dee and I left and went away to college [University of Kansas], we just thought we were normal people. We got up to Lawrence, and everybody would ask us, "Are you from Haskell?" "Do you go to school at Haskell [Indian College]?" I had never seen this side of it, and they'd tell me, "Well, why do you tell people you're Indian, you can pass? You could tell them you're something else." It was something completely new to me. It was a strange feeling. But that was what people would say to me when they found out I wasn't going out to Haskell to school. We were just a normal brown couple with all the white couples. And they didn't think anything about it; [at the University of Kansas] we just fit in because Dee was an athlete. I think, if [my parents] had their choice, they probably wouldn't have me marry an Indian man. But I knew from the time I was young I would always marry an Indian. I wasn't interested in marrying a white man. So parents try to teach their children one thing but may end up teaching them something else, maybe; I don't know how to explain that.

When I went away to college, Oklahoma State University, as a freshman, my folks took me down to campus and just dropped me off. I stayed in a dormitory. I was a home economics major. I'd been raised in the country, and studying cooking and sewing was a natural thing. And for that age in that year, that's what a lot of women did; they became teachers, so they were in home economics. And you stayed in home economics till you got married. And then you became a housewife. I like home economics. I like sewing, and I like fabrics and cooking, and so I thought it just sounded easy to me. So that was my major. And then [after marriage] I went up to the University of Kansas. I changed majors because they didn't have home economics; times were changing. So I went into liberal arts, but I never did graduate. I only went two years. Well, I went a year and got married, and then I took college credits here and there. I don't have a degree. I have a little over two years of hours. And as time went by, Dee was going on; he was going to be a teacher, be an educator. We had children. And I was happy with my role.

I wasn't career oriented at all, I'm happy to say. I'm industrious, and I've worked a lot of jobs.

When we grew up in Oklahoma, we thought we were the only Lenape people, that the only Delawares were in Washington County. We discovered Delawares in Nowata (County.) Nowata is about twenty miles away from Bartlesville. But we always heard about the Absentee Delawares, too, who lived in Anadarko. We heard about them. And we even heard about some that lived down in Mexico, and Grandmother even had gone down to Mexico and brought back yuccas. We knew there were Delawares other places. But it never made much impact to me until 1987, when we went back to New York. That's where construction workers found bones on Ellis Island. Ellis Island is the place where the immigrants from Europe got off the boats. The Park Services asked Leonard Thompson, our ceremonial chief, and Dee Ketchum, Leonard's understudy and tribal council member, to go to New York and New Jersey to rebury the bones that were unearthed. My sister, my niece, and I accompanied Dee and Leonard as the party from our tribe. We got back there, and it was the most incredible feeling. The Delawares from Canada came. The Delawares from Anadarko came, and here we are, the three tribes together for the first time in over a hundred years. It was an impacting thing. I wasn't prepared for it in my mind. I hadn't thought about the impact of being back together. But when we got back together, it was just like we were all little kids, just standing around, just talking to each other and looking at each other. And saying how wonderful; we all had these feelings; it's almost like getting butterflies in your stomach. That's how it felt the first time we all got together. Our elder, Leonard [Thompson], he was so knowledgeable. He hadn't forgotten anything. He identified the artifacts that he was asked about at Heye Museum of Natural History in the Bronx, NY. He knew what all the artifacts were; he knew where they came from. The other elders from Anadarko and Canada were not able to make these identifications because they had lost so much of the culture because of living among other tribes for so long. We participated in the reburial of the bones. The elder from each tribe wrapped the bones for reburial. They asked two women to be pallbearers—Linda Poolaw of the Western Delawares, and I from our tribe. Pictures of the tribal people came out in the New York and New Jersey area newspapers while we were there, and there was television coverage of the ceremonies. I hate to say this, but a reporter printed my picture in the *New York Times* in my Delaware ceremonial clothes with the Statue of Liberty in the background.

Indiana was one of the places our ancestors lived on their removal from the East Coast. Our tribal members have done presentations at Muncie, Minnetrista Cultural Center; Anderson, Indiana; Ft. Wayne, Indiana; and Conner Prairie at Fishers, Indiana. I did teaching in beadwork and Woodland cooking at Minnetrista and danced at the powwow several years. The

Miamis sponsored Kekionga at Fort Wayne, Indiana, and we danced at that powwow and took our Eagle Ridge Singers Drum. Our tribe did the River Walk at Anderson, Indiana, because many of us are descendants of Chief Anderson. The resurgence of interest for the Delaware Tribe in Indiana has been a wonderful opportunity to share the fact that the tribe and our people are still making history. We are not only a part of the history of the 1800s in Indiana. I feel good about coming to Conner Prairie, and I know that we are walking where our ancestors walked. Just like people that say they go to the Holy Land, and they walk where Jesus walked or they walked where the Apostles were.

Since I've been up here [at Conner Prairie], I've taught in the clothing and arts and storytelling. I was in storytelling for several years. I'm in language now. But our presenters can present more than one subject about our culture. We've broadened [the program], and we've shaped it and massaged it into areas that are more interesting for the students to make it more of a learning experience. So they can absorb more, we put it in a nice package for them. I only get a few minutes with each child, and I want to leave something with them. Some of the teachers have come back with new classes each year. They comment on how they like the change[s] we make and the delivery. They say they learn something new every time. Students ask us questions like, "Do you drive cars?" "Do you wear those clothes all the time?" I wear a buckskin dress or traditional Delaware dress. And they have no concept of how modern-day Indians live. I say things like, we go to Wal-Mart, we drive cars, we eat snack foods, and we live in houses. But we are also just as able to live in the Indian world where our culture is, and we go back and forth between those "two worlds." We go into our cultural world. We don't talk about the politics of the [U.S.] nation; we talk about Delaware politics. We don't talk about the latest recipes; we talk about Indian food. We talk about Indian subjects in our house a lot of the times. And we don't sit around and talk about our neighbors; we talk about our ancestors. We try to keep the genealogy straight, and we are always remembering. When I come up here, I know these kids aren't interested in our history as much as they are interested in our clothes, dances, singing. But they might go home and read a book about the Delawares, or they might go research Indian history. If so, we have opened their minds. You don't know what kind of seeds you plant. And that's kind of what it is—seed planting—the interest that you share. We're not trying to get them to take our culture as their own; we've been learning about their culture for a long time; now they're learning about ours; it's sharing. I guess that's what it's all about, sharing.

One thing that is really interesting to me and I take a big interest in is our foods. Preparing foods and passing on how to make the recipes, like we learned when we were young, and some of the foods that we eat in Oklahoma now, like the fry bread. I don't know when our people began to make fry bread, but [now] we make it with self-rising flour and water and a little salt and fry it in oil. Well, I think that they always had oil, from animal fat, to fry it. When I was a girl they fried it in lard. My grandmother made it. But when they were coming through [during federal relocation], at some point in time, they didn't have kettles. Back on the East Coast, I don't think they fried bread then. They probably made bread another way. They probably baked it. They had earthen pots and things. Pots and kettles were part of the trade goods. I think our ancestors were very progressive. When they saw a new kind of way to fix things, they went for it. And as they found a new kind of pan or a new kettle, they used it. They improvised. Even today, if I'm cooking at home, I do it in a certain way. When I cook out at the campgrounds I cook a different way; I have to use what I have out there; I improvise and use a wood fire, put a kettle on a wood fire. And if I'm at home, I use my oven or I use my stove. That's what they've done. Our people have evolved in that cooking, but we still have a lot of our old dishes, like the dried corn soup. We still have many of the greens in the spring, the wild onions and those kinds of things. We still go out and dig the wild onions and make wild onions and eggs. The Delawares started eating pork and beef after they met the Europeans. We still get deer from time to time. We can get buffalo from time to time. We can cook those kinds of dishes. It did evolve, but we still use the corn; we still eat a lot of squash; we still eat a lot of beans. We still eat all those same traditional foods. There's certain things that every generation was raised with, and every generation after that eats it. And my daughter does that, too. They have access to lots of venison. And she just fixes venison, all kinds of dishes in venison. I didn't have much venison. When I grew up, there weren't hardly any deer left in Oklahoma. And the generation before us, there were none. They had just completely died out. Now in Oklahoma, there's lots of venison. So people start using venison again. They use hogs and beef. We raised some hogs and some cattle at the farm and chickens and things like that to eat, and possums and raccoons and squirrels and rabbits. We ate about everything that walks, swims, and flies. We ate all kinds of foods. And we ate whatever we had.

One of the things I really enjoy about our culture is the dancing. We have fun. And when we're at a powwow, we can always tell all the Delaware women because we're all wearing the same kind of dresses. We have leggings and wrap-around skirts with ribbon work on them. We also have the gathered skirt with apron called a day dress. We always wear the same kind of blouse with the big collar and the big sleeves. We have to make those. The blouse has silver washers or buttons on the collar above the ruffle. The buttons are silver discs about ½ inch to ⅝ inch with the holes on the outer edge of the disc, not in the middle. The buttons or washers decorate the collar of the blouse, as many and in any configuration the lady wants to use. The washers are round with a center open (like a donut) and a pin in the middle that is put through the fabric to hold it on. Washers range in size from ⅝ inch to one inch. The buttons are about ¼ inch to ⅝ inch in size. The holes are at the outer edge of the button, not in the middle as a bone or plastic button.

When the women go out to dance, we dance to the beat of the drum. We don't jump around. The Delaware women do a very upright dance—we carry a shawl, a fan, and tulip purse. It is so-called because it is shaped like the flower with six petals or panels sewn together and opened and closed with a drawstring. It is made of deer hide and is beaded, decorated, fringed. We look very dignified when we dance, and the Delaware women are as attractive from the back as from the front because we wear an Ahsipulaun (hairbow and trailer) that is clipped to the back of the head so as not to be seen from the front, only the back. We put red spots at the point of our cheekbones—one on each side that range in size from a dime to a quarter size. The old people told us we wear the spots so the Creator will know us as Delawares when we get to heaven. The other dances that we do are traditional dances. One in particular is the women's dance, just for the women. And that's to honor our women. That's what they tell us, that we all started with a man and woman. And that's what our old people say, that we started with a man and a woman, and the Delaware honor their women. Generally, we wear shawls with that dance. Anytime a woman goes into the arena, if she's not dressed in traditional clothes, she puts on a shawl. We don't walk into the arena like the men do. Men can be in any clothing. Sometimes they'll put a blanket on. But the Delaware women can wear an honor blanket instead of a shawl. Back in the fifties, when I first started dancing and noticing what the women were wearing, they always wore black shawls. That was the only thing that I ever saw. I thought every shawl had to be black. Nowadays, a shawl is any color a woman wants to wear and may be decorated or not and any length of fringe. Part of that is because of contest dancing. They never had contest dancing back in the old days. Contest dancing was something that came probably in the seventies, maybe late seventies. Now, it's just what they do at every powwow—they contest dance. And so the colors get brighter, the things get bigger and better, and now a woman will have two or three dresses to wear. Every night you change dresses. And it didn't used to be that way. If you had a skirt, you wore it. If you didn't have a skirt, you wrapped a blanket around your hips, or you wore something else. You wore what you had. If you didn't have a blouse, you would just use what you had. We've evolved into being very correct. When I see a Delaware woman dressed, I know her from any other woman. I see an Osage woman dressed, I see a Cherokee woman, I see a Potawatomi—any woman I see, even the variation in the Woodlands, you can pretty much look at whether it is a Sac and Fox or a Potawatomi or a Shawnee by their clothes. You can tell by what they're wearing if they are a Woodland tribe or a Plains tribe, or Seminole.

It's interesting. The women dance all the same though. We all dance alike, but our dresses are different.

I guess things have gone pretty much full circle in my life, to some extent. I went from having a grandmother to being a grandmother and to having grandchildren. I have two granddaughters and three grandsons. The granddaughters and the grandsons are all special, but the granddaughters are the ones that I am transferring these transferable concepts to. And I started young with these girls just like I did with my own children. With my children, when they were old enough to hold a needle and start to put beads on there and put them on a cloth, I started teaching them how to do that. They hated it. But when they became adults, suddenly when they wanted to know how to bead, and they picked it up, it's like, "Well, this isn't so hard!" and I said, "Well, I think you've learned something. You must have remembered something." It was implanted in there someplace. And then the granddaughters, I did the same thing. It wasn't their mothers; they always say that it skips a generation, that it's not your mother that teaches you; it's your grandmother that teaches you a lot of things. And so, fortunately, I'm here to teach them, and since my little granddaughters and grandsons both, since they were little enough to hold a needle, I started to have them string beads on a thread. And they'd make necklaces. We started with large beads and we progressed up to smaller beads. The girls, they're ten and eleven right now [in 1999], last year they made a rosette about the size of a half-dollar or silver dollar. They call me Annie, and Annie has to sit there and tell them where to put the bead, and they do it. They really amazed me because it's not easy to do. And then the little boys are still wanting to string the beads, and they do smaller beads. I think it was during the seventies it was real popular to wear the strands of beads, and it's come back, down in Dallas. And they make bead necklaces for all their friends when they come to my house. So we've transferred that on. And same way with the cooking. I'd always let them sit right on top of the cabinet when they were little and sit right there, crack eggs, do whatever they were big enough to do.

I can remember one evening we were doing wild onions. We had the two little boys pulled up there to the island in the kitchen, each with a knife. They [the children's parents] say, "Don't let them have knives"; they were like five and six. And I said, "Just chop on that chopping block," and they chopped those onions up. If they come in and they crawled up on the cabinet, we'd just cook, right like that. I would be careful about letting them put things in hot grease, but everything is a transferable concept. If you start kids young enough, you get them hooked. And that is our whole plan in life, with our own children. Now with our generation, we were hooked already. We didn't have a choice. We couldn't get away from it. But our kids could have gotten away from it. But we hooked them young. And the same way with the grandchildren. They could easily get away.

I'm hoping my grandchildren will keep the culture alive. It can be lost. Like freedom, it's just one generation away from being lost. You can lose your freedom in one generation. You can lose all your culture in one generation. The Delawares came close at one time, but there was always that thread; there were always those traditionalists that were right there, and we've picked it up again and we carried it on. And it's a wonderful thing to see these children. One of the first things we teach our children: take care of your clothes because these Indian clothes have very fragile work on them. Your fan is very delicate. Take care of your things. If you don't take care of them, you're not going to get to wear them. We're not going to let you dress in them until you can take care of your things. So we'll have them up there at the powwow, in the night, with a flashlight, in the tent, getting their clothes and putting them back on the hanger and folding them. They don't just walk in the tent and throw their things everywhere. I've seen kids that did that. I wouldn't let my kids dance if they did that. I wouldn't let my grandkids dance. They know to put their things up. You won't walk into the tent and find dance clothes all over the floor. Maybe their other clothes will be scattered. We are teaching them to cook outside, too. That wood fire is awfully dangerous, you know, but they can start to learn to do things in the camp instead of saying, "Oh, you kids get away from here, just get away." We don't ever do that. We tell them to come on in and help us. And it makes them draw close. I let them play with my hair, too. The kids love to braid it. And they just play with it. And when I'm down in Texas, if I'm at one of their ball games, their friends come up, and they each take half of it and they braid it and play with Annie's hair. So we don't have a lot of silly rules about what they can't do.

Two of the most important things, possibly, that I would like to see my grandchildren be able to grasp and pass on, the daughters especially, is how to cook the food. It's passing away very rapidly. I belong to the Bartlesville Indian Women's Club, and one of the things that we talk about—we get these women in there that are eighteen, twenty, twenty-five—they don't even know how to do anything traditional. They're Indian young people. If we don't get them back and teach them how to make the food, then pretty soon they'll be carrying in fast food. They don't want to make a cobbler. But I think that my granddaughters, one of them at least, will learn to do it because her mother likes to cook. But the other granddaughter may be lacking in that department. So I will probably have to teach her those things. Another thing I want to teach them is how to make the traditional clothes. Our daughters keep saying they want to learn to do it. But to this date, DeAnn has made her own skirt and her leggings and trimmed them. But she has never made the blouse yet. And Kala is not too interested in sewing or cooking. But she is interested in looking good, so she may, out of necessity, eventually learn to do some of those things. Another thing I really want to pass on is my beadwork. That's probably one of the passions in my life. I love to bead. I want to pass it on.

Oral history interview conducted on October 6, 1998, at Conner Prairie, Fishers, Indiana. Annette Ketchum came from Bartlesville, Oklahoma, to participate in the Seventh Annual Woodland Indian Art and Culture Program.

JANUARY 2004, UPDATE BY ANNETTE KETCHUM

In August 2003, Jake Sears enrolled at the University of Texas at El Paso (UTEP).[2] He was eighteen years old and had graduated from Fredericksburg High School in Fredericksburg, Texas. Jake received several honors as a football player his senior year. They included first team all district and region, All West Texas, All State, All Centex, and All Southwest Texas.

He also played basketball in high school. When the UTEP recruiters came to visit Jake and watch him play basketball, they liked his speed, height, and competitive spirit on the court, as well as on the football field. UTEP coaching staff recruited and signed Jake to a five-year football scholarship.

In May his grandfather, Dee Ketchum, went to Fredericksburg for a graduation gathering. Andy and DeAnn had an enormous dinner and blessing ceremony. His grandfather set up an arena with seating. He explained that he was going to pray in the Delaware language and bless Jake, his first grandson, and that all who wished to join in could dance a special dance with Jake. Almost all the guests, none of which were Indian, except for the family, joined in and went through the line to shake Jake's hand and wish him well. Dee sang some songs and prayed. Then, everyone ate a traditional meal.

Many of the eighty-plus guests expressed how they were touched spiritually by the blessing ceremony. They had never seen anything like it. Dee wanted to leave an impression of how important graduation is. Few Indian students attend college, and of those who attend, a very low number graduate.

Jake has finished his first semester at UTEP and has made his grades. Since he is a red-shirt freshman he did not play ball this year. He still has four years of football eligibility. College life has been an easy transition for Jake. He is mature. Because of his brown skin, black hair and eyes, he fits into the largely minority student body. However, at six feet four inches, 240 pounds, he is among the largest athletes.

---

2. Jacob Sears is the son of Andy and DeAnn Ketchum Sears and the grandson of Dee and Annette Ketchum. The cover of this book features Jacob dancing.

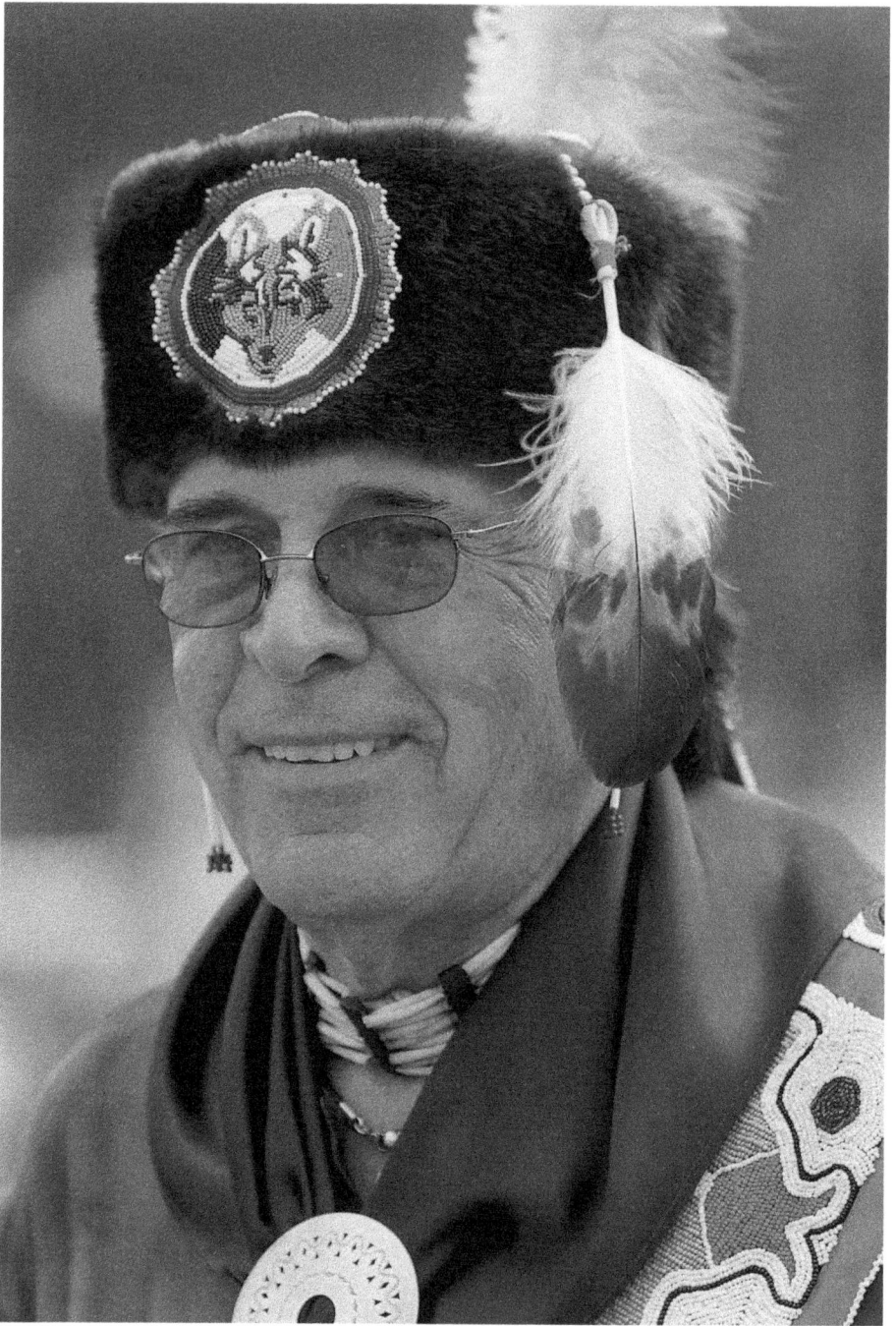

Dee Ketchum dances at the 2005 Andersontown Powwow, Anderson, Indiana.

DEE KETCHUM

Chief, 1998–2002

I grew up in Bartlesville, Oklahoma. Grew up in the city, even though the house that I lived in was close to a river, the Caney River there. I've always remembered, as a boy, spending all my days at the river. Playing in the river and making this or that at the river. My mother [Lillian Berry Ketchum] and father [Lewis Ketchum] were divorced when I was very small. I lived with my dad but always just remembered going to the river and playing ball. That's basically growing up in Bartlesville. And it was just as a little Indian boy; I spent all my time on the river.

I think that I always knew that I was a Delaware. You know, we use the term today "Native American." I didn't, never. That subject didn't ever come up as far as I was concerned. I was always a Delaware. My mom and dad always taught me that because they were both Delaware. And my Aunt Kate Curleyhead Berry, who's full-blooded Delaware, and she was like a grandmother to me because my mother lost her father and mother real young. And so consequently, Aunt Kate took my mom in and raised her. So she was like a grandmother to me on that side, and I spent a lot of time with her. But I always knew that I was a Delaware because they always taught me that, even though I grew up in a period of time when, in Oklahoma, it wasn't particularly fashionable to be Delaware, per se, or Indian for that matter, you know. We didn't go to a lot of dances because there wasn't a lot dances going on then. My Uncle "Fish" Ketchum, on his allotment, we'd go up there from time to time. But I can hardly remember a lot about that. We'd go up there and stomp dance a little bit.

But we didn't have the powwows and things to go to. My Aunt Kate spoke Delaware, but we didn't speak a lot of Delaware around our house because my mom and dad both went to Chilocco Indian School, which is a boarding school that our government put our kids in to assimilate the Indian kids into the white society. And what happened is they put them in a boarding school where they met and married other Indian kids, so that's why we're here. And so they actually perpetuated [the Delawares] in some degree, since we didn't have reservations in Oklahoma at that time. By virtue of my mom and dad both going to Chilocco Indian School, they were taught to not speak the Delaware language or do a lot of the customs there. I remember mom always talking about how she was punished at Chilocco by speaking the language or doing something that would be Indian, so to speak, or Delaware, even wearing clothes or so forth. She'd be punished and made to stand in the corner and other things. I asked my dad one time, "Well, did you ever, when you were over at Chilocco, did you ever dance?" And he said, "Well, we'd sneak off and go down by the river there (it was in Arkansas City) and danced down there by the river." I said, "Well, did the women have any cans or shells on there legs." He said, "No, we just sang. Didn't sing real loud." Because if they sang real loud, well, the teachers, and so forth, would come and get them and punish them. But I, just growing up in Bartlesville, I was just an ordinary Indian boy that went to school and played athletics and sports and so forth. I guess because of the splitting up of my mom and dad when I was young, I really engrossed myself in athletics and education. You know, that was my outlet. My brother was four years ahead of me in school, and my sister was two ahead of me. I just kind of dived into that athletic stuff and that was kind of my life, to some degree, for a long period of time.

Going to school at the elementary and junior high levels, there was no sense of separation between whether I was Indian or Delaware. I'm jumping over a few years here, going from grade school clear up to going to school at the University of Kansas. I never did feel special or not special in grade school. I didn't feel any prejudice when I was growing up per se in Oklahoma. When I went to the University of Kansas I didn't feel any there. Billy Mills was a good friend of mine, and he was Sioux Indian off of the reservation, and we roomed together for a semester and became real good friends, still are to this day. You know, he's the only American who ever won the 10,000-meter for the gold medal for the United States [1964]. He said to me one time, which was kind of shocking to me, "You know, I envy you and this John Tiger," a football player from Miami, Oklahoma, who was at the university. I was there to play basketball, and Billy Mills was there to run track.

He said, "I envy you and John Tiger."

I said, "Well, why do you envy us?"

And he said, "Well, you don't seem to have a problem with socializing, you know, when we have these outings."

And I said, "Well, no, I don't have."

And John said, "No, I don't have any problems."

"Well, [said Mills] I have a problem. I don't feel like I'm adequate enough out there."

And that's a little bit of what that reservation syndrome gave him and his attitude. Even when I was coaching at Bartlesville-Wesleyan College, years after that, I had a Sioux boy that worked as a manager for me. He was a full-blood Sioux. We were one time going to have lunch, and I asked Henry, I said, "Do you want to have lunch?"

He said, "Yeah, coach." He said, "Well, where are we going to have it?"

I said, "Well, we're going across the street."

And he said, "Now where is that?"

I said, "Well, we're going across the street to the country club."

He said, "Well, I can't go."

I said, "How come you can't go?"

He said, "Well, I'm not good enough to go over there."

I said, "Well, Henry, I belong over there. We can go over there."

And he said, "Well, coach, I can't go over there, I don't feel adequate enough."

That's why I feel very fortunate growing up in Oklahoma. There's a little bit prejudice, but I never felt that in Oklahoma. Not much unlike some of the kids from different parts of the country. Because I may, in grade school or junior high or high school, have been sitting right beside someone who had as much or more Indian blood than I had, you know. I never felt any prejudice at all growing up in the state of Oklahoma.

To go to college, athletics was my ticket to get an education because my father, mother, really didn't have the money to send me to school. No one had gone to college in our family, with the exception of my brother and myself. And so I had an opportunity. I was recruited by the University of Oklahoma to go play basketball there, as well as by Oklahoma State. I was recruited to play basketball, and Kansas had such a rich history of basketball there, with Phog Allen [Forrest C. (Phog) Allen coached University of Kansas Jayhawks for thirty-nine years] and Dr. Dean Naismith [James Naismith, first basketball coach, 1898] starting basketball there at K.U. And going back, to some degree, to where our last reservation was, I always felt at home up there. I felt that going back that direction, there were a lot people from Bartlesville that went to school at the University of Kansas, and so when they offered me a scholarship to go back and play basketball there, I accepted it. I feel that was one decision that I made right in my life, and I really enjoyed playing there for four years.

[I took a teaching degree.] It never ever crossed my mind that I would do anything different. I felt like that was my calling. I felt, you know, everybody has a little bit of aptitude toward something. I felt like that was something that I was always called to do, to coach and instruct young men. And so when I went to the university I enrolled in education and got my degree there. And went out and coached a high school a couple of years and came back and got my master's degree in psychology and felt like that if I wanted to stay in the field of athletics and coaching and teaching, then I wanted to try to have as much education as I could. And I felt that there were so many kids that I could see out of Oklahoma, both white and Indian, that during that time didn't go to school for one reason or another. And I really wanted to better myself. My mom didn't go to college. My dad did not go to college, except later on he went and got his degree through the mail, where he'd spend nights and do that. And he was very aggressive in that way. But he didn't go to college, per se. But he finally got his degree later on in life. And so, I observed him and said, "Well, I want to get my degree and be sure that I can see if I can be of some help in that by getting an education."

Annette and I always, by living outside the state of Oklahoma, always knew who we are and were. We'd always come back to Oklahoma for special occasions. Starting, I think, in the seventies, sixties, something in there, [the Delawares] had started dancing again. So we'd always come back and attend those dances. We started getting more interested, obviously, in our roots back in Oklahoma. But my job was someplace else. Consequently, there was a time when I was getting on in my career, and my brother [Lewis B. Ketchum] and I were in the business together, called Red Man Pipe and Supply Company. I wanted to really kind of get back to Bartlesville. So I told him that I wanted to sell my interest out in the company and move back to Bartlesville and get a little bit more involved with the tribe. He had been involved with the tribe. He lived in Tulsa and was acting chief at that time. And so I was so out of touch, by virtue of living in Dallas, Texas. Even though we came up once or twice or three times a year you have to live in the [Delaware] Nation if you're really going to make a contribution. So Annette and I decided to do that. We moved back to Bartlesville. As far as the connection with [studying with] Leonard [Thompson] being a relative of mine, it just kind of materialized. It seemed, prior to me coming back, there were some other men and women that were helping him do some things. For some reason, he started calling on me to go help him. The others just kind of dropped out. So consequently, Leonard, being our ceremonial chief, started giving me more responsibilities to be his helper and started talking to me about the different types of ceremonies and what you do and so forth, something that I was deeply interested in. He probably has forgotten more than I'll ever know, but he's been a wonderful man to be around. I've been very fortunate to have Leonard in my life and being also a family member that we feel good with each other. He shares a lot and has shared a lot of knowledge over the years with me and shared some of the experiences going to New York together and doing all that as well as doing the naming and the burials and all those things. Real significance in my life. But living in Bartlesville, one could only do that. When Annette and I decided to move back to Bartlesville, I immediately ran for a council position and was very fortunate [that] the people put me on the council. I got involved in that; it has been evolving for the last fourteen years or so.

Lewis moved [to Oklahoma] also. I think he moved back probably about four years before I did, back to Tulsa and got involved with the tribe, which was a wonderful thing. That was high on his agenda. Lew knew where his roots were as well. He went to Bacone Indian College [in Muskogee, Oklahoma]. Our folks didn't have the money to send him to college either; he went there on a football scholarship. Then he went to Springfield, Missouri State College. I think Lew made the decision to get involved with the tribe, and so he actively worked towards getting back closer to the Nation, and he ended up in Tulsa and got involved with the tribe. He was on the council when Mr. [Henry A.] Secondine gave up his chief's position. Lew served out his last two years, and he ran for chief and was elected on three terms and served real well. I think by virtue that he was an educated man, but yet humble enough to listen to the people, he had great leadership from that respect. I think he was highly respected in both worlds, in the white world as well as the Indian world. And I know he was talking to Chief Wilma Mankiller and even Joel Bird of the Cherokees as well as a lot of the other chiefs. When I moved around the country to go to some of these meetings, they'd ask me, when he was the chief, how he was doing, then when he passed on, their particular sentiments. He had a lot of charisma that was quite apparent, and he was very well loved. I think that there was over two thousand people at his funeral, and the interesting thing about the funeral was they were mostly men. There were obviously a lot of women, but men came to give their last respects for Lew. He was a good administrator, and I think that he could see that it takes good administrators to run tribes today. That's what I've observed. I think that it takes educated, well-educated, good administrators, and I see this happening more and more with tribes around the country. Yes, it's wonderful you know the traditions and songs and so forth, but you have to be a good administrator to be able to move your tribe forward and going into the twenty-first century. Lew had that; he was ahead of his time in my regard as far as seeing what we needed. He was a delight to work with, and I miss him a lot.

When this decision came down in 1979 to take away our [tribe's] federal recognition, it was a real blow to us. The chiefs and council people prior to then had always had a wonderful relationship with the federal government and with the other tribes around the country. When [Horace L.] McCracken and [Bruce Miller] Townsend and [Henry A.] Secondine and my brother, [L. B. Ketchum], all were acting chiefs, it was a wonderful relationship. But all of a sudden, in 1979, the federal government came out with their first publication for federally recognized tribes; our name was not there. So it was quite of a blow. Economically it was. However, we knew who we were. The Delawares knew that we had not assimilated in with the Cherokee Nation, as some of the [government] people were saying. We knew who we were. We knew that we were going to fight that. It has been long in coming, primarily because of economics. We just didn't have the money to go to court and do the things that needed to be done. But I can remember sitting on the council, and we had one small smoke shop that was actually [providing] the funding; that came from Chief Secondine, who helped with the financing of that. Eventually he turned the shop over to the tribe to run it. But we were actually running our tribe on the revenue of about $50,000 a year and keeping those doors open and paying the bills. I heard a lot of comments during that period, "Well, that council is not doing anything except just playing Indian down there," from a lot a people. But we kept working and kept digging. But what was one of our breakthroughs, I think, was that we applied for a federal ANA grant that would work toward doing the study that needed to be done to look into them withdrawing our federal recognition. And surprisingly, we wrote the grant for one side of the government to contest that, and they gave us the grant. We hired the attorneys to do the research. And we were well on our way. Obviously, my brother, being the chief during that period of time, was very instrumental in getting all that accomplished and getting that started on the legal basis. And he worked very, very hard toward that end. It was just unfortunate that he was not alive. He passed away unexpectedly of a heart attack prior to the federal government coming down and saying that "You are federally recognized again." But I know that he listened, he knows.

[The economic advances are] just so exciting. We have more people working for us today than we've ever had. We're repurchasing land. We bought eighty acres, and we're going to put a child-care center on that [completed in 2000] and hopefully have a museum and a cultural center there. But our people have been so used to doing without, so it's exciting to me to see that some of this work is actually paying off; some of the money now that we have coming in from the "638 Funds," the travel funds, and some of the grant monies. Now that we're federally recognized we can apply for those and receive them. It's really exciting. So it's coming to fruition that we're putting Delawares to work to lead these programs, and eventually we hope that more Delawares will move back within the boundaries of the Nation (in Bartlesville), and we can continue to put Delawares to work. This is the goal of all the council members. The self-governance we'll be working towards to where we will eventually be a tribe where we are self-governing [not under Cherokee Nation jurisdiction when dealing with the federal government]. Where we will have the funds and delegate the programs accordingly; that's in the future, but it's right around the corner. And so consequently we're trying to get our staff in a position to be able to do that. And I think that we have a very good start to be able to do that. We can see some real progress being made because we do have funds available today that we did not have for so many years because the Delawares were under Cherokee tribal governance, and funds were not given to the Delawares to improve their economic status as a tribe in their own right.

In terms of some of the [Delaware] artifacts in some of the non-Indian and Indian museums, the National Parks had invited me and Mike Pace and some other people to come back [to New York City]. Prior to Mike, a salesman and Leonard [Thompson] went back to New York. Going through some of those museums, that was something that I feel that our people need in Oklahoma. We need to bring some of these things back to our Nation so that our people can see those things, some of the [material culture] that was in the Big House. Even though that particular phase, the Big House and religion and the ceremonies and the things that went on there that our Elders don't want to bring back, seeing those objects would help them connect better with their tribe. So it is my interest to establish a museum for our people in Oklahoma, in Bartlesville, where they can come and see. We've had all these things in other museums in other places. Back in I think it was 1987, the National Parks contacted Leonard [Thompson]. So Annette, my wife, and her sister and daughter and Leonard and I went back to meet with the National Parks and some of the other Delaware tribes. There were some bones to repatriate, which were on Ellis Island, so we went back there. We really didn't rebury those bones; we just wrapped them again for a reburial. It was exciting, and I think that being able to identify and having people like Leonard around, even though he's ninety-four he's still very sharp, and he can identify those things, so it's exciting, and I'm trying to squeeze from him whatever amount of information that he can give me because it's going to be a real void in my life as well as the Delaware Tribe because he's been such a mainstay. He has been a real information source for us to go to. It's exciting to have eventually a museum we own, tribally operated, and we have our [cultural materials] in there.

Rachel Redinger was one of the ones instrumental in starting the Delaware Grand Council [with members from the various Delaware tribes]. I was a member of that council, and my brother was also, and I think Curtis Zunigha was as well, with our tribe. The theme of that was to get the groups together and have some type of annual gathering where we could share stories and songs and dances and so forth and so on. The theme was right for some reason, maybe the people that were pushing it were strong, I'm not sure, but it was exciting to have and be there with the Western Delawares or the Absentee, as well as the Canadian Delawares, and to share stories and so forth. That particular event has kind of died out a little bit; it's not as prevalent as it was two or three years ago, I don't know for what reason. But it was not so much tribally sponsored, it wasn't from council to council; it was members in the tribe that was kind of getting together, and some of those members in a tribe happen to be some of the leaders of that tribe that got them together, but it wasn't a council-to-council movement. And maybe, if that's ever going to have some substance in the future, it would probably have to go from council to council other than just some of the leaders in those tribes. But it was fun for a while. I haven't attended the last couple of meetings that they have had.

Talking about the role model and so forth, Lew and I came from a very humble background. Dad and Mom didn't have any money, and they were working people just like everyone else during that period of time, for what they made, they spent. Yet they instilled in us a great deal of pride, my dad and mom. So Lew obviously had that drive and determination and the will to better one's self, and he went to work with Bethlehem Steel Corporation right out of college and worked with them in their oil field supply division. He was bringing up a large family, four boys. And so he realized right quick that if he was going to make a difference, he was going to have to take some responsibility. He had worked for Bethlehem Steel Corporation for [nearly] twenty years. I can remember him calling me while I was living in Kansas City, and he called me and said, "Dee, how would you like to go in business with me?" and I said, "Well, what business you thinking about going in?" and he said, "Well, I want to start my own company. I'm going to go into the pipe business on my own." So he was willing to take some chances, here he has four boys and a wife, and he said, "Are you interested in investing in the company?" and I said, "If it's you Lew, absolutely." I actually went down and borrowed the money to invest in the company, and we didn't have to borrow a lot of money. He started that company on a shoestring. I remember so vividly, I didn't know anything about the pipe business, and he called me about four months later, and he said, "Well, I made you a lot of money. I got a distributorship from United States Steel." And I said, "Well, that's good, Lew; how's your family?" and he said, "Well, you don't understand." And I didn't. He was going through a time when President Johnson was really encouraging minority men to go into business, and so consequently he took that challenge and he stepped out there and made it successful. You know, in looking back, he had no guarantees. We didn't have a lot of money in the bank to take us three or four or five years if it failed. It was a small amount of money that he started out with, and he made it work.

We need more role models like my brother. We need more role models that can make a difference, that our young people can look up to and say, "This man, if you were not born with a lot of money, and if you were not born in a certain family, and if you're not born in a certain place, that you can go make a difference." And that's what Lew did. He went and got his education by playing football, and then he made that education work. He instilled that same drive and determination to his four boys, who all work now in the company and all have families. And to me that's the type of role model that our young Indian boys need to see and emulate as much as they can.

A question came to me the other day, it says, "Where are all the Indian athletes today?" And I said, "You know, I don't know where they are, but we have a lot of potentially good athletes. When I was coaching at Bartlesville Wesleyan College we had some Indian boys that I recruited to come down and work out, but for some reason or another they didn't feel like they were adequate enough to work out. That saddens me some just because we have so much potential out there with these Indian boys. We have examples like my brother that made it. He did it the right way. He didn't take any short-cuts. And he also kind of rolled the dice in a sense. He had a very comfortable job with Bethlehem Steel Corporation for twenty years, and he said he wanted something better for him and his family, and that's what he did. He went out and started a company that today is one of the largest minority-owned companies in the country. It was honored by President Reagan. It makes me feel good that I was a little bit of a part of that. I can see that he was a real role model.

I think that it is some of my responsibility now as the young brother to work towards that end and to make sure that I don't come up short, and try to be a role model for the rest of the Indian kids to go get an education, to have a family and have a home, and to be responsible and to raise your kids to respect your elders and to listen. You can live in this world very comfortably in two worlds, the white society and the Indian society. He did that, and I'm working towards that.

We always tried to have an Indian preference [in hiring]; however, if we weren't prepared to be able to provide a product at the best price and the best services, we don't deserve the business. That's why he was successful. Many companies that started out during those years didn't have that same philosophy, and they are no longer here. So consequently it made us tough. It made us know the business. We knew the service, and he surrounded himself with educated people, but yet there was an Indian preference, plus we always had a scholarship program that we started from day one that we would give to the universities to help young Indian boys and girls to further their education. And it's worked. I just attended [an event] at Oklahoma State where they dedicated a wing at one of the dormitories. It's one of the places that Red Man Pipe Company gave money towards helping Indian kids there.

It's important to see that some of this culture is passed on. I came through a period of time, and Lew did too, where it wasn't available. It wasn't in the home. We didn't speak Delaware, and we didn't sing a lot of songs. Consequently, when we moved back and really started getting involved, I can remember a time when there was an Indian, Delaware, gathering. This was probably twenty years ago or so. One of the ladies came up to me and said, "Dee, let's have a stomp dance." And I said, "Well, that's good, do we have any leaders?" And she said, "Why don't you lead, Dee?" and I said, "No, I don't know the songs." And so she made the announcement and asked if there were any leaders. And we didn't have one Delaware leader, and that was embarrassing to me because our history, the Delaware Tribe, we had wonderful leaders. We had some of the best stomp dance leaders in the country. And here we went through a generation where we didn't produce any.

So I made a vow right at that point to learn the songs. I went down to the Creeks and learned from them as much as I could and learned from other elders around that I could and got as many tapes as I could. I started to learn how to lead those songs. Now we have some stomp dance leaders, and we can have our own dances and enjoy ourselves.

So I am trying to take that same attitude [with my] three grandsons. Whenever the opportunity arises, when they come to Oklahoma, or I go visit them in their home, we talk about that. We talk, from time to time, about some of the songs. Of course, when they're young, they pick up real quick, and the only difficult thing about that is that they live so far away. One grandson lives in California, and another lives in Dallas. But they know that they are Delaware. And when I sit around and talk to them, and we talk about some of the songs and so forth, they know what I'm talking about and they're trying to learn. So it will just be a matter of education, and they know that their grandfather knows those songs and can teach them. That was one of the awakening things for me. As far as our songs where we went through that generation that they just passed on, and a lot of us didn't pay attention. We're starting to get them back and sing. Our people love it.

Being a head dancer and being in charge of the arena is a big responsibility, being sure that people respect that ground. I tell my kids, and my grandkids, if you have any bad feelings or so forth, we don't want them in that arena. If you're having a bad day, don't come in. So we try to educate our kids. So consequently when they come, they have good feelings, and that's what we want to create there as we dance around that drum and come to that center and that circle, that they come with really good feelings and want to be there. I've never forced my grandkids to dress. We've given them an opportunity if they would like to dress and so forth and come dance and we'll teach them, but they don't have to. But they all have come, and Annette has dressed out the girls, and I dress out the boys. And, of course, my two daughters have always dressed, since they were real small. And they like to come back and dance. But being a head singer is a responsibility. I'm not the head singer per se, or the drum keeper of our tribe. Doug Donnell, my nephew, is the head drum keeper, so to speak. But Doug and I sing a lot together, and we learn those songs and so forth. It's a little different on stomp dancing because he kind of took the initiative to learn a lot of those social songs on the water drum, and I kind of took the initiative way back there to learn stomp and kind of maybe teach some of our men the stomp dance, to get back into that again. And so it's important that they know the songs and the dances; then they know when you're not doing it right. When Lucy Blaylock was around, as far as stomp dancing is concerned, she helped me some with the right and wrong. She helped a little bit because she used to be a shell-shaker. So she was delighted when we really started that back up again. And so it's exciting to me to have a lot of Delawares out there dancing once again around that fire.

That word "powwow" is a Caucasian word. It's a gathering, a coming together, and we use it in today's society because they're intertribal powwows, and all tribes come in and dance in their culture. But to me the significance is sharing culture, or sharing being with other Indian tribes and so forth. It's hard, however, because we've almost become a melting pot, particularly the men, in some of the stuff we wear. The Delawares were always pretty much what they call straight dancers, which is the really old dance and the old style. But I don't know that it would've been any different than way back because if you see something that another dancer is wearing, you think, "Boy, that really looks good, I think I'll put some of that on." And so it's a little difficult today when you go up to a powwow for the men to be able to tell whether he is Shawnee or Cherokee or Delaware or whoever. The women pretty much stayed a little bit more traditional in their dress, so the women can pretty well depict what tribe they are. But the men, they're sort of borrowing and adding to their clothing. One thing that does kind of disturb me as far as powwow is concerned is the direction that we are going today. I can remember when we were dancing for the love of dancing, and we never spoke of money. [A dancer] went out and danced. I can remember George Allen, he was an old Kickapoo man. I remember watching him twenty or thirty years ago, and he had such a smile on his face when he danced. He was just so excited about being out there and dancing. I'd show him to my girls. I'd say, "Look at that man; he's enjoying himself around that drum in that circle." Today with the dancing for money, most of powwows today are contest powwows. I'm not real sure that we're sending the right message to our kids. I've seen and heard, "I don't think I'll dress in that because my contest is tomorrow." They won't dress. They are waiting for their contest tomorrow. I worry about that some. I think that some of our elders worry about that some. Are we sending the wrong message out there?

What I'm wearing is a ribbon shirt, and I'm not sure that I know a lot about it other than my wife makes them all, and I just wear them. This doesn't have the stand-up collar, but many of the old Delaware shirts had a stand-up collar, and they had some ruffles right here in front as well. I think that they are so hard to make, a lot of the women don't make them. There was a particular style that you could identify a Delaware man from his shirt even. And yes, the Delaware colors are red and black. We try to hold to that tradition. That is one thing that hasn't changed. Of course, we get that from the old Big House. Red on the right for good and black on the left for bad. It's colors that have stuck, and we're very proud of it. We try to wear as often as we can these black and red shirts.

From what I understand about the ceremonial chiefs, we had visionaries way back. We've pretty well gone through that with the Big House being shut down, and we don't have visionaries anymore. But the namers back then, I understood, used to be by family and you would pass that on from family to family. I think that we're in the process of probably changing that. Leonard, when he showed an interest, the tribal council appointed him to do that because he was the one that was quite knowledgeable about the ceremonies and was fluent in Delaware. So they kind of sought him out, and he was appointed by the tribal council. I suspect that in the future it will be the same. It won't necessarily come through family lines. It could. I happen to be a relative of Leonard, but it doesn't necessarily mean that I will be the next ceremonial chief, or if I even feel qualified to be the next ceremonial or even if we will have one. A lot of tribes have that phase that they don't feel like that they have qualified men to serve in that capacity, and so they don't have any. They leave it up to the council to try and take care of many of those things that they can. I don't know exactly where our tribe will go after Leonard passes on, but it will be pretty much up to the tribal council to appoint a ceremonial chief to try to help with some of the ceremonies. I think that someone needs to be a ceremonial chief or have that title. I think that there probably needs to be someone as a reference. It could be a reference in relationship to different things and procedures that they would know about. Like on burials and so forth, because if they want to be buried traditionally, there is a very set way that they should go about. I'm not sure. It started with family passing that down, and now I'm not sure where we'll go from that perspective. I'm learning all I can, not necessarily to be in that position, just because I want to know and Leonard is teaching me.

[The present] powwows are different from how the Delawares did them before. I'll talk about what's been passed on to me. Our drum, the big powwow drum or the big war drum, was not necessarily set in the center of the circle; it was set over on the west side, and the singers would face to the east because they really felt they wanted to be ready for the Second Coming. I was told that our warriors would dance out in front of the drum, and if they had a story to tell, and if they were singing a song, [a warrior] would go up and put his hand on that drum, and the singers would stop, and he would tell his story about whether he was going to war and he had a vision about what was going to happen, or he had just come back from war and he wanted to tell that story. Or if he had something that he wanted to share with all the other people, he would go up there and touch that drum. And the singers would stop. And then when he got through telling his story, the singers would start playing again, and he would then enact whatever [he spoke about] through his dance. That doesn't happen anymore. We have since taken that drum and put it in the center. But there is a protocol. The Oklahoma Indians pretty well set the stage for the rest of the country, I think to some degree. But we have our own style, and the tribes up north have their own style. Usually, the flags are brought in and the head staff is brought in, the ones that have been picked to lead the dances on that weekend. And we all honor that. There is a song that's sung, a grand entry song. The protocol is bringing the American flag in as well as any of the tribal flags along with the American flag, but the American flag is out there first. Then we will have a veteran's song. We're always very, very cognizant and very appreciative of our veterans, particularly the Indian men that have gone to war. So we sing a veteran's song there. We always want to honor our men and women in that way. Then we will have a memorial song for all the people, and then we will have a retreat where we take the flag out of the arena.

But there is a protocol, and the head staff will set the stage for when the dances start because they are the first ones to get up. You're not supposed to start a dance until they get up and start the dance. If that particular head man dancer went around the drum in a clockwise manner, then the rest, in respect for him, would go in a clockwise manner. If that particular head staff man went around that drum in a counter-clockwise manner, then the rest of the dancers would go in a counter-clockwise manner in respect for the head man dancer. I was told that the Delawares always went counter-clockwise around the drum, and the Shawnees as well. We always went counter-clockwise. I was also told that we wanted to go around that drum in respect to that drum being the heartbeat of our people. And it was on the heart side as we gave our sentiments and our wishes in acknowledging that drum as we went around counter-clockwise. There are a lot of things that are protocol. The arena directors are there to make sure all of those things are followed properly, and the people are there respectful of the drum. It's not a playground; it's a place to go and dance and have a nice time but in respect for our elders and for the men that are singing those songs they would not act up in the arena.

I feel respect is earned, and I think that it would be pleasing to me if [my grandsons] remembered me as someone that they could respect. Not just because they are my grandsons, but because of who and what I stood for. The decisions that I have made in my lifetime were more good decisions than bad decisions and that I had a love for the People and that I came back to serve the Delaware because I had a love in my heart. I speak to some groups from time to time, and I say, you know it's not how much Indian blood runs through your veins. It's how much of the heart that you give to it and what's in your heart. Don't be ashamed if you have very little [Indian] blood. Have a big heart for the Indian people and customs and traditions and carry that on. That's the most important thing. I just hope that they can look at my life when I am old and gone just like my brother's, and say I respect that man for what he stood for and how he lived, his contributions to his tribe and trying to make a difference.

Why was the Caney River important to Delaware people?

When the government, in 1866, decided to move the Delaware tribe to Oklahoma, [the Delawares] were always used to having and being around a river. When [the Delawares] were in Kansas, our last reservation, they were around the Kaw River in Kansas. Therefore, they were looking for something that would be similar. And so the Caney River is closest to that [need to live by a river in the Oklahoma Territory]. So consequently that's where they decided to move when they had the choice of where, not the choice to whether they were going to move to Oklahoma or not, but where in Oklahoma. So they felt like the Caney River would be as close as they could get to what they were leaving in the state of Kansas.

Describe the Silver Lake and Curleyhead cemeteries.

When the Delawares came, they actually started living around Silver Lake, which was just to the south of that cemetery. And the church was in that area. When they would have services and so forth, and if they had someone that did pass away, well, they'd take their covered wagon and go up to that cemetery. But that particular cemetery is rather unique; it's not all Delaware. There are some whites buried there. It's mostly Delaware or friends of Delawares. But it's one of the older cemeteries in that region, and some of the real prominent families in the Delaware were buried there at Silver Lake Cemetery.

The Curleyhead Cemetery started as a family cemetery, which is much different from Silver Lake. The family started it, but it kind of diversified a little bit. We were very fortunate in the last couple of years to have a Boy Scout that was working on his Eagle badge to go out and clean that up, and it looks good. It made all of us feel very good when he got through cleaning that up and mowing it. And we've kept it in good shape now. So we're able to go out there and show people our ancestry, where our people were buried there.

Our Delaware people that wanted to be buried traditionally always had their head to the east and their feet to the west because it was our belief that when the Second Coming was coming that they had humility, that they didn't want to look him straight in the face when he came. So that's why they wanted to have their head looking away at the Second Coming. I think that it goes back to say just exactly what Lenape stands for, the Common Original People, and that they don't feel like they're anyone special anymore than anyone else, that they are real honest people that have been given the opportunity to live on Mother Earth here, and they were appreciative of it and humble; that's why they do that. In that humble way.

Oral history interview conducted on October 6, 1998, at Conner Prairie, Fishers, Indiana. Dee Ketchum came from Bartlesville, Oklahoma, to participate in the Seventh Woodland Indian Art and Culture Program.

Coleton Thomas prepares his roach for dancing at the 2007 Delaware Powwow near Copan, Oklahoma. Thomas is Dee and Annette Ketchum's grandson and the son of Kala Thomas.

Lewis Ketchum stands to honor the color guard and dancers at the 2002 Delaware Powwow near Copan, Oklahoma.

LEWIS KETCHUM

Tribal member
Born in Woodword, Oklahoma

◈

[Woodword was] where my mother's parents lived, and she went back there for my birth. She lived on my father's allotment northeast of Dewey. As far as I know, shortly after birth, she went back to the house on the allotment [his mother was Bertha Scovel; his father was Charles C. Ketchum; and his grandfather was Abraham Ketchum]. I went to elementary school, Wayside Country School, through the eighth grade. At that time of the year, things were pretty poor. We didn't have transportation like a lot of people had. I would have to go from seven miles northeast of Dewey to high school. I don't know where I got the information on Chilocco Indian School. Anyway, we had to send in to Muskogee to get an application to fill out to go to school at Chilocco. That was in 1928 that I first went over there. I finished twelfth grade there in 1932. My parents, in 1929, had sold their property and moved to Bartlesville while I was in school. And so, [after graduating from Chilocco] when I came back, I came back to Bartlesville. Instead of pursuing any further schooling, I went to work for my dad. He was a contractor in the oil field. I worked for him until 1935. I got a job at the Reda Pump Company and worked there until 1977. I've spent the biggest part of my life right here in Bartlesville and working for the Reda Pump Company.

The move from Kansas to Oklahoma [about 1866] was the one my parents [grandfather and father] was in. But he did not talk about that move. My grandfather, Abraham Ketchum [1848–1921], at one time was an interpreter. But Grandpa Ketchum didn't teach his children, which is my father and his brothers and sisters, any of the Delaware language. He said that you have to learn to live the white man ways. He said that you need to speak English. He would not teach the language. There was a time that people hesitated to acknowledge that they were Indian blood because they were taught not to speak or do the ways of the Indian. And that's what my grandfather taught my dad and his other children. [His grandmother was Roxie J. Ketchum.]

The allotments were all in one section. My father's brothers and sisters, and we [cousins] all played together and went to school together out in the country schools, and we didn't live much by the Indian ways. We lived mostly by the white man's ways. When I got ready to go to high school there were other children that had gone to Chilocco, and we wrote to Muskogee and got an application to make out to enter Chilocco. It was pretty tough to get in school at that time. They were pretty full. But myself and my sister and a couple of cousins went over there, but they didn't stay. They got homesick and came back after a year. Of course, we just stayed there through a school term, and in the summer we were allowed to come home for three months. There was not much talk about the move from Kansas to Oklahoma. I don't recall my dad even talking about it. He just accepted the move as they had instructed us to do, and that was it. They didn't make any comment about it.

We, as a family, had participated in the powwows and the stomp dances that they were having in this area, quite a bit. And my oldest boy—L.B., we call him—he got interested in the activities of the Delaware Tribe. They were having meetings. I don't remember how he got word they needed someone to head the Delaware Tribe. At one time they [the tribe] kind of dropped interest, but he came in and fired up the interest to rejuvenate the activities. He got acquainted with the other officers, and he worked very hard at being in a chief's position. During that time he had started his company in Tulsa, and he got so busy with it. They opened stores all over the country; when the election came for re-election, why he kind of dropped interest a little bit, and he was defeated. My son Dee was with my older boy in the business to start with. And then he decided to get out of the business. He had joined in with him, though, in the Delaware board of trustees and the council and was on the board. They talked to him, after the oldest boy died, about running for election. He talked to me about it, and I said, "Dee, I don't know. You need to do whatever you think best, but whatever you decide you want to do, I'll be behind you and help you with whatever I can." And he said, "Well, I don't think I will." And it went on that way for a couple of months or so, and then finally one day he said, "They've been asking me about running for chief. I think I will." He was elected chief.

I don't think I was involved very much with the tribal council. I attended the meetings and participated in their activities, but I was not actually any officer, anything of that sort. When the boys got up of age, I was in retirement age and took retirement. And at that time I didn't feel like I was physically and mentally able to take part in any of the activities of the tribal council.

I would say that it [my knowledge of Indian culture] did come from being at Chilocco and the ways that the people lived and did up there and your communication with different people. While we were there we would go down in the woods and stomp dance and parch corn. It was one way of entertaining ourselves. And I think that I probably learned more about the Indian ways and means by the Indians in Chilocco rather than at home because my parents just didn't take part in any of the Indian ways.

A few of my grandchildren have taken up the Indian ways. I have some grandchildren that don't. But the ones that have taken up the Indian ways, I have encouraged them as much as I could to take part in the singing, drumming, and learning songs. I have one grandson that's real good in singing and drumming, and others have taken part in the drumming and singing in the tribal meetings and their get-togethers. Annette and Dee, their grandchildren have participated in the powwow tradition and taken part. I remember her and her mother, they always took part in the Delaware meetings and their powwows and their dances and their songs. It's been very nice having the grandchildren take part. I am really proud of it.

My grandfather, Abraham Ketchum, was alive when I was growing up. I think I was probably five or six when he died. I don't have any memories of Grandfather doing any Delaware traditional things. I was just told that he was an interpreter. But I never had witnessed any myself, being that small. I do remember him standing at a pedestal with his arm on it. They took a picture of Grandfather. I remember that very well. I was telling Mr. Brown [James Brown] here earlier about the Delaware powwow. I was thinking that it had started sooner than thirty-six years ago because I remember going up there to Falleaf's place, and I don't know if it's the same location or not, but it was in one of those brother's place and stomp dancing when I was probably ten, twelve years old. And we'd get on a flatbed truck. It'd go around the section, and guys would just go jump on the truck and ride up to the stomp dance, and we would stay just about all night just stomp dancing. There were other places that had stomp dances, too. My uncle, Fish Ketchum [Abraham W. (Fish) Ketchum, 1899–1975], he had a stomp dance at one time, and I remember going to it, which is located about seven miles northeast of Dewey. But his children have not taken part in Delaware traditions. But he has one boy that does take part, and he is an officer. That is Benny Ketchum. He's an officer of some sort in one of the committees here.

I don't know who was doing the drumming and singing [at Falleaf's]. One of Falleaf's boys went to Chilocco, and that's where I met him to start with. I had met him not knowingly when we were kids at the stomp dances, and then when we got over to Chilocco I remembered him. And there was also another boy named Ray Elkhair [1914–1974] was over at Chilocco, and he was Delaware. [Ray Elkhair was Michael Pace's uncle.]

I just remember meeting him in Chilocco. I found out he was from the same area here as I was. But at that time I was not taking part in Indian traditions. We were all struggling to live and trying to make a living. My dad did not take part in the Indian ways or traditions. He hardly ever went to a powwow or a dance or any sort of that. He was very busy back then. He had teams that worked in an oil field, and they moved these drilling rigs and this sort of stuff, and he didn't have time for the Indian traditions. My family had allotments I lived on. There was oil on our allotment. It was leased out.

I don't remember who had the lease on that property, but there were several wells on our allotment property. They were pulled out later, but at the time we were there they were pumping and producing oil. But I don't remember who had the lease on it. The allotment passed on.

I guess [the federal government] passed a law or some sort of legislation that my father could sell the allotment and his other property. He had bought quite a bit of land at the time, but the stock market went down, and he went with it. He had to give up the allotments. Of course, they had borrowed money to buy cattle to put on the land. When the stock market went down, there wasn't any way to get the money.

Oral history interview conducted on May 30, 2000,
at Bartlesville, Oklahoma.

Trey Johnson's scarf slide at the 2007 Delaware Powwow near Copan, Oklahoma.

Beverly McLaughlin dances at the 2005 Delaware Days at Conner Prairie Living History Museum, Fishers, Indiana. She carries a bald eagle fan made from the white tail feathers.

BEVERLY MCLAUGHLIN

Tribal member
Born September 1, 1946, at Claremore, Oklahoma

It's kind of funny because I don't know how I've retained my Delaware heritage because my mother so discouraged it. Mike's mother [Thelma Elkhair Pace] and my mother [Leora Elkhair Barnes Toon] were sisters. They went to boarding school, and they were punished there for being Indian. She would never teach us anything about language, never say a word. I know she spoke Indian, but maybe she didn't [teach us] because she was so punished for doing that. She also always told me and my brother that if you can pass for white, do it. So I realized that she had a very hard time in life because she was Indian. It's just a shame that she's not alive this day and age when everyone is proud of who they are, no matter what ethnic group they are of. And to be ashamed and [your heritage] taken away from you to the point that you would tell your kids to pass for another race, it's very sad. I don't think that the younger people can relate to that, and I really can't either.

I've lived on the reservation; I lived in North Dakota for fourteen and a half years after growing up in Tulsa. I married very young, living on a reservation after growing up in the city, and having to get bigoted towards white people just to survive because off of reservations they normally don't like Indians. They have their set ideas and everything about what an Indian is, [thinking] we get free money and we get checks every month and nobody works and drive nice cars, which has never been true in my life. But [whites] are still like that today. My daughter lives there [Sioux reservation]. She's visiting me right now, and I can sense that in her now, just from [her] experiences in the last two years. So, it's been a learning process for me to learn my Delaware heritage because I know so much about Sioux, having been married to a Sioux and living on a Sioux reservation and living that life.

Mike [Pace] and I have been back together for about two years. We happened to make contact at a powwow in Tulsa. I happened to see him across the way, and they announced his name, and I thought, "Well, that's my cousin, and I need to see him." So I went over, and we've made contact since then. He's encouraged me to come back around to meet the people and to see the people. I've always known all my relatives. I'm probably related to all of the Delawares. My father was Delaware, and my mother was Delaware. I really don't know them [the Delawares in Bartlesville], [but] they know my parents. So, to me it's been a real relearning, and I've been doing that.

I've been traveling. I'm a Christian, and I just went to a conference two weeks ago, the first of May 2000.They sent for me; they sent for Delaware women. They couldn't find another one. I laugh because I'm not the only Christian Delaware woman. A lot of my family is Christian. I am the only Delaware that they could find. So they sent for me because, at this conference at this church in Silver Springs [Maryland], they wanted to honor the indigenous people from that area, so there was myself representing the Delawares and some [women from] other tribes that I've never heard of from Virginia. So as we were on stage there [also] were Dakota, Sioux, people from Alaska, and several other tribes. They [white people] came and gave us gifts and honored us, and it was just wonderful. I wore my aunt's traditional dress, and I was so honored that Mike has let me wear that. I'm probably the only one that will wear it, or can wear it.

It's just really been a learning experience for me to learn about my people. My mother said she didn't really want us to marry Indians, and all of us did. I don't know her reasoning behind that; maybe it's the hurt again, the pain. I'm sure it was, but we all ended in divorce, so maybe she was trying to tell us something there, too. She also didn't want me to go to boarding school. My brother and sister had to because of financial reasons. When [my mother] passed away, she was thirty-seven years old and I was thirteen. I chose to go to boarding school because I was pretty much an orphan at that time. I had aunts and uncles who I was not close to and was not allowed being close to because of my stepfather. When my mother passed away, my Uncle Howard and my Aunt Betty [Barnes] stepped into my life and became a part of my life. And Aunt Peggy Toney that lived in Dewey, I lived with her. That's when I probably got more familiar with my mother's family. I did go to boarding school at Chilocco. That's where I met my former husband. He was a Sioux from North Dakota. I got married when I was sixteen years old, so I have a son that's thirty-six years old, and I have a daughter who is thirty-two, and I have a granddaughter that is two and a half years old. I'm very proud of them.

I grew up in North Tulsa until I was thirteen years old. I have a half brother who knows nothing of this [Delaware] family. That's a whole other story with him. The process of reconnecting [has been] with my heritage and the Delaware people and my family, especially with Mike Pace. Mike Pace and I are first cousins. I remember visiting him when we were children. He has wanted me to pull back in and get to know more of the people and the people know me from our tribe, and to get a little more involved, which is a little bit difficult for me because I live in Claremore. It's about an hour's drive. But last year [1999], he invited me to Conner Prairie with him. I didn't know why they wanted me because I knew nothing. But he really encouraged me to go. He told me not to worry about it and just go. Getting the outfit together was fairly easy. Then on the way up, the ten hours of driving up, I had to learn a few Lenape words, and I had to learn a few stories.

This is the story of the duck and the turtle: There was a duck and a turtle, and they were very good friends. They played together, they chased bugs together, they swam together, and they just had a real good time during the summer. Well, it starts coming towards the fall; the duck told the turtle, "My family's going to fly South. We fly South every winter, but we'll be back." The turtle said, "Can I go with you?" And he said, "Yeah, you can go." So the duck and his family took off flying, and so the turtle started, and he walked and walked, not realizing that he could not fly, so he just walked. And you know that they have very short legs. And he got very tired and said, "Well, I don't think I can walk this, so I think I'll just stay and plan on something next year." So the winter came and went, and the duck finally came back in the spring. So they found each other; they resumed their friendship. They played together, chased bugs and ate bugs, played games, they swam, and they were really good friends. So the turtle asked the duck, "Is your family going to fly south again?" He said, "Oh yes. We always do." He said, "Well, I want to go, but I need to prepare." So the duck said, "OK." They tried several things. They tried the turtle getting on the duck's back, but by then he had gotten bigger. The duck tried to run and take off and fell forward 'cause the turtle was too heavy. He said, "Get higher on my back." So he got higher, and he still couldn't take off. He got lower and still couldn't take off. He said, "That ain't gonna work." So he thought and thought, and the turtle said, "Well, I have a real sharp beak, and I can hold a stick in my mouth really tight." So he was thinking and he said, "Well, if you could hold one end of the stick in your mouth, and I could hold on real tight, maybe then you can fly with me." So they practiced that. They could actually take off. The duck got stronger and could work with this. Come fall, they could do it. So they took off. So here is this duck, and he has this turtle hanging from this stick. So the other ducks are cruising along and looked over and said, "Well, what's that?" Well they saw and said, "That's a turtle. What's he doing?" Well, they said, "That's great. Who thought of that?" The turtle was going "mm mm." He couldn't say anything. So many ducks passed by and said, "Who thought of that? That's brilliant. Who would think to do that?" Finally after a day or two, the turtle couldn't take it any more. So when someone said, "Who thought of that?" He opened his mouth and said, "I did." And at that moment he fell to Earth. The moral of the story is to keep your mouth shut. That's a good little message right? I think, in Indian humor, we make fun of ourselves and each other as Indians, but not to hurt the other person. Usually you make fun of yourself more than you will the other person. I really don't know how to explain it. It wasn't all that stressful. I was a little bit worried about it, but I love seeing the children, and I love sharing my heritage, whether it is Sioux or whether it be Delaware. I'm probably more comfortable with the Sioux because I lived it and I know the people very well, and I know their ways. And just sharing with anyone interested in Native people, I want them to know as much as they can or as much they can get a hold of because, nowadays, people are very interested in that. I'm finding in the Christian conferences I go to, it's a real awakening to the Native people, and with honor they've called us the host people, especially the Delaware because we're the grandfather of all tribes. So, it's been very interesting and very honorable to me. I'm very proud to know my bloodline and to know who my grandfathers were. So it's just kind of interesting how everything pulls together and a little bit more than you think it is.

[The] conference in Silver Springs in Maryland is called "Many Nations, One Voice." It's a Native/Christian conference that they've just started. The next one will be in mid-June [2000] in Canada. From history books we know that when Columbus came to America, he came with a purpose. We know and we believe that because of greed and many other things that purpose got aborted, whether it was through him or through others. But there was a plan, and God had a plan for the Native people. But through that greed and wanting the land and wanting this and that, the plans got aborted, and evil came from that.

I went back two years ago to Ohio. A Christian woman researching that area of Ohio massacre sites, Mardee Alff, sent for me there, and my Uncle Howard Barnes went with me. We did reconciliation there. There were people from that area whose forefathers had lived in that area for I don't know how many generations. Also, they were there to ask for forgiveness for the massacre of the Delaware people there. It was very nice. A lot of tears were shed. A lady whose great-great-great-grandfather's name was on the list of the militia that was responsible for that, she came and she said, "We speak of this with shame. We don't hardly ever talk about it in my family because we're so ashamed of what happened." And she asked us to forgive her and her family and that she'd be released from the curse that she felt that was on her family. The scripture says when someone has been murdered the blood cries out from the land. And Christian groups right now, that's what they are believing is going on in America. The atrocities against the Native people that were caused mainly out of greed, that God is showing them what is happening right now. So there's a lot of repentance going on all over the United States right now with many tribes.

Then a man named Darrell Fields called me. He is a minister, and he wrote a book called *The Seed of a Nation*. It's about William Penn being a Quaker and the Delaware people and how he was the only one that ever kept a covenant with them. But when he passed on, his sons weren't the same type of man he was. Darrell Fields spoke. He did a lot of research on them, of the atrocities and what had happened to the Delawares. It's an excellent book. He's actually the one that sent for me. I had never met the man before. I had talked to him twice on the phone and was highly honored in his church and by many other people by just giving me gifts, just crying and weeping and saying, "We didn't know this happened in our land." And they could not find a Delaware in Pennsylvania. I thought that was real interesting. I thought maybe they're so ashamed or whatever. I think there are some there that they aren't real sure of, so they would rather send for someone who they know is of the bloodline. So it's been an interesting two years for me. I tell them I don't really know a lot about my people, but I feel free to represent them. I talk to Mike about this and share with him how I feel about it and what these people wanted, to repent and ask forgiveness on behalf of their forefathers and see a healing come to this land. And I said that they're doing everything they know to do, from paying my expenses, to honoring the Delaware people by giving me gifts just beyond belief. And he totally agreed. He told me that I have a right to do that. I felt good about that. I don't feel all the bitterness and hurts that a lot of [Native] people do. But, I've also lived on a reservation and know how it feels to be looked upon as a drunken, dirty Indian, too. It really does something to you when people put that expectation on you. And still today I cannot stand for any Indian to be looked down on just because of the way they're dressed, or alcohol on their breath or whatever. It's just a state of being for a time, hopefully. I have great hope for our people, and I have great hope for this country because of what's going on right now.

I think to me, especially, going to the Conner Prairie Museum, I was very honored that it is a wonderful museum. I was just in amazement of how they honored the Delaware people and how everything was done really right. They have checked into things and found out how the regalia [clothing worn at powwows and ceremonies] are to be and all this. I just appreciated that. And I really appreciate how they honored the black people, the slaves there. I was really taken with some of Harriet Tubman's quotes. I was just walking around there. I had never seen anything that honorable before. When I got home I was telling people how I felt so honored by this museum. But I think it had more of an impact on me when I went back to Ohio where the [Gnadenhütten] massacre occurred. I really didn't know a lot about it, but Mardee Alff, who wanted to have this reconciliation, researched it and would send me packets in the express mail, two to three inches thick, copied out of text books, highlighted and circled so I wouldn't have to read everything, just the most important things. She sent three or four of those, and when I would get them I would try to read them right away because I thought that if this was so important to this lady that she's willing to take the time to do this, then I need to read it. And so I read through it, and that's when I learned a lot of what had gone on there and realized my people being a Christian and trusting people. Back then it must have been very difficult to be separated from your own people because of your religious beliefs. And so for them [the Christian Delawares] to become more trusting of non-Indians, and then to be massacred [by Pennsylvania militiamen]. We went twice. We went in March on the anniversary date [March 8, 1997], and then we went back in September 1997. At that time in September she brought in the four chiefs. Curtis Zunigha [from Bartlesville]. The chief from western

Oklahoma was represented (he wasn't able to be there), and two or three came from Canada. She brought them all in. They really didn't know what they were doing there. But she paid for the trip. She paid for everything. A busload of Munsee Delawares from Canada, she brought them in also. So, at that point she had the reconciliation, and the [non-Indian] people [now living in Ohio] did repentance. They had the chiefs sitting to the side together. From just reading everything in the textbook and the literature she had given me, [I learned] the [Christian Delawares], when told that they were going to be massacred the next morning, asked if they could sing and praise God. And [the Delawares] did that then. They repented to each other for sins they may have committed to each other or different things in their life, and they did this all night knowing that they would face death in the morning, because they believed in God. They had to accept their death. I doubt if I could do that. I would like to think I could, but that's pretty much a dramatic thought. What would I do? Because you think how much of a stand are we willing to take for something you believe in? These people were put to death, and being on that same ground, probably not the same building, but the very ground that had been a bloody mess, that really impacted me. I know when I went into one building where they murdered the women, and I didn't know one building from the other until we got started, I just wanted to scream. I broke down and started crying. I thought, you know, people shed blood here for believing in God, when their own families had left them because they had joined the Moravians. So I guess it was a martyr thing that I admired. It didn't sound like they tried to run. They couldn't have gotten away, but I think being shot would be easier than being bludgeoned to death, with a rock hatchet or whatever [Pennsylvania militiamen] used, and you're standing there waiting for this to happen. So that had a very big impact on me. We went over to the house where the men and boys were executed. That was a log house. It looked older than the other ones. I don't know if it was the original building or not, but surely the ground and the dirt were still the same. It had that same impact on me. I just wanted to scream and cry. I am sure, like the Jews that were executed by Hitler, I am sure if you went there you could still hear the blood crying out from the land for righteousness and a righteous stand to be taken. But yet knowing that they wouldn't want unforgiveness because they were forgiving these people that were going to hurt them. They had already prayed and forgiven them. That's pretty awesome. That had a real impact on me, knowing that maybe I am not even worthy to stand here because of what this people willingly did. And they could have denied [their Christian beliefs], I'm sure.

My mother's name was Leora Barnes. My father was Bernard Adam Barnes. Every body called him Joe. My stepfather, he was not Indian. His name was Arlis O. Toon, called "Red." Everything that I have done I want to say that it was God because I haven't had the time to research it. People send me the research, and I just read what they present. My brother is Carl

Barnes. He lives in Tulsa. He has been battling cancer; he's still working, but he's been battling lymphoma cancer, which my father died from. He is six years older than I am. Probably my mother spoke to them a lot more because I was more of a child; I'm the baby of the family. Every once in awhile he'll come up. I don't visit him a lot, but I know what's going on in his life. My sister is Sharon Hanns. She is retired, living in a motor home in Branson, Missouri. But their home base is really in California. They just retired a year ago, and they're on the road. I have a half brother; his name is Stephen Toon. He lives in Texas. His wife is in Georgia until the house sells; then she'll be moving with him in Texas. He is usually here for the powwow. He came for the past two years, and he didn't know that he had any family. I made contact with him ten or eleven years ago before my stepfather died. His dad didn't tell him he had any brothers or sisters. I made contact through one of my mother's sisters, May Brown [1908–1986]. Luckily, I got the address before she passed away and contacted my stepfather in California and from there contacted my stepbrother, who was living in Georgia. It's really kind of strange to contact someone and say, you don't know me but I know you! I just had to write him a real long letter and tell him who I was and what I had been doing, what my brother and sister did, and if he wanted to contact me, that would be great, but if he didn't, that would be fine also. I guess when he got the letter he called immediately. And we've been in touch, and I'm more like his mother; I'm eleven years older than he is. He doesn't remember his mother at all; he was three years old when she died. So two years ago he came to Copan to the powwow. He wanted to come this year, but he was in the process of moving. It was kind of neat. We were up there last year [1999], and Mike [Pace] came over and was talking to us; he was in his regalia. He had been dancing. Two ladies were sitting next to me; I didn't know who they were. When Mike left, one of them said, "Are you related to him?" And I said, "Yeah, he's my cousin." And they said, "Well, how?" And I told them that our mothers are sisters, and they started naming this big whole family and saying, "Well, we're related to so and so and so, so we're related to you." So it seems like I'm related to everyone here [Bartlesville]. And I was telling my half brother that, and he was realizing that he had a lot of family. So he's trying to get some roots. He's very proud of his heritage, too. It was completely taken from him, not by his choice, but he's very interested in it.

Kenneth and Lisa [are my son and daughter]. They're very proud of being Delaware, also. I think when you're mixed blood, you're proud of whatever you are.

[Their connecting with the Delawares is] not really happening because my daughter is living on the Sioux reservation right now, and that's very much a lifestyle because of the isolation. My son has just come back with me. He's thirty-six years old and has been with me for the past two years. He works in Tulsa; he's a motorcycle mechanic. He tells the men he works with about living on a reservation and how it's like a third-world country, and they cannot relate to any of it. So he's just more or less getting used to the white world and a whole different way of living. It's good for him. He's learning a lot of different things.

It's really hard for me to express [my personal] adjustment, moving back [to Oklahoma] after I was married for fourteen and a half years. Living in North Dakota on the reservation, I worked for Indian Health Service. When I went through a divorce I transferred back down to Claremore, Oklahoma, and interesting enough that was the place I was born. I had never lived there; I grew up in Tulsa. But there was an adjustment there because I was used to working with nothing but full-blood Indians. There was a few of us that weren't Sioux, but I lived there for so long and I got married so young, they would even ask me, "Well who did you vote for?" [in tribal elections]. And it would be, like, "I can't vote, I'm not Sioux." So I was very well accepted there, and I still am. I go back about once a year to see my granddaughter, and the people are always very glad to see me. Sioux are not very hospitable people. I tell people that they aren't going to welcome you with open arms. They're very mistrusting and probably with good reason. And so for me to come back and live in a suburb of a large city after living on a reservation and [now] working with non-Indians, I just miss Indians. [Growing up] I was proud of being an Indian, [but] then to move to North Dakota and to be, like, "you steal, you guys are all drunks." And still to this day, they watch you when you go shopping; I don't care how nicely you dress or what you're driving, it's just an expectation they put on Indians up there. And then you come back to Oklahoma again and realize that it's a place where everybody wants to be at least Cherokee. To me that's honorable. So it's very hard for me to go back [to the reservation] and go to the city and go shopping when I know people are watching me just because of who I am. Of course, I want to get up in their face, just waiting for them to say something to me.

I know it's a time for all Indians to be honored. It's a time when people are searching for the reasons for violence in America. And people that are researching and Christians that are searching are realizing the atrocities, the blood that's spilled on this land. Because God placed us here and had given us this land. [To] many groups, we're the host people, and when you're the host of something, it's like the host of your home; you invite people in, and then to have them run over you and kill you for your land and your house; knowing there are people who don't even know if they were related to those people, and they come up and ask for forgiveness, that's been pretty awesome. And knowing that we should forgive and knowing that God created us to be Indians and black people to be black and Asians to be Asians. But we have to forgive of the past and go on towards the future or we will be held in the past.

Oral history interview on May 28, 2000, at Bartlesville, Oklahoma.

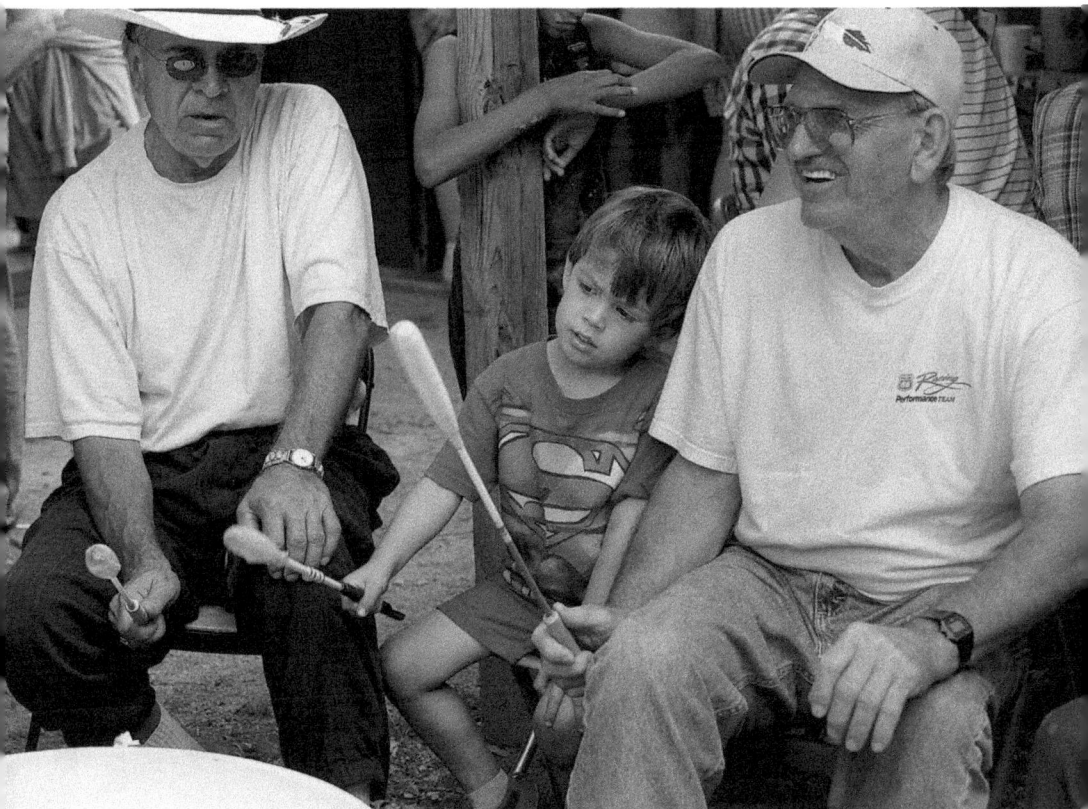

Deacon Floyd Crabb sits between Dee Ketchum and Forrest Yearout who are guiding his drumming. Adults readily teach youngsters when they want to learn. Adults stress keeping to the beat, which represents the heartbeat of the Delaware people. (Below) Crabb studies a butterfly at his family camp at the 2004 Copan Powwow.

Joanna Nichol at the Ketchum Camp near Copan, Oklahoma, circa 2000.

JOANNA J. NICHOL

Tribal member
Born September 12, 1919, in Hogshooter, Oklahoma
Died January 27, 2004

My mother was Josie Curleyhead. She was Delaware. My father was Alexander Benjamin Pambogo, and he was Potawatomi. They met at Chilocco Indian School. I forget what year they were married in. I think it was 1914 or 1915.

My father was three-quarters Potawatomi, and Mother was seven-eighths Delaware. To go to Chilocco, you have go clear down to the last drop, and that's why I know my sixteenths of my [Indian] heritage. I had an older sister, which she only lived two weeks. She's buried in the Curleyhead cemetery out near Hogshooter. Then I had a brother that would have been older, and he lived to be about a year and a half old. And he died in the flu epidemic of 1919.

My Grandfather Curleyhead had two wives. I think he was one of the last Delaware Indian men to have two wives. And he had Grandma Pomp [Pom-pa-noc-qua; Mrs. Lizzie Curleyhead], who was the first wife. She was barren, and so he had to marry another wife. So he'd married Grandma Lilly Thompson. So then, she was the one who had all the children. My mother was pregnant with me during the time of 1919 that my brother died. In fact, they had his funeral in the living room, because I think Mom and Dad couldn't get out of bed, they had the flu. So it was hard, but I grew up right up there on that hill. My dad had a stripped-down Model T Ford, and Grandma Pomp loved to drive that Ford. She and I would go out. She couldn't speak English. I couldn't speak Delaware. But I knew when she said something to me, I had an idea what she wanted me to do. Evidently, it stuck, because in the language class, Lucy [Blalock] used to tell me, "You always get the accent right. You don't always say it right, but you get the accent right."

So anyway, we would go tearing. We had no fences at that time. Aunt Kate's allotment was right next to Mamma's, on top of the hill. We used to go tearing over to see Aunt Kate [Josie Curleyhead's sister], and Grandma Pomp was so old then, and she looked through the steering wheel to drive, and we'd go through tall grass, just flying. Just a flying. She threw me through the windshield one time, 'cause we hit a stump.

I would love to remember the language, 'cause, like I say, whenever they tell me what the word is, I could always say it. But I'm getting to the age to where I'm seventy-nine now. And I'm getting to the age where I don't remember the language. But I miss it. I loved to hear it. I just love to hear. And the dancing. I remember Momma dancing sideways and swaying. I don't know what the name of that dance was, but it was always at a stomp dance. The women had a dance of their own that they did at a stomp dance. It was so pretty, and it sounded so great. I went to sleep to stomp dance for years and years, as long as I was here. I remember when my little sister was born. My daddy used to tell me, "Be sure and keep her down on the floor," 'cause then we had a Model T touring car, "leave her down on the floor; you can sleep on the seat and don't raise your head." And I'd always thought, "Why can't I raise my head?" Finally I asked him, "Why can't I raise my head?" He said, "Oh, some of these guys get some liquor in them," he said, "they get to shooting." And he said, "You might get hit." And I remember one time, a bullet came right through where I would have been if I'd been sitting. I could hear it go "Psheeew," and I thought, "Boy, I'm going [to] lay still like Daddy said, go to sleep; I'm not going to look anymore." But I used to hear some of the fights. In those days, at a stomp dance, they did have a drum. But the drum would be back in the trees. I never got to see who was on the drum. But I always got to do the stomp dance at the end. All of us children had to be at the end. And that was really strictly enforced. My daddy was a great leader. He had a beautiful . . . he had a trained lyric tenor voice. And he sang over at Enid Radio. But it was beautiful. Later on, after he'd married my stepmother, he started a quartet up in Arkansas City, Kansas. And they used to sing at weddings and funerals and all that stuff. So he sang his entire life. And I have sang it all mine.

I wasn't here during the 1940s and '50s. I was in California. But I was really upset about what was happening because the Bureau of Indian Affairs was relocating everybody. They was offering everybody, making it sound like heaven, "Here's a one-way ticket, go to San Francisco, Chicago, wherever you want to go and into the big cities. Here's some money, and you can get yourself an apartment, and you will really enjoy it." They didn't have a return ticket. They didn't know how to use a telephone. They didn't know how to find a rest room. They didn't even know how to order in a restaurant. Because some of the tribes that we had at that time did not look at people in their eyes; they would look down and wouldn't speak until they were spoken to. I was working with the Indians all the time. In fact, I had a newspaper going. I had a newspaper going, and I occupied Alcatraz. I occupied their communication center, where the D-Q University is now.[1] I was active all the

1. D-Q University was a non-profit, private, two-year community college, accredited since 1977 by the Accrediting Commission for Community and Junior Colleges of the Western Association of Schools and Colleges. D-Q University was also a founding member of the American Indian Higher Education Consortium. The institution was supported by numerous tribes and tribal organizations. D-Q University lost its accreditation in 2005 and closed.

time. And I had my own cell at Alcatraz. We all threw our gear in the cell, and that was our room, you know?

I worked; I had a Title IV program for the whole county of San Mateo, which I worked on and started several good programs there for the Indians. We taught the teachers how to handle the Indian children because our children was not taught to try to be first or smartest. They were taught to be polite and only answer when they were supposed to. And when they were in a school situation they acted that way. And they were accused of being the mean kids because they wouldn't look the teacher in the eye. And so we had to teach them those things. That's where I got the name Momma Jo. They got me a "Momma Jo #1" California license. I still have it. Can't use it anymore, but I still keep it. But we had powwows, and Stanford has a big powwow every year. We used to have powwows and art shows and so forth. We got the Indian Council started, 1950, a little bit before 1950. It was really after the war and after the Korean War; it seemed like every time the Indian people partook in powwows they remembered the way it used to be at home and wanted it back. That's what D-Q University is now. You can go into the library and find a book about almost any tribe and their culture. Titus used to teach singing and dancing at D-Q. We share D-Q now with the Mexican farmworkers because Cesar Chavez, he helped us occupy, he helped keep us fed. I was working at the post office at the time of the Alcatraz thing. But I spent all my weekends on Alcatraz.

I work with children all the time. Like I say, I have "children" all over the country. I got children named after me at Rosebud. I got children named after me at Pine Ridge. And I worked with all the tribes in California. I had a store up in Redding, and I had a customer that was Miwok. She was married.

Do you remember that little Indian boy used in advertising [the] Santa Fe railroad? His name was Lloyd Stevens. When he grew up he married this Miwok lady. They were sitting at the bar having a beer, and over the radio came an announcement by the Forest Service, "If you go to Yosemite, be sure and stop at the Indian exhibits because several of the tribes are extinct, like the Miwoks." Edith liked to blow her top. Man, I'm telling you, you never saw a mad Indian until you saw her. She went down there, storming down there, and told them rangers off right then.

I always teach that in school [being in harmony with the Earth and taking care of the Earth]. I always tell them that the Creator made the animals, just like he did us. And they have just as much right on this Earth as we do. It's something that the children have to know, grownups have to know. I really got a good kick out of when Arizona went after all their coyotes. And they killed all their coyotes. Then they started griping 'cause they has so many rats and mice in their houses. And the Indians finally told them. The Navajos finally opened up and told them and said, "You killed all the coyotes, and that's why you got so many rats and mice." So now, they're not killing coyotes anymore. But this is something that they have to learn the hard way. I don't know why, but they do. If people don't have that feeling, because the children, when we was young, that's the way we was taught. We were equal with the animals. Not better, not worse. And whatever the animal could teach us, we were supposed to listen. And we respected the elders, and we didn't ask questions until some situation came up that would encourage such a thing. Mother saw to it. Mother was very clean. My daddy was a house painter, and my mother would starch his overalls and iron them and put a white shirt on him. And a black bow tie, one of those kind that you just snap on. And that's the way he went to paint a house. Our school, when they were still together, was right there by the shale pit in Bartlesville. And our backyard backed onto the baseball field, and I was the top baseball player in the sixth grade there. And when she seen me slide into second, she come right out, and the ball game would stop, and she'd take back in the house and take my dirty clothes off, put clean clothes on me, and then she'd put me back in the game, and we'd go again. Everybody got used to that.

One of the things that shows why years and years ago, before the white man ever came, the other tribes used to try to steal the Delaware women, because the Delaware women was known for their wisdom. The council was men, but the men got their instructions from the ladies before they left. And then, if they couldn't come to an understanding, they went back to the ladies and asked them to give them an answer. And this has been going on for thousands and thousands of years. That's why we're called the Grandfather Tribe. Because we have given counseling. We have gone and learned languages in order to help the government and the tribe that they were trying to move out. We would go to listen so we could counsel them and make them understand what was happening to them. And wouldn't let them do like they did Potawatomis and drive us like a herd of cattle. The only thing lucky with the Potawatomis, so it seemed, we would not travel without a priest. So we have written history . . . total . . . daily, of who died on that trail of death.

I think the [future for our Delaware culture] is going to be good. If you build what you're supposed to build, and keep your classes up, and keep these children learning this stuff, let them go on and go to university, because that's what one of the things Momma always said. You have to learn how your enemy acts before you can beat him. And so, we have learned that the hard way, haven't we? So we will be Delawares forever, and so will our children. And I don't care if they get clear down to one-sixteenth or one-hundred-twentieth, you know, they're still going to be Delawares. And the Delaware will be more, they will be more looking for a culture then, than now. We need to leave books, we need to leave dances and records, and we need to leave all this for these children. Because we have some wonderful children here now. And I think it should continue. All of the dances, because you don't know how good it makes you feel till you get out there and stomp dance. And you don't know how good it makes you feel when you get there and hear the drum and dance at the powwow. Those things have to be kept; they have to be kept. And if we live it, then our children will live it. There's just no other way. And another thing, when an elder speaks to any child that's been raised the Indian way, that child minds. If that child is doing something he shouldn't be doing, the elder is supposed to tell him or the medicine person. 'Cause I been to many conferences in California, and I've spoke to many children, and they listen, they listen, it's wonderful.

I thank the Creator for all of those things. When I lived in California, and even after we got D-Q, it took us twelve years in court, but we made it. We didn't get all, but we got half of it. It was three hundred forty-five acres, and they gave us half of it and all of the buildings. We also have burning privileges, even on a non-burn day. Because they know that our sweat lodge is not going to catch anything on fire. That's something I miss here is sweat lodges. I think we ought to have a sweat lodge right up here so that whenever people want to have sweat lodge ceremony, they could do it. There was a Red Eagle from Pine Ridge, was at D-Q. I was sitting there with a pair of slacks on, and he didn't say it to me, he kind of looked out to the sky like this and said, "We don't allow anybody to wear pants like that at Pine Ridge, especially for sweat lodge ceremonies." So I didn't say anything either, but I was parked pretty close, and I had a muumuu that I always used when I go in a sweat lodge. And so I went and changed, right there in the car, right after supper, broad daylight, nobody knew what I was doing, but I changed. I came back out and sit down with a dress on. This Mr. Red Eagle didn't say anything, didn't say anything. And I waited for about thirty minutes; finally I said, "I don't want anybody talking about me being in pants instead of a dress when they don't notice when I come back in a dress." And Mr. Red Eagle said, "I'm sorry." He said, "Thank you for getting the dress on."

I was part of the AIM Movement with Dennis [Banks] and all of them, and I never saw such hard-working guys in my life. And it was so great to see Dennis totally sober; he never took another drink. We had a conference for all the indigenous people of the world at D-Q, shortly after we opened it. And we had a crowd. Dennis was the one that was cleaning the toilets and sweeping; he never said anything. When it was his time to speak, he got up and spoke strongly, 'cause he's a trained lawyer. But they gave him such a bad time over Wounded Knee; they couldn't get him; we all kept working not to get him, and they kept him, like they're keeping Peltier now. And we write to him every day because if our mail is returned, then we know that they've done something to him. And that's what we did there. That was the way we did with Dennis. We write every day, the whole gang, all of the tribes. And that's the way we kept them from hurting the people that they had so-called said were outlaws or something. We have to do that.

I think the Woodland people were a lot kinder, compassionate. I'm not saying anything wrong about the Plains people, but they had to be tougher;

living on the Plains and the desert wasn't easy. But I think the Woodland people were; our religion was more like the white man's religion, only we believed really in praying up to the Creator and looking up and sending the smoke up to him, and we didn't have to have a house of worship, and we never asked for money. And those are the things that Indians needs to remember and to tell their children about so that their children will know that you go through life. And when you want to give money to somebody for something, you give it for a particular thing. But don't just give it just because they asked you. That's a white person thing that we just do not need. I could talk for hours because things come up in my mind that I have run into living in different places like I have. Like Leonard Thompson here, ask him about when he was in the war and what kept him going. Smokey was Miwok, and he used to come down to where my summer place is in Northern California. He'd come down and get a six-pack. And he knew I was Indian, and it took him about five years before he'd speak to me. Finally he spoke to me. He worked at a ranch up above where we was. And then he was telling me about having to walk through China, through south China from India, because they were part of the marines. And he said, "We had to walk, and without food a lot of times." And he said, "I just kept saying, 'Just let me see Mount Shasta one more time.' That's all I want, just to see Mount Shasta one more time." And he said, "That's what kept me going." So that's the Indian way of thinking, and I'd like to think that that's the way all of us, all of us think of the woodland and the trees and the things that we are blessed with. That's all we need.

Oral history, September 1998, at the powwow grounds near Copan, Oklahoma.

Joanna J. Nichol also has an oral history in **Always a People** *(pages 151–159).*

Former chief Curtis Zunigha, a Vietnam veteran and a member of the Delaware Color Guard, carries the colors at Grand Entry at the 2007 Delaware Powwow near Copan, Oklahoma. Mothers of veterans dance wearing blue blankets with red trim in the background. Delawares revere service to the country in the armed forces.

Deborah (Deb) Nichols-Ledermann holds an antique quilt with blocks sewn by her great-great-grandmother Rachel Ketchum Wolfe Anderson. The quilt represents five generations of her family who have owned it, going back to Rachel, who originally removed from Kansas to Indian Territory in 1868. (2005, Maryland Heights, Missouri)

DEBORAH NICHOLS-LEDERMANN

Tribal member, historian

My Delaware heritage is through my mother's family. When the Delaware were removed from Kansas in 1868 (following the 1867 treaty), my great-great-grandmother, Rachel Ketchum (Wolfe, Anderson), moved with them to what is now northeastern Oklahoma. Her maiden name was Rachel Ketchum. She first married a Delaware by the name of James Wolfe (Wolf), who was active in the tribal government in Kansas. He was a horse dealer and drowned in a river while trying to escape men who were after the large sum of money he was carrying from the sale of some horses. Captain Wolf was listed among the Delaware who accompanied John Fremont on his 1856 expedition across the Rockies. The Jewish photographer Carvalho chronicled the journey and wrote about Captain Wolf, a horse trader, on several occasions. I believe that he may be related to the James Wolfe that Rachel married. Rachel and James had two children, Henry Tiblow Wolfe and Elizabeth Wolfe Barker. I have a photo of Henry Wolfe with my great-grandmother, Rachel Wilkins.

One of Elizabeth's sons, Herbert Barker Sr., wrote about his memories of growing up in Indian Territory/early Oklahoma in a little book titled *Paradise Remembered*.[1] It is a good portrait of what life was like northwest of Welch, Oklahoma, as many of the things he speaks of are similar to the things my own mother talked about when I was a child. Herb's wife, Marie Barker, did research into Delaware history. They were friends with Cornelius Wilson, a Delaware minister, and Betty Bullette, the granddaughter of George Bullette. Herb and Marie lived in California for a number of years, and when Cornelius Wilson (they called him Grandpa Wilson) visited them, they made a tape of him saying things in the Delaware language. They also recorded him singing hymns in Delaware. Marie donated several older cultural items to the tribe that were left to her by Betty Bullette. My family also

---

1. Herbert Barker, *Paradise Remembered: A Lenape Indian Childhood, and Other Stories.* Published 1991 by Dan Barker, PO Box 429, Madison, WI 53701.

knew Sarah Kinney, called Aunt Sarah by the older ones. George and Betty Bullette, Cornelius Wilson, and Sarah Kinney were all descended from Mekinges Conner (through her daughter Eliza). Marie also gave me one of Richard Adams's books which originally belonged to George Bullette. Inside was inscribed, "George Bullette, Tulsa, I.T." The title of the book was *A Delaware Indian Legend and the Story of Their Troubles*. It told some of the history of the problems between the Delaware and Cherokee over the land in Indian Territory. I gave this book to the Delaware Tribe, as I felt that was where it belonged for future generations to see. Marie Barker was very kind to me and always willing to share her Delaware history.

After the death of James Wolfe, Rachel married a white man by the name of Alexander M. Anderson, originally from Ohio. They had six children—Charles Journeycake Anderson, John Martin Anderson, Anna Anderson Siegel, Rachel Anderson Wilkins (called Bonnie), Nancy Anderson Nading (called Dottie), and Lizzie Anderson, who died as a young child. They settled about ten miles northwest of Welch, Oklahoma. The community was called Kinneson, after the family who ran a country store there. Her daughter, Rachel (Anderson) Wilkins, was my great-grandmother. My mother, Nadine (Wilkins) Neil, was born there in 1920 on my grandfather Robert Clay Wilkins's Indian allotment. She had one sister, Erma, and two brothers, Robert and Leonard. Leonard was killed in World War II, when his son was just a baby. Several members of my family died in that war, as many Delaware died in the wars of the United States, even before we were citizens of this nation. My family has been in the Welch area for around one hundred and thirty years. Two of my brothers, Robert and Merle, still live there today. My son, Chris, lives in Tulsa, and I hope that his interest in the history will increase with age.

Rachel and Alexander did not settle northwest of Welch first, however. The story is a bit sketchy to me, but I believe that they first settled over near the other Delaware. They had rented a house from a man named Coker, who was married to the sister of William Adams (the grandson of Mekinges Conner, through her daughter Nancy). Coker was the Cherokee who killed Isaac Journeycake. I think that there was a mob after Coker, and they went to this house by mistake, burning it down. From the information in a book by Helen York Rose, I know that Alexander Anderson gave testimony about it in court, but I have not researched the case yet to get the details. After that, they moved northwest of Welch, into an area where many of the descendants of the Shawnee or Shawnee/Delaware settled. The house where they lived still stands there today. I have a copy of a photo made in front of the house in 1898, on Charles Anderson's wedding day.

As I learned more history, I realized I had been surrounded by descendants of the Shawnee, like the Bluejacket twins who were my classmates at school. We were close to Miami, Oklahoma, where many of the smaller tribes had lands. My sister, Twyla, was first married to one of the Captains, who are Eastern Shawnee. So my niece is Delaware and Eastern Shawnee. My brother Merle's wife, Phyllis, is related to the wife of Charles Dawes, the Ottawa chief. When her parents died, she was "adopted" into their family, and they took on the role of her parents. I have rarely seen people as nice as the Dawes, and I think very highly of them. After I left Oklahoma, I realized that when you grow up surrounded by Indian people, it feels completely normal, and it is only after you get out away from Oklahoma and get older that you see most people do not grow up this way.

One of the most interesting experiences I had was when I spent about a month on the Navajo reservation doing a clinical rotation for pharmacy school. I was at the Indian Health Service hospital at Fort Defiance, Arizona. I really liked the Navajo people, and I was happy to be surrounded by them. The cattle are free-ranged, and I woke up the first morning to find several of them lying in the yard of the little house where they let us stay during our rotation. While I was there, I realized their language and culture was in a stage that our tribe must have gone through about a hundred years before. I had one girl tell me that her grandmother only spoke Navajo, her mother could speak both English and Navajo, and that she understood it [Navajo], but did not speak it. It hit me that this was exactly what happened in my family with my great-great-grandmother, great-grandmother, and grandfather. One of the other students was a girl with Chinese ancestry. When we went to Gallup (New Mexico), all the little Navajo grandmothers would stop her on the street and make over her, thinking she was a Navajo. They ignored me. Then we would go into a shop, and I would have to explain to her what all the Indian things were and how they were used. After a while, I just shook my head and laughed over it.

Rachel Ketchum's paternal aunt, Sally Ketchum Raccoon, accompanied her family to Indian Territory. Sally's husband, Big Raccoon, was a tribal council member in Kansas, but he died before the tribe was moved. I have a copy of a very old photo of Aunt Sally standing in front of a log cabin. She died in 1887 and is buried at Walker Cemetery northwest of Welch, as are Rachel and A. M. Anderson, along with their descendants. John Anderson and his wife died when their daughter, Rachel C. Anderson, was just a baby. She was raised by Grandma and Grandpa Anderson. She wrote years later that her father's dying wish had been that Grandma Anderson teach his little daughter how to speak Delaware. She did learn it, but after the older Delawares died off, she lost most of it as the years went on. Her name was Rachel Cherokee Anderson Adams. One of her cousins on her mother's side was Belva Secondine, the wife of Henry Secondine, who was always very kind to me and very helpful in my history research.

Rachel Ketchum was the daughter of Howard Ketchum, the son of Capt. Ketchum. According to family stories, Howard was murdered on a hunting trip while the tribe still resided in Kansas. Rachel's mother's name is not recorded that I have found. Her uncle, probably a maternal uncle, was named Tonganoxie. The Kansas town of Tonganoxie is named in his honor. He ran a sort of stage station there, and many people passed through it on their travels. One of them noted that he wore silver half-moon ornaments in his ears and nose. He is listed as one of the Delaware who served in the Seminole War. He was a very respected man in the area and was actually elected by the tribal council and other chiefs as a chief of the Turkey clan, but the federal government would not approve it because they had the chiefs in place that they wanted at that time. There are several accounts of Tonganoxie helping people during the "Bleeding Kansas" period before the Civil War. One incident was called "the Martyrs of '56." Three free state men were taken prisoner on the road between Leavenworth and Lawrence by a group of roving pro-slavery militia. They stopped at Tonganoxie's home that night with their prisoners. Later in the night they marched the captives further down the road and attempted to execute all three. One man died right away; one was badly wounded and died several days later. The third man was wounded in the neck and escaped, making his way back to Tonganoxie's house. Tonganoxie showed him where to hide in the brush until nightfall to escape the militia. He also gave the man a blanket and instructions on how to find his way to Lawrence, the haven for free state men in Kansas. When you stop to think about it, that was years before the Civil War was officially declared. The Delaware and other emigrant tribes lived all those years in a virtual powder keg, surrounded by the free state and pro-slavery militia who constantly roved the area committing violence, stealing, and wrestling for political control of the future of Kansas.

Rachel Ketchum and her siblings lost their mother at a young age and were raised by Tonganoxie and an aunt. Rachel's two brothers, Simon and Best Quality Ketchum, were listed as living with Tonganoxie on the early 1860-era tribal rolls. Also listed was a girl by the name of Nancy, who may have been her sister. Louisa Ketchum Lundy was also believed to be a child of Howard Ketchum. A railroad claim lists Tonganoxie's widow as Wus-car-le-tah. She was the half sister of a Delaware named Frenchman.

Capt. Ketchum was born in Tuscaroras County, Ohio, in 1780, according to his gravestone. His Lenape name was Tah-whe-la-len. He was a band chief in Missouri, after the death of his brother, Lapenahile. In Kansas he was listed as the chief of the Turtle Clan. He was the principal chief of the tribe at the time of his death in 1857. He is buried in White Church Cemetery, which is located in present Kansas City, Kansas. You might like to hear the two different versions about how he obtained his name. The early trading post ledgers in Missouri list his name as Catchem. One story attributes his name to being such a fast runner that he could catch a deer on foot.

The other story is mentioned in one of the local county histories in Kansas, quoting a writer who passed through the Delaware Reserve while the tribe was still there. According to that man, Ketchum was captured as a child by enemy soldiers and locked in a storage room. He pried up the floorboards and escaped. The soldiers spotted him as he ran away and shot at him, yelling, "Catch him!" Knowing the time period in which he was born and the turmoil of the area, I can easily believe the latter story. Another thing this man wrote has me puzzled. He stated that Capt. Ketchum was Tecumseh's second-in-command at the Battle of the Thames, where Tecumseh was killed. I am not certain about that, because I have read that William Conner commanded a group of pro-American Delawares at that battle. I think he might have been second-in-command of that group, instead. Ketchum did claim to have served with the Americans in the War of 1812 and as a scout for Louis Cass to Canada. The Delaware Tribe had a silver pipe presented to them by William Henry Harrison in 1814. From that information, I believe the writer passing through Kansas might have gotten his notes confused and that Ketchum was part of the American group at the Battle of the Thames.

I think Capt. Ketchum must have been a very extraordinary person. Several authors mention having long, interesting talks with him, but they fail to tell us what he had to say. One of the rare glimpses of him comes from George Manypenny in *Our Indian Wards*. He wrote of a long conversation where the old chief spoke of the "thirteen fires," or thirteen original American colonies. My favorite passage is where Manypenny said he asked Ketchum what message he might convey to the government in Washington, D.C. The chief's reply was to indicate that he wished those in Washington to act on Earth in such a manner that he would meet them in heaven. Obviously he did not meet many politicians in heaven. In our reprint of Delaware Indian legends I used his quote about having no written histories and keeping the stories "written on our hearts," to be transmitted to our children. That oral tradition was vital to the survival of the tribe's culture and sense of identity.

The old Delawares are my heroes. Men like James Secondine, James Swannuck, Capt. Falleaf, Black Beaver, and the others who hunted, trapped in, and explored the old west. There is one group that went up trapping in Iowa in the early 1840s. They were a party of fourteen Delaware and one Potawatomi on a fur-trapping expedition, and they were mistaken by a Sioux war party for a Potawatomi camp. It was a long and bloody battle. Even the wounded Delaware who could no longer shoot crawled to the campfire to mold lead into bullets for their tribesmen. After an exchange that lasted all morning, between fourteen Delaware and about two hundred Sioux, the Delaware were finally all overcome and killed. Estimates on the number of Sioux killed ranged from forty to sixty, which would be about three Sioux killed for every Delaware. Francis Parkman Jr. mentions being told the story by Paul Dorian in his book *The Oregon Trail*. Lt. J. Henry Carleton provides more detail in his *Prairie Logbooks*. According to Carleton, when the old Delaware were asked why they did not send war parties after the Sioux to revenge the death of their men, they proudly replied, "They revenged themselves!"

[My interest in the legends of the Delaware] was a long process, which began with my mother. She told me that we were Delaware, and one of the things she always emphasized to me was that her grandmother, Rachel (Anderson) Wilkins, believed it was important to remember that although we had been forced to register as Cherokees, we were actually Delaware. So it came down in my family that even though the government had put us on rolls as Cherokees, that we were never to forget we were actually Delaware and not to get mistaken about our identities. One of my friends likes to talk about his "little Delaware grandmother." We all had them, or our parents did. They were remarkable and strong women who made sure the younger generations remembered their identities and culture. I remember when I got my C.D.I.B. card. I took it out of the envelope and looked at it. It said "Cherokee." My immediate thought was that someone at the B.I.A. had made a mistake. I started to call them and ask them to correct it. Then I remembered that they made our ancestors register on Cherokee rolls. That made me angry and sad. I wanted something done to correct that. Many years later, when our tribe was putting together history and information to prove our sovereignty, I did all that I could to locate or suggest records that might help.

My mom told me stories about growing up northwest of Welch and attending a one-room country schoolhouse as a girl. She attended Iron Post School. They walked to school and rode horses or rode in wagons for transportation. She told me the Delaware words that she could remember from her grandmother, such as the names for rabbit and squirrel, and the numbers to ten. She told me that when it snows and just a little snow lingers on in patches while all the rest melts, that the snow is "waiting for its friends," and more snow will come soon.

I wish that I had grown up in a more traditional Delaware family, because I would have been more aware of the stories, history, and spiritual traditions. One of the earliest memories I have was from one night when I was only about four or five years old. I woke up in the middle of the night and started down the hallway. I only got to the doorway of the bedroom, because there in the door were two images. I stood there looking at them in the light from the nightlight on the hallway wall. They were there side-by-side, about my height or slightly taller. The one on the right was an owl, like a very big horned owl. The one on the left was a sort of winter being—a mass of whirling and swirling snow and ice. Kind of like a little winter tornado. I still carry a mental image of them, and that was over forty years ago. The owl spoke to me, and he told me that this spirit beside him wanted to get me. It meant to do me a lot of harm, maybe kill me. He said that he was there to protect me from it and would keep me safe, but I should run back to bed very fast so that it would not get me. I ran as fast as I could across the cold hardwood floor and dived into bed, absolutely terrified. After a while, I looked at the door, and they were gone. I was afraid at night for many years after that. I was afraid that thing would come back. If I had been in a more traditional family, I might have talked to my parents about it and learned that sometimes Delaware girls have spirits appear to them when they are very young, and to see them is not a bad thing, but more of a normal thing, at least it was in the old days. This subject is not easy to talk about, but a few years ago I did have the chance to discuss it with an older traditional person, and that was very comforting. The sole reason I tell this example here is because I seriously think it is very important for people to understand when they read the old accounts and legends of spirits and guardian animals appearing to Delaware, or of ghost whoops (the spirits of the dead who call to you in the woods), or premonitions that someone will die or something bad will happen, or dreams that carry a message—those things were real. Our people really experienced them. As someone who is normally skeptical, from a scientific education background, I felt that I owed the old Delaware a voice of support on record in saying that their visions were very real things, and I can understand that they wanted to recite and sing about them in the Big House.

My grandparents married at a young age. My grandmother, who was non-Indian, was fourteen, and my grandfather was sixteen years old when they married. Mom told me that when her grandmother wanted to say something to her father and didn't want her mother to know what it was, she spoke to him in Delaware. Grandpa understood Delaware but did not speak it fluently. He had one brother, William Henry Wilkins, and a sister, Bonnie Wilkins Dotson. Grandpa was known for being a really good hunter. He always shared his game, fish, and garden produce with other people. Marie Barker sent me a copy of a letter from a couple in Chetopa, Kansas, from the 1930s, I think. They were telling her how Grandpa brought them the nicest big fat possum for Christmas dinner, and they were very happy to have it. He also trapped in the earlier years. My mother recalled seeing furs stretched out to dry all around the outside of the house when she was young, and my older brothers remember him trapping when they were younger. My oldest brother learned it from him and kept traps until he was in high school. Grandpa was still driving two Model A Fords when I was a child (I was born in 1956), and he kept them up through the early 1960s. One was his hunting car, and the other was his "town" car. He was not a car collector; these were his means of transportation, and he drove them every day. My cousin, Leonard Wilkins Jr., recalled that when he was out hunting with someone other than Grandpa, they could tell if he was out and about because they would see his narrow tire tracks, which were quite different from the tracks of other cars and trucks.

Mother also told me that one of my ancestors was a Delaware chief, buried in Kansas City, Kansas. That caught my imagination quite a bit as a child, and I was determined to see that place when I grew up. I used to wonder what it might look like, and hoped that the people at the church took care of the grave so it would not be lost. One day I would actually help with a historic project to try to preserve that cemetery. We got a grant from the Kansas Historical Society to clean and repair the remaining Delaware gravestones there. When we finished, they looked so much better. We had a dedication, and it was wonderful to see the Delaware at White Church again. It had once been the site of a Methodist mission to the Delaware. Delawares like Charles, James, and Jacob Ketchum preached in the Lenape language in the original church during the early 1800s. Many of the local people helped with the project, and it was a very moving experience for us all to come together for such a good cause. Also with us were the descendants of Isaac Munday, the blacksmith of the Delaware, who died on a hunting trip with them. One of his descendants happened along as we were planning the project and was able to gather his family members to help us celebrate.

We hoped that our work would preserve the stones for the next century so future generations of Delaware could see some of the few remaining historic grave markers from our time in Kansas. Tragically, several months later some vandals broke two of the best stones, those for Charles and Jacob Ketchum. They were both Delaware Methodist ministers. It was truly heartbreaking to see those rare pieces of our history destroyed in such a senseless gesture. The historic society does have photos and slides on file to record how those stones looked after restoration, but they can never be replaced. More recently they added smaller granite markers to each of the graves so that as the older marble markers grow too faint to read, the graves will still be identified.

To continue my story, after my mother went to a residential care home, I got one of the family Bibles. It was dated from the 1890s in Indian Territory. Originally it appeared to belong to Nancy, my great-grandmother's sister. It contained poems, some hair mementos, notes, bits of lace, and a friendly letter that had been started to "uncle" William Adams. Also in the Bible was my great-great-grandparents' wedding certificate. William Adams was the Delaware Baptist minister who performed the ceremony. He was also the father of Richard C. Adams, who originally published the book of Delaware Indian legends we reprinted with Syracuse University Press (*Legends of the Delaware Indians and Picture Writing*).

William Adams was the son of Nancy Conner, who was the daughter of Mekinges. So he was a cousin of Rachel Ketchum. His father was a Delaware by the name of Wilson. An application to the Sons of the American Revolution by Richard Adams provided some interesting family genealogy. According to it, the mother of Mekinges (and so also Capt. Ketchum) was Ah-ke-che-lung-un-a-qua. Her name is spelled phonetically different ways, depending on who is writing it. The affidavit with the S.A.R. application also stated that Ah-ke-che-lung-un-a-qua was the daughter of White Eyes, a Delaware chief from Revolutionary War times. Perhaps additional research in the future will shed more light on this genealogy. I think I should say that Capt. Ketchum was not named Jack or John as some historians have speculated. There was a John Ketchum, but he was a younger and totally different person who is buried on his own allotment in Kansas. He died about the same time as Capt. Ketchum, and some have confused the two. John Conner, who was chief afterward, sometimes went by Jack, I believe. There was also some confusion about his Lenape name, which has always been signed Tah-whe-la-len, though the spellings may differ slightly from document to document.

Although the last name Ketchum began as a version of Catchem, the old chief's name, it seems to have evolved into a family name that was used by various branches of his family, possibly including his brother's children, cousins, and others. One of several ways in which children obtained Christian names was to take the translation of their father's Lenape name as a last name and add a Christian first name. Thus the son of Capt. Ketchum was Howard Ketchum and his daughter was Sally Ketchum. Another common way to obtain a Christian name was simply to have one assigned to a child when he or she attended a mission school, as was the case with William Adams. Sometimes the missionaries gave their own name or their wife's name to the children in their school. Some of the last names came from traders or trappers who visited the tribe and took Delaware wives. One book that I saw about the history of the Ohio falls region of Kentucky told about a man named Bullette who was part of a group of men who went to visit the Shawnee and Delaware. And one researcher has suggested that the last name of Charles and Isaac Journeycake's mother, Jane Socia, was actually Saucier, the last name of a Frenchman who traded with the Delaware in Missouri and who was related to the Chouteau family.

My curiosity continued to grow concerning Delaware history in Kansas and Oklahoma. I learned about William Adams's son, Richard, and became interested in his work for the Delaware Tribe. I was attending pharmacy school at the University of Missouri–Kansas City, and during some of my free time I explored Miller-Nichols Library, across the street. They have the Snyder Collection there, which is a wonderful collection of western history books. Among them were copies of several books published by Richard Adams. One of the books was an original collection of his records from the tribal claim for $150,000 around 1905. It resulted in the 1906 roll which today is the basis for membership in our tribe. Included in these records were minutes from several tribal council meetings at that time. It was completely fascinating to me to read the words of our tribal leaders from those days and see how they spoke. One of the most interesting things was that they divided the Delaware into three geographic/political districts: the Grand River, Verdigris River, and Caney River districts. They had to have representatives from each of those districts at a tribal council to conduct business, so that people in every area had a voice in the business.

When I read Richard's collection of Delaware Indian legends, I thought they were really great stories. I wished that I had been able to hear these stories as a child. I wondered how many Delaware children had grown up without hearing these stories which were a part of their heritage. It is a rare book. When I talked to Richard Adams's grandson, William Adams, he told me that he found one copy of the book, but it was in a university collection, locked in a glass case. They refused to take it out for him to see. It seemed terribly sad that the man's own grandson was not even able to read his stories.

Not long after that, I bought a book by Laurence Hauptman about the Native Americans in the Civil War. It was titled *Between Two Fires*. It contained a chapter on the Delaware in the Civil War, and I was very happy to see some of our Civil War history brought to light for modern readers. I had done some research in that area and wrote to him about it. He was preparing to write some articles for the *Civil War Times Illustrated* and asked if I would like to help on the one about the Delaware. I agreed, and we co-authored that article. Then I told him there was this book of Delaware legends, and it needed to be reprinted. He was a series editor for a group of Native American books for Syracuse University Press. I sent him some photocopies of the stories, and he showed them to some of their people. One of them took the stories home and read them to her son. She said that he would not let her stop reading them. He loved them so much that he wanted to hear them all. They agreed to publish them and asked me to edit the book. They also asked me to write the introduction containing the research I had done on Richard Adams and his work for the Delaware tribe. Time had dimmed the memories of his contributions, and I wanted to make people aware of his work, especially the younger generations of Delaware people. I admired his spirit and his determination never to be defeated. He always got back up and kept going. Maybe I admired him because I had just finished pharmacy school (I already had an associate degree and a B.S. in education). It was very hard to get through it as a single parent. I had no money and had to work my way through it with the help of scholarships, grants, and student loans. The first two years I worked all night at a medical lab and then went to school full-time during the day. So I admired someone with the determination to keep going and never give up.

I wrote the introduction and chose the pictures. Some of them are from his record books at the University of Kansas. These books have a lot of the government records for the tribe copied in them. He used them to research his cases. There are twenty-three volumes in that collection, each volume being about the size of an encyclopedia. When he brought suit against the Cherokee Nation and the U.S. government, they did not have copying machines. He hired people to make typewritten copies of the tribal records in the Interior Department. If you can just imagine the time and the work it took to do that. Then they were bound into these volumes. Some volumes were scattered to other places, like the Snyder Collection at U.M.K.C., and some are at the University of Texas at Austin. Others may exist that we are not yet aware of, as Adams mentioned in one of his writings that he had thirty-two volumes of tribal records.

Other photos in our book of legends were of objects in the Victor Evans collection in the Smithsonian. Richard Adams had been given some artifacts by the tribe in appreciation of his work. After his death, they were sold to Evans, who eventually left his Native American collection to the Smithsonian. I should also mention the wonderful drawings of John Hill from the original book which tell his adventures with the Nez Perce and in a battle of the Civil War in Indian Territory.

One of the luckiest things to happen in reprinting this book was that we were able to include four of the stories translated back into the Delaware language by our native speakers. Nora Thompson Dean had translated one of them, which Jim Rementer offered to let us use. He had been working on several others with Lucy Parks Blalock. To me, these stories in the Lenape language are just irreplaceable. We will never have the same people for these resources again. They were a precious gift from these ladies, and we should treasure them.

We printed each line of the stories in the Lenape language, a literal translation, a modern-day translation, and then the way it was printed in Adams's book from the turn of the century. It gives the reader a much better understanding of the Lenape language. In English we might say that we held a torch. But in the Delaware language we would say literally that we held a "stick on fire." It is important for people to understand how the language was constructed. Adams stated in one of his books that he wished he could convey to people the beauty of his native language. Perhaps this way we were able to give them a glimpse of it.

I should also mention that we were lucky to have the artwork of Ruth Blalock Jones for the cover of the book. We liked the traditional dress of the women in her painting as well as the coloring and setting. That helped to make it truly a Delaware book. I wanted this to be the work of various Delaware people. If you think about it, it was actually the collected efforts of many generations to collect the stories, publish them originally, translate them back to the Lenape language, collect the history and photos, and do the artwork. Syracuse Press was very good to work with and did not try to chop it up or make it into their version of Delaware legends. I cannot say enough good things about Laurence Hauptman for his help and interest in this project. It would not have been possible without his support. Many other people gave me help in my research, and I owe them a great deal. Hopefully, seeing these legends once more in circulation for present and future generations to appreciate will have made it worth their effort.

Oral history interview conducted on May 28, 2000,
at Bartlesville, Oklahoma.

Oral histories by Lucy Parks Blalock, George J. "Buck"
Captain, Eastern Shawnee, and Charles Dawes, Ottawa, appear in **Always**
a People *(pages 35–38, 56–62, and 76–83). Both are now deceased.*

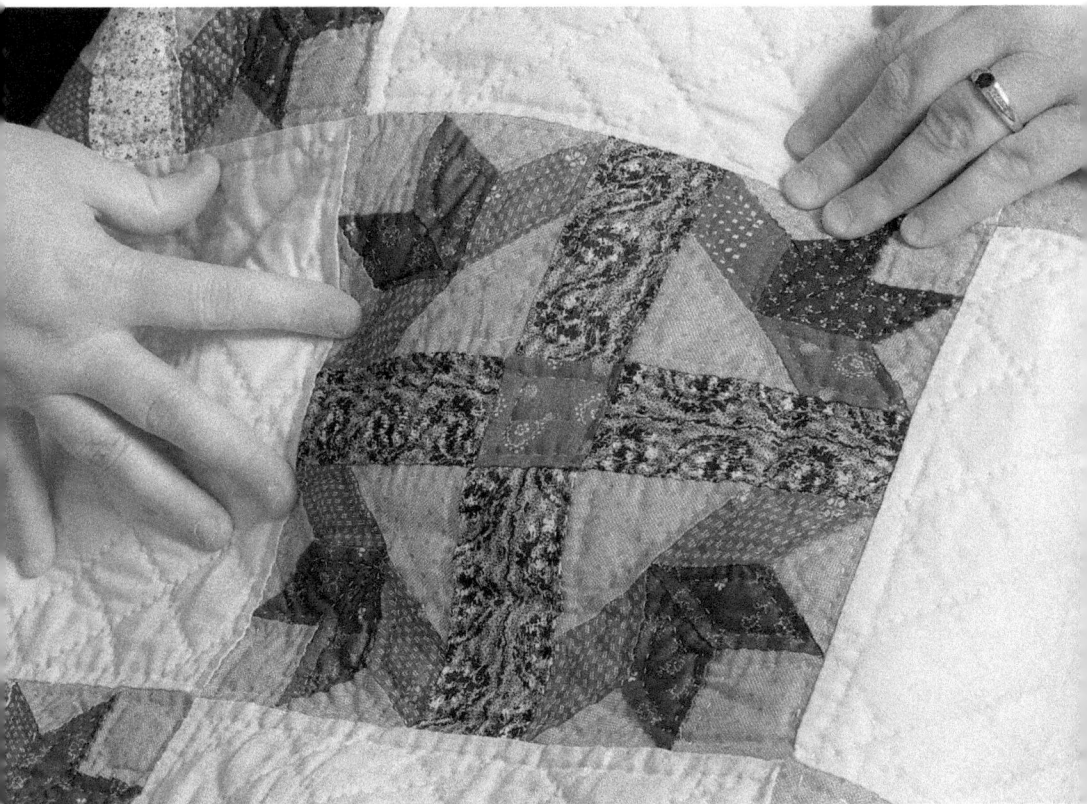

Michael (Mike) Pace at the Lenape Village, Conner Prairie Living History Museum, Fishers, Indiana, in 2006. The brooch Pace wears on his otter hide turban was handed down by his great-grandmother Susie Elkhair.

MICHAEL PACE

Former assistant chief and Cultural Preservation
Committee chair
Born in Los Angeles, California

When I was two, my earliest memory of traveling to powwow was over in Quapaw, Oklahoma. In those days the powwows lasted about two weeks. I asked my Aunt Anna Anderson Davis—Anna Davis, as she's more commonly known—about that memory because I wasn't sure myself, but it was the first thing that I recall. I remember waking up by the fire, and my aunt was over me, and she was handing me my bowl, and she said go get in line. But I do remember waking up by the fire and the smell of that fire and the aroma, and even today whenever I hear that sound and I smell that smell, it always reminds me of that particular incident. In those days, they used to have communal feed, and so you'd just get up and go in line, and they had these huge kettles that they cooked. Women got up very early, and they cooked all these meals three times a day, and it worked out very well, and people had a great time. Those are certainly my fondest memories of that time.

When I was also at a very young age, I think back about probably when I was ten, my Uncle Ray, Ray Elkhair, was a very well-known stomp dance leader, and he traveled around all over the state of Oklahoma, and, in fact, sometimes he even moved down to those areas and found work and enjoyed himself down there singing with the Creeks. And the Creeks, of course, are most notably famous for stomp dance because to them it is a ceremonial dance. But all tribes in Oklahoma, the eastern part of Oklahoma, usually have stomp dances. The Shawnees, in particular, too, and the Delawares. Uncle Ray was very well known, always liked to sing, always enjoyed leading every one of them if he had the chance because he just loved it so much. At that time, my family had a farm southeast of Dewey, and we used to go out there practically every two weeks or sometimes once a month and have a stomp. And, of course, the rest of the family would come, and many other families related to us would come, and we'd enjoy ourselves. Those dances were very special. We usually would have a very simple meal, usually just cooking hot dogs over an open fire or something, and then we would start stomping. And sometimes those events were so popular we'd have maybe one hundred people there, and the sounds that was created by the shell shakers was really special to me. And I do remember one particular incident where, since we lived just on the southeast part of town, the highway ran about maybe two hundred yards away from us, and one night we were down there in the little glen where we held these dances right by the river, and we were down there stomping, and my Uncle Ray noticed as he turned around, he looked up on the highway there, and he said, "What are all those people doing there?" And we all kind of turned around, and I guess we were such a curiosity that people were stopping along the side of the road, and there were probably thirty or forty cars up there, and they were just sitting there watching us down there dancing, probably wondering what we were doing. But as time moved on, we moved on, too. We held those dances, you know, up at the place where we used to live northeast of Dewey at that time, on the Holly farm. And those dances usually we started Saturday afternoon, and we would have [an Indian] football game, and quite a few people attended. And those were very special times. That's what being a tribe is all about, was that sharing. And sometimes those events would be along with maybe a hog slaughter. The men would come over and bring their hogs over, and they'd slaughter them all and hang them up and do all the cutting and the slicing and the fixing it up, and the women would cut them up for hams, and it would be a big sharing time. People enjoyed that. Then we would get down to the socializing and then the stomp. Football games were really tremendous, and we had a wonderful time with those. I still recall a lot of incidents when my women cousins would get aggravated, and sometimes they would actually drag us off the field and beat us up. But we always recall those times and always bring it back to them today. We say, "Yeah, remember the time you hauled me off and beat me up on the side?" We always enjoyed ourselves with this, and that was a more special thing. That was the true Delaware spirit that I remember. Because those songs were special to us, and the social dances that we did were, we didn't do a lot of the social dances that we do now, only because we weren't really using water drums at that time. We would usually stick to just a rattle and just the regular stomp dance leading. So, I do recall those with a great memory and due respect, and I do miss those. There was a point that it did die off. It did fall away from everyone, and people began to move to different areas, and that passed for us for a time. But over the last ten years [1990s], probably, that has made a great comeback, and we're starting to see that again. Individual families are not working on social events where we all do it together, but they're having them at their own place, and their own families are doing those things. So, there are little pockets that are popping up again, and that's something that we haven't seen for awhile. I think that pride is coming back to them, and they are wanting to do that, and I'm very happy to see that.

At a very early age, since I was raised by my Aunt Anna, I was always very proud of being a Delaware. I did not experience those things that some people have gone through where they were raised in areas where there was a certain lack of pride in your history, your family. That was brought on by the society at that time. It was a bad thing to be an Indian at that point. This probably really began at the turn of the twentieth century where there was a definite effort on the part of the government to acclimate tribes into mainstream society. Because of that, they tried to break down those structures within the tribes and to bust those tribes up. The allotment system was used to spread the tribes out so they couldn't commune together as a tribe. Spread them out all over the place so that they would lose that sense of tribal identity. In Oklahoma, the allotment system was used to break those things up [tribal identity]. The young were sent off to boarding schools and forced to give up their languages and their songs and any identity with the tribes. So, for a long period it was not a healthful thing to even admit that you were an Indian. But, in my particular instance, my aunt who raised me was a very traditional lady and instilled that pride into me. I never experienced those kinds of things that happened to other people where they were ashamed to admit that they were Indian. I was always very proud of who I was. I knew who I was, and I wasn't afraid to say so. I couldn't understand why anybody couldn't say that they were Indian. I probably drove my friends crazy because I was always talking about Delaware history or something that we had done, and sometimes they would tell me to shut up. They were tired of hearing it. I was always happy to pass those things on.

Today we work with the Cultural Preservation Committee that was part of a master plan from our trust fund. We set aside 10 percent of those monies from our trust fund to help restore some of the cultural preservation and to protect some of the cultural items that we get, too, that are sent to the tribe from several of our people. We're talking about artifacts from families that want to preserve them. We're also looking at artifacts from all over the country that are held in museums. Under the NAGPRA[1] act we are allowed access to those items, and if we ask to have those things restored to us, they will. So that's one part of why the preservation committee came about. The other part is to help restore and provide funds for the socializing and the things that we have lost for a long time. It's also a way of archiving information for our people. It gives them a little better access to their own history, and it gives them an avenue so that they may come and learn a little bit more about their own culture. It also includes language. We've had a great resurge in the people wanting to learn the language because there are very few speakers left. There are a few of us that know quite a bit, but we don't really consider ourselves fluent speakers. If it can get five or six people

---

1. Native American Grave Preservation and Repatriation Act.

who would study the language in depth because, as in learning most foreign languages, to be truly fluent it probably takes, for an adult, about ten years. The Cultural Preservation [Committee] provides opportunities for people to learn about themselves. Because the tribe is spread out all over the country and it's hard for people to participate in a lot of the programs and events that we have, probably the main event is the Delaware powwow every year over Memorial Day weekend. If we can provide access through the Web or Internet for those people, then we're accomplishing that and that's part of the project, too. But anytime they can come and enjoy themselves with us, that's the top priority for us because a lot of people have lost their tradition. They're proud of who they are, but they don't quite understand their own history, and it's not really their fault. It's just something that happened in the past, and they've lost touch with that. But their willingness to come back and try to learn, that is evidence that they are proud of who they are, and we want to provide that opportunity for them.

One of the important things that we like to stress is learning the social dances of the Delaware. These dances are very, very old, and they've been around for a long time. We've tried to restore that to the tribe and make that more accessible to the people, to get them to learn more about themselves. We've started having monthly dances to allow those people to come in and learn those songs and to learn the dances again. We also do the Go Get 'Em, the Cherokee Dance, the Woman Dance, the Turkey Dance, the Duck Dance. The Stirrup Dance is another one that's very popular. Those songs are the same, passed on, and we will pass those on to our young folks, and hopefully they will, in turn, keep those and pass those on to their children. But those dances are very important to us. That shows who we are, and we have shared those dances with a lot of tribes, and we know that a lot of those dances are, at the very least, two hundred years old because there are other tribes in the East that still do a lot of those songs, and they acknowledge that those songs were given to them by the Delaware, the Lenape people. Today we have that opportunity to pass that on to our own people. Just like we have Delaware Day every year, we also have the Delaware powwow, and we do those same things at that event, too. But the important part is that those songs are ours, and no one else sings those except us, and that's a very intimate part of being a Delaware. We're happy to socialize with these songs with other tribes because today, when you have a powwow, those powwows are really inter-tribal, and they are what you consider a pan-Indian event. It means that we're sharing with other tribes, and so no one tribe controls everything. And the songs that you hear are inter-tribal, and whenever you sing at a powwow drum, the songs that you hear are from very many different tribes. They might be Kiowa, it might be Arapaho, it might be Ponka, it might be Cherokee, it might be Delaware, and so those songs that you sing at powwows are kind of like the Top 40. Every year, there's new songs that are being written by singers, and those are passed on. And then there are old standards, the golden oldies, we sing a lot of those. And those songs are very special to a lot of people. There are family songs, memorial songs, veterans' songs, and many inter-tribal songs. Everybody has their favorites, and those things pass on. Because of this inter-tribal nature of the tribes we know a lot about each other's culture. We have probably at least fifty or sixty different tribes represented at the powwow. We all know each other real well, and we are happy to see each other because we're all old friends, and it's a great way of sharing. And that's probably the last bastion of what you'd consider a tribal ideal. It's a wonderful feeling to go anywhere in the state of Oklahoma, and you see friends. They're almost like relatives because we know each other so well. We're so mobile today that tribal feeling today is in sharing with not only your tribe but many other tribes. And as in any time you do this, there are certain things that you pick up that you add to your own tribal identity. You see things that you like so you say, "I would like to use that in my own way." So, there is a great deal of mixture. We all know where it came from, and we also acknowledge that, so if we have something that we use as a special way, maybe it's a ceremony or we're smoking off or a blessing ceremony, we always acknowledge this is not ours, this is given to me by one of the Sioux, one of the Osage, or we acknowledge those things because we appreciate them sharing that with us. But it's special to us, and we hold it in great respect, and that's why we acknowledge these things.

Back in the 1790s, the Delaware were living in Ohio at that time. After the Battle of Fallen Timbers they were forced to move on into Indiana and actually had already started migrating that way and were living at the plea-sure of the Miami. They invited them to come in to live with them in Indiana. So we lived south of Fort Wayne and kind of east of Indianapolis today. Anderson, Indiana, was named after my great-great-great-grandfather Chief Anderson, who was a very reluctant chief. He did not want to be the chief at that time, but he was a very honored man and very respected, and so he took up that responsibility he may not have wanted. He was probably in his early fifties at that time. But he did lead his people and did handle all those things, dealing with the government or the tribes. The events that took place in that area was probably the third or fourth move that the Delawares had been forced to move since they were originally in New Jersey. All of the state of New Jersey, the lower part of New York, eastern part of Pennsylvania, northern part of Maryland, and Delaware, those were the original grounds of the Delaware. The Lenape people—Lenape is what we call ourselves; the Delaware name is just a designation because we lived along the Delaware River—so we had several events that forced us to move. Probably the most trying incident on the Delaware Tribe was the fact that we lost a great deal of the tribe, almost completely decimated by German measles because we had no natural immunity to that, and we probably lost almost half the tribe from that single event. So, from that point on, the Delawares were very careful in what they did and the wars they fought in because there were so few of them that they preferred to move on and keep together as a group rather than try to stay and live within the white man's boundaries. So they progressed across the country until eventually they were in Indiana. They spent a great many years there, [developing] the town of Anderson, Indiana, and then Muncie, Indiana. We call the northern part of the Delaware tribe the Munsee. So those names stuck, and they are still there today. We're very happy that those names are there. Our legacy, of course, stretches all the way back to even Manhattan. Very few people know that Manhattan is really a Delaware name. It's Minnatan to us. It had just been anglicized to Manhattan. But Minnatan means a place that is an island. All those names that are still there are very familiar names—Hoboken, Pasaic, Susquehanna, Monongahela—those names are Delaware names. It's actually kind of fun to go driving in that area, and you come across a Delaware name people don't know what that means. But if you understand what that means, the legacy is still there. I had the opportunity to come back to Indiana and to be in Anderson and to see the legacy of my grandfather, and, of course, at Conner Prairie, we come back to that museum and do special events there. Mr. Conner was married to my great-great-aunt Mekinges. When we think about how far our tribe has been pushed west and how far we had to walk west, it was very difficult for me to imagine, especially even in Indiana, my mother, being at an elderly age, trying to walk that distance back to where we are today. I don't think she would have survived. That's just exactly what happened to a lot of Delaware people. They were forced to move. They had no food. They had no wagons to carry them. They had no horses. A lot of the transportation was provided by riverboats. But they didn't take you very far. So, it's difficult to even imagine the problems that they faced. We don't really understand that today, how much those people suffered. We don't understand how they truly felt because we have not experienced those things. That's one of the things that I really do in a sense regret that I cannot really truly be like my ancestors. I cannot have those same kinds of feelings. I cannot really share those feelings with them. The sorrow that they must have felt. The starvation that they must have felt. The bone-weary tiredness that they must have felt in having to deal with this every day. And then there were times of great joy when they did arrive at where they wanted to, and they rebuilt their lives, and they brought themselves back together and shared and had good times again. But they knew in the back of their mind that eventually it was going to change again and that this event would happen again, and it did happen to us many times before we arrived here in northeastern Oklahoma. I cannot really be like those people. But what I can do today is to honor the legacy that they have given to me and to remember their suffering and remember their hardships and to remember that what they did they actually did for us to preserve their history, to preserve their legacy, to preserve the culture,

Mike Pace serves as the Delaware interpreter at the Conner Prairie Living History Museum Lenape Village. Three visitors learn about the unique Delaware water drum.

preserve the language. Those things are very difficult for people to understand. But we try to pass those on to our young. I try to explain that to them. It's very difficult for them to understand because they live today in a world of plenty. They don't understand that kind of heartache; they don't understand that kind of hardship. And they truly don't understand until they get to an older age. I'm a fine example of that. It took me awhile. I was very proud of who I was, but I did not understand what suffering my ancestors went through so that I would be proud of who I was. So, that's what we try to do is to bring that to the people, to share that with them, to make sure that they understand what they have today is very special; to be a Delaware Indian, to be a Lenape Indian is very special. There are not very many of us left, and we always talk about that. As Delawares pass on we always say, "Well, there's one less." There may be younger people coming along, but we're hoping that they would take up the tradition to learn their culture. But it doesn't always happen. A lot of tribes have that problem today.

It's kind of interesting that the Delaware Tribe, although it was originally from New Jersey, today has been welcomed back home not only in four, but in six different states. It's very interesting that people are recognizing the Delawares for their contributions to their state's history.

People are beginning to look back at their past, and they're proud of the heritage that they have, and sometimes they're even surprised that it includes Native American history, and it rightfully should. We were there in those areas. There were other tribes that were displaced from those areas, too, and they've been welcomed back because they did play a great role in each one of those histories. The Delawares, in particular, were very well known because they were one of those who had had first contact. In fact, I've often recalled Buck Captain, the late chief of the Eastern Shawnee, who blamed the Delawares for all the events that have happened in the last three hundred years because he said the Delawares had very poor immigration laws. I always recall that. Prior to that point, before colonial contact, we were a very powerful tribe, and we were considered a Grandfather tribe. We handled a lot of affairs. Because we were a small tribe, we did not hold life as useless. We've held life very precious. We would rather work out a problem than have to solve it by a war or any other method. We developed that aura as the peacemakers. In colonial times even more so we became the intermediaries between other tribes. Since we developed the first contact with the Europeans, they relied on us to help them meet other tribes as they passed across the country. Therefore, in the history of the United States, Delawares were always on the frontier. They were always that buffer between what you would generally consider the civilized Indian and the wild. They really did not want to have any part with the European culture. They preferred to stay with their own culture. That's why we were always on the frontier moving out away from [settlers]. We had a great deal of contact with many different tribes. We were always used as scouts. The Delawares were even scouts for General Custer in Oklahoma. They were very well known here. The Delawares also scouted for Zebulon Pike and General Frémont, Captain Frémont at that time. They actually led those expeditions all the way across this country. They truly spanned the whole of the United States. Because of that, we have our very rich history that we like to recall. In fact, there's probably more books written about the Delawares, but it's not very well known because they did not have the glitz and the hootzpa of the western tribes because the Indian Wars were highlighted. But the Delawares were part of American history for two and three hundred years because they were always on the frontier. So, we do have that history, and it's time for us to bring that up and say, "We played a great role in the history of the United States." We're proud of that. We're proud that states are calling us back and appreciating our effort. We cleared the way, we eased that path so that the United States would grow as it moved westward. We did not really take a part in Manifest

Destiny. That was something that came a little bit later, but we knew that we had to move away to maintain who we were. Sometimes we had to do things that we really didn't want to do, that was against our nature, but in order to preserve the tribe you did those things. That's why I'm here talking today, because of the efforts of my forefathers and the things that they left for me to learn and to pass on.

When I look back at the trials and tribulation of my own family, I am one of the fortunate few. Because of the nature of my family and the responsibilities that they took, we are always at the forefront of the things that were done by our tribe. It is very easy for me to trace my history, even back to Philadelphia. I know a lot about who we are and what we have done over the last two or three hundred years, and that's the burning desire behind me trying to teach young people. Kids just don't understand that they need to take this up as a responsibility because they haven't experienced that. I wouldn't want to abuse a child because of that, but it's why we don't have visionaries today. At one point when you were twelve years old, they kicked you out of the house for two weeks, and you survived on nothing but what you were wearing, and you came back, and if you had a vision then you would be able to tell that in the Big House, and they would tell you your path in the future and what those things meant. Today you can't do that; if you did that, you would be sentenced for child abuse. Even though the child may understand it, those things have passed as an opportunity that has just gone on. We can't do that today; that's part of our nature, and we should be allowed to do that, but it's not in our right for us to do that today. Here again, maybe that's part of freedom of religion that you're not allowed to share those things. That's the thing that I truly regret. I can't step back. I don't truly know the feeling. I am honoring them by what I am doing, but I just can't, I don't have that feeling, and that's what I regret more than anything.

Oral history, September 1998 at Bartlesville, Oklahoma.

Oral history by Mike Pace also appears in **Always a People**
(pages 160–167).

*Beginning in 2003, Mr. Pace joined Conner Prairie as a
Lenape interpreter. Conner Prairie is a living history museum
set within the early nineteenth century.*

Jenifer Pechonick puts a coat of paint on the totem at the Pechonick Camp at the 2006 Delaware Powwow near Copan, Oklahoma.

JENIFER PECHONICK

Tribal council member (2002–)
Born September 17, 1976, in Winfield, Kansas

My parents are Joe and Paula [Martin] Pechonick.

I think some of my earliest memories are probably before I could walk, being at the Delaware powwow near Copan, Oklahoma, just having all my relatives there, hustling and trying to get ready to go dancing at night. I'd probably be asleep before we danced, and Mother would be trying to get me ready and trying to get herself ready and trying to dress all the women in the camp. That certainly impresses on my mind.

I remember falling asleep to the powwow drums a lot. And then finally getting put to bed and sleeping all night to the sound of the drum; it was always very peaceful, and I could always sleep and never be scared, up there in the woods. Also, just having almost a sense of autonomy because I could run around and do whatever I wanted to do up there, even though there were thousands of people there. It seems like everyone knew me, and everyone knew who I was, and everyone knew my camp [Anna Anderson's camp]. It was just always a really good feeling up there, up at the powwow grounds.

I can remember being very young and learning things from my great-aunt, Anna Anderson Davis, and I know that she had a lot of influence on my mother, Paula Pechonick. My mother has been a great influence in my life. I've always lived with her and my father and been involved in the activities in which she was involved. I think my earliest exposure was with, like I said, the Delaware powwow. Mother got into the tribal politics, and I became involved at the Delaware Tribal Center in Bartlesville, Oklahoma. I even worked up here as the secretary one summer, and I got involved with the gift shop. I've been to a lot of council meetings and trust board meetings and General Council meetings, seeing, kind of, the other side of the tribe, the more political side versus the traditional side. So I would say that my mother has been the greatest influence in both aspects, the political and the social aspect.

I used to be able to attend the language courses that were taught at the tribal center. But now [1998] that I'm out in Weatherford [College, in Weatherford, Oklahoma], I don't get to attend very much any more. Mother and Dad still keep me up to par, I guess, as to what's going on within the language aspect, which I really enjoy. I enjoy my traditional clothes, and I really think that it's just all a big circle; you really can't have one without the other and have a full, whole feeling about yourself. And the music, I love our music and dances.

I'm really disappointed in my peers that they don't participate more in the tribal activities. I feel like if I didn't have the tribe, I would have a void in my life. It gives me a sense of spirituality; it gives me a goal, almost, a purpose in life. And I feel like without my involvement in my activities, that part of me would just be missing.

I really enjoy getting to travel for our tribe. Getting to go back east to Indiana and to Ohio and to Ellis Island and to Washington, D.C. I've really had a lot of exposure to different parts of the country with that. We usually go back to Indiana; we go back and talk to the schoolchildren, and I find that to be very fulfilling, to go out and educate people to what a modern-day Indian looks like, I guess. I really like to meet people and see their reaction and answer their questions. And I feel by doing that it helps spread tolerance to different cultures, and it helps people understand why I do what I do everyday.

When we're in Indiana, we're usually in the Indianapolis area, and it's so metropolitan there. I don't really feel tied to that area. But in Ohio, when we go back to eastern Ohio, it's not as populated. There's still a lot of the original countryside there. And it just feels like home every time we go there, it's just beautiful.

When we do get outside of Indianapolis to go out to places like Conner Prairie, there is more of a feeling there with the way that area is constructed to be like back in the 1800s when my ancestors were there. There's a neat feeling about that.

I just love to work with the schoolchildren. They seem to have a little bit of knowledge before they come in. But some of their questions, you just have to not laugh because I have to treat every question as genuine. But when they ask my uncle and our chief, "Well, have you ever killed anyone?" Just makes me wonder what they're learning in school and what they're seeing on TV. They really do get a sense of what a modern-day Indian is [with our visits]. One of the children said, "Where did you get your ears pierced?" And I told them at the mall. And they were like, "WOW." That's neat, just to see that I was a real person. They're so reverent when we walk in, they're just amazed and wide-eyed at these real-life Indians standing before them that it's almost like they can't imagine that something like that really exists. And they're always concerned whether I ride horses and live in tipis and what Oklahoma is like. So I try to just draw them an accurate picture of how I really live. They spend the whole day with us, and by the end of the day they're just coming up and talking to you like a normal person rather than just as an icon almost.

Our Lenape tribe has always been called the Grandfather Tribe. I believe on the East Coast we were the tribe that knew how to do things and how to solve problems and conflicts. We weren't a warring tribe; we were problem-solvers. A lot of the other tribes looked up to us, and we were very influential in their ways. I think that comes into my contemporary life. I'm a leader and a problem-solver and not a warring person. I really hold high respect for my ancestors in that way. I'm proud of the fact that we were the people that met the settlers that came to the United States, that we were the people that signed the treaty with William Penn. I wonder why everyone doesn't know that, how influential the Delawares were in the beginning. You hear a lot about the Cherokees, and you hear a lot about the Iroquois Confederacy, but you don't hear a lot about the Algonquian tribes, the Delaware tribe, the Lenape tribe. I think that they played a very important part in the settling of the United States, if it needed to be settled anyway.

I want to say something about how I appreciate the historians. At all of our symposiums that we've gone to, I've been so impressed with the historians. They come up to me and say, "I've started out as just a general historian, and then when I discovered the Indian culture, I decided to be an Indian historian, and then I started studying the Delaware, and I have not studied another tribe since I started studying the Delaware." I really appreciate that those men and women are out there, and learning and promoting the Delaware culture and really trying to get into a society that sometimes is closed off to individuals that haven't always been a part of it. I appreciate their perseverance in getting the ways documented.

Our tribe has gone through a lot of changes in the last decade. It's really an exciting time to be a Delaware. I look to the future and just see it getting better and better for our tribe, for our tribe to kind of come out of the blanket that they were under, almost all during my life; our name getting out there and people knowing who the Delaware tribe is and knowing what it means to be Lenape. I see our group coming together as a people, and once we do come together as a people, then we can move forward. I hope the tribe focuses on education and helping their young people get into school because I feel that education is the only way to succeed in the modern world. We really need to focus on that. And definitely to teach our children what we know and not let our traditions be lost. I think that if we can work together for that common goal, then we can survive in the future.

Oral history, September 1998, at Bartlesville, Oklahoma.

After college graduation Jenifer Pechonick
returned to Bartlesville.

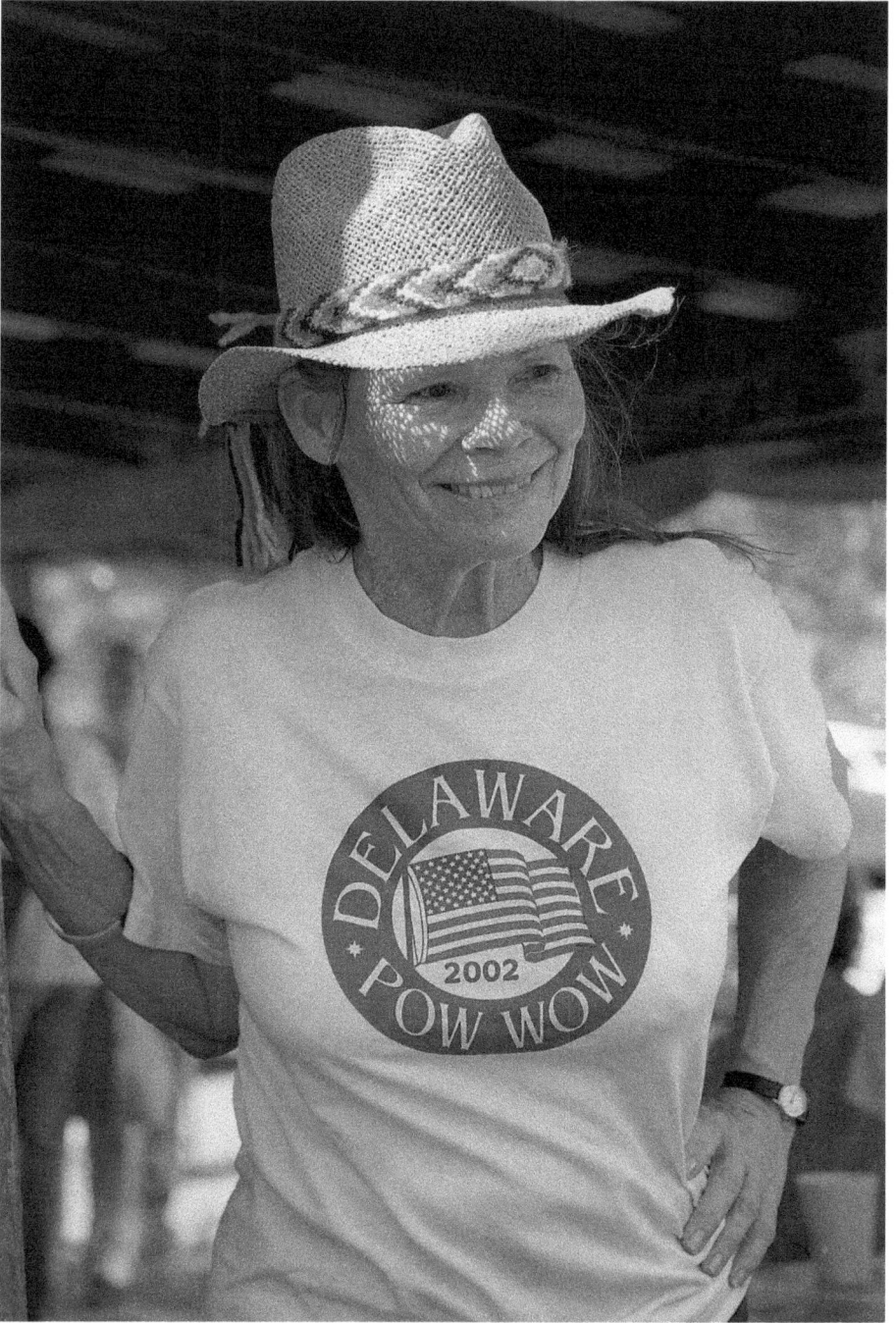

Paula Pechonick at the 2006 Delaware Powwow near Copan, Oklahoma.

PAULA MARTIN PECHONICK

Tribal member; elected to Delaware Tribal Council

I was born outside of Dewey, Oklahoma, many years ago on my Grand-mother Minnie Willits's allotment. She was a Delaware Indian woman that was born in Oklahoma. My mother was born on the allotment, and my sister and I were born on her allotment land. We lived there for several years until the war came, World War II, and people moved to town because they didn't have any cars, tires, or the transportation was bad. My father didn't have to go to the war. But he moved us to town, and then he went off to work on the Big Inch Oil Line that was up in Alaska. So we lived in Bartlesville for a while. One of my earliest memories, I suppose, was when he came back from Canada. I was two and a half years old, I believe, at the time. We were all excited when he came back. My sister and I are just a couple of years apart in age, and we had both grown; he had been gone for nine months. He came in and saw me standing there and called me by my sister's name. He said, "Annette!" And I said, "No, I'm Kathleen!" My middle name is Kathleen. He was surprised to see his Kathleen had all grown up.

My father's name is Frank Martin. He is a white man.

My mother's name was Violet Jean Woody, and she was born out there on the grandmother's allotment, like I said. She was quite an intelligent little girl. My grandmother was raised in a convent. She was kind of a child that nobody wanted, I guess you could say. Her mother had lots of children and several husbands. And this little girl came along, and she lived with some other people for a while, and then they sent her to a convent. And when she wasn't at the convent, she'd come home and she lived with this old Indian lady. Her name was Ora Spybuck. So she lived with the Spybucks for a while. But then she went to this convent. She went to Bacone College [Okla-homa]. And then she had a guardian in Bartlesville, a doctor, and he sold her to my grandfather's family. It was not a marriage made in heaven, I guess you could say. They were married a few years and built the house out on the allotment. My mother came along, and they had a kind of rocky marriage. My mother was the only child. My grandmother was an educated woman. They would go to Kansas City to the opera on the train. My mother had many childhood memories that she could remember, that were nice things to remember. My mother was a very, very intelligent woman. I just said today [to students visiting Conner Prairie] that she didn't allow us to talk what I would call Oklahoma slang. We weren't allowed to talk like other children talk when we grew up. She tried to teach us proper things. She wanted us to have the things she didn't have when she was a girl during the Depression, like dance lessons, music lessons, and piano lessons. So my sister and I had all those things. The grandmother lived with us, and she was a very traditional type woman. So she's there in the background teaching us lots of old Delaware things, and the mother's up front, taking us to dance classes. We had the best of both worlds, I guess you could say.

I learned lots of traditional things from my grandmother and her sister. She had a sister that was a few years older, and she was a very traditional woman. My grandmother had gone to the schools where the Indian children weren't supposed to be talking their language or talking about anything that they knew traditionally. But as the girls grew older, they went to school together, and their allotments were close together after they got married. So they visited back and forth. My Aunt Anna, her name was Anna Anderson Davis, was a few years older than my grandmother, and she [Anna] was really the keeper of the moccasin making and the traditional clothing. When we got older, she helped us learn this. I had a great interest in this. Their grandmother, Mary Bullette Brown, had been a moccasin maker. She was one that came to Oklahoma when the Delawares originally came down from Kansas. She died in the 1920s. She had taken her moccasins over to Pawhuska, Oklahoma, west of Bartlesville, which was quite a mecca for the Indian people in the area. They would sell their Delaware moccasins and purses and clothing over there. I suppose tourists came in at that time because the big oil boom was going on. That was the story that they used to tell us. Aunt Anna was a moccasin maker, and she also taught the language to the people in the sixties and seventies. I was raising my children up in Kansas at the time and just really homesick to come home and learn these things. I wanted to come to Bartlesville and work with my tribe and join the Bartlesville Indian Women's Club, which was another goal of mine. It seemed like every time I came to Bartlesville to visit, the Bartlesville Indian Women's Club was in the newspaper, doing some kind of activities. My sister and I came back to Bartlesville and got involved in the Bartlesville Indian Women's Club. We have three generations of our family involved in this club. This was fourteen years ago, and we still have the three generations involved. But they're getting older now. I have enjoyed this activity with the Bartlesville Indian Women's Club and helping with the moccasin making and the clothes. I participate in their style shows and activities that raise money for scholarships for Indian children.

After moving back to Oklahoma, I went to Bartlesville, and I sat in the council room for over eight years, just trying to learn about the tribe and what was going on with the tribe in this era [1980s.] As a young child I had gone to different Delaware meetings in the Washington County Courthouse, in Bartlesville. They were pretty exciting meetings. Sometimes our mothers would just have to spirit us out of there because the activities got a little in an uproar, I guess you could call it. So they would take us out of the court-house. Those were the old meetings they had. They were over claims mon-ies for our land right here in the Indianapolis area. We had looked for that money for many, many years, and the old people said, "Oh, you will never see that money. You will never see that money." But we did. We actually had the claims from Indianapolis and places in Kansas where the government had just paid the tribe like a dollar an acre for the land where Indianapolis now stands. But [in the 1980s] I sat there in the council room and learned about the tribe and the politics. I did not want to be involved in the politics because it is just messy. It's just difficult. I had need, I guess, to be accepted, and politicians aren't always accepted. I sat there for many years, and it fi-nally became apparent that they did need a new person on the council. So, one day I was appointed to be on the council. Two and a half years later I ran for office, was elected, and now it's time, four years later, for new elections. But in that time, I've learned quite a bit about the tribe, and, of course, we did get our recognition reclaimed two years ago, in 1996, which was a won-derful thing for the Delaware Tribe. I've been involved in Native American Graves Protection and Repatriation Act, what we call the NAGPRA, the re-patriation of the human remains and the funerary objects. We're just getting started trying to travel around and find out where our possessions are. Our main goal at this point is just to reclaim human remains [from museums] and get those ancestors back in the ground and put them to rest again. We had been involved several years ago, back in 1987 [with another U.S. government project in New York]. They were trying to restore Ellis Island, and Ceremonial Chief Leonard Thompson was asked to go back there. My daughter, Jenifer, was eight at the time, and we were asked if we could par-ticipate in the ceremony that they were going to have. All we had to do was pay our airplane fare because the room would be free when we got there. So we got to participate in that, which was quite a treat because this was the first time that the four groups of Delaware people had been together in two hundred years. We met the Canadian Delawares from Munceytown and also from Moraviantown. That was the first time we had met, and it was quite an experience. It felt really good for the four groups of the Delaware people to get together again. Since that time, we have gone to Canada twice [after the Ellis Island meeting]. We had seen these Canadian Delawares several places down the trail [at powwows at different locations]. Finally, we just had to quit and decide we're going [to the Canadian Delaware's] powwow over the Labor Day weekend. So two years ago [1996], we went up [to Ontario, Canada], and we had such a wonderful experience and such a wonderful time. Sandy and Richard Snake [of Moraviantown] are wonderful hosts.[1] We were able to get with them and talk and visit, compare the tribes, and see where we were with our language and clothing and different aspects. We had such a good time, we had to go back this year and visit with them again. They had a really nice powwow, and it was really good to be together.

In the spring of 1997, we came up to do an archaeology dig for Prophetstown [near present-day Lafayette, Indiana]. It seems as though Prophetstown had been lost all these years. It had been burned twice, originally back in the early 1800s, and it had just disappeared. They just didn't know where it was. They knew it was on the Wabash River, and they knew the confluence of the Tippecanoe, down on the Wabash about three miles. But they just didn't exactly know where it was. So they were going to do a dig. Several tribes were invited. It was cold and rainy and quite an experience. It was the first dig that my [now former] husband [Joe Pechonick] and I had been to. I have not seen the collection that we actually [dug up, that] they prepared after we left into a collection. I don't think we found Prophetstown, but we did find the location they are going to put the museums. I wanted to be involved in the Prophetstown Museum because if the Delaware people were going to be portrayed in this museum, I thought I knew how they should be portrayed, and, therefore, the tribe needed to be involved.

I like to see the clothing accurately portrayed. Not that I'm an expert. In fact, I would just love to be able to counsel with my grandmothers and see what they would like there. I like to think I'm making my Aunt Anna and my grandmother proud with what I'm doing with these different things I've learned along the way. I feel like Prophetstown could get out of hand and things wouldn't be portrayed the way they should be. Just a lot of times I know historians, traders, whatever, came back to Oklahoma and bought things, and the Delaware people told them that they were Delaware articles. But maybe it was just something another tribe had given them. And I think, along the way, some of these things that are portrayed as Delaware aren't. I've been to many, many museums, and with many Delaware people, and we can see that some of those things aren't labeled right. But Prophetstown is not looking for old articles. They don't want antique things. It's just going to be reconstructed replicas of things that used to be. In this museum here at Conner Prairie, I was asked to make the clothing for the men's and women's clothing, sort of in the period of 1836. So I worked on that project.

---

1. Sandy and Richard Snake are now deceased.

The Delaware moccasins are unique. There's just a pattern there that makes them Delaware. I told you that we went to New York, and we went to the Heye Museum [George Gustav Heye Center] and walked in the door, and here was all these moccasins in this case. They said they were Iroquois moccasins. Well, it was a learning experience for me. Because, over time, I learned that the Iroquois moccasins and the Algonquian [Delawares are of the Algonquian group] moccasins weren't so far apart. They were both a soft sole moccasin, and they were sewn up the front. They were what some people like to call a "pucker-toe" moccasin. I don't like that term very well. But they both had lots of quillwork on them. The big difference, though, that I have learned about the Iroquois moccasin and the Algonquian moccasin is that the Iroquois moccasin is sewed completely up the back, and so they're turned down, and it forms a cuff in the back. [But] the Algonquian moccasin is just sewed up the back half way, so it turns into a flap. Nowadays, of course, we have the beads on them. Cherokees (Iroquois) wear rather plain moccasins in Oklahoma these days. I've made several pair for one lady that has lots of Cherokee friends. And they're just plain. They're not beaded at all. That's the way she wants them because that's the way they were by the time they got to Oklahoma; they didn't have any beads on them.

When I say the Iroquois or the Algonquian, those are language groups. Amongst the different Algonquian tribes, they have different dialects of the language. It's a similar language, but they do have different dialects. And then the Iroquois; they all have a similar language with different dialects.

We've been coming back here to Conner Prairie to do these children's programs for a week, for six years now. It's kind of a job for us. Myself, I have been doing similar things for several years. Maybe I have done a little more history in the past. But we do have the clothing; we show clothing to the children. The group this year was just a wonderful group. I thought that all the children were quite well behaved. They seem very attentive. They just really seem to listen. They are interested. I don't know how much they will retain from the groups. I hope they do retain some because they were attentive, and I know they were interested. So I'm hoping they will learn. This was quite an experience to be able to come back to Conner Prairie. Because it was right here, at this land, that William Conner had married this Delaware woman [Mekinges] and had six little Delaware children. So I was quite anxious to come back and see this. We were going to Muncie [Indiana] before we started coming here. We've been to Anderson [Indiana] for programs. But when we were invited to come over to Conner Prairie, we knew that the Delaware people [also] had actually lived right here on these grounds. It's kind of a sad story that the wife went with the [Delaware] family. But that's the way it is, that we have a matriarchal system. The women stay with [their mother's family]; the children stay with the mother, and the mother passes on the learning to them. And she decided to go with her family, go with the Delaware people, when they had to leave Indiana. And Mr. Conner decided he was going to stay here. So it's kind of a sad story. In fact, we don't know that Mr. Conner ever saw any of his children again.

I'm not sure that the [Conner] name is actually on the roll [the list of current Delawares in Bartlesville]. But recently, we did run across some Conner people. Our great-great-grandmother Willits was a Conner. But we haven't ever been able to really research that. Although we do have a lot history from our side of the family, we can't find anyone that knows enough about William Conner and John Conner to go back to David Conner (our ancestor). Some of the names that are on those family trees really are the same. But we can't really find that specific connection, that specific relative.

It really is a strange thing when you think about people walking. They did take a very bad trip when the Delawares had to leave Indiana. It was sad to think that when they got to the Mississippi River and had to cross, it was at flood stage. When we did get to Missouri we had bad land, and it flooded. Chief Anderson begged the government to give us another place to live. The Delawares [had] some bad years there. Chief Anderson took us from Indiana to Kansas and had bad years [in between] in Missouri. So when we got to Kansas, he was really happy, because we had about a million acres across the top of Kansas, and we had another million acres that was a hunting range. We had lots of land, and it was rich, lots of animals and game. It was a wonderful terrain. Very good to grow lots of crops. Chief Anderson died a happy man because he thought he had taken us to a place where we could live the rest of our lives. But it wasn't very long until in comes the railroad and the settlers wanting more land, forced us to go on to Oklahoma. When we came down from Kansas, we came right there, outside of Copan, and there's a big hilltop. I think about that. I look up there at that hilltop and think about those Delawares standing up there. There's a pile of rocks up on top of this hill. It's on the Mullendore land actually. My mother said, "Well, I guess you know women were with them because those men wouldn't stack those rocks up like that. It had to be Delaware women." I can stand there and look up on the hilltop and think about the men who stood on that hilltop and surveyed the land around in that countryside, thinking about that's where they were going to move. This was just a party that came to look at the land. And they had to agree to come down from Kansas, and a lot them didn't want to come. They knew they had to leave. There was a bunch of them that wanted to go to Colorado. But instead of going to Colorado, we had to come to Oklahoma.

We've been coming up here [to Conner Prairie] for six years now. We go back [to Bartlesville], and we try to tell people how this program is done and why we do it, and [about] the schoolchildren and the experience and how it's accepted up here and how the program is going forward. You know, there's a lot of Delaware people that just don't want to do it. We have a new man this year because a couple of our regulars just couldn't make the trip this year. It's kind of sad; I would call it apathy; there's lots of apathy in our tribe, and I suppose it's that way in all tribes. They think, "Well, let somebody else do it." Then when we do it they're kind of jealous that they didn't do it. But they won't step forward. You can't even twist their arms to go work for the tribe and let [non-Indian] people know about the [Delaware] people. I watched an Indian girl today; she came up to me at the first session, and she said she was Crow from Montana. I told her that some of our people went to her Crow fair this year. And oh, she was so excited. She said that she was going to go back. She wants to go back to the Crow fair next year and have a traditional wedding there. The [other] Indian people seem to be interested in learning more about the Delaware people, as well as the schoolchildren; the grown people will come up to you and ask you a few questions about the tribe. I know a couple of years ago when we were here, we went out to a restaurant before the programs ever began, and this woman came up to me, and she said, "Oh, I know you." I said, "No, I'm from out of town." And she said, "I know, you're from Oklahoma. I was out to Conner Prairie last year, and you presented a program." She really did recognize me, and I didn't even have on my Indian clothing. She remembered from the year before. So it made an impression on her as to what we're doing and presenting. I had another lady this year come up to me, and she said, "You know, I've been coming for several years with several different groups of schoolchildren." She said, "I learn something new every year." So I think maybe it was [not] repetition for her. The schools were just clambering to come out when this thing first started. The first time we came out, we just came for a couple of days. And then they had to expand it to a week because the interest was so high in the area. I know schoolchildren all over America, in the fall, study the Indian people. But this is more like a hands-on for this tribe. We were the tribe that lived here in their area, you know, their ancestors knew our ancestors probably, if they were along the White River. So I think it does make an impression. It's a fun thing for us to do.

One thing I try to get across is that we're standing in these, what I think are beautiful clothes, and the different things we're carrying and showing that these were really things we used in everyday life. This isn't a costume we have—it's our clothing. We try to tell them the practical side of what we do and what we think. The different things we're showing them have a practical side that was everyday life. It's just part of history.

This program we do is kind of a fast thing. The classes this time lasted twenty-five minutes; in years past, maybe they lasted thirty-five minutes. But it's not enough time for them to have much hands-on and really learn something. In times past, sometimes they made a little craft item to take home, like a headband or a bracelet or little vest, some kind of clothing item.

My sister and I make the clothing and the moccasins. We have grown children and grandchildren. [In Bartlesville] we teach these classes hands-on and actually teach people to make clothing and moccasins. We just hope we can pass this on to someone. And, of course, we hope, eventually, that it'll be our own grandchildren. But if not, then let's pass it on to someone that's in their generation, even if we can't pass it on to our children. Right now, the children are busy and doing other things. My daughter is in college, and she doesn't hardly have time. She did take a fast beading course a couple of springs ago. I was just so overwhelmed to make a lot of moccasins and clothing before powwow time. A lady came to me wanting this Ansipelaon—a hairbow with a trailer that was very highly beaded. She wanted it done, and I didn't have time. Jenifer, my daughter, said, "Mom, I could help you." So I said, "Well, great," because she was out of school for the summer. She had a couple of weeks before powwow, and she really wasn't that busy. She pitched in and took a nice beading course from me. As time goes by, she'll have a little time here and there. I'm thinking that of all people, Jenifer will learn to do these things. My great-aunt Anna, that I talked about, has a daughter named Annette [Reeve]; my sister was named for her. She said she didn't really learn this stuff from her mother because her mother did it. Her mother made the clothing, made the fry bread. She said, "I never learned to make fry bread because Momma was always there to make it." Annette Reeve was learning these crafts and things because she actually helped me. Aunt Anna had died by the time I moved back to Oklahoma, and I was wanting to perfect my moccasin making. I had made many pairs of moccasins that weren't up to what I do these days. I went to Annette Reeve's house, and she sat down with me and helped me, and I learned. She was teaching my daughter Jenifer to finger-weave at the same time. I was listening and listening, and I could hear her telling her all these things about finger-weaving. So when I got ready to learn to finger-weave, I'm sitting there, and Annette Reeve's voice is going through my head. I could hear her repeating those things that she had repeated over and over to Jenifer with the finger-weaving. So it was kind of a memory thing. And someday, I think, Jenifer will have some time, and this will come natural to her to do some moccasin making or finger-weaving again.

Oral history interview conducted October 9, 1998,
at Conner Prairie, Fishers, Indiana.

Paula Pechonick came from Bartlesville, Oklahoma, to participate in the Seventh Annual Woodland Indian Art and Culture Program.

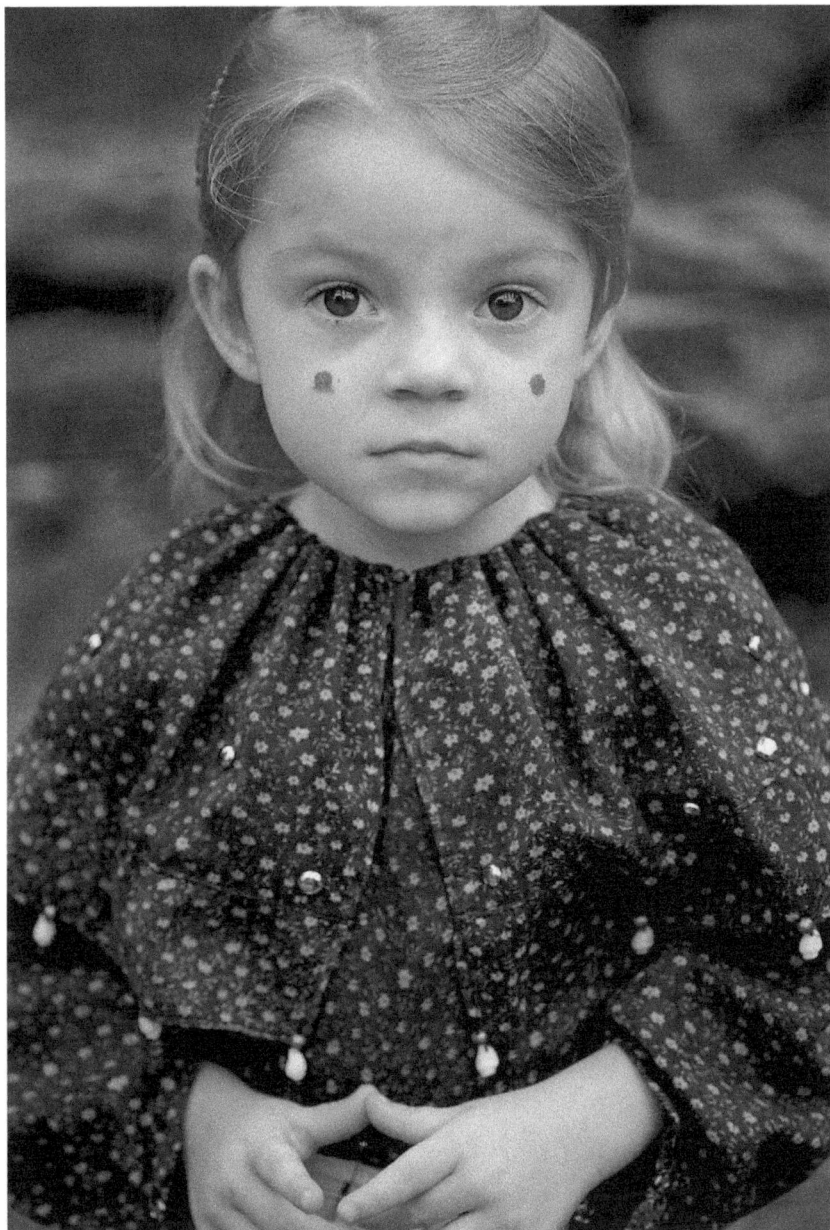

Anna Pechonick, three years old, has been dancing since even before she was born, according to her mother, Jenifer Pechonick. Her dress was made by her grandmother Paula Pechonick. Anna began dancing and attending powwow at three months of age and especially enjoys traditional Delaware social dances such as the Bean dance and the Go-get-'em dance.

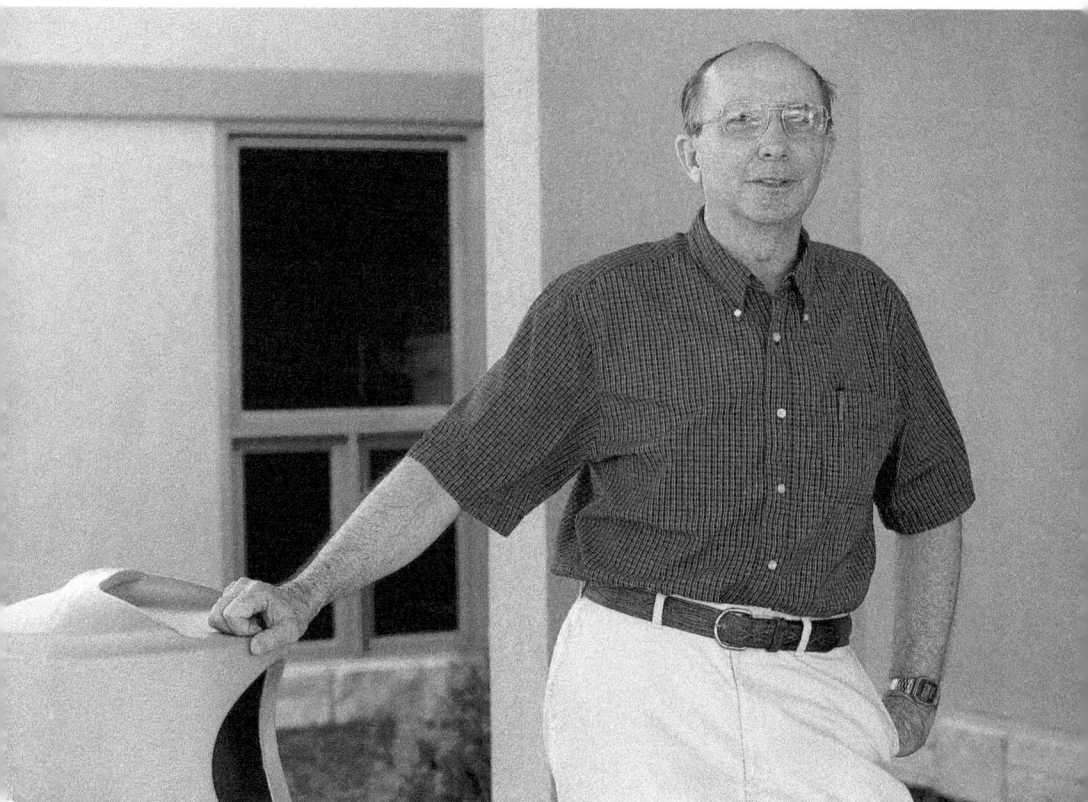

James (Jim) Rementer at the Delaware Tribal Center. (2006, Bartlesville, Oklahoma)

JAMES A. REMENTER

Language project director
Born July 26, 1940, in Germantown
(now Philadelphia), Pennsylvania

The thing that led me to this [Delaware Indian language project] was that my great-aunt Emma, and this was back in Pennsylvania, told me one time that we had some Lenape blood in the family. Of course, that got me very interested in learning more about the Lenape people. Now that I look back after all these many years, I wondered if she was just indulging me, if I was pestering her, "Aren't we part Indian?" And this could have all stemmed from the fact that, as a young boy, I went to a camp called Camp Lenape. Anyway, I developed an interest. I started doing some research on the Lenape, the Delaware Indians, where they had gotten off to. I did research in Philadelphia at the American Philosophical Society Library. And I found correspondence that said that the Delawares, the main group was in Oklahoma. I found also some correspondence between a Delaware man and the anthropologist Frank Speck. So, just on a chance, I wrote to this [Delaware] man's [Freddie Washington] address, which was probably thirty years old, and he answered, and he said to come on out. So, in 1961, that's exactly what I did. Hopped on a bus and came to Oklahoma.

Near Copan or Wann area is where he lived, out in the country. Not too far from where the powwow grounds are now.

There is a little story about my trip out here. It was a lengthy trip, and it took about two and a half days or three days on the bus. I was very tired and I was excited. I didn't sleep much. And he [Freddie Washington] said he didn't live too far from Dewey, Oklahoma. So, when I started inquiring around people at Dewey, Oklahoma, I met a Delaware man—in fact, the uncle to Joe Baker. The man's name was John Fugate. And I said, "Do you know Freddie Washington?" He said yes. And I said, "He lives near here?" He said, "Well, yeah, he just lives up north and east of Copan; it's about, oh, twelve miles from here." So, [Freddie Washington's] idea of near and my idea of near were a little bit different. But after further inquiries he said, "If you go wait at this filling station, there will be some workers getting off of work, and you can probably hitch a ride up there." And that's exactly what I did. I showed up at Freddie's door, very tired. I introduced myself, and we chatted for a while and I was about to ask him if he had a place I could stretch out for a while when Freddie Falleaf, who now runs the Delaware powwow, came by. He told Freddie Washington that they were going to have a stomp dance tonight. And [Freddie] said that he had company, so Freddie told him to bring the company over there. So, I started asking Fred about the stomp dance, what it was. How long does it last? He said it lasted all night. And I thought, "I'm never going to survive this." But we went, and I guess I got re-invigorated with all the activity. We came home about three in the morning. So that started my work on the Lenape language.

As far as any special studies on the language, I had not had any college at that point. I guess I just had a general interest in language as a subject. I had studied several in high school, became proficient at none, because we mainly conjugated verbs, and other things kind of gave me some clues about what not to teach if that ever came up, which it now has. I took some French. Well, if they'd plunk me down on the streets of Paris right now, I wouldn't be able to order a meal. I could stand there and tell them, "I have," "you have," "he has." They would probably look at me very strangely. "My brother's pen is on the table," nice things like that.

Yes, I spent about two and a half months [in Oklahoma] that first summer. I went back to Philadelphia, and I took some courses at the University of Pennsylvania. But during that winter, the more I studied about it, I thought, "Well, the university's been here for about two hundred and fifty, three hundred years, probably be here that much longer." But even that first summer, I realized that the number of Delaware speakers was fast decreasing. And so in 1962, in May, I decided to come back. Again maybe just to do a summer's work and go back. But somehow it didn't turn out that way.

Going back to 1961 again. One of the old speakers that I met was Nora Thompson Dean's father, James Henry Thompson. So, when I came back in 1962, I went to work with him. He was born in 1867. When we started working, I guess he was about ninety-two. So, the way things developed when I came back, Nora and her family told me that I was welcome to stay there. As it turned out, I guess it was meant to be, because I was able to help her with her dad a few years later, when he became feeble, not able to take care of himself as much. I stayed in the Dewey area.

How did I go about learning the Lenape language? Well, initially a lot of it, besides asking words and sentences, involved just listening to her and her dad talk. Or, Nora and other Delawares, when they would come by, or she would go to see them. And then a few years after I had been out here, we had linguists showing up: Bruce Pearson, from the University of California and Ives Goddard from Harvard. Bruce Pearson worked extensively with Nora, somewhat with Lucy Blalock and some of the other speakers. Ives Goddard had some other speakers that he worked with. I did learn a lot from the linguists being here, especially Bruce. He kind of took me under his wing and taught me more about linguistics than what I knew and taught me how to elicit forms and things like this, and how to analyze them. But unfortunately I tended then to follow what the linguists did, and I did not try and record day-to-day conversations. I tended only to record texts, stories, and maybe conversations between two people. But I should have gotten out the tape recorder every time words were said, because there have been many a time since then I wish I had done that.

I guess the difference between the way I was working and the way the linguist would work is that I was actually living in a Delaware household. And I was using the language on a day-to-day basis. Where the linguist would tend to come for a few hours, or in Bruce's case it was sometimes as many as six hours a day, asking the questions. Frankly they are a lot better than I am about analyzing some things, because they can compare with other Algonquian languages, which they have also studied and I haven't. So, a lot of times we exchange information that way. I also do a lot of information exchange with some of the Munsee Delaware speakers [in Canada]. We will call each other and ask, "Do you have a word for this?" Or, "What's your word for this?"[1]

Lately since helping with the classes, we have been trying to come up with words for modern appliances. Sometimes we get funny responses. With Lucy Blalock, we had come up with a word for "computer." Then I started asking her about television. So, I was trying to explain to her what the underlying meaning for "television" is and so on. So, I said, "Lucy, if you have to come up with a Lenape word for 'television,' what would you say?" She said "TV." For "computer," it's *pĕnaelintamahikàn*, "the thinking machine." *Hikàn* indicates it's an implement of some sort. It's something to use, and this could be anything from a saw, scythe, anything like that on down. So this would apply to machinery like a computer.

Dianne Snake is one of the main people at Moraviantown [Ontario, Canada] I contact to go over words. And, speaking a different dialect, a lot of times she will say, "Well, we would say this." And I would have to alter her dialect to make it understandable to me in this dialect. And in some cases, they use an entirely different word.

To give examples of the different dialects, three of the numbers from one to ten are entirely different. For example, nine is *noli* and ten is *wimbat* in Munsee; *pèshkunk* (nine), *tèlën* (ten) in this dialect, the Unami dialect. I remember one time we were having a little joking debate with some of the elders about the word for "tick." Several of us were up there at Moraviantown, and I found a tick on me. I picked it off, and I was showing this one elderly woman, and she called it by the Munsee name, which I don't recall. And I told her *sùktukw*. She kept saying no, no, and whatever the Munsee name for it was.

---

1. Oklahoma Delawares speak the Unami dialect.

The word that we use here for "shake hands with me" would be *òn-kumi,* and the Munsee dialect sounds a little different. They say *wankumi.* But it doesn't mean "shake hands with me," it means "kiss me." So I had to caution some of our people who were learning the language, and tell them if you get up there in Canada, be careful what you say. In another case, Dianne Snake had sent down a coloring book for children, and she said, "Feel free to use this, and you can substitute your dialect for our dialect." So, I called her about a week later, and we were going over a few of the words I wasn't quite sure about, because there was no English in her book. She said, "Well, how would you say this?" We went through several pages, and we got up to a page that had two little boys sitting at a table, and one was telling the other to please pass the milk, and the one boy was saying something like, *Yoh linih muluk* in Munsee. When I read her that page, I told her that we would say, *Mili nunakan.* She said, "What?" I said, "*Mili nunakan.*" And she said, "Do you know what you're saying?" And I said, "Yeah." She said, "But do you know what else it means?" I said, "It means, 'give me the milk, pass me the milk.'" And she said, "Well, don't ever say that up here because in Munsee that would mean 'give me a breast.'" But here we use the same word for both "milk" and a "breast." So, again that's a word you have to be a little cautious with. Munsee adopted the English word "milk" and turned it into *muluk.*

Comparing the two languages, Dianne and I both take notes when we talk with each other. Here [the Delaware Tribe in Bartlesville, Oklahoma], we have a language committee. In some cases, if a new word comes up, I'll run it past some of the members of the language committee and say, "What do you think?" In some cases, there might be birds or animals that we don't have here, or tribes that we haven't known for a couple of hundred years. We find out what they call them, and maybe we will adopt that word, maybe not.

Apparently there were at least three main dialects. The Munsee was spoken in northern New Jersey and southeastern New York State. South of that, there was a dialect called the northern Unami dialect. This was the main dialect that the Moravian missionaries used in their material. Then there was the southern Unami which is the dialect spoken here in Oklahoma by both groups. There is actually very little difference between the two forms of Delaware used here in Oklahoma [Bartlesville and Anadarko]. When there are differences, usually you find that they can be accounted for on a regular basis. A lot of the words that we [Bartlesville Delaware, eastern Oklahoma] say that begin with the sound "ah," [the Western Delaware] put an "h" in front of it and say, "ha." Like we say *alàpsi,* and they say *halàpsi.* It means "hurry up."

Lenape, as a growing language, an evolving language, pretty much ceased maybe in the 1920s or 1930s. By that I mean the number of speakers was decreasing. You had a number of the parents that were telling their children, "I don't want you to learn the language." Parents were getting brainwashed into this thought that seems to permeate a lot of parents in the United States, that if you learn more than one language you'll never be fluent in any of them, which is totally absurd. Consequently we now have people in their maybe sixties or seventies who never learned the language. The language that was spoken even by people in Nora Thompson Dean's generation had become fairly static, it was not growing because if you had two Lenape people come together and they wanted to talk about a refrigerator, they'd probably just say "refrigerator." For TV or television or radio, there was a catchall term, *sëkahsën,* which means something like "on the wire" or "on the iron." It was so easy just to throw in the English word because everybody was bilingual by this point. There really wasn't much of an interest among the younger people up until the late 1960s or early 1970s. Suddenly, Indian things became popular. We had people suddenly interested in reclaiming their Indian heritage. One of the things that I helped with, around that point, was when my Aunt Nora decided to go ahead and do some Lenape language lessons. There were no funds of any sort to help with the publication on these. So, it was pretty much a self-funded project. This [he holds up a booklet] is a book that comes with a cassette tape, so you not only see the language—you also hear it.

Actually I think Nora herself was a little unsure as to whether there would be much interest in these. And when we found out that probably the best way to do them would be to have them run off by high-speed duplication, the minimum order was two hundred copies, and it seemed like such a tremendous amount. And yet they continue to sell, [and they're] into something like their fifteenth printing at this point.

In 1992, under the sponsorship of the Culture Preservation Committee, Lucy Blalock used to come over and teach language classes about every two weeks. We had a class initially of about thirty people. But, as in most other cases where you have people coming to learn a language, especially one that is difficult and as different from English as Lenape is, you have a tendency to have dropouts after a while. I'd say we wound up with a core group of maybe twelve to fifteen. And of those, we had some exceptional students; one was Mike Pace, and another one was Jan Brown. Jan Brown helped put together this little mini dictionary [he holds up *Conversational Lenape*]. Some of the people in our class had said, "Oh, I wish I had a little dictionary that I could just carry in my pocket or purse." Jan got a [computer] program, and she took the words that we had in the class and put them into this little dictionary. And it has basic information on the spelling system. We sell this for all of two dollars [at the tribal gift shop].

It got to the point after about two and a half years where Lucy's health and age prevented her from coming over to teach classes anymore. So some of us from the language committee would go over once or twice a week to her house, which was ninety miles away over in Quapaw, Oklahoma, and work with her on the language.

It's hard to say the number of speakers we have now because how do you qualify a speaker? Do they know fifty words? Do they know a thousand words, ten thousand? I would say that people who have a fair knowledge of Lenape, at this point, in this community, probably don't number over about five. But fortunately they're mostly younger people. People in their forties and fifties and so on. We only have one person left, Leonard Thompson, who grew up with Lenape as his first language.[2]

He prays at some of the ceremonies, and I've done some language work with him. Sometimes he has a difficult time remembering some of the more obscure words. And he's quite deaf, which presents a problem in itself. But, thank heavens, he can read and write, so I can write the things down for him, too.

[Lenape did not start out as a written language]. There have been a number of attempts over the years to write Lenape. The earliest was the Lutherans in New Jersey. Then probably it would have been the Moravians, then the Baptists in Kansas. Of course, each group had their own spelling system. And, unfortunately with people like the Moravians, they restricted the teaching of the written language to people who joined the missions. I often think about how much better it would have been if they would have provided reading and writing to everybody. Delaware might now have a written language, even though it would have been based on the German orthography. It would still be a written language.

[Regarding the church texts,] each group apparently felt what another church used wasn't proper. The Moravians might not even have been aware the Lutheran catechism had been translated into Lenape. But even if they had, would they have used it? I don't know. And when the Baptists started working with the Lenape in Kansas, they apparently did not want to use what the Moravians had put down. So it's kind of like re-inventing the wheel with each new church group that comes in.

About the only thing, I guess, that still exists are a few of the hymns [in Lenape]. Some of those have been preserved in some of the old hymnals. Unfortunately, with a lot of them, we don't know the music that goes with them. I remember a few years back some of the people at the Indian Church in Dewey were interested in Delaware hymns. When they had people come to sing hymns, they would be Choctaws or Poncas or some other tribe. One woman made the comment, "It's too bad we don't have any hymns in Delaware." And I said, "Don't have any hymns? We have over a thousand that have been translated into Delaware. The Moravians did at least seven or eight hundred and the Baptists added about two or three hundred on top of that."

---

2. Leonard Thompson is now deceased (2002).

She was amazed to find that out. But with a lot of the old hymns, we don't really know the music that's supposed to go with them. Now we have adapted in a few a cases. Working with Lucy, we took one of the hymns out of the little Delaware hymnal from Kansas and slipped those words right into the melody of "Amazing Grace." Of course, some people wondered about this because they thought that the translation of "Amazing Grace" should be exact. The same way when we did "Silent Night," they wondered why it didn't mean exactly what it does in English. I've tried to point out to them that the English version does not make an original translation of the original German, because the line that reads, "holy infant so tender and mild," [in] the original German was the "little lad with the curly hair." [In Lenape] we used something like "the pure child," because "pure," in this case, would mean spiritually pure. That's probably about as close as we could get to "holy."

Now, in our language classes, our latest thing is a Lenape language CD [he holds up *Lënapei Lixsëwakàn*].[3] We worked on this with the Miami Tribe of Indians. They had produced one, and we expressed an interest in it. So, discussing this with their language committee, they came to an agreement for us [to] supply what they needed, [and] they would put this together for us. But, of course, we had to do the language part ourselves. We'd have to isolate the Lenape words in different sources and put them on there. These are all native Lenape speakers on here saying these. [The speakers are Nora Thompson Dean, Lucy Blalock, Leonard Thompson, and Fred Falleaf.] It's not me or some of our students in class. I always feel it's best to use a native speaker, someone who grew up with Lenape as their primary language.

This is rather limited because the [Macromedia®] Authorware® program that this is written under only allows for stills, as far as I'm aware of. And you can just show so many things as a still; it's hard to show verbs. You might show washing your hands, combing your hair, eating. How do you show sleeping? For that matter how do you show water? That was one of the problems. We wanted to show water in here, but do you have it in the glass? Since there is no English used, the person looking at a glass of water might think this is the word for "glass." Do we show it in the sink? Well, once again they might think it's the word for "sink," or in a lake? Sometimes words can be a little difficult to illustrate. So a lot of these are names for things: "horse," "dish," "tree," and so on.

This CD is just a very basic introduction to Lenape and Lenape vocabulary and basic phrases, kinship terms, and so on. The hope is, and especially since we're making these available at five dollars a copy, that people will want to buy these and learn some. And once we've piqued their interest,

---

3. *Lënapei Lixsëwakàn,* Lenape language CD © 2002, Delaware Indian Tribe of Oklahoma.

they will want more. From here on it gets more difficult because we have to start introducing fun things like grammar, which is usually a big turnoff to most people. But as one young Delaware man jokingly said, "Oh, I speak Delaware. Chair. Table. Book. Bird." So you do need grammar.

We need to show, how do you put them together? How do you say something about them? What are they doing? What about them? Is it a good book? What's the bird doing? Is he flying? Is he sitting there? You have to get into verb forms. And your verb forms have to agree with the nouns that you're using. And the participles that go around that or describe that also have to agree. People have to learn the concept of animate versus inanimate, which is not used in English. And in Lenape anything that is alive, of course, is animate. But some things are animate that would be considered inanimate, like a spoon is animate, a wagon is animate. People ask me why; I say I don't know, that's just the way it is. There are no genders in Lenape. That I guess would be Lenape's gender, animacy versus inanimacy.

The revival of the language promotes not just an interest in the history, but also the culture of the tribe. And fortunately, I'm happy to say, most of the people who came to Lucy's class, one of the first things they wanted to do was learn how to pray in Lenape. We have a number of people now who have said prayers in Lenape and do it at public occasions and so on. I'm glad for this. It was a rather difficult subject to approach with Lucy because in the Lenape belief, prayers are supposed to come from your heart, your self. Lucy said, "If I say a prayer and they learn it, that's not going to be their prayer." So that kind of put us back a little bit. We had to sit down and think how we were going to do this. So we decided and discussed with Lucy to work out a prayer where we gave the people a prayer format. So that as you go through this prayer, we take some basic prayer words that they used in their normal sequence and then give them options of words. For example, you can say, "Dear Heavenly Father, help me, help him or her, help us." Pick the word you want, then when you go down the line a little bit, "so that, I can, he can, we can stand up well." Which in Lenape, doesn't mean physically standing up, it means to be an upright person in life. So Lucy agreed to that, so that's what we did. We created a prayer format. A lot of people used that. Sometimes people will do this with Lucy and with me, where we tell them to write out what you want to say in English. And I told them to just not use those big abstract words that you might find in some prayers, because they're hard to translate into Lenape. For example, the two words, "amazing" and "grace," would have made the whole first verse of that hymn if we had used that. Because they are abstract concepts, they would be rather long words.

Going through the oral history [moving from Ohio to Indiana to Missouri to Kansas to Oklahoma], not too much was remembered. And sometimes what was remembered were things like in any folklore or legend tend to get merged into one huge cataclysmic event. There were a number of things that happened at the time the Delawares were in Indiana, bad things. There were the meteor showers, which is supposed to be not a good sign. There was the earthquake. There were the witch burnings that took place. And by the time oral history had come down through the generations that I worked with, these just kind of emerged into one big event. They all happened at one time. Also, if you base the things on oral history, the Delawares apparently gave up the Big House at the time they moved into Indiana, or shortly thereafter. Then, all these bad things started to happen. So they revived, rebuilt, the Big House Church. Then you also wanted to bring it down to the more present. I would have to say that I think one of the reasons that a lot of the oral history was not handed down was because there was so much that was happening to the Delawares after they left Indiana. Every place they went, they were told that "This is your home from now on." First in eastern Missouri, then in the southwestern part of Missouri, then Kansas. They thought Kansas was the permanent home. They moved into Kansas in 1830. Even as late as 1865 [the federal government was] allotting lands to the Delaware, which I could never understand because the government knew full well that the Delawares were being kicked out of Kansas. Two years later they were. Then [the Delawares] got into a situation down here where they were to buy a piece of land from the Cherokees that was ten miles wide and thirty miles long, pretty much what is Washington County, Oklahoma. At the time this treaty was to be signed, the three chiefs who were taken back to Washington, D.C., were kind of placed over a barrel and forced to sign this treaty, which meant that the Delawares would become citizens of the Cherokee Nation. When word reached the Delawares still on the reservation in Kansas, they immediately got up a petition signed by over two-thirds of the tribe. But, of course, the Indian agent who was in favor of the merger and getting the Delawares out of Kansas immediately wrote to Washington and said to ignore the petition because it was coming from the unfettered class of the tribe. So the government did just that. And the Delawares wound up merged into the Cherokee Nation, even though they paid a double sum of money to the Cherokees so they would maintain their Delaware identity. This was a situation that up until four years ago [1865–1996] they were trying to get themselves out of. Most Delawares have a lot of Cherokee friends. This is more on a political basis. This is not a struggle between two groups of people, this is more of a political and governmental fight. Finally [1996], the Delawares were able to regain their federal recognition.

The history that most of the Delawares now know comes from the C. A. Weslager's book, *The Delaware Indians: A History*.[4] This was probably one of the first complete books about Delaware history that was ever written, and unfortunately the publisher had Weslager cut way back on this. He had enough for about a four-volume set. But the publisher said that they couldn't publish something that big; no one could afford it. He had a number of other photographs of people and so on, that he wanted to use in there, and they were cut back. Fortunately, Weslager became aware of the traditional Delawares' role in a lot of things and their struggle to preserve the old traditional ways of the tribe. He brought those into the history, even though those weren't as well documented as the historical data that most historians like to use.

Other than occasional meetings or get-togethers for all the groups [of Delawares], I would say they're still much independent from each other. Again, there has been some political differences between this group of Delawares and the Western Delawares.

My primary concern is with the language. We do have people like Deborah Nichols, you interviewed her yesterday, who is very good on history, especially with the Delawares in Kansas and during the Civil War era. If people call my office and ask for some simple answers to historical things that I can easily look up, I'll do that. But if somebody wants to know, for example, how the Delawares dressed during the French and Indian War, I will refer them to someone like Don Secondine, who has made an extensive study on that. I think maybe this is something that I learned from Nora Dean, because, if she didn't know something, she would just say, "I don't know," where some people that I've worked with will just kind of make things up as they go along. I know one man, I asked him how do you say "cattails"; because he didn't know, he just put "cat" and "tail" together and told me *pushisi shkwĕnay,* which means the tail of a cat. Which is, of course, not what I wanted. I was very explicit with what I wanted, the plant, so he knew, but he just created a word.

What I see as the long-range plan for the language, and this may alter according to whatever type of funding we can get because funding agencies have their own little theories about the best way to preserve a language. Total immersion is one of the things that they are really stressing at this point. That's fine for groups like the Cherokee or the Hawaiians where you have a number of speakers who are middle-aged or whatever and can come to class for a couple hours a day and sit down with the kids or the adults and talk nothing but that language. We're not in that situation. Our people are so scattered. We've got almost a thousand Delawares living in California from this group; we've got almost an equal number in Texas. Holding local classes, while it's a good idea, only benefits a few. So, what I envision, first of

---

4. The Weslager book is considered to be flawed with errors in fact and therefore interpretation.

all, we have any number of audiotapes and videotapes of our speakers, our elders, when they were speaking Lenape. These need to be preserved; they need to be copied, put into visual format, so that they can be easily edited. And then individual words and sentences [need to be] extracted from those. And probably create the multimedia database, which would allow us not only the written word, but also a sound file so people can hear the word and, in some cases, pictures to illustrate what it is, what it refers to. Then from this, we should more easily be able to put together language lessons. That then can be used to teach the children or the adults, whoever wants to learn. It's hard to say with the way things are changing, what the future is going to be as far as the media we'll use. The one that people still want at this point is cassette tapes because that's what most people have an have easy access to. So that's what we've been working toward.

I've been working with language preservation. The tribe has very little funds to work with. I do wish that there were more funds available. It doesn't have to be government; private, foundation, whatever, for language preservation; it seems like a lot of it is more geared to tribes that have a number of speakers. Are you familiar with the situation with the Miamis, where they have basically no speakers that grew up with Miami as their first language? You have people like Daryl Baldwin who have learned the language and are attempting to teach it. But, that makes it difficult for them to find funding. We're about in the same situation. To preserve the language, to me, is a very important thing. It goes along with the culture. It explains a lot of things about the culture. Whether there will ever be a community of all Lenape-speaking-Lenape people [including] their spouses and children, I don't know. But I would like to leave this world and leave behind the material that they could use to learn their ancestral language if they want to. I would prefer using the voices of the elders and not just me repeating some word list that I've written down.

Oral history interview on May 29, 2000, at Bartlesville, Oklahoma.

DeAnn Sears at the Ketchum Camp, 2002 Delaware Powwow
near Copan, Oklahoma.

DeAnn Ketchum Sears

Tribal member
Born in Lawrence, Kansas

I was born in Lawrence, Kansas, where my parents [Dee and Annette Ketchum] were in college. As I understand, they were trying to finish up education and start up a family. I love Lawrence and I love Kansas. I feel like it was a good beginning for me. I have a lot of good memories there. I lived there until I was in high school. And then we went to Kansas City, [where I attended] high school. I went back to KU for college and didn't finish there; I transferred to Texas and met my husband, and I'm still there.

I can't remember not being exposed to the Delaware family, the extended family, my parents both being Delaware. My sister [Kala Thomas] and I were brought up in a lot of influence from our family. I think that we were always very aware that we were Delaware Indian, very proud of that. I can remember going to school, and when they want you to mark on your enrollment card your ethnicity, my mother was always, like, "now don't put white." And so, of course, that's what I tell my children, too; they know who they are, and they're proud of that. We travel back to Oklahoma all the time because of family. And holidays we were with my grandparents. So both sides of the family had strong ties to their Delaware roots. I think even the meals we ate were influenced [by Delaware heritage], but we didn't talk about it. Now that I'm a grownup, I always think about how we used to have cabbage and stews and that kind of thing. We started going to dances, this dance in Copan, I think when I was about four or five. I haven't missed one, I don't believe. I think the one year when I was getting married I might have missed one. But then when I was in my grandmother's home or my aunt's homes, they would tell stories, and we would sit around and listen to their stories about what they were doing when they were young. We were always going through and looking at pictures and looking at who the old grandfathers were that were no longer living, and whose names came from who, and who you looked like, and things like that. I remember in Kansas we were brought up in a middle-class environment, and I remember thinking when we would come back to Oklahoma, especially for gatherings, I would look around and think, "Hey, I look like these guys." Just kind of a refreshing thing for me. I was always amazed because my Grandmother Lil, my father's mother, went to a boarding school, and she told us they whipped them if they spoke the language, so she was trained early that that was not acceptable, and my grandfather, too. I was always amazed that that wouldn't be okay [to speak Delaware]. They couldn't practice their ways. I think they were even encouraged not to come home. My mother's mother, Violet, she's just an extraordinary and a wonderful woman. I remember Great-grandmother Minnie being around, and she was a quiet woman. I couldn't wait to go in the other room so we could look in her room and look at her things; she always had really neat things. She just represented the past, real strong.

I have three children: a fifteen-year-old boy [in 2000] who looks a bunch like my dad; looks so much like a Ketchum. I have a thirteen-year-old daughter. I have an eleven-year-old boy. All of them look a lot like the Ketchums. I'm hoping to pass [Delaware heritage] down to them even though they're very busy with their own world, full of sports and friends and schoolwork and their musical pursuits and all, but my husband and I make a really huge effort to be involved with the culture. My parents are so strongly involved in the culture they have helped me keep my children in touch and grounded with their Delaware heritage. Some of their dancing and some of their songs, my parents write letters, they put in language. Both my parents are very involved in helping me with that. At Christmas [1999], they had just been to a burial, and so we set up the table, and my mother was telling them what they experienced, and they just listen and take it in. And sometimes I hear them [the children] telling their friends. They're very aware of the culture. We haven't mastered it. We're not experiencing it as much as I would like. But they're getting it, it's sinking in. I'm happy about that. I would like more influence, but we're kind of in an area where there isn't much.

I'm married to Andy Sears. We don't think that he has any Indian family. But we're not sure. He has some interesting names in his background that my mother thinks he might be. She's been trying to track that down for us. But his family has not celebrated that or embraced it or tried to find out. He has pretty much identified with my family in the Delaware people. And he has taken on more of a support role. Any dances that we go to, he is dressing the boys. He hunts; he likes to keep the hides and tan them so we can make the boys leggings. I even made a buckskin dress. So he's very involved from that viewpoint.

My great-grandmother Bertha Ketchum married Charlie Ketchum; lived to be a hundred and something. She had some interesting stories, but one of the most amazing things that she told us was coming over to Oklahoma in a covered wagon pulled by horses and just enduring that hardship and not knowing really where they were going to land or when they were going to quit moving, and ending up in Oklahoma. And in my day of computers and jets, you just think, "grandmother?" But when I would press her for details, she just didn't have many. She's gone now, and now I regret not pressing for more details. She had this potato she would wear on a string under her blouse, that she believed helped her with her health and that it pulled out all her arthritic aches and pains. And she lived for so long. She had some interesting practices like that. I don't know if someone taught her those things and where she got them. I don't know many stories about their travels here to Oklahoma. I do know that my Aunt Anna Davis spoke the language; she was the elder in the camp, and she ran things. She was a beautiful woman. And she told us about her allotment, and they found oil on her land and made her a wealthy woman. She did a lot of burials; she paid for them. I just remember looking at her and thinking that she was an amazing woman. I think about the past, it was overwhelming. I took it for granted.

My father being chief currently [2000] is kind of a mixture of feelings. I'm thrilled for him, and he is completely capable. He's an excellent leader, and I've always known that he is a very strong man. He's a beautiful blend of tradition and understanding of it. But also he's a man that has visions for the future. He's not trapped in the past. His education helped him to be futuristic, a visionary. I always remember him speaking of moving forward. My Uncle L.B. [Lewis B. Ketchum], chief of the Delaware Tribe, 1983–1994, achieved for so long. I don't remember who was chief before my uncle. Uncle L.B., he was a loving, playful man. He was my dad's older brother. It seemed appropriate to be chief, being a big brother. He knew what was going on. This is how I viewed him. He has four sons, and they're our cousins. He did talk about political matters of the tribe with us. People came over to shake his hand and talk to him. Now that he passed on and Curtis Zunigha took [the chief] position, I could see in my dad's heart, a time of waiting, but we all knew that he was feeling called to run. I really do think it's a calling and it's an appointment, something bigger than yourself, something bigger than you just want to do. It was his time, and he knew that. I have now noticed a difference in the way he would do things than L.B. would do things. I might not have ever recognized the differences if my dad wasn't chief. But my dad, he's more of a public speechmaker. He does blessings and prayers. He wants to dance; he's been dancing for years. He wants to sing; he wants to play the drum. He's got all aspects, whereas my uncle ran the tribe as a business. My dad's very hands-on and relational. He's not as easy-going as L.B. was. He let's me know, he let's my children know, what is appropriate and what is not, what he expects us to be at. He's very sweet about his expectations, fatherly, but you can tell sometimes that he wants us to understand that we have a responsibility and he takes on my boys, he takes an interest in their understanding of what's going on as we do it. And I appreciate that. My mother's constantly teaching, constantly talking so she's always right there by his side. And I think they see it as, in my opinion, a partnership.

My mother is an excellent craftsman. She understands the technique on how to do ribbon work, the beading, the blouses, the skirts, the colors you use, the designs. She's teaching us those things. We are a bit lacking in our actual skill for making beautiful beadwork. Every year she still reviews, and I'm still trying to conquer that. My daughter Hannah, I think she's gifted and she has an aptitude for it, so my mother seems to be directing her. She's totally teasing me. But my mother's never disappointed, and she never gives up. I think both my parents are good teachers, and that's probably why my children will understand what they're doing. Not so much as what I've taught them, but because of their grandparents. This last dress, my skirt, my mother helped me do the ribbon work, but I had to put it on, and I'd bead it around the bottom, and she supervised, but I did it. And I'm proud of myself, every time I put that on, I think wow. I did attempt, with her help, a pair of moccasins for my husband. My husband has made the boys' dance stick, and he beaded a fan for my daughter. He picks it up quicker. We're not going to forget any of it. I'm slow.

We come back, and I become very aware of the fact that I will have grandchildren someday, and I will have parents that aren't as physically capable to jump up and do all these things. My sister and I both have been paying attention quite a bit to the protocol of dancing and the arena and the drum and how to respect that. How to wear your clothing, why you wear what you wear. Things like that so I won't have to rely on my mother because I realize that she won't always be there. It seems like the last couple of years I have thought that more intensely. And then with my father and my mother being such leaders, I wonder at times if that will be expected of me. I'm not sure that would be expected of me. Sometimes I'm even overwhelmed with understanding. My parents understand who, even among their friends, among their peers, who the grandfathers of those people are, and they understand their names and where they came from. And when I say, "Mother, I need to understand this. Could you tell me again?" she understands that she has to tell me another time. And I feel, "Will I ever get there?" We've done some teaching in the classroom for my children in their own schools, and I have felt so inadequate. And yet my mother is saying, "No, you know so much more than you realize. You just haven't taken the role of teacher on yet." And she's very encouraging like that. I look at her and feel like I will never get there.

My oldest son is Jake; he's fifteen today [May 28, 2000]. My daughter's name is Hannah Kate. She was named for my Aunt Kate, my Grandmother Lil's aunt who raised her. I just loved that woman; she was a beautiful Indian woman. My third child is Clayton Ketchum. We gave him my maiden name so that we could have a boy with that name. My grandmothers and my aunts were very strong women. So that sometimes makes me feel I can't live up to them. But on the other hand, I go home, and I know who I am, and I don't really have to prove anything, so I feel at ease with that and I enjoy it. But those women, the way they cooked, the way they dressed, the way they danced in the arena, everything about them. And they would tell us, "We don't wear our shawl like that," or "We don't pick our feet up like that." Every detail they understood, and they were very subtle, but they knew who they were. They just lived it. It's very encouraging.

Sometimes people say, "Delaware? I don't know that tribe." And I used to think, how can you not? Because we grew up with such a rich group of family that understood so much about who they were that I would think, how can you not know? How can you not understand our blouse, why we wear this, why we wear these colors?

My grandmother always told us we have to wear our red dots on our cheeks so that the Creator will know that you are a Delaware. But then you don't want to go to bed with your red dots on because that might mean that you are ready to leave the world.

The language is very interesting. My mother has sent me books and tapes, and the kids will try out language, but it is coming back stronger among the people who are living here together [in Bartlesville], where they encourage one another, and they are helping each other remember and talking to each other in the language so that it's not going to die. And I love that. I don't remember that many times that we would pray in Delaware or speak in Delaware when I was much younger. I think because, like I said earlier, my grandparents weren't encouraged at all, they were supposed to forget those Indian things, especially the language and especially some of their customs and traditions, especially their worship. So those were discouraged. But they're not discouraged any longer; in fact, they are very encouraged. And I think because of that it will remain at the surface, and you will hear it and know it. Some of the underground things around with the elders, you just hear one word, and they would nod at each other because they knew what they were saying.

I consider my dance clothes to be clothing for a specific purpose. Everything that you wear has meaning so I don't consider it in any way a costume or a show at all. We were always encouraged to understand that they are Indian clothing. We took good care of them. A lot of work went into them, and they were meaningful.

A traditional Delaware woman's dress would include a wrap-around skirt of wool. Sometimes we make them out of different fabrics, depending on availability or maybe the heat. If you're encouraged to do things the most traditional way, you're going to be wearing your wool. It has ribbon work down the left side and sometimes all the way around the bottom and sometimes not. The blouses have the huge collars; cloth blouses with the large collars decorated to your taste, to your personality, but most all blouses will include silver washers or little studs all the way around. You can add other particulars to the blouse, beadwork, or anything that you've had time to put on the blouse, or something meaningful to you. So there's some freedom that makes it sort of your personality. I think that we copy each other. I copy my grandmother. The men's clothing is very complicated; some of the things

that they have to have on. All three of my children dance, and they are loving it. I really rely on the elders in the camp to help me get them dressed
properly because sometimes I'm not totally sure straight and traditional.
Some of the obvious differences [for boys and men], the bustle or no bustle,
that's easy to figure out, but some of the extras like the trailer and the otters
[a fur piece], their beads, the little beads that they wear crisscross, if they're
not wearing their roach. They have so many details, it's kind of complicated.
I've got the girl stuff down; I understand that; [for example,] the tulip bag.
Your tulip bag should have four sides, and it should have something on it
that represents your life, your family, something personal. So my mother has
made us all bags as a gift. They were a gift from her. She decorated them,
and they're all different because of who she made them for. And then our
fan; my dad made me an eagle fan as a gift one year, and it's got some of the
old feathers that he had out of a fan passed down that he needed to rework.
And he told me exactly whose family it came from. And my mother beaded it
all for me. To me, those are irreplaceable, beautiful items that have meaning
behind them. The colors that we wear, my mother told me that she would
have me wear red because I'm first born.

Oral history interview on May 28, 2000, at Bartlesville, Oklahoma.

DeAnn Sears talks with a friend at the 2007 Delaware Powwow near Copan, Oklahoma. Powwow is a very social time where families and friends catch up on their activities since they last talked with one another.

Don Secondine at the Natives and Newcomers area at the Historic Sauder Village, Archbold, Ohio, in 2004. Don is a silversmith and gunsmith.

DON SECONDINE

Tribal member, silversmith, flute maker
Born January 27, 1952, in Nowata, Oklahoma

One of my earliest memories of my childhood was getting into the chicken house when I was just maybe four or five years old, and the chicken house wasn't ours. The chicken house belonged to a lady that lived back behind us there in Nowata. It was my grandma's house. My mother's mother. And me and my brother were just wanting to pet these little chicks, you know, these little yellow fluffy chicks. In the process of chasing them around inside this little bitty coop, why, I guess we stepped on some of them and killed them before we realized what was going on. When we did realize it, it was too late, of course. So, we hustled home, hoping nobody noticed, I guess. And this lady brought these, I don't know, probably about six or seven little chicks and come walking across the yard. She came into to the kitchen and laid them on the kitchen floor there, and that really made my mom mad. And I guess she wanted Momma to give us a spanking right there in front of her to make sure we got paid for what we did wrong. She wouldn't do it, she wouldn't give that woman the satisfaction. But we caught pretty good when that old lady left and got out of earshot. That's one thing I remember.

My grandfather, Henry Secondine, was chairman of the tribe. That was back in 1970s and early 1980s. That was before we called them chiefs [again]; we called them chairman of the tribe, chairman of the business committee. And I guess he was probably the chief for about twelve years or so, if I recall correctly. Grandpa had always been real active in tribal politics and was on the board, business board way back before that. I don't remember ever a time when he wasn't involved in tribal politics. And my Grandmother Belva [McBurney Secondine] was always interested in doing research on the tribe and genealogy of the family, the family history. And a lot of the stories that she showed me and read to me that she found were very interesting. The Secondines had been leaders of the tribe clear back into the Revolutionary War time period. We're direct descendants of Captain William Anderson [who was chief of the Delawares and for whom Anderson, Indiana, is named]. His oldest son is where we get our last name, our surname Secondine. Of course, it's Anglicized from what his Delaware name was [Sagundai]. And there's a lot of Shawnees over around White Oak that are Secondines. We're all related—we all go back to that same old man, James Secondine [1800–1858]. Our family is both Delaware and Shawnee. But some of the Secondines that live over around White Oak [Oklahoma] are more active in the Shawnee tribal community, and ones over around Bartlesville and Nowata [Oklahoma] which is our family, were more active in the Delaware community. Filmore Secondine [1842–1928] was my great-great-grandfather. He was active in both communities; he led the Buffalo Dance at White Oak in the early 1900s. Seems like the families did a lot more traveling back and forth than we realize at this time period, by wagon. When they went by wagon, of course, they stayed for a week or two, I'm sure. That was a long road between Nowata and White Oak back in those days. Of course, the roads weren't near as good as they are now. The Secondines are active in both Delaware and Shawnee tribal politics, historically and even today, too.

I never stepped out of the boundaries of Oklahoma, I don't think, until I was eighteen. Oh, I'll take that back. We went over into Arkansas one time to visit, but it was just for a day. Basically, stayed in Oklahoma all my life. Then, when I turned eighteen and went away to college, I went to what was then Haskell Indian Junior College in Lawrence, Kansas. Now it's called Haskell All Indian Nations College or University [Haskell Indian Nations University]. That was back in 1970s. A lot changes. It's hard to believe that it was twenty-eight years ago. I went back to Haskell and visited several years in a row here a while back and took part in their homecoming and their art show there, the Lawrence Indian Art Show. It's put on by the Natural History Museum at Kansas University and the art museum there. They have a big outdoor art show and sale on the campus at Haskell. I couldn't believe how much it had changed. A lot of the old buildings that I remember are no longer there. A lot of new modern buildings. The campus has changed quite a bit. But it was good to go back because a lot of the same people that were teachers and instructors at that time and a lot of the guys that I went to school with are now working there in different capacities. So it's always good to go back and see that. Then after I graduated from Haskell, I went down to Texas and worked on a horse ranch for a while and just kind of kicked around. Went back to Bartlesville, Oklahoma, and worked at Reda Pump for a little while. Then I decided I wanted to go back to school. So I went to Kansas University. It's just up the hill from Haskell, right there in Lawrence, Kansas. Studied art there. One of my favorite instructors, and very good friend, was Nick Vaccaro, who's an Italian from northern Italy. He was a real interesting fellow, and he loved Indian art and Native American culture. He collected Indian art. We'd sit for hours, me and him and his wife, and visit. Just a really great guy. But I learned a lot from him about good design, about the American mindset about what art is and what it isn't. I think that for the most part how Indians, Indian people, look at their artwork is a lot different from what mainstream American people see in artwork.

I think that has to do a lot with our whole vision about where we came from and our whole outlook about the Earth and the animals that walk on it, and that we're a part of that. We're tied to the land somehow that I think European people are missing. When they see our artwork, they don't see that. They don't see all of the traditions and all of the old people talking to us all of our lives. They don't see any of that, and they don't understand that. I think for the most part, Nick understood where I was coming from with my artwork, and I think that's why he spent so much time trying to help me understand more about how New York and different schools of thought run here in the mainstream, about what art is. At that time, I was painting traditional Delaware ceremonies and pictures that were in my head from different stories and things that the old people had taught to me. That's one thing about the stories, they come from different sources. There's no such thing as a professional storyteller or story-keeper or anything like that in the Delaware Tribe. All of these stories are handed down to the young people from different people; different elders in the tribe have different stories to tell. So you glean all this information from different individuals and process it, and it becomes a part of you. Of course, that was spilling out on the canvas and watercolor paper. Anyway, after I graduated from Kansas University, I went down to Wichita, Kansas, and worked there at the Indian Art Museum. I was a curator of exhibits there. Also, I taught some of the art classes in one of the back rooms; taught ribbon work and silk screening. The techniques of different Native arts that I knew and picked up from different sources, different people. No one person has it all. Then after spending some time in Wichita, Kansas, I decided I wanted to go full-time art, and so I moved to Ohio. I was doing a lot of work for the Ohio Historical Society and also at different sites. Not only myself, but other people of the tribe would all be invited to come to Ohio and go to places like Gnadenhütten and Schoenbrunn Village and Flint Ridge Memorial Park, their state park, to share cultural ideas and dances and our artwork with the public at large. So I liked it here, and the more I learned about the history of the Delawares when we lived in this area of Ohio, I decided to move to here. I lived along the Tuscarawas River for about five years. All up and down the Tuscarawas River. Of course, when the Delawares lived there, it was called the Muskingum River. But there were Delaware towns all up and down the Tuscarawas and the Muskingum River, clear down into the Ohio River. I got to reading more about the Delawares at that time period; found it very interesting. Every time I'd go hunting, I'd be sitting there in the snow and just all quiet, the hills and the trees all around. I'd think thoughts like, "I wonder if one of my great-great-grandfathers hunted on this mountain two hundred years ago?" So that's what I mean, there's a kinship with the land that European people may not understand. Sometimes I don't think they get it. But those kinds of thoughts went through my head. And sometimes when it was foggy and real early in the morning in the woods, you get to feeling, it feels real secure, 'cause you're all surrounded by fog, and it feels like you're the only person in the world at that time, you know? You feel like you're really close to your Mother at that time. If you want to call her Mother Earth or whatever, but you just feel real secure, all wrapped up in her arms there, kind of like. A lot of times I wouldn't come back with a deer, but that was okay. But there were times when we did come back with meat, and you know, you thank, thank God for those times. But you also thank God for the times you have in the woods, and you don't make meat because you had that opportunity to just look inside in fellowship with the Creator, just you and Him alone. Enjoy what He made. And sometimes it's like He made it just for you, you know? *[Big smile.]*

Jewelry was introduced to not only the Delawares and the Shawnees but to all of the Great Lakes people back during the fur trade. Our form of jewelry is actually an old style of jewelry for Europeans that they don't even remember anymore. They don't know how to make it anymore. The techniques that I use were taught to me by Ben Stone. He studied jewelry made by old Delawares and Shawnees; that, and looking at their tool kits, and looking at the backs of the jewelry, and just kind of put two and two together and figured out how to use the tools. It is a series of punches you punch into lead block or into the end grain of hardwood, so it would cut clean to do the pretty piercings. This, I guess about 1800, is when Delawares started making their own jewelry instead of buying jewelry already made from European craftsman through the fur traders. They started trading just blank silver sheet to the old timers. Lots of times they'd take bracelets and arm bands that got crushed, or maybe they got torn out or something, because a lot of the old trade silver was paper thin. Of course, they were trying to make it as cheaply as possible. It was turned into nose jewels and earrings and other items after it was no longer an armband. So they were re-manufacturing silver from other silver pieces, too. But I've read where by 1820 there was a Delaware silversmith in just about every major Delaware town. It was a very popular trade item that had become very quickly an accepted commodity, and nowadays it is just a traditional part of our ceremonial clothing. The armbands and, of course, there's new pieces made out of silver that used to be made out of bone, like roach spreaders, hat bands, brooches of all descriptions, sizes, and shapes. A lot of those are very much Celtic in origin. The Luckenbooth, you know, the double-hearted crown, the crown double hearts were betrothal brooches in Scotland. And the Claddaugh, it's a single heart with a crown on it. We call them Owl brooches nowadays. But those brooches were directly from Europe, and they're still being made by Indians today, and they're called Indian jewelry, you know, Delaware jewelry. A lot of the old brooches, the great big ones that the ladies wear. That was the main reason I got into jewelry and silverwork was because there wasn't enough of those great big brooches being made by silversmiths from other tribes because they didn't use them. They used the smaller ones. Anyway, the big ones, I like making those for the ladies back home. And even though I live in Ohio now, I have done work for a lot of the ladies back home over the years. That's what motivated me. When you go to Copan and see the ladies all lined up in a row, dancing together, you see all of the silver and the ribbons fluttering in the breeze and the red paint on their cheeks. It just makes your heart swell. Makes you so proud of them. It's a beautiful sight.

I have had some paintings in museum collections over the years. People ask me if I'm still painting. No, I haven't painted in quite a while. I don't know if I'll ever go back to painting again. I mean, I still have that urge to paint, but right now, my creative drive is fulfilled by making those big brooches and jewelry, powwow jewelry if you want to call it that. Also, I make flutes. And where I work now, at Sauder Village at Archbold, Ohio, I'm a trading post operator. It's the earliest exhibit in the complex. It's dated around 1790s to 1820s. We research all the trade goods that were available to the old Delawares there in Ohio. Not only the Delawares, but other Great Lakes people, too. We tried to make it look just like a trading post. When visitors walk in there, we want them to feel like they're walking right into a trading post in early Ohio, the old Great Lakes area, and ready to do some fur trading. You see all of the trade goods laid out on the counters and hanging on the walls.

I make flintlock long rifles, too. Those are usually special order items for people who want an old flintlock-lock rifle. A lot of my pieces go to re-enactors, the people that re-enact history for educational purposes on historical sites. Some of them go to collectors that never shoot them, just hang them on the wall. But I like making the Christian Springs rifles. They were rifles that were made by Moravian [United Brethren] settlers in Pennsylvania. A fellow by the name of Andreas Albrecht founded the gun shop there at Christian Springs or Christiansbrunn. There's a lot of evidence that there were several Delawares that were gunsmiths there and studied under Albrecht, some of the other gunsmiths there. The old Delawares and Shawnees picked up pretty quick that a long rifle was much more accurate than a smooth-bore trade gun. So the old Delawares and Shawnees started carrying rifles pretty early. But I like to build those because of the connection with the Delawares. I like building the trade guns, too, the old French trade guns, the English trade guns. Any of the guns that were connected with the Delawares in any big way during the eighteenth century is what I try to re-create at the trading post.

One of the biggest influences on my life as an artist was Dr. W. Richard West Sr. A lot of people know him by Wah Pah Nah Yah, Lightfoot Runner. He's a Cheyenne artist. I love that old man like he was truly a relation, like an uncle or something. But he had a great influence on my life when I went to school at Haskell Institute. In fact, I went to Haskell because he got transferred up there from Bacone College. When I was going to Sequoyah High

School there in Talequah, Oklahoma, I was going to go to Bacone at Musk-ogee, Oklahoma. I'd hitchhike all the way from Talequah and catch a ride to Bacone at Muskogee, and I'd take a painting with me. Dr. West, or Doc as what I call him. Doc would take a magic marker and mark on the painting and correct my anatomy on horses, people, and what not. I remember the first time he did that I about passed out on the floor. But I didn't show any emotions or nothing; I didn't want him to know that I was upset, 'cause I truly wanted to learn from him. And he took a brown felt tip and drew on my painting. Anyway, I graduated from Sequoyah, and Dr. West said he was going to go up to teach at Haskell Indian Junior College; in fact, he started the art department up there at Haskell. So I went up there and studied un-der him for three years. It's only a two-year school, but I stayed there three years so I could study under Dr. West. Anyway, he's the one that got me to build flutes. I'd go to his house and visit. Not very often, but when I did, he was very generous, very hospitable; he'd open the door and ask me in. We'd sit there in the living room and visit. I'd only had three or four flutes that he had made. He was, besides being a great painter and a sculptor, an accomplished flute maker. He had one flute that I remember, that stood out in my mind more than the others. It was stained bright red, kind of a deep, rich red color. It was a beautiful thing. I remember as a child, when I lived in Tulsa, going down to Philbrook Art Center and seeing the Indian Art show they used to have there every year. They had a big showcase down in the basement where they had all the Indian art. And they had all of these flutes in this case. They were the most beautiful things I have ever seen before. Different shapes and colors. So I just started building them; he showed me how to build them. Showed me a little bit about how to finger them and play them. And it just kind of took off from there. But I would have to say Dr. West was the one who got me started on that. I use the same wood now as when I was back in Oklahoma and Kansas; cedar wood for the flutes.

Ben [Stone] got me started on using German silver. German silver was introduced to the Indian trade in about the 1840s and '50s. You see the same objects being made that used to be made in the early fur trade out of sterling silver and coin silver, showing up in German silver. And also, they were trading this white metal, fake silver basically, in sheets to the old-time Indians in the fur trade. And they made stuff. There was a real famous Dela-ware silversmith that lived down around Anadarko, Oklahoma. There's a photograph of his wife and daughter. They have silver all over the cape on their blouse, and its all along the ribbon work on their dance blankets. All these old designs, you know, were still being made.

You'd look at the early, early photographs from around the turn of the century, a lot of the older ladies had the great big brooches on. You didn't see those brooches being worn anymore. It really bothered me. It was al-most like a tribal badge, saying these are Delaware women, they've got the big brooch on. And so, I started making those. A lot of the gals wear them now; they have big brooches again. It makes me feel real good. Feels like I accomplished something for this generation. I hope that somebody else will pick it up and just keep it going. I hope it doesn't start to slow down or die out again.

When my son, Isaac, lived with us in Ohio for a couple of years, I tried to get him interested in silverwork, and he was real good at it. He picked it up; he's a natural. And he came up with some design that I started copying him, really good, just natural ability and design of silverwork. I'm hoping that he will pick it up again someday. Right now, he's busy surfboarding and playing basketball and doing all that kind of stuff everyday kids do. But I really believe that some day he will pick it up again. And I've done some workshops in the past at Minnetrista Cultural Center in Muncie, Indiana. And had a lot of students from different Great Lakes tribes, Potawatomis, Miamis, Ottawas. 'Course, they're from all over the Great Lakes area, Michigan, and New York. Who knows where all they're from. But a lot of them were really good at what they did. They picked it up, and they were excited about it because they knew it was a Great Lakes tradition. I really think that will make a difference for future generations. I really hope it does. That was my whole reason for doing it in the first place.

None of the elders really remember the flute having that big of a place in our culture as far as ceremonial or anything. The flute, mainly with the Delawares, was an instrument that was played along with storytelling, for entertainment. The old-time Indians, they didn't have TV; they didn't have radio, HBO, Showtime, all that. So what they did in the wintertime was they'd tell stories and entertain each other. Pass on things that way. The flute was very much a part of that wintertime entertainment. There were certain lullabies you could play on the flute to lull the babies to sleep. I try to stay away from those though when I'm playing it for crowds of people, because I don't want them going to sleep on me! Try to steer clear. That was another thing that the flute was used for, activity. You hear pro and con about the courting thing. Some say the Delawares never used the flute for courting, and then others say, "Yeah, they did." So maybe some of them didn't, some of them did. But at any rate, there was an old man, I don't know how old his flute was, but his name was Ed Wheeler. He was Oklahoma Delaware, and I never did meet him, but I saw a flute that he made. His widow had it. A friend of mine took the measurements, Jim Rementer, he's a linguist back home. Jim took the measurements from the flute and drew it out pretty good and clear for me and sent me the measurements. I started making Delaware flutes off of Ed's design. Later on, several years later, I believe it was C. A. Weslager [Delaware historian] sent us some photographs, some color slides and Xerox copies of black-and-white photographs of different Delaware flutes in the Smithsonian collection. The similarity, the sameness of the flutes that were in the Smithsonian collection, one of them was dated clear back to 1760. It was collected from the Delawares at Fort Pitt in 1760. The fiple system, the tuning block and the reed, the way it was made, looked just like the one Ed Wheeler made, way back in the 1930s or whenever. I just couldn't believe it. So consequently, the conclusion that I came to is our flutes haven't changed a bit, in what, two hundred thirty years? And that's something that we've retained over half a continent and two hundred thirty years of migration westward. We retained the same flute. And our moccasins are the same as they were, cut the same, center seam moccasins. Our style of leggings, our ribbon work, our jewelry, is still pretty much the same as it was when the old people lived here along the White River here in Indiana, in the 1830s, 1820s. You look at drawings by George Winter that were done way back in the early days of Indiana, 1820s and '30s of the Ottawas, Potawatomis, the Miamis. You see the same style of clothing that the Oklahoma Delawares are still wearing today at powwows. All that ribbon work and everything, it's all Great Lakes people that had it. When the Delawares moved out that way, the Delawares and Shawnees, they took that with them. And now, a lot of people call it Osage ribbon work. But when you look at the Osages in the 1830s and the old Catlin drawings of them, you don't see any of that ribbon work on there. But it was introduced to them by the Delawares and Shawnees and Cherokees after we moved out to Kansas and Oklahoma.

Oral history interview on October 9, 1998, at Conner Prairie, Fishers, Indiana. Don Secondine came from New Philadelphia, Ohio, to participate in the Seventh Annual Woodland Indian Art and Culture Program.

Don Secondine, a nationally recognized Delaware artist, offers comments on a student's brooch during a workshop he conducted at the Conner Prairie Living History Museum in 2006. Secondine joined the faculty of Haskell Indian Nations University in 2007 as an art instructor.

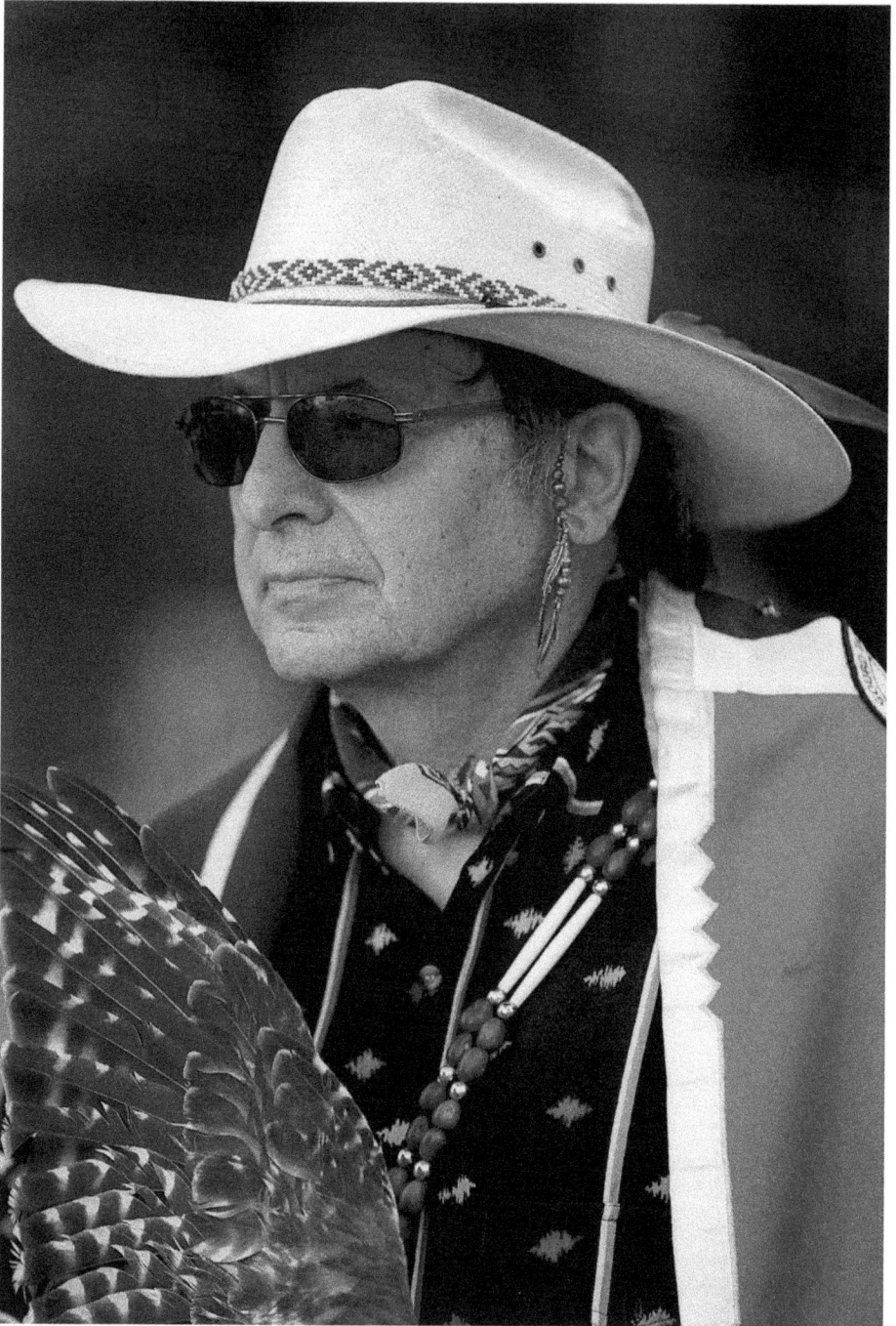

Jack Tatum dances the gourd dance at the 2004 Delaware Powwow near Copan, Oklahoma.

JACK TATUM

Tribal member
Born in Oklahoma City, Oklahoma

My mother ran away from Indian School very young. My mother went to Indian School in Tahlequah, which was a Cherokee school at the time. I am Cherokee and Delaware. My father passed away before I was two years old. Consequently, like many Indian children that was in an earlier age were raised by their grandparents, I was fortunate enough, my mother being a young widow at eighteen years old, [to be] raised by my Delaware full-blood grandmother Jeanette Whiteturkey. My grandfather at the time was my step-grandfather, and I didn't realize he was my step-grandfather. That was Preston LongTail, a full-blooded Shawnee chief and a speaker of the Shawnee language. I, up until I was six years old, I thought I was like my grandparents, both full-bloods.

I didn't learn that I was at least half white, and about my father, so much, until I started school and realizing that I wasn't like my grandparents. It was somewhat of a traumatic experience for me at the time. I remember because I didn't have a whole lot of respect for being white. And I really wanted to be like my full-blooded grandparents, who were my heroes at the time. My earliest experience with the Native American culture was with the Shawnee people, who treated me just like I was Shawnee and a member of my step-grandfather's family, who I thought was my real grandpa. I participated in, like many of the Shawnee children, in that culture at that time. This was in the early 1940s. This was before World War II. I can remember hearing about the war over the radio that we had. At that time we lived very rural. Had no electricity. We lived like a lot of rural Indians in Oklahoma did at that time, without running water, without electricity. We did have a car. My grandfather farmed, was a tenant farmer, essentially on his own land that he leased to a white farmer that hired him to farm his own land. He farmed with a team of horses. Those, the earliest times, were about that farm and about growing up in a rural Indian community.

[When I was] thirteen years old, my mother remarried and was in California. I relocated to California with my mother and started high school in California and lived in California pretty much most of my life. When I did that, I got away from Native American culture in Oklahoma. I married a second-generation Norwegian lady and had two children by her. During this time, though, I had a problem that was common amongst my Indian heritage; my folks, that I can remember, had a problem with alcoholism. And I also have a problem with alcoholism. And it became acute by the time I was in my early forties, and I was desperately trying to overcome that addiction. And couldn't overcome it; just had such a battle with it, that the people who did overcome alcoholism attributed that to a higher power. In searching that higher power and studying the different philosophies, I'd already had experienced Christian philosophy. Christian philosophy and the Christian way weren't bringing me about. Being as desperate as I was, I took up Buddhism and Eastern philosophy. In that philosophy, I found where those that don't know their ancestors may be lost and that they don't know where they came from. And they don't know where they're going. Anyway, I came across that and I thought, "Hey, maybe it's time I go back and learn something about my Native American ancestors that were so influential." All this time I knew, pretty much, that I was Native American and felt a very closeness to the Native American culture, even though I didn't participate in it.

So I went back to Oklahoma, joined the Native American Church, and got involved again with my own Native American culture and philosophy. While doing that, I also overcame my addiction to alcohol. For better than about twelve years now, I haven't had any connection with alcoholic beverages, which I attribute to the culture that I started participating in. And that's how I came back to my tribe and my folks. Before coming back to my tribe, I had had a lot of experience with computers, [especially] when I spent several years in the military, [which I left] in the late '50s. By 1960, I was working for General Electric's computer department and with their first commercial, solid-state system in those days. I had been associated with that high technology for forty years approximately when I returned home. And I thought, "Well, maybe I can be a benefit to my tribe with the experience that I had." And so was encouraged to run for a political office in the tribal council, and I became a member of the tribal council. I encouraged my tribe to get involved with high technology. Well, coming back home was a real experience. There was someone that said, "you can never go back home." And I did experience that. As a child, I grew up on my grandmother's allotment. She owned quite a bit of land east of Bartlesville that is now a very affluent area. She sold her land as she needed money. She wasn't an educated woman. She didn't have an education where she could get a good job. She did have land. And over a period of time, she sold all of her land. So when I returned home, which was right after my grandmother's death, which is the sad part of it; she always wanted me to return. I didn't return until after her death. That's the sad part. But I still feel her spirit is there with me in that country, although everything has changed; it's not a rural community anymore that I grew up in. Where there was once a dirt road that ran through my grandmother's, my great-grandmother's property, and my great-uncle's, is now U.S. Highway 75. And there's neon signs from one end of that land to the other, where once all of my folks', my family's, allotments had been, where I grew up, spent a lot of time as a child. So everything is essentially gone. And that is kind of a disappointment. The other disappointment has been that I haven't been able to make very much headway with my tribe as far as the high technology that I've always encouraged them to get involved with. There seems to be an attitude that, "Well, Jack is Delaware and he's Indian, just like the rest us," and "What does he know as far as this technology. He couldn't know much more than the rest of us," and "We don't think we need to get involved with it," or "It's not that important that we should get involved with it." In fact, there are some Delawares who feel like some [other] people that technology, like communications, like the Internet, for instance, which I've encouraged my tribe to participate and get involved with, has a lot of bad information. Consequently, they shouldn't get involved with it because children might be exposed to information that is not good for them. And they have an attitude of that sort, that I personally feel has hurt the rest of the tribe. But these are some of our tribal leaders that have an attitude like that and have made the decisions really not to get involved.

I'll talk about what it's like to be Native American and recognizing that my ancestors had much at one time as far as wealth and land and playing such a role in this country and seeming to have so little now. My ancestors settled Bartlesville, Oklahoma, and essentially started that community on the Caney River. The history behind that is my white [and Delaware] Journeycake family that I'm a descendent of and a member of played a major role, with Charles Journeycake picking that site to settle in and starting that community and Jacob H. Bartles marrying into the Journeycake family [the widow of Lucius Pratt, who died in Kansas, Nannie Journeycake Pratt] and starting his mill there in Bartlesville. Then sometime later, after oil was discovered and the Phillips Brothers came and the first oil well was drilled on a Delaware allotment, all of a sudden, the Phillips Petroleum Company blossomed into a multi-million dollar company with skyrises and buildings that are huge. To come back, knowing that [once] my folks owned most of that land around there, but now my tribe has a very small, little building in the city that has these high-rise buildings and multi-million dollar people that make such tremendous amount of money. Yet, my family or my tribe is one of the poorest, I feel, one of the poorest Native American tribes in the country.

Coming to cities where my ancestors once had land and were made to move from, like Indianapolis or the outskirts of Indianapolis, here in Indiana and many places in Indiana. And seeing the affluence, the wealth, it's such a great country and everything, but I think, "Well, what happened to my folks?" They were forced to move from a country that's so beautiful and has produced, it seems like so much, and they didn't get to really participate. At times I have to suppress a resentment. And every once in a while it will start to boil out, and I'll start resenting, and then I have to say, "Well, that was a long time ago; everything has changed, and it's not the same," and not to harbor resentment because I know that can hurt you. And so I throw it off and realize that the people here in Indiana are so friendly now and so nice, I sometimes wonder, "What happened? They wanted us to move and didn't want us around. They forced us out of the state essentially." And these people that are here now are so beautiful and so wonderful. It's difficult to explain the dichotomy or the absurdness of the whole situation. But I really appreciate coming back and participating with organizations like Conner Prairie organization and with children; having an opportunity to tell young children, some who never heard about the Delaware people that lived here in their own community, that once owned this land around here. Tell them about my ancestors and the cultures my ancestors participated in. I have found, through my own analysis, and what I knew as a child, that it was an exceptional culture.

I am Cherokee and Delaware. I have met Delawares that claim to be Cherokee Delaware. Well, Delawares got involved with the Cherokee Nation back in the 1860s, and at that time the Cherokee Nation said they adopted the Delaware people. Cherokees felt that they had adopted the Delawares into their tribe. Well, in my case, it's not that I don't feel that I'm Cherokee by adoption, I'm Cherokee by blood. My grandmother, who is a full-blooded Delaware, married my grandfather, who was part-Cherokee. And I've re-searched some of my Cherokee background, which goes back to the signing of the treaty with the Delawares. One of the Cherokees who was a great-uncle of mine, Riley Keys, signed that treaty representing the Cherokee. And another great-uncle of mine that was a Sarcoxie, John Sarcoxie, that was Delaware, signed that treaty with the Delaware. Consequently, my ancestry is really on both sides; they're the Cherokees and the Delawares. I've re-searched where the Delawares fought with the Union during that Civil War. And my Cherokee folks, like my great-great-grandfather, fought with the Confederacy, and my great-great-grandfather on my Delaware side fought with the Union, and came close to shooting each other in one case. If that had happened, I wouldn't be here right now. But it was real interesting their coming together and how that all happened. And how I came about and am here today to talk about it.

I'll give you a little history with the Cherokee-Delaware situation in Oklahoma, which has not turned out so well for the Delaware people. The Delaware, my Delaware folks, were always on the front of the frontier, right on the edge of the frontier. In Kansas, they were forced to Kansas [from Indiana]; they were in the way of progress, in that the railroads wanted their lands up there. So the Delawares had to move. This was right after the Civil War, and the railroads were moving into that area and wanted that land that the Delawares were on. I'll try to tell a quick story here about that situation. The government said that the Delawares could move to Indian Territory and should move to the Indian Territory. The only place at that time that was available to move to in Indian Territory was in the western part of the Indian Territory, or the state of Oklahoma now. My Delaware folks didn't want to move to that part. They knew that where they really wanted to move was further west into Colorado, and the government was just not going to allow that to happen. So they chose to move into eastern Oklahoma, the most fertile part of Oklahoma, and they chose to move along the Caney River, in the eastern part of Oklahoma. And the Cherokee, they didn't really want to give up any of their lands. But they fought with the Confederacy, and the government was coming down hard on the Cherokee for supporting the Confederacy at the time. At that time, [the federal government] forced the Cherokee to free their slaves and give them Cherokee status, just like any other Cherokee, and they became what the Cherokee called "Freeman." They were Cherokee now, not slaves, but free Cherokees. The Cherokee called them "Freeman." They got allotted; I mean they got lands in the Cherokee Nation, just like any other Cherokee, to live on. And the government told the Cherokees that essentially the Delawares would get land in the Cherokee Nation, and the Cherokees were just going to have to accept that. The Delawares picked out the land that they wanted, which was all contiguous. They paid the Cherokees for that land at the time because they were paid for their lands in Kansas. The quick story about that is [the Delawares] were paid something like a dollar an acre. Before they were even moved off of it, the railroads were selling that land for $5 an acre. [The Delawares] complained about that, so the government finally agreed to give another 25 cents an acre. And so, they got some more money, like around $1.25 an acre. They ended up in Oklahoma, thinking they were going to get a contiguous land that they had specified, but they didn't. They got land that was non-contiguous. The Delawares were spread throughout the eastern part of the Cherokee Nation. Like most of the Delawares, my family ended up on the forks of the Caney River, between the Little Caney and the Big Caney Rivers, which became the site of Bartlesville. There is a lot of history involved with how that all came about. The Osages were in that area. The Cherokees went along with it because the Osages were still making raids into the Cherokee country and were still fierce Indians, compared to the Delawares. Delawares came in there and buffered the Cherokee between the Osages. So we were in between, and we had confrontations with the Osages, at that time. Many of us nowadays are married into the Delaware and Osage tribes. I have cousins who are Osage and Delaware. But back there at one time it was very [much like] the cowboy and Indian period, where you could easily get killed by going out into the Osage country.

There was some stories [about that time]. My great-grandfather was a close friend of Frank Starr, who was an outlaw, or considered an outlaw, during that era. It was the era of the cowboy and Indians, or right after the

Civil War, essentially. It was Indian Territory, but there were whites who came into that area. They married into the Indian families and became assimilated into Indian communities. A lot of those white people were, you might call them "frontiersmen," but there were a lot of old cowboys that were hardy, very hardy people. And many of them were outlaws that were on the outskirts of white society, essentially, and were forced out of white society and could easily go into the Indian Territory, which wasn't policed so much by the federal police, although the Cherokees had their own police, and many of the Indian tribes had their own police forces at that time. But they were a lot more lenient, and they didn't bother people that kind of stuck to their own business. But a lot of whites started infiltrating into the Indian Territory at the time because it was again on the edge of frontier and was beginning to be settled. And that land was beginning to be valuable to white settlement. As it became more white, had white settlement in that community, there were gangs, I guess like there were white gangs and Indian gangs. There was shoot-'em-ups and things like that. My great-grandfather got involved with some gun battle in Bartlesville where the whites were going to run off the Indians at this party. And someone got shot. They couldn't ever prove who pulled the trigger because there was a gun battle. But they got my great-grandfather. I guess he was kind of in the lead. They knew of him and put him in prison for about a year, from what I understand, and then let him out because they never really had any proof that he shot the man that was killed. But there's other stories. One story about my great-great-aunt that tells of being in church and the cowboys shooting up the church at the time. It was an Indian church, and the Indians ran out. Well, they never heard of those cowboys anymore, you know. But there was a lot of stories of that sort where there were clashes between the whites and the Indians. But then sometimes there was a lot of whites that were with the Indians in those clashes. I mean, we had, you know, white Indians essentially.

I grew up with my grandparents. I learned, early on as a child, I didn't have a whole lot of respect for the law. My grandparents, in some ways, were almost like outlaws. What I learned, early on as a child, was that laws were made by those that had the power to make them, to keep those that didn't have the power from getting the power. And consequently, it was an attitude that I have to this day that I haven't been able to shake exactly and feel there was a lot of truth in that. And that's what happened in Oklahoma essentially, being Indian Territory. Just like Indiana was at one time Indian Territory and was set aside for the Indians. The Oklahoma Indian Territory was destined to experience the same kind of thing as white settlements found those lands valuable. [The federal government] came up with the Dawes Act back there around 1887. They wanted to get that land so they made a law that would allow the Indians individual ownership of that land rather than being owned by tribes. They knew at that time, I think this was all planned

out, the Indians were naïve enough to not really understand. Some figured
it out, not many did, that they would have to give up that land if they were
assigned it individually because they had no way to maintain the land, to
pay taxes on the land. Things like that changed as far as making that land
all available to whites and Indians. Indians could sell their lands, and that's
what happened. I heard stories about great-uncles that sold their land for
a wagon load of whiskey because they were addicted to alcohol, and they
just didn't know the real value of holding onto their property. Many of the
Indians were not educated nor knew enough about business and how economics really worked to keep their land. Only very, very few did so. Consequently, the land eventually came in to the hands of white settlement. And
that's what has happened to Indian Territory essentially. And being Native
American, well there's a resentment, yeah, that I feel that my folks were essentially taken advantage of back there, and I can resent it. I resent the state
for allowing that to happen and not recognizing that it did happen. Not even
making any allowances, [because] the state doesn't have programs for our
Native American children, education programs that gives them a chance to
become economically independent to purchase their lands back again. It's
a resentment that I have, and it's hard to overcome it and maintain being
good-natured about it and be able to smile and say, "Well, *c'est la vie,*" like
the [French] or that's just life.

I can tell you one of my favorite Delaware stories that was like a prediction or prophecy, that goes back, hundreds of years ago, that was told to
me by a Delaware speaker that has since passed . . . elderly lady . . . that
since passed away. Reminds me a lot of my great-grandmother in that she
had humor. She could laugh and talk about the Helusis which is kind of a
"no-account" in Delaware. Helusis. But the story has a moral and not exactly the moral that you might think it has, that pops out at you right away.
It's about the tribe that goes back a thousand years ago or so. But the tribe
was in very bad shape, in that there was famine all over. They didn't have
enough food to exist. But the spiritual leader and wise man at the time realized that there was a powerful creature that had a powerful spirit connected
with it that once terrorized the community. If they could find the remains
of that creature, the bones, if they could find even a bone from that creature, prepared properly, they could get whatever they wanted with a wish.
So they sent the men; all went out looking for the remains of this creature.
Who should find it was like my Delaware elder referred to as Helusis, which
is like a "no-account" or "old no-account." Anyway, this character comes
back, and everybody's elated about him finding the remains of this powerful creature and that he's going to get whatever he wishes after the spiritual
leader prepares the bones. And he did, he prepared the bones properly. And
everybody gathered around to hear what this guy was going to request in
his wish. Everyone was looking forward to the tribe really prospering and

getting all the food that they wanted. He gets ready to make his wish, and he wishes that he was so attractive to the women that they would fight over him. They're dumbfounded; I mean, like, they can't believe this character would do such a thing when they're all starving to death. They're really disgusted with him. Why would he do such a thing? They're asking why would you do this to us? And he's saying, "Well, I've never been attractive, and women have never liked me very much, and I've always wanted to have women want me, and this is what I wanted." And they're so disgusted with him they leave. Sometime later, they hear noises that are hideous, screaming, and the men think, "Oh my goodness, offspring of this creature must have come back to terrorize the tribe again." So they rush over there where all the noise and the screaming and the commotion is coming from. And they find these women have been fighting over this man; they have torn him apart. One of them is carrying his head, another one a foot; pieces of his body are going in all directions with these women that have carried him off, fighting over him. After hearing that story, I thought about it a lot. There's a lot more to it than just getting what you wish for and being careful of what you wish for, which jumps right out at you. But it's like what happened to my own people. We're scattered all over. We got people in Canada. We got people in southern Oklahoma; we're not together. We got people that have even been lost, down into Mexico. And what has it been over? Essentially greed. And that's what greed or thinking of only yourself can do to you.

Oral history interview conducted on October 9, 1998,
at Conner Prairie, Fishers, Indiana. Jack Tatum came from
Bartlesville, Oklahoma, to participate in the Seventh Annual
Woodland Indian Arts and Culture Program.

Clayton Sears's scarf slide was given to him by his father, Andy. It features a star design representing Texas, the Lone Star State, where they live.

Kala Thomas is dressed to dance at the 2007 Delaware Powwow near Copan, Oklahoma. Delaware women carry a shawl over their left arm as they dance. The decoration on the shawl indicates she is a member of the Turtle Clan, the clan of her mother, Annette Ketchum.

KALA KETCHUM THOMAS

Tribal member
Born in Lawrence, Kansas

My early memories were my dad [Dee Ketchum] being in coaching and my sister [DeAnn Ketchum Sears] and I and mom [Annette Ketchum] going to the games and that kind of thing. We didn't probably hit a powwow until I was six. I remember that very well because it was very exciting. There were lots of cousins and relatives around. It's always been that way, as powwow is like a reunion for us where we get to see people because we didn't live here where it was going on. There was just a lot of play and fun. We got to dress up and dance. I watched Mom putting all those things together; you just kind of reap all the benefits as being the kid and having no responsibility. And then some important people like my great-aunt Anna [Anderson Davis] who would be there, and she would always set us down, my cousin, my sister, and I, and teach us some of the Delaware words like how to count. I just thought that was fascinating that she felt like such an extension of the culture. At that time I wasn't really raised in a real heritage-aware atmosphere. It felt like we just came to powwow and played Indian for the weekend. But she made it a realness to me in just hearing some of her stories as a little girl. I was fascinated about that. My Great-grandmother Minnie [Willits Woody] had passed away a year before, and I kind of started understanding her uniqueness, and her uniqueness was because she was a Native American. I felt really privileged that I had that in my family. I really remember Aunt Anna and watching her cook, and her hands—she just had these old Indian hands that looked like she'd just done so much work.

My dad coached basketball. He was a big-time basketball guy. Of course he was always golfing on the spare time.

I think because I always felt like I should have been the boy child, I retaliated at that. "I'm going to be girlie; I'm not going to be sporty." And also it wasn't that big a deal for girls to get real involved in sports as it is now. They weren't that encouraged. I knew my dad really wanted me to be athletic, and he encouraged me to play basketball to some extent. I did it to whatever level I wanted, but I didn't pursue it much.

Well, Haskell Indian School is at Lawrence, Kansas, and I felt that influence of having a college there, and there were a lot of Indians that lived in and around the area. But I was so young I didn't have much involvement with it. And I don't really remember hearing too much about the Delaware history in Lawrence either. It's more of a college town because of Kansas University. I don't have a lot of remembrance of the Delaware history there.

My mom was sewing, and she and her sister [Paula Martin Pechonick] were putting together outfits. I think that's how it came about. I know that they consulted with my Grandmother Martin; and Grandmother Minnie had passed on a lot of things, too, because she used to dance at powwows; and then they kind of went out of fashion for a period of time, and they were bringing it all back, and that is exciting. We could sense that.

1965–66. I'm not sure what the date or the year of the first powwow, the Delaware powwow, was. After that, my mom was sewing a new outfit pretty much every year. I don't remember where the first outfits that we wore went. But if you go into my mother's cedar closet now, you'll see some of the dresses that we wore when we were probably ten or eleven. And it's kind of funny, because the fabric represents the time a little bit, too; the early seventies. We have our old fans; they were kind of scrappy looking. But you get them a little more polished the more you go, and you start looking around at what everyone else is wearing and carrying. It is a bit of a fashion statement even out there.

I think that it wasn't until probably about eleven years ago I became a little more aware because I was in my late twenties. And the reason I think that is because I lived in Europe for all through the 1980s, and I would come back during powwow. I would skip Christmas even just to know that when I would come back I would hit powwow. That was the beginning of my year, powwow time. But I kind of relied on my mother, and I still do. She's the craftswoman and my dad, too; they are both very involved in it, and we rely on them way too much. We're starting to realize that we needed to learn how to do ribbon work and beadwork. My sister and I were just having this conversation yesterday, because our daughters are very concerned about what they'll be wearing next year because they've outgrown their outfits this year. I was always aware, but I kind of relied on my mother to make sure that I had something appropriate when I came in, because my life, outside of that little time when I came back, was far removed from the culture. I would wear some of her stuff, too.

When we went to school, of our friends that we ran around with, I think that I was the only Indian. There weren't any Indians in our school district that I know of. If there were, it wasn't something that we came together on. Really, there weren't a lot of people that were involved with anything [Indian]. It was just we lived there and conducted a normal lifestyle, and we would come back here, and I would feel through my roots or my heritage more because they were living in it more in Bartlesville that in Kansas.

We moved a few different places outside of Lawrence. We moved to Kansas City when I was in ninth grade. I had graduated school in John Michigan School District.

I went one year to Kansas University. My parents had moved to Dallas the year before that. I decided I wanted to move to Dallas, and I pursued my modeling career at that point, and then I stayed a year in Dallas and then moved to Europe.

I started out in London, and then I went to Milan and Paris, and then I ended up spending time in Switzerland. Then I found myself in Germany for a few years. You bounce around a lot when you're in that industry. You always have to have an agency.

I was a catalog queen, to be honest with you. I always wanted to be gracing the covers of *Vogue* and *Harper's Bazaar,* but that didn't happen. I did commercial work. Just different apparel jobs and some runway.

I had a little house in Dallas, and I would come back in between seasons. Then I would go back over when work started picking up again, and I did that for a good nine years.

I got married in between there. My husband was a model as well. And when I found out I was pregnant, my last trimester I came back here to Oklahoma to stay with my mom and dad for three months before I had Whitney, my daughter. She was born in Claremore because we didn't have insurance, so that was always great that the Indian hospital took care of me. I think there is a lot of things that Indians don't pursue because they just don't know what's available to them. I do know that all my daughter's immunizations we had done at Indian clinics, and they were all free. It was like, "Wow, this is a nice provision." My mom knew some places and contacts so I followed up on them.

I am really proud of my parents and my relatives and my forefathers. I believe it's a privilege to be in this family, to be related to real leaders. How it affects me, I don't know, I haven't had a calling to get involved, and I never lived in the core where the political issues were being brought up. But I care about it, and I have an opinion about it. I just really observe, like my uncle when he was chief. I think there is a real difference between him and my father that I see. My dad was kind of getting in there and really being active and learning the old songs. He came in from another angle and perspective than my Uncle L.B. Ketchum. Uncle L.B. had a lot of business knowledge, and he brought a lot of class, I think, to the tribe.

I think that what my parents did was observe this huge void within our people. We didn't know how our forefathers did things, traditions, and when my dad got involved, and he had this hunger to know more about how they did things. He wanted it to be authentic and true, not just some made-up thing that one of the elders had vaguely remembered. He wanted to really know it. So they started doing a lot of exploration themselves, digging into the history and doing research. Then, really pulling out the elders, interviewing them on what they remember and what songs can you share with us. He really studied it. It was amazing; each year I came back my dad knew more. Just his ability, the way he just jumped in. He could just do it; he just learned it. I mean, it's not easy, the language, the songs. I think it was in him. His passion to learn the culture became almost like a full-time job to him. He has been in the ceremonial position, assistant to the ceremonial chief, Leonard. It is something that he wants to preserve for us and for his grandchildren.

Honestly, I don't have a lot of recall of the language. My parents, I hear them saying words here and there, but I tell you what, it's kind of mean, because I'm the person that lived in Europe for nine plus years, but language is not my forte. I don't have a good mind for remembering language. I have decided to get the tapes, and I really want to challenge myself to learn. I know that's not a strong point with me, but I do think it would be really neat to translate some things into the native Delaware tongue.

Europeans are just fascinated with the Indian culture. That would come out because people would say, "Oh you're American." Or I'd be mistaken for being Italian or some other nationality until I opened my mouth; then, obviously, I was American. So they would ask my ethnic background, and when I would say American Indian, they were just awed. It was really warming to me. Suddenly they were fascinated, and I because important. So that did come up. And that is one of the reasons I didn't really work that well in Dallas, because I was always being asked what my ethnic heritage was, or I was too dark, or I'm too this. I looked just enough too ethnic for the All-American look they were into at that time, whereas now it's very cool to be exotic or different.

I remember little Indian ways, little things, little remedies, little bits of culture that would just come into everyday life kind of situations, where they would talk about how they handled things. Like, my Grandmother Minnie would say that she had a smooth rock that she kept when she would remove her hair with it; she'd just rub it on her arm, and the hair wouldn't grow back. The stuff just sounded like some made-up silly things. I was not educated on that. I just think that in a way I feel a little slighted that my grandmother and my great-grandmother didn't share what I have. I think they just took it all for granted. Certain ways of life, things they just knew, and maybe they didn't even think it was pertinent to share. Plus my time here was limited. We came on Christmas, and we came for powwow once or twice a summer. So it wasn't like I lived the days in and the days out where those things come up, and they share them with you. So I thought like that maybe I was a little more removed.

Wild onions and eggs, which I couldn't stand, hominy, which I couldn't stand; there was a lot of food that I didn't like. I always liked fry bread. And the stew, my great-aunt Anna made great stew. I don't think we've ever had a pot to match that stuff. Things were real good. The foods my Grandmother Martin, that was Minnie's daughter, she cooked with a lot of spices, and she always had some unique flavors go in there. I think my sister and I kind of cook like her. I didn't have a whole lot of training in that. We just make it up as we go.

My daughter Whitney and my sister's daughter, Hannah, are so into making fry bread this year, which I'm so glad. They just begged to enter the fry bread competition at this year's powwow. Annette Ketchum was a little particular about letting them make the fry bread for the dinner. But I don't know what the big stigma is on making the fry bread just so. It's like a reputational thing. So anyway, it's a big challenge. You can make good fry bread. And my daughter just steps up to the plate on any kind of challenge, so that was her end on getting some recognition. She's very big on that. I think it's become a big hoopla. It's kind of funny. It started in our camp. Indians are big braggers; you know how they like to brag a lot. So it was sort of like a challenge; to make the best fry bread that was put out there. It just kind of naturally occurred, and one Saturday morning we had a bunch of people come over. So we had to pull in some outside folks and judges, and it kind of happened and it was fun. It was just lighthearted basically. So now every year we do this because it kind of brought us together. But then we made it into a big thing. Now we have to have plaques and aprons made, and we have to give consolation prizes, and we have to have an official fry bread drum song. Now it's like you don't want to win, because you're going to have to host it at your camp and have to think up all the prizes.

My mother didn't want my daughter and my niece to go there because her family might win. So she's discouraging them. The deal was that they were the first ones in the fry pot, and the oil was too hot so their batch got burned. So they said that didn't count. So they went back and made another batch of dough. Meanwhile the other contestants were frying up theirs, so when Hannah and Whitney's bread was the last in the pot, so it was the most hot and fresh that the judges tasted, and so therefore they won. I think that had everything to do with it.

The judges are the elders that really know their palate and have authority on that.

Next year we'll have to have the plaque and the apron made up and the first-runner-up prize. We have to provide the oil and the cooking facility. Mothers worry; we have to make our camp presentable.

We originally started camping at the Davis camp on my mother's side. My dad would just kind of come in for a token appearance. This is in the very very early days, and my dad was into making money. It just all of a sudden, with my dad, it seemed to just hit him that he needed to be involved with this. His mother would always come out, but they wouldn't camp. Then I guess they collaborated together on making a Ketchum camp. That was a good twenty years ago, or longer. We just shifted over from the Davis camp to the Ketchum camp. It originated on my mother's side of the family, that whole interest and draw to come to these powwows.

My dad and his mother saw the need to make their own campsite. And that's where we have camped from that point on.

We're eating and in the powwow. We always worry about what our meal is going to be. My mom is the head cook and will plan the meal and will delegate who needs to do what. It's pretty healthy, don't you think; except for that fry bread it's all pretty healthy. A lot of desserts, though. Cobbler is a big dish around camp. My Grandmother Lillian could make a great cobbler. I think that Indians were really into good food, vegetables.

They used to have rations. That's what we were talking about the other day. It used to be that Friday morning or Saturday morning they would call over the big speaker, "Come and get your rations." And it was, like, you could tell who the "in" families were because they would get the big nice pieces, cuts of meat, a lot more vegetables. So my mom started sending me and DeAnn into separate camps because they kept giving us such slighted rations. So we would pretend we belonged to another camp so we could get some more. But "they" used to hand out meat and potatoes and carrots and all kinds of stuff for your stew; onions and the whole bit.

The "they" was the powwow committee. The all-powerful powwow committee. They determined a lot of things.

To be honest with you, I felt like I was "city girl" who came in at this specific time, and it was a big playtime for a while. But as I've gotten older I realize the importance, and as I see my parents' involvement in the things that they've learned, it's come alive for me and real for me. But one thing I always remember is the drum has a certain effect on you. It's like the call of the drum, and it will call you back year after year. Maybe people who don't have [Indian] blood don't understand that. You just have a real appreciation for the drum. It's the heartbeat of the people, and I really felt that every year. I start having a sense of responsibility to my children. As much as I love my husband, I feel, like, why wasn't I more aware? I sometimes wish I would have married an Indian man to keep that blood running, because it's just such a family-centered thing, and he doesn't feel part of it. Sometimes that makes me feel sad. But because I want the traditions to carry on, I encourage my daughter to have prerequisites, to find an Indian man to keep it going.

My son, Colton, he's eight. He just got roached this year. It's like he's come of age. They decided it was time for him. He's been dancing since he was little bitty. He gets a lot of the hand-me-downs from my sister's boys. Which is kind of nice because they always had something for him to wear, but nobody really paid that much attention to what Colton was wearing until this year. He has to look good out there, and he's officially dancing now. And he really took that to heart. I think the roaching ceremony signifies that you're seriously wanting to be a dancer. I didn't get a solid explanation for that myself, so I probably need to hear what Dad really has to say about that. Colton danced alongside my dad. We practiced in the living room. We play the tapes, and Dad shows him the steps. Dad is a coach. He really coaches his grandsons and expects for them to pick it up and put it into practice. But we live in California, and we're not around to do too many powwows with my family. So Colton doesn't get a lot of practice, but he's picked it up pretty good. The roach is a headdress made out of horsehair that stands up and has a little ridged roach that comes down, one or several feathers on top. For my son it was one eagle feather. My father had it made for him, and it's a little smaller size. He finished off some of the details on it.

Eventually Colton will go into whatever he wants to. It's like Clayton, my sister's son; he's doing grass dancing now, and he's learning a whole different style of dance.

I showed Whitney, my daughter, how to dance. We all showed her; she watches. There's plenty of us to emulate. When she was really small, she and Hannah would go around in their little outfits, and they kind of had their own beat going there, but they were just so cute.

She's [Whitney] talked about fancy dancing. I was kind of thrown into doing some of that. They need different styles represented, and because it's quite aerobic, my dad thought I could handle it. They gave me a videotape about two minutes long, and I had to watch her footwork, but I'd been seeing it all my life. I always admired them so much, and I thought, I could do that, and so I pulled it off. But it does come with practice and learning the beat of the drum and that stuff. Sometimes you feel like you're being an imposter. It's a lot of little issues. You have to have permission to dance. And it's not my tribe. The older I've become, I've wanted to stay more traditional with what's Delaware.

The shawl is extremely important. I did make one of my shawls, and I took a lot of pride in it. I've made one that I really like a lot. And probably because I made it that means a little more to me. But my mother has definitely done a lot of the work for my daughter. Of course, she leaves a lot of detail work to me. If we want our shawl to be tied then we can do it. Like our blouses, if we want beading on the edge or any whatever details, we have to do that ourselves. She'll make the base of it, and anything extra we do.

I think that my kids are probably even more aware of traditional things and dress and what things mean and things that are sacred than I ever did. But my parents know a lot more now than they did when I was my kid's age now. So it's a good thing. It's really coming back now a lot more than it was when I was real young. My parents are living it now much more than they did then. And I think that is calling my sister and me to a position where we need to keep it going. That's the thing that's just so great about preserving our culture. You feel it; it's heartfelt.

I think in my younger days the cosmopolitan pursuit of a glamorous career was the forefront for me, but as I have settled into a family, I see the importance of the drum. I see the importance of being close to my family. I've lived my entire adult life far away, and I'm only able to come back once a year and it's at powwow time, because that's in my heart to come back. It's like a big family reunion. The older I've become, the more I want to be close by. I will be back.

Oral history interview on May 30, 2000, at Bartlesville, Oklahoma.

Whitney Thomas carefully places red dots characteristic of Delaware women on her cheeks before entering the dance circle. The dots are worn so that the Creator will recognize, after death, a woman as Delaware.

WHITNEY THOMAS

Tribal member
Born March 1, 1988, in Claremore, Oklahoma

What does the powwow mean to you?

It's like family, the only thing that I follow. It's the only traditional thing we have in our life. [The Thomas family live in California.] It's something inside you. When you get here [the powwow], you feel like you're at home even though it's all dirty and gross [the outdoor campsite]. It means a lot for me to come because it's the only time I see my family, and then, like, it's kind of soothing to be out here.

Talk about making fry bread.

I started making fry bread when I was ten, with my cousin Hannah. They wanted us to enter the fry bread contest 'cause, I don't know why, they thought it would be fun, and it [the contest] originated in our camp. My auntie [DeAnn Sears] actually didn't want us to win because you have to host it [the next year]. My grandma [Annette Ketchum] told us it was a good traditional thing, and that's the first step in learning—like, passing everything down. It was really easy for her to pass that down to us, and ever since we entered the fry bread contest, now we have to make it every night [of the powwow], but it's okay. And, um, it's just, like, a gooey icky mess until you eat it, and then it's good.

What does it mean to you when you can get dressed in your Native clothes and go to dance?

It feels like, it's, like, something inside you. I've been doing it since I was, like, four years old; this has been a part of my life. I know it means a lot to my family. It's kind of like an adventure; you come out here, and you're not really playing dress-up because it's, like, something inside you—holding up tradition and everything. But it's not something I'm required to do; it's something I want to do. It makes me feel important.

Can you imagine yourself being in your grandmother's shoes someday, and you'll be the one passing these traditions on to your grandkids?

Well, I don't know; it's, like, I better learn the traditions before I can pass them on because she's kind of got big shoes to fill. She does everything. Her and my grandpa do everything; they know all the ceremonies. They know how to speak and everything, and that's a really big spot to fill. I don't think we could fill it. I think our moms will probably not learn it as much as us, but they're going to be a big part of passing it on, so we'll have a little more time to wait.

Your mother and aunt say sometimes interest in tradition skips a generation.

That's their own little excuse for not having to learn anything. *[Annoyed facial expression.]* Skipping a generation. "I don't want to learn to cook fry bread. Oh, it skips a generation." "We don't want to learn how to make the clothes; it skips a generation."

What do you enjoy about traditional dancing?

I kind of enjoy getting dressed 'cause it's, like, I'm kind of girlie, and I like to play dress-up. Like the clothes; they're so pretty and everything. I just like when you walk around with your family, and you feel like you're part of something. The drum—it's like something inside you; you want to be there all the time. But then sometimes, you want to go take a shower. When you go out there it feels like everyone's your family even though they kind of are—like everyone's my cousin. It feels like it doesn't really matter what you look like, what you're doing, or anything. It just matters that you're in touch with your heritage, whatever that means. I think my favorite part is when you go out and dance—the feeling that you're doing something that's important to your family, and to you, and to your ancestors. Not that I think they're, like, spiritually there or anything. But I think it's important to keep the tradition alive. That's the main reason we come out here besides to have fun and be kind of weird. But we come out here to keep it going so it's not a lost thing.

You don't get a chance to see your grandparents that often. What do your grandparents mean to you?

I really respect them more than a lot of [other] people because they've learned so much, and they're a really big part of this whole tribal thing 'cause you know my grandpa's chief and all that. Besides the fact that they're my grandparents and I love them, they're just awesome people. I really respect my grandparents because they've taken it all upon themselves to make this whole tribe [more traditional]. I think that they're the main thing that's been keeping it alive [tradition] 'cause they took the time to learn the language. My grandma spends all year making our clothes and the bandoliers with all the beads all over it and everything. It's just, like, they've learned a lot of it from Leonard [Thompson], but without them we wouldn't have any of that; it would kind of be lost. We wouldn't really have a point of being out here because a lot of the tradition would be lost. So, I mean, I don't think everyone out here realizes how much they do, but they really do a lot. I think without them it would be missing.

Oral history, May 2002, powwow grounds, near Copan, Oklahoma.
Oral history conducted by Michael Atwood during filming for
the documentary **Long Journey Home**, *produced by*
WFYI Public Television (Indianapolis).

Whitney Thomas shows great-grandfather Lewis Ketchum her family album pictures.

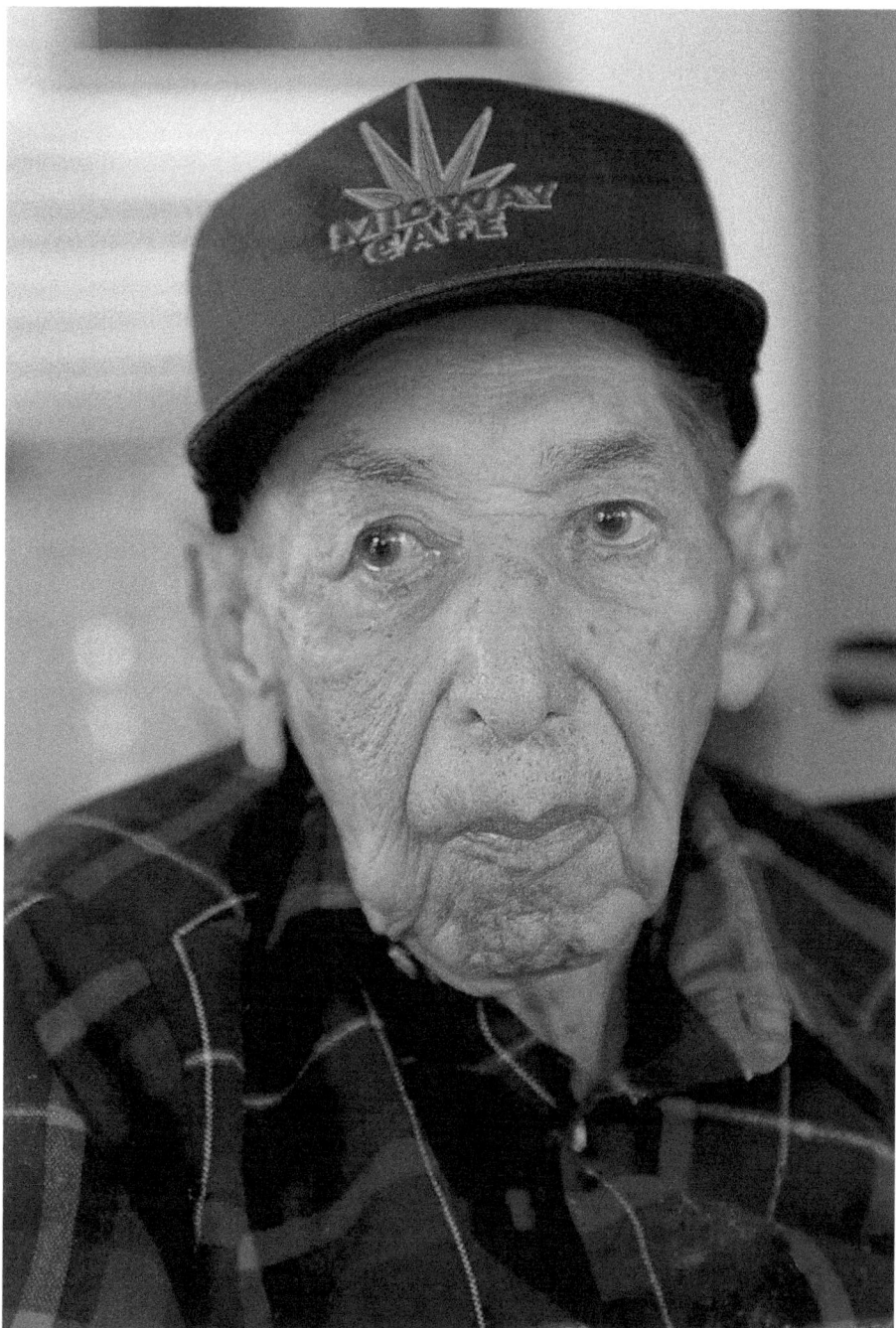

Leonard Thompson at the 2002 Delaware Powwow near Copan, Oklahoma.

Leonard Thompson

Delaware elder, ceremonial chief
Born April 13, 1904
Died August 31, 2002

My name is Edward "Leonard" Thompson. My Delaware name is Sa-sakipahkikámën, "the one that walks in the forest kicks up leaves." I was born about eight miles east of Bartlesville in the neighborhood they called Hogshooter district. 1904. April 13. I must have been five or six years old. I was out playing east of the house, about one hundred yards when I was a little boy. An old tree that had fell over, kind of like a log, and I was close to it. I would say I was fifty yards from it. I looked up, and I noticed that there was an old Indian man sitting on this log, and he had all-Indian, buckskin clothes on and a feather in his hair. Must have been tied. Must have been the spring because the wind kind of blowed that feather like that. Well, I looked at him a long time, not too long, but about ten minutes or five minutes. I got scared and run to the house. I told my dad, James H. Thompson, that I seen an old man sitting on a log down there, and he says, "Son, that's the man, that's the spirit (that) will help you throughout life. When you're in a bad place, a bad fix, he will appear to you." Well, about, oh, it must have been after I was a man, about forty-five, I see the old man again, and I said, "Well, here he is again, good." Just for a little bit, and then he was gone again. And the next time, heard him, but I didn't see him this time. While I was in the service in Asia, the big coast in Iran, the place called Karachi, India. It was India then, now it's Pakistan. We was moving one night; it was rainy and cold, and (we) was walking. There was no Indian boys in my outfit, just all of them from the New England states. While we was walking along, I hear somebody whoop real sharp. I say, "Well, that's him, I bet you that's him." I said, "You hear anybody?" Nothing. "Did you hear anybody?" Nothing. Well, that's all I know about that.

I can't remember how old I was. But ever since I can remember, we had wagons to go on. Some Studebakers and (some) spring wagons. If we go to Dewey, we took all day, went to White Oak, to go to Summit it took two days. We would stop at Hayden and Verdigris River overnight, and we would have breakfast and supper there when we were going to White Oak. And far as that, we used the Studebaker and the spring [spring seat] wagons also to haul grain and everything else with. Wood and everything.

I don't know the dates but [the Delawares] first moved from where Pennsylvania is on down, [and] plumb up to New York State. And right now in New York City there is a lot of Delaware names on the streets. From what I read and what they've [the elders of his childhood] told me, they must have took about a year or so to get here [Oklahoma from Kansas]. It was slow, and one old feller told me that a lot of people died on the way coming. Instead of moving in the summertime, they moved in the wintertime in the cold. They died on the way, of pneumonia or something. They couldn't dig; [the federal troops] wouldn't give them time to dig so that [the Delawares] had to hang [the dead] up on a staff or something, so that the animals wouldn't get them. Well [the federal government said], "We're going to give you this land here [Kansas after Delawares came] from Pennsylvania, Indiana, parts of Kentucky till they got here in Kansas." Well, they was going to give us this part, [but] more settlers come in, and [the Delawares] had to move again. [The Delawares] got to Kansas, now I don't know the date. They had a good reservation up there; what they told me, they liked it, the Delawares did. Right up there where Lawrence, Kansas, is now. There's a river there, I believe it's called the Kaw River. That's the Consicipo, they called it. They liked [Kansas], the Delawares did. And the settlers come in, and the railroads stole the trees and wood and everything, and [the Delawares] finally had to move away from there. Down into Oklahoma.

[Speaking about the role that the men played and the role of the women in Delaware society]: The Delaware men went out and got the game. He hunted all the time, mostly, got to provide the dinner. And the women were supposed to take care of their house; they had reed houses made out of reed. And the women would take care of the house, and the house belonged to the woman, and not the man. And when she got ready to divorce him, she threw his stuff out the window and that was it. And she carried everything, the business, through the woman's line. In the clan system, Wolf Clan and Turkey Clan and Turtle, there were certain places in the meeting that was just like pews in the church. The men sat all together, but the women mostly sat in the back of this old Big House [sacred place]. The boys could sit with their papas or their uncles, something like that. I always sat with the Wolf Clan. [His mother was Wolf Clan. Children took their mother's clan.] The Turkey Clan sat over in this southeast side, and the drummers sat right in the middle. And the [Turtle] Clan sit on the southwest side. And the woman she done the cooking and making clothes, sewing cloth and skins to make clothes. But the man, he really done his hunting and first carried his bow. If he brought anything, his wife would run out and take the bow away from him; put it away for him, and sit down because they know he was tired. Same way when they had a gun. She took his gun away, put it away for him, then give him a big dinner. That's all I can remember the women done. The women made a lot of decisions, mostly. Except something like war or moving or something like that. Then the chief took part in it. But he always had some guys, I forget how many, I think it was four of five, they called the wise men, Lupawenowok. Before they moved [to Oklahoma], the chief didn't have all the authority. He'd ask the wise men, would we move or would we do this or would we do that? So I believe.

If you was a name-giver you had to have a vision when you was young, you know, when a boy.[1] Then you were eligible to be a name-giver. But now days, we couldn't do that anyway 'cause, four- or five-year-old little kids, you have to go to school. They can't turn him out and say, "Well, go out and have a vision, and the guardian spirit will take care of you through life." You couldn't do that now. The vision gives us authority to give names. Well, you couldn't name anybody with a name of a person that's passed on or somebody that already got a name. So, it's pretty hard to do 'cause you had to think, "What if I am naming him somebody else or somebody else's name." So I'll give you a little instance. This boy is living now, JoAnn Markleys's boy [grandson]; she wanted me to name him. I still [have a] little of my original allotment out east of Bartlesville. I would go out by myself and talk to the Creator, "What shall I give this feller's name. Help me so that I won't get mixed up now." So she wanted me to name this boy of hers, he's about grown, he's a going to school or high school down there . . . And I went out to my old place, sat under a little walnut tree there, and I talked to the Creator. I said, "Heavenly Father, help me, give me a name for this boy . . . young man." I sat there for about an hour. There was this woodpecker up in this walnut tree . . . Tap Tap Tap *[makes tapping noises],* and it was up there, why it, I guess, just sit there for an hour. I hear him pecking around up there. Well, I still wondered what I'm going to give that boy [as] his name. Woodpecker, he flew off pretty soon. Tree about high as this. When he flew off, he flew about from here across to, oh, about here to that car, and a feather fell out of him and hit the ground. And I went over there and got that feather. Oh, what a pretty feather, kind of a golden-looking feather. It is what we call a golden woodpecker, you know. And I looked at it and, well, well, that's what He wants me to name that boy, Pretty Feather. Good Feather. *Shiki Mikwen,* Pretty Feather. So that says something right there; name this boy. So that's how you had to name, you couldn't name somebody that passed on. Or if somebody passed on, don't name him before noon. But you could name him after noon. I don't know why, but they said that it wasn't good.

It's very important [to know the Lenape language]. A few words anyway, that showed we were Delaware Indians. And it's important whenever you're in ceremony to give these names. You've got to talk, and when I pray to the Creator, I talk to him in my own language. And if I'm giving thanks

---

1. Both Leonard Thompson and his sister, Nora Thompson Dean, had a special gift for giving traditional Delaware names.

[when] some different kind of people [are present], I talk to Him in my language, and I translate myself into English, and that's quite important. The scriptures even say to translate yourself. [When I was a boy] Mama and Papa talked English; they talked Delaware mostly, mostly in their own tongue. They were both full blood. My mother was Sarah [May] Wilson, her maiden name, and James [Henry] Thompson, my dad. They were both full-blooded Delawares.

We played the football game. I always played games and dances and songs that [Delaware ancestors] give to us, and [we] thank them for it. Well, the football game, the old story was, long ago the old ones say, "In the beginning," they'd say, "He [the Creator] says, I'm going to give you the games so you can play and amuse yourselves, football. Make this ball out of deer hide and put deer hair inside of it. Use it for just one game, and when the game is over with, have the oldest lady in the tribe to take the deer hair out and give it to the wind." And that's one I did, that would be a game played here. But they can't do that now. Now we have to use the same ball all of the time. And the dancers. They give us some dances to sing, different dances, war dances, stomp dances, and different other kinds of dances we brought before the tribes.

I believe they are [now dancing more, using the language more, singing our songs more than a few years ago]. They're taking more interest, and I'm really glad they are. Seeing the younger people taking interest. I like to see the things that we borrowed from the Creeks and stomp dances, where they shake the shells, you know. But when I was a young boy we would go down to this side of Tulsa to stomp ground, Shawnees. But there would be a lot of Creeks there, and I got crazy with a Creek girl, and she was a shell shaker, and she put turtle shells on her legs. And in the evening, just before sunset, she'd take the turtle shells, twelve of them, and set them out in a little row and talk to them and say, "Well, we didn't kill you for nothing. We killed you to use you in these ceremonies we got, and we'll give you some water, too." So she would pour water, talk to them and pour water on their back and take good care of them shells. But now they use cans. Different kinds. [Small Pet] Milk cans mostly. It's a religion with the Creeks, but we borrowed that from the Creeks. We had a buffalo dance, so the Delawares did, like the Shawnees. That, let's see, that was in the kind of fall, if I remember right. But anyway the boys would put clay all over them, you know, mud and a little cloth on [their hips like a breech cloth, now they wear jeans] and [in the center] hominy, plenty [of] hominy and dance around that hominy and go "whoo, whoo" and kick the dirt up like the [buffalo] bulls, you know. And the women would try to go in and get little pieces of hash [meat ground up]. "Whoo," and push them away and get the hash. And, of course, after the dance, everybody get to rush in [and eat hominy and meat hash].

The water drum is what's used by the Delawares and the Shawnees, that I know of. The drum is usually made—well, they tell me; I've never seen it—was made out of a stump, and they burnt and hollowed it out until it was about that big and this high and put in water just about half full and used a little drumstick with a knot on each end on it. Need it to pound away on it [the drum]. But now you must always set the drum on the ground. Don't pick it up. A different drum now; we use a crock. You'll see it tonight [at the powwow in Copan]. It's a drum [made from a crock] with deer skin over it and about that much water. That's a Delaware drum. And the Shawnees use the drum, too, the same kind. Joe Washington was a drum keeper. He tied those drums and took care of those songs. And he kept other things, too. Things from that old Big House. But I think he took them to New York to that museum up there [Smithsonian National Museum of the American Indian]. I seen everything that the Delawares had when we were up there [as invited delegates]. I seen the things we used in the old Big House, and I seen the witch funnel, too. That feller [museum curator], he was afraid of it. And, of course, it was in enclosed glass; you couldn't touch it. It was about from like this post to that post and about 10 by 12, full of stuff that the Delawares had. And I seen the old prayer sticks there and Kieko and Wampum and the thing women carried wood with, on the back, you know. And I can just remember, while sitting, I just looked at them. Talked to them. That there man, [who] was overseer, he was afraid of that witch, just like I was. Of course, you couldn't touch them, they had the glass up there, you know. But I was afraid of it. There's still a lot of people that says there ain't no witch. The Bible said it in the first, the Old Testament, that there's witches. "Suffer not a witch to live," it says. Well, there was always mean people in all kinds of tribes and nations of people. Well, there was people, Delawares, that wanted to the Devil, I guess, or wanted to be a witch. If they did, they sacrificed the one, most lovable, the one they loved most in their family.

I can remember [a few years back, back in the time when people were made to be ashamed because they were Indian]. Just prior to World War I. Yeah, [the Indians] were ashamed to go to school, you know, the way they was dressed. But they would send them to boarding schools sometimes, like Chilocco [at the Kansas-Oklahoma state line], that one in Pennsylvania, in Carlisle and also Lawrence, Kansas, you know [Haskell]. I like to see the young people carry on [be proud to be an Indian and to carry on the traditions]. Makes me feel good. I pray for them all the time. I'm a great [one] to ask Him for things, even when I was overseas in wartime, I'd talked to Him. Well, it's hard, hard to say it, describe how I feel. I feel glad, you know, when I see them dancing. But we danced a little different War Dance like they do now. They dance with the water drum. The warriors would carry the tomahawk, war club in the dance—boy, they were going. And pretty soon the feller [who] was ever in battle, he'd go up there and hit that drum, "PAH" . . . stop, he'd tell his story . . . where he served and what happened during the battle, how he felt and how scared he was at first. And he said, pretty soon he would begin to feel glad in battle. I heard one old feller say, "Then I'd whoop." That's all I can remember. That old feller said that, George Falleaf [1875–1963]. Well, the signs are that the younger people are catching on. But we can't expect them to go like we did before, but to carry it on as much as they can. Of course, later on, it'll be shows, just like it is now. But anyway, they'd be Indian. Different tribes, different ways, you know, but nevertheless, they'd be Indian people. Do you want me to tell you some songs? These are kind of like a vision, too. My dad knew a man who told what he'd seen when he was a boy. Said he was out by his house. And he'd seen a squirrel run in a hole, in a log. And he went up there and put rocks in that hole, so that squirrel couldn't get out. Well, next day he said, "I'm going over to see how the squirrel's a doing." When he got, oh, ten or twelve feet away from that place with a hole in the log, that squirrel was singing: "Little boy, Little boy, you'll never starve me to death. Little boy, little boy, you'll never starve me to death" [English translation].

So he went up there and took them rocks off, and he won't eat squirrel now. That's like me with turkeys. I won't eat a turkey. Me and a boy [who] was [the son of] a white man [who] lived on our place, I said it was about four o'clock in the afternoon, and there was a path going down to the pond where the horses and cows go; it's a dust. And they had turkeys, too. And the turkeys would go down to get a drink out of this pond. We were talking, standing in kind of a barn, shed-like, you know. And there's a path about like this road here. And pretty soon, here come a turkey, had a little dead turkey in his mouth and an old hen turkey following him. They got about even with us. The old gobbler, put that little turkey down, went to digging in and put it in and covered him up. And here's what got me, they looked like this, oh I'd say a half of a minute, which they'd quit. I said, "They're praying now." And white boy, even he'd said, "Yeah, I guess they're praying." And [those two turkeys] went back on up to where the rest of them was. I won't eat turkey now.

I'd like for them to make me feel glad in my heart if the young people would carry on the dances, the songs and games of ours. Carry on as long as they can. Of course, we don't expect them to do like we did, say, twenty years ago. I ask the Creator every time, I ask Him to pray for anybody. Especially pray for the young people to carry on . . . the songs, the dances, and ball games. That's it—Nah Ninney.

Here's an Old Man Elkhair Big House song.[2] Now this is his song and his story I've heard a lot of times. When he was a boy on the Kaw River, the

---

2. The reader may hear the late Leonard Thompson singing the song by visiting the Long Journey Home website at: http://brownimages.com and on the video documentary, *Long Journey Home*, available from http://www.wfyi.org or ctaylor@wfyi.org or 317-636-2020.

one that is on that Delaware Reservation. He says, "I lost my brother, my older brother," and he said he loved his brother very much, but he passed on. He was walking in the forest; Delawares are always in a forest. While he was walking along, he was kind of crying. Something hit the ground, right there beside of him, "Pah." He said, "Boom." He came to later; found out it must have been a hawk that hit the ground. And it told him, "Young boy, don't feel thataway. We want you to live to be an old man and sing these songs in the old Big House, your vision song."

So he sang this song. That was his song. When I was a boy, I seen and heard that song about hawk that hit the ground and it told him, "not to worry." [Old Man Elkhair] talked in the old Big House, [Delaware] church. They claim that these visions he had was given to him through the Creator, our heavenly Father. Yo.

Oral history conducted September, 1998, powwow grounds, near Copan, Oklahoma. Verified and corrected by Dee and Annette Ketchum. Their corrections appear in brackets. Leonard Thompson's oral history also appears in **Always a People** *(pages 233–243).*

Jesse Townsend at the 2005 Delaware Powwow near Copan, Oklahoma.

JESS TOWNSEND

Tribal member
Born 1925 in Delaware, Oklahoma

I was born on my father's allotment. My father was Jess Townsend, half Cherokee. My mother was Ida Mae Miller. She was three-quarter Delaware and one-quarter Shawnee. My father's name was Jess, same as mine; he was senior, I was junior. We lived in the country on his allotment, on his farm. Dad farmed, and he was also a blacksmith. He raised various crops, wheat, oats, and had an orchard. There were four of us kids survived, three boys and one girl. I had an older sister, and I was the oldest boy. Father died when I was quite young, eight years old.

My mother was quite fluent in the Delaware language. She was bilingual. She could speak English as well as Delaware. Anytime she and her sister-in-law, Aunt Martha Miller, would get together they spoke the Delaware language almost exclusively. The Delaware language is real humorous. You say some words in the Delaware language—it's much more humorous than it would be in English. They talk backward. German sentences are sort of backward the same way. They had a big time visiting. My grandmother spoke fluent Delaware. Grandfather spoke real fluent Delaware. My maternal grandfather, Stephen A. Miller, was acting chief of the Delaware years ago. They had a pretty good-sized family, too. I believe there were six of them. The three older children in that family could speak Delaware much more fluently than the three younger children.

My brother, Bruce [Miller Townsend], he was the youngest in our family. He was chief of the Delaware tribe [during the 1970s].[1] They lived in Tulsa. He was a practicing attorney there. He would spend a lot of his time in this area and going to Washington, representing the tribe. [See Mary Townsend Crow Milligan, page 73.]

I've participated in Indian culture quite a bit. When I was a teenager, my cousin who is half Osage and half Delaware, he got me interested in the Indian dances. Along the way we learned how to sing stomp dance songs. At first we designed our own "costumes" for what they call fancy dancing. That's not the Delaware regalia for dance. Delawares wore leggings and the

---

1. The title then was chairman of the Delaware Tribal Business Committee.

shirt, beaded belt, and moccasins. I have that costume, most of it, yet. But he was Osage. See, the Osages, they copied their costume from the Delawares. Delaware helped them make a lot of their costumes. Their [Osage] dance costumes are primarily Delaware. That's what they tell me.

I've danced fancy dance and what they call straight dance, both. I learned how to sing the stomp dance songs. Delaware are quite a bit into the stomp dance. That's traditional to the Delaware. In this part of the country, it is a mixture of what languages they sing in the stomp dance. A lot of it is Creek, and there are some words in Shawnee, some words in Delaware. There's a mixture of the Indian languages common to this part of the country. But they pretty much sing the same words, the same songs, so they can sing with each other. They have the shell shakers, that's the only rhythm they have to go by, besides the singers, that is. It is kind of interesting. There are so many other dances that go on at the powwow. Round dances, buffalo dance, and all different traditional dances.

My cousin, who was maybe a year older than I am, he was pretty well versed in that already. He had learned dancing from a small child up. He was mainly responsible for teaching me that. Then you'd pick it up on your own, just trial and error. When I was younger we would just follow the powwow in the summer. During the summer vacation, when there wasn't school, we'd attend numerous powwows. Summer is powwow. We'd always go to the traditional powwow at Pawhuska in June, their traditional powwow. In later years they had one at Copan, at the Falleaf place, but I don't know exactly when that started. Some ten, twelve years ago.

I lived over in Nowata County. My mother was bilingual. My mother was real concerned about trying to teach us the Delaware Indian language. We comprehended and learned quite a bit about it. Just the basic language. Delaware greeting: *"Kulamalsi hach"* to say "Hello, how are you." We had Indian names. We could count to twenty. We didn't know a lot. She [also] concentrated on learning the American way, the English way. That's what she was concerned about. Not so much as some of the other tribes. They go traditionally. Everything is down to 100 percent Indian traditions, folklore, and all that. Ours is limited, because they were trying to get us in the mainstream. Good, bad, or indifferent, but that's what they practiced. *[Chuckles.]*

We were taught to live the tradition of the American way and try to get away from the Indian traditions. My mother was quite a bit for that. She wanted us to get an education and be able to compete in the white man's world. She didn't do a whole lot in passing on Delaware traditions. Just hearsay, just tales that they told us. But all these Indian traditions, I pretty well learned myself.

I went to school at Haskell Institute in Lawrence, Kansas, in my senior [year] in high school. It's completely Indian students there. I learned a lot about different Indians there. Indians from up north, from Minnesota, Wisconsin. Quite a bit from all over the United States. Majority of them was from Oklahoma. That's where I got my high school education. I went in the army for three years. I served in the army infantry. I was wounded on the Philippine Islands, so that kind of slowed down my choice of vocations. I went to school, three years of college. Worked various occupations. Something I could handle. I was a disabled veteran.

The job from where I retired was Sequoyah High School in Tahlequah, Oklahoma, as a counselor instructor. Sequoyah High School is a boarding school. All Indian. It was a government boarding school. It is an accredited boarding school, like Haskell. People would send their children there if they wanted to. Since I worked there it changed over to the Cherokee tribe, which took it over. Now I don't know if it is only Cherokee students. It was co-ed, boys and girls. I was a counselor. We had the children part of the time. I just pinch-hitted, study halls and stuff like that. They had a regular schedule of classes. They had some children that had problems and some didn't. We didn't know which one was which. There was a social worker in there. Some of the time the kids would get in trouble. It was a mixed crowd. It was a regular high school sponsored by the federal government.

I went to Oklahoma State University. I went to Southeastern State in Durrant. I had decided to go to Haskell on my own. I decided to go up there [to high school] to get special training, to learn a vocation before I went in the army. It didn't turn out that way. I learned auto mechanics. I was drafted into the army after they issued me a deferment to finish high school. They sent me directly in to the army at Fort Sill, Oklahoma. When I got in the army I was placed in the infantry. My mother went there [to Haskell]. Years ago it was quite common for people to go there. It's an old, old school. My brother went there, too. I was drafted before I finished high school. I went to Oklahoma City for the physical. I went directly on in to military training at Fort Sill.

My grandfather, Stephen A. Miller, was a big farmer. He got along with people. He entertained a lot. At that time they didn't have any hotels. He'd put them up and feed them. He's quite an entertainer. A linguist. He'd sing a song. Some of these salesmen that would come through, he'd have them sing a song in their nationality, and he'd sing a song in Delaware. He entertained a lot like that. He was bilingual. He could sing church songs in either English or Delaware. He was real religious. He'd do that. Up real early in the morning, and he'd be singing church songs in Delaware. He knew all the people in the community. He was kind of a community leader. Matter of fact, mother tells a tale. We lived at Delaware [Oklahoma]. The Rogerses, Will Rogers's parents lived down around Oologah, which is some twenty miles away. They'd come down and trade horses. My grandpa used to tell about Will Rogers and his daddy looking for horses and trading livestock.

Will was a little boy. He'd be sitting up there with his daddy. Up there to visit Grandpa. He was pretty versatile in that line.

I'm a great believer in education. Independence and education. Grand-children, children that I had in school, I stressed education very thoroughly to them. Teach them that if they get education they can be independent and self-supporting and live a more comfortable life. Also they could offer more to their community and their fellow people.

[The tribe has] their Delaware Business Committee. Then they have their chief and vice chief. They limit big decisions to general elections. Special issues, they will have a voting from the registered voters. I participate in tribal affairs by voting.

I never have heard too many tales about being on the trail, like the Cherokees. They [Delawares] were farmers; they'd get settled, they'd live a place several years. They'd get established, and [the government moved them] on West. Then they [got] moved as far west as Kansas City, where Kansas City is today. They moved into Oklahoma. This section area, Dewey, Copan area, and also around Nowata County. So I never had heard too many tales like that.

The U.S. government had already closed the rolls down as far as giving allotments. My mother, her brothers and sisters received allotments. Her younger brother was considered a "too late." In other words, the Dawes Commission roll included him. I guess they extended it a little bit, let him get on it. That was probably in 1905 or 1906, when they shut that down.

I don't have a Delaware allotment. My mother and her brothers and sisters had allotments.

I married a white woman, by the way. My children, their Indian blood is split again. They got Indian names and so forth. I'm seventy-five years old.

Oral history interview in May 2000, at Bartersville, Oklahoma.

Tristen Tucker, nine-year-old Delaware Tribal member, rests between songs at the Delaware Tribal Center. Tristen started dancing as a Fancy Dancer at age five. He was introduced to the drum at age six and has been a Gourd Dancer since age seven. Families gather every Tuesday evening to share a pitch-in supper and to practice singing, drumming, and dancing.

Joyce Williams at her home in Okmulgee, Oklahoma, in 2005.

JOYCE WILLIAMS

Tribal member
Born August 18, 1928, in Muskogee, Oklahoma

My mother was Dixie McCracken, the youngest daughter of John and Oneida McCracken. My father was Francis Hartgraves. When I was born, my mother died in two weeks. She never was able to leave the hospital. I was not raised, or familiar with, my heritage. I visited my grandparents, the McCrackens, when I was very young. My father and his in-laws were not close. Everyone wanted that baby, and everyone didn't want that baby; it was kind of a pull and tug. My dear Uncle Horace and his wife did not have children. They told me, in later years, that they really wanted to take me, but my Grandmother McCracken was a very strong-willed lady, and my Aunt Bonnilyn said she knew that I would never be hers. At that point, of course, my dad would not have it. It wasn't a choice to them anyway, but it was a big discussion. So I was raised by my father apart from Indian culture and the McCrackens. Uncle Horace was always very considerate and very close, and in later years, after my children were older and I had a little more time, Uncle Horace was instrumental in getting me and my children enrolled into the Delaware tribe. I became more interested, and it was not really because I felt suddenly that I was a Delaware, but from an artistic point, we became interested in Indian artifacts. We have an interesting collection of Indian baskets, and if you collect baskets, you're going into pottery and a few rugs. That pretty much is my background. As I said, I didn't start collecting because I was Delaware, but in collecting I became more interested. We have done some researching. My husband has done a family tree the best that we could. I have particularly one daughter that has been very interested in her heritage, and one of her sons was involved in local, state, and national history day, and he was second at national history day for his story of the Delaware. We are so proud of that project, and I hope to give some of his work when the tribe is interested and has a place in their archives for his contribution. He was able to use some of Uncle Horace's papers. Horace McCracken was chairman of the tribe for many years. Aunt Bonnilyn gave me a lot of Uncle Horace's papers after he died. My grandson Zachary Ornelas was able to use those papers in his projects. Of course, that sparked a real interest in that part of the family. That's pretty much my story.

Aunt Bonnilyn had sent me the book [*The Delawares* by C. A. Weslager] with Uncle Horace's picture that was written about the time that Uncle Horace had died. It was to me, knowing so little, volumes of information that led me on this path. And this enabled us to do a family tree. Also, my mother's aunt, who was my grandfather's half sister, did a story that Uncle Horace had recorded and had notarized about her family. In that, she talked about the family of William Conner and his Indian wife, and having read more, I question if this is correct. Because, in her affidavit, she said that they had started a trading post, which was later named Indianapolis. Well, in reading the little that I have, or as much as I have, I think their trading post was ten miles or twenty miles from Indianapolis. We had talked about this, and we hope sometime that we can go back and do some research of our own. But little things like that have led us from one place to another in trying to understand the heritage.

Mekinges's [youngest] daughter was Eliza Conner. Eliza married Bill Halfmoon. They had a daughter Sarah. Sarah married William McCracken. William McCracken was John McCracken's father, who was my grandfather. Each time I try to get those in order, I either leave someone out, or add someone in. Because I wasn't there to hear the stories, the only thing that I do have are two affidavits. That's my only knowledge of my background. The affidavits Uncle Horace McCracken did. I think he knew the importance of the heritage and wanted to preserve it and wanted some accurate, firsthand information. He just had the foresight to do it, I think; he was quite a man.

The [affidavit] that I was first familiar with that I always thought was interesting, this was by Laura Fields. Laura was the half-sister of my grandfather John McCracken. It is my understanding that Uncle Horace had them retyped. Uncle Horace says: "My family information supplied by my aunt, Laura Barnet, my father's half sister [and, of course, Laura Barnet had four different last names]. These are copied from her notes and statements exactly as they were received. [Mekinges] married William Conner. They settled in Indiana to make their home. For at that time, Indiana was their own reservation, the Delaware tribe, I mean. And this special couple set aside to get ahead in life. So William Conner picked a site for a general store and built it, and went into business in a general way. And he called the place of his establishment Indianapolis. This is, as it stands today, a large, a beautiful city."

This makes wonderful reading. As I said to you earlier, after doing more research, I question this because I think their trading post was north of what is now Indianapolis, whatever that might mean. But this is interesting reading. And the other affidavit gives that family history of who the children of the Chief Anderson are on down. They are both interesting.

I have several copies at home; this one does not have the date on it. Probably early 1920s or 1930s, I don't know.

In all fairness, when my [four] children were young, I didn't share this as much. As I said, there was a bit of a conflict within my family. My father remarried. And my grandparents McCracken. And I was always very careful not to offend either. This probably isn't the sort of thing that you're looking for, but it might be. I know at one time my aunts were coming; one was coming from out of state, and they wanted to come to visit us, and I was frankly in a twit. My children were young and impressionable, and I wanted them to know them. And yet my stepmother (who was never my stepmother—she was my mother), my stepmother was always afraid of the fact that the children never knew that she wasn't my mother, so she really did not want my children to know. So I was not going to ask the McCrackens not to come. But I asked them to call me when they got to town, and I would direct them to my house. Well, I was going to ask them then, when they called, to not share this with my children. But instead they knocked on my door. The day went beautifully. I called them aunt, and later my children were confused, and I said that they were very good friends of your papa's and nana's, and I've always called them aunt.

After my mother died, and after my dad died, I told my children the story. The girls, being young women and curious, were really disturbed that I had not asked my parents more questions. It just isn't my nature. Uncle Horace, as I said earlier, was instrumental in enrolling us in the Delaware Tribe. And it goes without saying, that created an interest. At the time my children were small, I was raising them, and the interest was not long lasting, but I was pleased. Then when my grandson became very involved in history day, that renewed an interest in even my daughter's other siblings. It created a real family interest there, and everyone was a little more interested. But the big thing that has helped my journey, my husband has been wonderful to help me understand and look back and try to find the history. He probably knows more about the Delaware than I do.

My oldest daughter, Diane Ornelas, lives in Broken Arrow, Oklahoma. She teaches in Tulsa at Bishop Kelly High School. She has four children, one grandchild, and is expecting two more grandchildren. My second daughter, Terry Teresa Gilly, lives in Shawnee, Oklahoma. She teaches special ed in Shawnee public schools. She has two sons, Justin Goodman and Berry Gilly. My third child is our only son, and he's Jim Williams; he lives in Henryetta, Oklahoma. He has three children, Bradley, Tara, and James Michael. And my youngest daughter, Patricia Wilburn, lives in Tulsa. She has two daughters, Abigale and Haley. And that's our family. My dad was an only child, and I was an only child, and my only cousins are Dan Arnold and John Arnold. So I had my own family, and it's big.

I had quite a few things that belong to Uncle Horace. Uncle Horace, before his death—well, it's my understanding—had given some things to the historical society, I think at the Bartlesville Library. Some of the papers, some of the telegrams from the representatives and so forth, I do have and I plan to give those to the tribe. And also Zachary's story. I have not asked him, but I am sure that he will want to give that to the tribe. The personal things I will keep, and I'm sure that some of my children will want them.

When your grandson Zachary was researching and you were able to share with him some of the materials that you have from your uncle Horace and your aunt Bonnilyn, did he express anything to you at all regarding what it felt like to touch some of this?

Not in that respect. He is a very enthusiastic, he was a little boy then, about everything he does. And in doing this you could tell that he became pleased with his heritage. But no, at the time he didn't share in words anything in that respect.

[My grandson's history project] was the story of the Delaware coming west, and he was able to use maps and timelines. For example, early on, Uncle Horace worked very hard for the tribe. In the papers I had were telegrams and letters from, for example, Representative Edminson from Oklahoma and from Senator Harris from Oklahoma. He used those things to show what took place in that period of time.

Oral history on May 30, 2000, at Bartlesville, Oklahoma.
See Dan Arnold oral history (page 107).

EDWARD WILSON

Tribal elder
Born 1928 on a farm west of Copan, Oklahoma

OPENING REMARKS FROM DEE KETCHUM: I am here with Ed Wilson, one of our full-blood Delaware elders, visiting with him concerning his life, being the last person living that can remember the last Big House ceremony that was put on in 1944 during World War II.[1] I have some questions I want to ask Ed. We are sitting at a location not far from the old Big House that our ancestors used in 1927. Ed's property that was allotted to his family during the allotment era, which he still owns, is not far from here. A couple of weeks ago I tried to do a recording similar to this and didn't succeed. We are now closer to the old Big House overlooking Copan Lake. Ed said the old river channel is not far from here. Tell me about that, Ed.

EDWARD WILSON: It is right next to us, and the reason the Big House is right on the other side of this ravine is because this ravine led down to a crossing because there was no bridge on the river, so people came from the other side of the river and they crossed here. About a mile down farther there is another crossing. It was sandstone outcropping that caused ripples, and the water was real shallow so they walk and bring their wagons across it. You can still see that large ravine down there. See that oak tree? Those post oaks probably existed during that time and probably before that.

DEE: Beautiful, big oak trees. I would assume this river did supply water for our ancestors.

ED: Yes. Right over here about three football fields away, three hundred yards, is where the Big House was, and that is where they camped, and some of them may have even camped on this actual bluff next to the crossing when there was a large crowd. We are pretty near the original place. There is a ten-acre strip, and my grandfather came down here from Kansas; he walked here barefooted. He was just a kid. All of his kinfolks—cousins, aunts, uncles, parents, sisters, brothers—were all killed on the way down here. They were attacked by Osages and killed. Out of the 1,000 who started down here, [it] is estimated, they don't want to tell the truth, at least 250 were killed. They say it was from disease, but they traveled during the

---

1. Mr. Wilson requested that his photograph not appear in the book.

winter, and they were actually murdered. They either came on horseback, walked, or in wagons. They were rich people because in Kansas they were farmers and well established. They [the federal government] just removed them [Delawares] because the railroad wanted their property, especially the Kansas Outlet, a ten-mile-wide strip from Kansas to Colorado.

My grandfather, when he got here, the Delawares had bought land at $1 per acre, which was a very highly inflated price because the Choctaws got land for a nickel an acre. We paid $1 an acre for a strip that is ten miles wide and thirty miles long, which is presently Washington County, Oklahoma. When our people moved here, they were under the impression that they bought it—160 acres for everybody that was coming down here, and they would own it and pass it down to their heirs. My grandfather had lost everybody, and my grandmother lost all her family, too. We don't know what her last name was because she was just a child. Someone took her, and when she was an old woman she didn't know either. We claim that he [the grandfather] had 5,000 acres here, which is a large area. He was a big person and owned the best horses there was. Because he had all these fine horses, all the outlaws wanted good horses, so they bought them from him, and he was good friends with them and hid out in those hills just west of here, Buffalo Hill. The hill I live on is called Butterfly Hill. I am telling you this to give you some background about my dad.

DEE: One of the things for people who don't know, and they are listening to this, we are in a location just three miles north of Copan, Oklahoma. How far from Caney, Kansas?

ED: Nine miles south. This river here is called the Little Caney River. Sometimes it is referred to as the Little Verdigris because that is where it empties into it.

DEE: Now all of that changed when the Allotment Act came in.

ED: The Dawes Act was 1904, and Statehood was 1907. One hundred and sixty acres was given only to those people who came down here [from Kansas]. Then everybody else got what the Cherokees got, which was 80 acres. They couldn't figure a way to only give them 80, because they had already bought 160, so they said we will give them 160, but all their children will get 80 acres. My grandpa lived on Highway 10 in a big white house. He owned all this [land] around and had all those horses; I guess he was wealthy. He was a man who gave things away. He gave the land for the school, which was right near where the Silver Dollar Restaurant was [across the road from Ed's allotment]. He gave them the ten acres for the Big House. But when they allotted it, they allotted that ten acres to a Freedman, which was a Cherokee slave. So then it passed on to people called the Larges, who were outlaws, bootleggers, and all that. But they lived on it, and their heirs now own two and a half acres.

I think this is all important because my dad was just a little boy. Since the Big House was just like his back yard he went over there, and at an early age he started chewing tobacco. He didn't have any money and no way to get money, so he would go to the Big House and take it from the Mësingw. That was the way they made offerings—they put tobacco in its mouth. It was always a good source of tobacco that he got to chew. He ran loose all over this [motion to the land]. My grandpa used to send food to those outlaws that lived there, and he [my dad] was the one who took it to them as a kid. I want to relate stories so the people can understand the conditions back then. He only spoke Delaware and only went to the third grade because he had a problem with hearing.

DEE: Let me introduce your dad, Reuben Wilson. He was obviously from one of the traditional families here in Indian Territory. He certainly was a full-blood Delaware and fluent in Delaware [language]. He was one of the leaders in the Big House eventually. He conducted, sang songs, and helped with the Big House. I remember your dad dancing up at the Delaware powwow at Copan. He danced with one leg.

ED: My dad grew up near the Big House [within two hundred yards]. Not only did his dad give the property; they were involved in the building. His brother, Uncle Tom, drug the logs from the river bottom with horses up there to build the last one [second Big House]. My dad brought in the logs and got injured, and he lost a leg. Since he [Reuben] was near that old Big House and knew all the traditions, he ran around like a little wild kid, and everybody loved him. He was just trying to be helpful, but he had no fear because a big part of the camping was to scare the whey out of the little children so they would be good the rest of the year. Part of the ritual of the Mësingw was that. Everyone except the little kids knew this, and they stayed in line the rest of the year because it was only held twelve days out of the year. This is where my dad learned all this. Later in life he carved the Mësingw. Very, very large ones that are in museums now. And he made models of the Big House. At least three of them he built are in museums.

DEE: What kind of wood? Do you remember?

ED: He always carved out of ash because ash is a close grain and it lasts a long time. That is what axe handles are made from because it is so strong. Other people who built—I know of one—built of willow because it is easy to work. It almost dry-rotted and disappeared. He did his of ash and one out of slippery elm. It was solid. It was a great big tree, and he had carved the outside of it and carved it so you could see in it. Nobody knows what has happened to that one. He did that and carved a big Mësingw.

DEE: In talking about the Big House, I know Reuben was quite instrumental in conducting that last service in 1944 when you were in the military, which was similar to the old Big House service.

ED: What they were doing as I understood it was to pray for all the boys to come home from the war because they were scattered everywhere. I was in North Africa in the air force and in England. They brought me back to Washington for thirty days for some reason that I can't even talk about even today. They gave me special treatment. There was a bomber. It wasn't a B-26; it was an A-26. They built them in Tulsa. They was taking one back to Washington for some reason. They brought me back and let me off in Bartlesville and then flew on. I was only here for six days. During the time I was here they told me to call them everyday, which I did. They said the plane is going to be there, and you are headed to the West Coast and to the Pacific. I wasn't very observant [about the Big House Ceremony] during that period because I had just left one theatre of the war and was heading for another that was just starting up real good. I wasn't in any mood to reflect or try to understand it [Big House Ceremony]. Plus it was all in Delaware, and there were very few people who understood Delaware.

As I reflect on it, I think they had the full twelve days, but I was only here for four of those days. I was staying with my dad. It was the only home I had. Every night we would go over there. The services were in the evening.

DEE: Talking about "over there," the location was at Minnie Fouts's just north of Dewey. They didn't try to restructure the old Big House; it was in a tent?

ED: Yeah, they had a big old army tent. It was big to me then, but not big by today's standard. I would say it was at least ten feet by ten feet. The only problem it wasn't made to have an open fire. If anything, it was made to have a stove with a pipe going out. There was no way for the smoke to escape. It was smoky. I couldn't understand what they were doing because the smoke was so thick. And the women that came in, you could see that they didn't like that smoke.

DEE: Was this in October or November?

ED: I can't really recollect, but it was kind of cold so it must have been November. Every once in a while they put too many logs on the fire to keep warm, and then there was just more smoke. A catch-22 thing.

DEE: Who came?

ED: To this day, I can't tell you any man that was there. But I can tell you by their absence.

DEE: With the exception of your dad.

ED: Yes, with the exception of my dad. But I don't remember any of the men. I remember them sitting there. Not very many of them sang except they kind of picked up. They didn't sing their own song. Dad was the only one who had a song.

DEE: His visionary song?

ED: Yes. The visionary thing; he hardly talked about that. But he talked about the purpose when I questioned him later about this—why are we doing this? He said, "Well, the reason is that we have a certain time to do this. We get a message to do it. It isn't exactly the same time in November. Some family calls it, and once they call it, people come and we hold all the rituals." Basically, what we are doing is everyone is sitting around here, and everybody has his place to sit. Of course, we weren't really observing that [the seating at the 1944 meeting] because there wasn't very many people there, and they didn't know what clan they were from anyway. But what we do is like self-confession, and whenever you have the terrapin rattle in the palm of your hand, you shake it and put your hand over it. Whenever you do that, you get the floor and you get to talk. What you do is tell what you did in the last year, especially the bad things. You confess your faults; it's a public confession. And then you shake the rattle and set it back down with your hand on it. It fit right in the palm of your hand; it was just that size. You can pick it up like a basketball player can pick up a basketball with one hand; you pick that terrapin shell up. It didn't have any decoration on it—no decorations whatsoever. It was just a shell with some river pebbles in it.

Then you tell the good things that you were going to do next year, which would put everybody there on notice that you were going to be a better person. You were going to be good to everybody and everything 'cause they didn't talk about just being good to each other, but good to your horses, your cows, animals, wild animals, the trees, to everything.

DEE: And giving thanks to Mother Earth for all that, all the good things.

ED: And being in harmony. People don't understand that Indians, especially Delawares, were in harmony with their environment. That was part of their life. Then he would shake it and hand it to the left. They went left.

DEE: Counter-clockwise.

ED: Yes, I can remember that.

DEE: That's what they did in the original Big House.

ED: Yes. My dad was kind of conducting that. Because he had built, over the years, connections with Frank G. Speck and M. R. Herrington and anthropologists from the University of Pennsylvania. He told them about all these things. Plus he made, I hate to use the word, but the word he used was "paraphernalia." It was the instruments they used in the ceremonies. One of the main things was a deer hide with the hair still on it. It was rolled up, and it seemed to be about eighteen inches long and approximately nine to ten inches wide. They rolled it up and then took strips. In this case Bodark, which is hedge, very hard wood. They used to make bows out of it. Then they put four—four is a very important number—they take four thongs and tied the sticks on there. They had a drumstick which was a special stick because it had sort of a fork on it. It had a Mësingw on it. It was about fourteen inches long.

DEE: They probably made that of ash, too?

ED: If not walnut. Walnut was very common back then, like it is here. We are under one. It is fine wood and it lasts forever.

He also made prayer sticks. They were made out of sumac that is sort of a brush that's poisonous in a way, but at the same time it is medicinal. They used it in the sweats back before. I don't know if they use it any more.

DEE: You mentioned that it was somewhat difficult for you to understand because they were all just talking in Delaware.

ED: No English used in the symbol of the Big House. I can only remember my dad was the only one who had his own song. Prior to that the only ones that could speak were the ones who had their own song and—from what people tell me, I don't know this—they'd have had a vision. I don't know if that is correct, because everybody has visions. Not one that's induced, but they had visions. But they didn't have their own song. He never did tell me what the song was about. He was a singer; he liked to sing. His dad was a great, well-known singer throughout northeastern Oklahoma. Him and Spybucks, Charlies, people around Skiatook who were Shawnee-Delaware people would go out where there was an Indian gathering, or they would just call one so they could sing. They were great singers, and people would come from miles around to hear them.

Well, he had heard these songs, but since he was deaf he heard them different from other people. That's why he was a good soloist, but not worth a darn singing with a group.

DEE: I hadn't heard that.

ED: Oh yeah, I want to add right now that I have never told anybody, and this is the first recording—I may have mentioned it—but I have never told anybody the entire story. I have been sort of recluse, but I will put it on a recording because I know this is going back to Indiana. It is a message from us Delawares here that our spirits are still there.

DEE: In reflecting on that last resemblance to the Big House . . .

ED: Well, we need to call it assembly.

DEE: Now you are thinking it was twelve days, and they did try . . .

ED: Well, I can't tell you for sure because I was only here for four [days].

DEE: It is interesting to note that they were not only praying, as you mentioned earlier, for the bad things that they encountered during their lifetime and then they were praying for the good things, but were they also praying for the war during that period of time?

ED: They weren't praying for who was going to win; they were praying for the children.

DEE: Not long after that the war stopped . . .

ED: . . . and they came home. Most of them came home. There were very few Delawares killed during the war.

DEE: That's interesting to me. Now reflecting back . . .

ED: Let me say one other thing. It is very important. People don't understand. They have the intellect, but they don't take the time to get into the depth of it. Your thoughts are like your acts. It's not just what you do, it's what you think. Whatever you think is just like doing it. So all the bad things you think you have to try to clear all that away from you. The bad spirits get control. That's one reason they had the Mësingw. He had power to chase them people away. He had power to chase those spirits away. He looked over the animals or wildlife, but he also looked over the Delawares. That was his mission. He wasn't a god. He was assigned for the Delawares. I'm sure it (the Mësingw) was just a symbol. The Mësingw rode a deer.

DEE: It was a cleansing. Cleansing of the mind and body and the spirit.

ED: Yes, and people don't understand that. They try to equate it against what they know, when it's entirely different, and their minds can't comprehend it. That's a very, very important message that if the Delawares ever bring it to them, and I think the Indian world is bringing the message about the condition of the world, and they need to do something about it. That thought is a very important message, and the old people that lived in Indiana knew it, and they will be very glad to hear it is still here and alive.

DEE: I don't know how much information your dad shared with you concerning the old, original Big House; the one that fell in to disrepair in 1924–27. Did he ever talk to you about why they shut that down, why they didn't want that any longer?

ED: There was a schism between those in power who were Christians. They were preachers, Baptist preachers. Journeycake, at that time, was only a fourth [Delaware]. All these people were a small part Delaware, and the government gave them control of the tribe. The people on this side of the Little Caney River came back to what [land] they bought. They [Delaware Christians] went somewhere else that the Delawares didn't even buy. They went over to Nowata, over in there . . .

DEE: Miami?

ED: Well, the ones that went up in Miami [Oklahoma] went up there because they couldn't stand the Cherokees—they couldn't stand the treatment—they went up with the Peorias. The rich ones who followed Journeycake and were mostly white, they settled in the bottoms of Nowata and Craig counties, which we didn't buy. They aligned themselves with the Cherokees. A lot of people who are not looking into this or thinking about it don't understand the history. The history is that the Osages owned where the Cherokees moved into. The Osages and the Quapaw had all of Arkansas, Kansas, and Oklahoma. Those two tribes, originally. When the Cherokees were removed here by President Jackson, they came here, and there was great resistance from the Osages. The Osages were still kind of nomads. We had a long-term thing because one of the chief's sons [Chief William Anderson's youngest son, Shoanock] was killed in one of these skirmishes. So when they came down here this strip—this may be the reason those people in leadership didn't move here—this strip abuts the Osage Reservation.

DEE: To the west.

ED: Two miles [points west], that's where the line is. They put us here on the strip between them [Cherokees] and the Osages. The Osages didn't like the Cherokees. We had several fights with them [Osages], whipped them bad to the point that we met over at Young's Flat Lake, a body of water where the ground happens to be lower there, not dug, it's natural. When the river rose up in the spring and the fall, it would fill it. It would go down and be full of water lilies. Anyway the Osages like these special type of water lilies, called yonka pins. You ever heard of them?

DEE: No.

ED: These are the greatest delicacies for the Osages. Like pawpaws. Ever heard of pawpaws?

DEE: No.

ED: This is a fruit that grows on a certain tree, like a banana. When they [Osages] hit oil, they used to get the Delawares to bring them [pawpaws], but after they [Delawares] whipped them, they [Osages] made peace, and they had what they called "Coffee Days." They would meet over here at Young's Lake. They would come from over there, and we would come from here, probably only the people on this side of the river, and we would exchange coffee gifts and became great friends. But the Osages never got along with the Cherokees. I believe secretly we gave them right to passage to build that lake over there. [Dee and Ed laughing]

ED: This is kind of interesting about the history and why they got rid of the Big House. Like the present chief [Joe Brooks]. It was his great-great-great-grandfather and other Baptist preachers in their coat and tails, they were rich enough to have coat and tails; it was the dress of the wealthy people of that time, and beaver hats. They would stand outside of the Big House and yell and try to disrupt the meetings by saying they [Delawares] were practicing idolatry there. So that was the reason . . .

DEE: Influx of Christianity was one thing and . . .

ED: Yes. Because people were dependant on the leadership because when we came down here from the land that we sold [in Kansas], we were promised annuities every year. We only had one annuity, and it was controlled by the people in the Journeycake leadership. That was the reason for the great division. But there were a lot of Christians who also came to the Big House. Because on this side of the river even though there are a lot of Wilsons, we are all separate groups, not kin to each other. We are scattered all down the river all the way past Dewey to where the Buffalo Ranch is—all the way down there are Wilson families. But most of them kind of moved out and went to town 'cause they were Christian, but they attended.

DEE: They attended the Big House?

ED: Yes, because they understood that it wasn't in competition with Christianity; matter of fact, it was a higher level *[laughing]* of Christianity. It's a ritualized thing to get the behavior of people directly in tune with the Creator. There has been many, especially among the Swedish, who came here as settlers, that made comments that the Delawares' religion was so similar to the Christians. It's not in competition.

DEE: When the Moravians came and started talking to the traditional Delawares, it wasn't hard for them to accept the concept of one God. They were certainly in tune with that. One of the things that has never been talked about, but for a lot of people who haven't been to Oklahoma, they have a little bit of a misconception of what the Indian population looks like today, but even back then, I think because of Hollywood, makes it appear that we had feathers and war bonnets and that type of thing. That certainly was not the case. When they attended these meetings they just came in their regular clothes.

ED: Regular clothes. They didn't have costumes because they cooked, ate, socialized, and had different days for different rituals. They even had a day for the women. They had an important ritual, which is the Doll Dance. It was important for the children. Through these dolls they found out who the healers were. There is one thing that is kind of interesting. We are sitting a few miles from the Osages line. Hollywood cowboy and Indians started in Pawhuska, Oklahoma. That's where the movies started. Tom Mix and all of those others came from ranches around here and went to Hollywood because they had the wild, Wild West shows at the 101 Ranch. That was a forerunner to the silent movies, and they [the cowboys who worked on the ranches] all moved out [to Hollywood]. So they took that perception [feathers and war bonnets] with them. Even though they knew it wasn't true, it made a good story.

Interview continues after a break

DEE: Today, Ed Wilson, who I am talking to, still lives on part of his ancestors' . . .

ED: Yes, on my dad's allotment. Eighty acres. My Grandpa William— you see that flat place out there, he got the best 160 acres—was surrounded with his family of five children. His boys and daughter were farther down south, and this place we are sitting on was his son who was in World War I, Walter, this was his allotment. Right over there on the other side was . . .

DEE: Pointing north.

ED: was Tom's. And around it, which is a half mile long and an eighth of a mile wide, is a strip east and west, and a strip north and south, the same size which is forty acres was my dad's. He surrounded himself with his children, so he had all of the land together.

DEE: You are following a lot in your ancestral heritage by virtue you are farming.

ED: I am going to be seventy-six in a short while [in 2004]. I have had a very successful life in the military. Also a successful life in business. I worked in defense mainly because I was trained in electronics, especially on bomb sights and secret kinds of things. They still use that bomb sight. Also different kinds of armaments controlled by electronics, such as the smart bomb. I was involved in the air-to-air missiles, the ground-to-air missiles, the cruise aircraft. I was involved with the Sperry Gyroscope and bomb sight (electronic radar sight). I went to work for American Airlines. I went to college. I came from Sequoyah Indian School into the service. When I got out I went to Bacone Indian College to keep my heritage alive. All my brothers went to Bacone Indian College, and even though we went there at different times, we stayed in the same room. Room 35 in McCoy Hall. Mc-Coy Hall later burned down.

DEE: That was in Muskogee, Oklahoma?

ED: Yes. Then I went to Oklahoma University; from OU, I went to Sperry Gyroscope. I was in pre-med—that was my training—but I couldn't get the money together to go to medical school, even though I was admitted. I was second in the state. Back then they only took seventy-five from the whole United States. I didn't have the money so I worked to pay off my father's debts. [He overextended over a long period of time.] I was an advisor/consultant at Sperry and then went to American Airlines and worked for them for forty-three years. They changed the term from "electronics" to "avionics," that's aviation electronics. I was involved with all things they developed. I was involved in the Transport Workers: Local #514 Union. I served as [union] president when I was a young man. I served as vice president. The president died, and I only served about eighteen months in 1964. I didn't serve again until probably 1978. I had served in minor positions. At that time when I became president, I was president fifteen years. I negotiated big contracts, not only with American Airlines, but with Zebco and many other big companies.

Since I dealt with these big companies, my biggest achievement was that I made a model. I never had an original idea in my life. I took other people's ideas and melded them together, sorted them out, and got rid of all the objections so that I would have a consensus—which is the Delaware way of leadership. Once we have consensus, we can move a project forward. I took this [model] and used it with the major corporations. Whenever you have people who are missing work or have family problems, alcohol or drug problems, any of the problems that people have that interfere with their ability to work together and produce usually becomes a union problem because they are fixing to fire these people. When they fire them, we have to represent them, and when they go back, they are usually fired again for the same reason.

Well, I thought about this for a long time during that period that I wasn't president. I was in the office talking to people from the Alcoholics Anonymous and all those people who worked on crises. I put that together with a cost analysis on how much it costs to train a new employee and get him up to that level as the one's knowledge that they just fired. I took it to them, and my first try was a total failure because the leadership in the union was a failure. *[Chuckles.]* They didn't want that because they lost their function of representation. Then I went to Florida Power and Light. I have some connections with them, and they said, "Let's do it." Then I took it back to American Airlines and, without the approval of the union, they accepted it. Today, it's probably in most the major companies, all the Fortune 500 companies. They call it the Employee Assistance Program. So when people are discharged, you find out the reason, get counseling and everything, and if you finally can't get along, you separate them. When you separate them, you let them go home with pay. Used to [be], whenever you discharge someone, you sent them home without pay. [With] this system you sent them home with pay so they could reflect. And then if they come back and say, I tried and tried and tried, and I just can't do it, they give them a stipend of $500, which was a lot of money back then, give them traveling expenses for them and their family to help them find another job, and ship them there. Well, that was my biggest achievement.

I've been involved and friends with people. President Johnson was a friend. He considered me his friend. I was friends with Martin Luther King. I was scheduled to go on the march in Selma, but some other business happened here that I couldn't go there. Some of the people I was associated with through my influence attended that march. Also, my best friend was Stuart Symington. I first knew him as secretary of the air force. That's how I got to know him. He treated me like a son. He became a senator from the state of Missouri. Also, I not only had friends in the labor union, but President Clinton sent me personal notes from his desk. I've still got them.

DEE: How many brothers do you have?

ED: Four brothers and no sisters.

DEE: Do you have any children?

ED: Yes, I have five children. We raised three of my ex-wife's cousins, too. In addition to that I have raised six Indian families.

DEE: That's kind of the old Delaware way, isn't it?

ED: Yes. Too poor, dysfunctional, whatever. It's kind of strange that out of that six families only one of them didn't go to prison, because of the dysfunctional thing that occurred. Indians are so susceptible to the wickedness of the white men.

DEE: I know your one daughter did work for the tribe.

ED: She's an attorney. My brothers all went to college. Lester Jack became the civilian head of Tinker Air Force Base in Oklahoma City, Oklahoma. He wanted to be a doctor. We all wanted to be doctors, but none of us ever made it. He became an industrial engineer and a clinical psychologist. A very, very important job.

DEE: Consequently, your folks instilled the importance of education in you . . .

ED: My dad did. My mother died in 1929. She left the day after I was born because she was so sick. She went to kinfolks over around Lenape and Delaware and that area [north of Nowata, Oklahoma]. She stayed there and died one day after I was a year old. I never remember seeing her. She went to school at Haskell. [It is now Haskell Indian Nations University in Lawrence, Kansas.] My dad only had a third-grade education in a little school that my grandfather gave the land to. He was self-educated, even though he only read the *Kansas City Star Weekly*. It was free and came in the mailbox. That was his only outlet to civilization because he lived out by himself, away from people, and he didn't have communication with newspapers, radios, but the point is that he knew more about current affairs—when I came to visit with him he knew more than I did, and I was in contact with it. I never understood that until recently when my son [William Victor Wilson] being an artist stated to me when I asked him, "How can this be?" He replied, "There is universal knowledge. People know a lot of things." He said, "Socrates didn't read any books." *[Laughter.]*

DEE: I want to ask you a question. Our last ceremonial chief elected by the tribal council [Leonard Thompson] passed away at age ninety-eight [in 2002]. He always told me (he was my cousin) we are losing our full-bloods. I am sure you have observed the same. We are missing a lot.

ED: There is a simple answer to that: "Indian men like the blonde, blue-eyed women with white skin, and the white man likes the brown woman that works." *[Laughs.]*

DEE: Well, don't you think that there was a little bit of thought from the government through the allotment checker boarding throughout the Indian Territory mixing Indian family, white family, Indian family, as your next-door neighbor?

ED: They had a plan, and that plan was to do several things: The main thing in the Delaware history that people could never comprehend is that the agreement between the Cherokees and the Delawares that was signed by the leadership was rejected by the General Council or the people—the Traditionalists. Well, they went back because the Indian agent was some kin, whether a father-in-law or I don't know, of Journeycake. They took that, and Journeycake's rationale was, public-wise, we want to do this because as soon as we can Christianize them, we can get rid of their pagan ceremonies, we can separate them, and then they will be Christians. That was the reasoning behind that, except what happened was a few escaped that net.

DEE: I wanted to visit with you because you are one of the last fullbloods that we have still here in Oklahoma, and I think the history that you have and your traditional family has, are so valuable, with your particular insight. Today, in the later years of our country you are somewhat still holding on to some of those traditional things by living on and working the land.

ED: I guess it is kind of important for you to understand this, I'm here because I am driven. I'd rather be in Tahiti picking up shells. And I could easily do it. I could travel. I could get on any airplane, and they will take me anywhere I want to go for nothing. But I came back up here and moved within thirty yards of where I was born. I came up here because they told me I was going to be dead within three weeks. I brought my little bed and some clothes. I moved up there, but you can look at me—I am as healthy as a horse. You wouldn't know I have cancer. Nobody can tell. I have been diagnosed with severe type two diabetes, which in itself is a bad disease. Plus, I have multiple sclerosis. All of that together, I shouldn't be able to do the things I do.

DEE: I will let the audience know that you have a wonderful garden.

ED: A big garden, an irrigated garden on top of a hill that the dirt is only four inches deep because this is just a great big hill.

DEE: As a matter of fact, today I picked up some of the produce, some of the things you have grown . . .

ED: Beans, peaches, peppers . . .

DEE: I am taking them to the Delaware Elder Nutrition Program in Bartlesville to help them out. I have big boxes in my truck, and I will be delivering them this morning. You are not only living in an area which your ancestors came from, but you are resembling what they did best: growing and sharing.

ED: I don't sell anything.

DEE: Giving it away. Where you live today, there are some stacked rocks up there.

ED: We don't want to talk about them. All kinds of people have speculated why they are there. I know why they are there. There is also another pile of them, right straight that direction.

DEE: West.

ED: Right through there on top of that hill there's one. I am probably the last person that knows the significance, but I haven't been impressed to release that. They need to know. The spirits are still there. This morning, first of all I live in about a thirty-one-foot trailer with pretty primitive conditions. I won't let people on my land. I'm purifying it and restoring it to what it was. The grasses, birds, all the vegetation, the trees, all the shrubs that people would kill using pesticides, is what I am restoring. I haven't brought things back, but I am making a place for them to come to. Some people call it "pelated," but I call it a "pilated" woodpecker. I've got a whole colony of them over there.

I don't have a TV, I don't have a radio, I don't read any newspapers or magazines. Occasionally, my son brings an article from the *Nations* magazine that I scan over. It's stool reading for me. [*Laughs.*] You can talk to me; I know about all what's going on probably more than people who study. But I have tried to use my brain, a big open computer that stores everything. I can't seem to recall it all, but it's stored, a big hard drive. I have taken all of the junk and erased it. I've erased all the things I learned that were useless.

I have developed a philosophy. I thought I'd found something. I found out people already knew it. All religions are the same. Really, all the same God. But I live up here trying to cleanse my mind and make an environment for the birds. I've got birds that aren't supposed to be living up here. I won't kill anything. I won't even kill a tick, a mosquito, or a fly. They are creatures of God. I am trying to chase all the bad spirits away and take care of the animals.

DEE: We are now returning to talk about Ed's immediate family.

ED: My brother Vic [Victor] is older than I. He was the smartest. The next brother, Oliver Dean, was two years older than me. He worked for Oveta Hobby, first secretary of health and welfare, and owner/publisher of the *Houston Post*. Oliver was managing editor of the *Galveston News* and employed by the *Houston Post* as the managing editor after going through all their departments. He then had a car accident that impaired his ability to withstand the stress of the newspaper. He ended up being a sports editor and retired from the *Washington Post,* which was a great achievement for anybody, much less a little Indian school Delaware.

My daughter, Fawn, the oldest one, is an accountant. My next son, Edward, died of a heart attack. He was a world-class chess player. That's all he was interested in. He played people like Bobby Fischer. He beat Bobby Fischer.

Then next is Carolyn; she's an attorney. She was very successful in advertising. She went to college and went to San Francisco to the biggest advertising firm in the world. She had many big accounts. One day she decided she was going to law school to help Indians. She worked for Larry Oliver, a noted criminal attorney. She gave up a promising career and went to work for the [Delaware] Tribe. I think she told you that she just wanted to help her people.

DEE: Absolutely.

ED: What she went to work for, an elephant wouldn't work for in a circus because it was peanuts. [*Laughs.*]

DEE: Well, there was no questions about it. It was a real coup from the Delaware Tribe's perspective to get her to come and help the people. She didn't come to work for money, but came to work for her people, and that's exactly what she did. She developed a program for the tribe to help the less fortunate Delawares who couldn't afford an attorney. I think it was one of the first programs of any tribe that I ever heard of that had an attorney on staff who would help tribal members who couldn't afford to hire an attorney for themselves.

ED: Or didn't want to. I need to tell you one thing about Carolyn. She is brilliant.

DEE: I noticed I always had a hard time talking to her. *[Laughs.]*

ED: She is such a kind person. You notice how she laughs. Her laugh is a Delaware trait. That was the trait of my Grandfather William. He called himself Willum. He didn't go ha ha ha. Delawares go hee hee hee hee. There is a story about him going home one day, and they told him someone had stolen six of his horses. So he didn't even dismount. He said, "Which way did they go"? Four days later he came back with the six horses. They asked what happened to those three men that stole them horses. Grandpa said, "Hee hee hee; they won't be stealing any more." *[Laughs.]* I say this because Carolyn and him laugh exactly alike; they laugh all the time. It's not a nervous laugh. Sometimes I think they know something we don't know. *[Laughs.]*

DEE: Talk about your other son.

ED: My other son, Will, is named after my grandfather. He lives on Grandfather's allotment on the road. He designed what everyone calls a hut, a little building designed so he can work. He's a stone artist, as well as being an artist, painting.

DEE: He is in San Francisco as we speak?

ED: No, in Santa Fe. He took a large, large, probably a 4½ foot, 800-pound head of a horse carved of limestone that not everybody can work with. He entered it in the "Trail of Tears" [art show] and won third. They had pictures on the website of him unloading it because it is such a feat. Loading and unloading is such a feat that no one could figure out how because of the balance of it and traveling over the Oklahoma roads in a pickup. *[Laughs.]*

But anyway, he's a great one. He did something that comes to my mind that is very important. He made this Mĕsingw out of stone. We went up to the quarry in Minnesota to get steatite or soapstone used years ago to make bowls because it could absorb the heat. This was the pots that they had back then. They used it in furnaces because it holds heat. Anyway, he built it, and we have it now. Everyone remarks of its power. You've seen it?

DEE: No, I don't think I have seen that.

ED: They need to get that up there [in Indiana at the Eiteljorg Museum]. It's significant to us. It's a work of art.

DEE: He is a wonderful artist. I have seen a lot of his work. I think, as modest as you can be, a lot of your talents have certainly rubbed off on your kids.

ED: I have another son, my youngest son, who is a cook. I'll tell you what, he can make a steak that is almost a joy to put a tooth into.

DEE: I am about to wrap this up, Ed. I really do appreciate your time that you have taken to reflect about your life, the property you are on, some of the rich history you have, and about the Wilsons being such a traditional family still toiling at the soil or land and giving personally as you have. I want to thank you for the time you have taken to reflect on your life because it has been a very successful life.

ED: I am not going to do any more interviews or write anything down.

DEE: Thanks again, Ed Wilson.

EDWARD WILSON: Thank you.

Oral History, June 23, 2004, at the Wilson allotment
northwest of Copan, Oklahoma, recorded by Dee Ketchum,
transcribed by Annette Ketchum.

Bucky Buck's trailer was beaded by his wife, Sandy, and incorporates her turtle design (lower left). The black diamond with the white cross symbolizes a cross. The intersecting black design on a red background and the cross are historic Delaware designs. Sandy Buck beaded for two weeks to complete the trailer. The trailer drapes from the back of a man's collar to just above the ground when dancing. In this picture, Buck draped the trailer over his leg while resting between dances.

The Passage started as an 18,000-pound block of Kansas limestone when Will Wilson, Delaware artist, began work. He has worked 800 of an estimated 1,000 hours needed to complete the piece, which he is carving in Sedan, Kansas.

WILL WILSON

Artist
Born 1961 in Tulsa, Oklahoma

Opening remarks: Dee Ketchum conducted the interviews with both tribal elder Edward Wilson and Will Wilson, his son.

DEE KETCHUM: Will, I want to ask you some questions about your art career and your work. I know your dad, Ed Wilson, is Delaware and your mother is Sioux Arickara. Do you have brothers and sisters?

WILL WILSON: Yes, I have one brother deceased, one brother in Tulsa, a sister in Reno, Nevada, and a sister in Tulsa.

DEE: Where were you born, Will, and where do you live now?

WILL: I was born in Tulsa, Oklahoma, and I live at Copan, Oklahoma.

DEE: Do you live on your family allotment?

WILL: Yes, on the original Indian allotment. It's been handed down. It feels good to live there. It's like living in your own little country. You don't have any codes or anything like that.

DEE: Where did you go to high school and other schooling?

WILL: I went to Hale High School. My art training is from an old man named Clarence Allen. He taught me how to paint. There was another old Indian guy named Dick West [Dr. Richard West]. He was a renowned Indian artist. Basically, he was one of the founders of Indian art. He was the head of the Bacone College Art Department for over forty years. So he taught a lot of Indian art. He was a full-blood Cheyenne. He did flat, traditional style of painting. A lot of his teachings to me was basically old Indian stories, and history and things of that nature.

I was in high school between the ages of fifteen and eighteen years when I was trained by these men. They were both eighty years old. So they were as old as the state of Oklahoma. They are both passed on. Dick West's son is the one who is chairman [president and CEO] of the new [Smithsonian] Museum of the American Indians in Washington, D.C.

DEE: So those men were the ones who really inspired you to get started?

WILL: I wanted to do art when I was even younger. I mowed Clarence Allen's lawn when I was young, and I asked him to teach me. He told me, "Learn to draw and come back, and I will teach you." So I drew for about two years and went back, and as agreed, he did teach me.

DEE: When you were young, did you sit around sketching things?

WILL: I did very little. I didn't think I was very good. I had a good eye, but I didn't have any skills. What really inspired me was a few of my friends my age and a couple of years older picked it [art] up in a very short period of time, six months to a year, and they were pretty good. When I saw them do it, I thought, well, it can be done.

DEE: Was there a particular type of art that you were doing at that time?

WILL: I experimented with most two-dimensional mediums: scratch board, pastels, watercolors, oils, acrylics. Basically, I have done a little bit of all of it. Not just the mediums, but different genre, too: landscapes, figurative painting, abstracts.

DEE: Has living in Oklahoma been a plus for you and an inspiration, living around so much culture of different tribes and so forth?

WILL: I definitely think the Oklahoma artists have a lot more to draw from with so many tribes here. When I go to the Southwest, I love Pueblo, Zuni, and Navaho art, but after a while it seems to get a little more generic. In Oklahoma we have a lot more experimentation going on. It raises the question, What is Indian Art? Lots of discussion goes on about it.

DEE: Since you have a rich Indian background to draw from, does that inspire you?

WILL: Yes, but I take a lot of my inspiration from western art, too. I incorporate that into the Indian ways of doing things. It's a mix. It goes back to when I make an abstract. It will have the Indian thought behind it, but it is still pure form. The argument is that there isn't an Indian or a buffalo in it, so is that Indian art?

DEE: How do you come up with the creativity?

WILL: I have ideas all the time that I want to do. Of course, I can come up with a lot more ideas than I can sit down and do, so there is always that selective process. Lately, I have been doing a lot of pieces that I've wanted to do for a long time. I come across that certain piece of stone, and I am limited to the stone—whatever I can get. Once in a while, I get inspired by the stone itself. I will sit and look at that rock for four or five hours. Some people don't consider that working, but it drains me sitting and saying to that stone, "Give me something."

DEE: One of your pieces is in the Eiteljorg Museum in Indianapolis. Has that been an inspiration to you, too?

WILL: Yes, that's what I've worked on for years and years and years— finally getting work in a museum. People place a value at large on that recognition.

DEE: Tell me a little bit about what inspired you to do that piece; tell me about that piece.

WILL: The piece, the Mësingw, is a symbol that goes back a thousand years. It is the protector of the forest and the Delaware people. The real inspiration for me to create it goes back to when I was a child and my grandfather used to make real big ones [of wood]. After seeing his, that image was burned into my mind. I think of it often still. I always wanted to make one [Mësingw] in stone, which had never been done. It's my medium, and it was a matter of coming up with two just right stones that I could put together—one in black and one in red. I used catlinite and steatite. I can get the steatite in fairly large pieces, but that one side of the mask in catlinite is as big as those pieces come, as far as thickness, and it is an anomaly to find a piece [of catlinite] that is that big and that thick. I had those two perfect pieces [of stone], and I put them together and made the Mësingw. I found the catlinite in Minnesota. I drove up to Minnesota and got the stone. I knew the stone was there, but it usually only comes an inch and a half or two inches thick. To get a piece that was four or five inches thick—well, I hadn't seen anything like it, and I've seen a lot of that stone.

DEE: What kind of tools did you use and how did you work that piece?

WILL: I used the basic hammer, chisel, files, sandpaper, and a few little grinding stones.

DEE: Did you draw it [the Mësingw] out on paper before you started?

WILL: No. I rarely start like that. I believe in using minimal preliminary work. I had the image in my mind, and I just started working the stones.

DEE: How long did it take you to complete the piece?

WILL: A piece like that runs about sixty to seventy hours. Even though it is a relatively simple piece, I just rechecked it and rechecked it on the finish and did the very, very best job I could do on it. Plus, I had to make that granite base. So it took eight to ten days. I have made a couple of smaller Mësingw, and my vision really is to make a big one. I will probably make one more, and that will be all.

DEE: It had to be a proud moment when you completed the Mësingw, right?

WILL: Oh, yes, I couldn't stop looking at it. I would walk back a hundred yards and look at it, and still it would jump out at me. It is one of the favorite pieces I have ever done. I put that in with the best of any of my work. It is simpler to do than other work, but as for the presence and power of it, I found it was unequal to anything I've ever done.

DEE: I felt the same way about Mësingw when I first saw it and when I donated it to the Eiteljorg, I was proud because I know the piece means so much to the Delaware people.

WILL: It doesn't just represent my work, it represents the tribe, the history, and my grandfather. There is just so much more behind it. To have it represented there [the Eiteljorg] for other people to see and to represent the tribe in that setting means a lot to me. That museum is one of the nicest in the country.

DEE: I agree with that, and I have been to lots of museums. The Eiteljorg and its staff represent and showcase the most marvelous work.

WILL: Everything they have is top of the line in that museum. Whoever designed the place originally created a building that is a masterpiece. It is impressive.

DEE: Do you work on one sculpture at a time or more than one at a time?

WILL: I try to work on one at a time. But right now I have five pieces that I have started. When I get like this, it gets to where I am just working on finishing for over a week and that gets tedious. I try to start one piece and finish one piece at a time.

DEE: Do you have a favorite type of art?

WILL: Stone is definitely my favorite. It is the collaboration between nature and man. When I'm working with it, I'm pushing on it; it's pushing back at me. The finished product has so much warmth. It has so much more warmth than a bronze that's cold; it's hard steel. Stone has life in it. That's why it's my favorite.

DEE: I know you are working on a piece in Sedan, Kansas, a large piece. Tell me a little about that.

WILL: I call that *The Passage*. It represents the Delaware people coming this way. She is looking back over her shoulder. I wanted something that had a tribal significance and historical viewpoint.

DEE: So it represents the Delaware Trail of Tears as they arrived in Indian Territory in 1867.

WILL: Yes, but we just don't cry about it as much as the Cherokees do. [*Laughs.*]

DEE: Your inspiration comes from the piece of stone itself, and you think about it a lot as you . . .

WILL: Yes, a lot of pieces I am doing now, I wanted to do ten years ago. The idea is still there. Those tend to be some of my best pieces. All the time I am filtering through those ideas. There is no way in ten lifetimes that I could do all the ideas, a least not in stone sculpture. I have seen artists that work in mediums that are extremely fast and can complete a piece in a couple of hours. Their process is so much faster that they can complete thousands of pieces where I can probably only complete a thousand stone sculptures in my lifetime.

DEE: Do you have any future plans other than continuing on with what you are doing?

WILL: Yes, I would like to move on to do some bigger monumental pieces, which is harder to do because I can't create one of those pieces and haul it over the country until I sell it. I have to have a place where I'm going to put it. The funding, of course, is up into the tens of thousands of dollars just in the cost of making a certain piece.

DEE: Is finding the right stone a large part of your work?

WILL: Well, that is one of my favorite parts. It's like a giant Easter egg hunt. I go out there, say a prayer, head in a certain direction, knowing that certain stone is out there. More often then not, I find what I am looking for. I've hit the back roads out in western Oklahoma, crisscross crossed, gone here and there, got out the binoculars and looked. It's old-time prospecting. It's a combination of luck and faith. I just put myself out there in the elements and wrestle that rock once I find it.

DEE: Is there a certain stone you like to work more than another?

WILL: I like to work with alabaster, and I am moving more to working with marble. It is harder and can be stored outdoors. Marble is more durable.

DEE: Do you go looking for a certain stone with an idea in mind, or do you see a stone and create an idea after you find it?

WILL: Sometimes I go out looking for a stone of a certain shape to make a sculpture, or I need a certain color, or certain qualities in the stone as to how it works. But mostly I go out for a certain type of stone. As I am out in the field I have all the ideas cataloged in my head, and boom, there's a buffalo, or there is a rabbit looking at me over there. It's a field of visions; they are already out there, but I have to be out there [with the stones] for the process to work.

DEE: Do you see yourself staying here in Oklahoma, or do you plan to go to other areas of the country?

WILL: No, I basically have been all over. I have seen everything that's out there. I came here to stay. I don't plan on going anywhere.

DEE: We are blessed with your work in the Delaware Community Center. Also, I know you had work at a gallery in Tulsa. Where is your work?

WILL: I deal with two galleries in Tulsa. One is downtown on Fourth Street, Native American Art. I deal with another gallery up on Sheridan. It is the Art Market. I deal with a gallery in Santa Fe. It's the Shush Yaz Trading Company. I am always taking them something new and keep them stocked. They all prefer something a little different.

DEE: You are young in age and old in experience. What would you tell the young artists today who think they have an interest in art, either Indian or non-Indian?

WILL: First of all I would tell them to learn the basics well and thoroughly. That includes all the science behind art. Once you are there, find your own way. Don't try to emulate someone else's work. Try to find your own style, something you really like to do. Just as importantly, if they want to be a professional artist, learn how to put yourself out there and talk to people about it.

DEE: Is it better to have diversification in one's art, or is it better to be focused in one area?

WILL: The market will always reward redundancy. The market really wants artists to do the same thing so it can recognize their works. They want that signature style. That's been a real challenge for me because I've never had that. I change the way I do things. It's been more difficult for me [to have a signature style]. I gave up on that a long time ago. I don't necessarily have to chase the money so much if I make everything top-notch quality. There will always be people out there who can recognize that.

DEE: Do you think having a mentor like you had is what is needed by young boys to learn basic skills of art?

WILL: Well, everyone has their own way. That's hard to find, what I had—someone who knew everything about artwork and had a lot of time to spend teaching it. It is whatever resources you can pull together. Some people will go to New York City and go to the Art Students League, which is probably the best training. The Institute of American Indian Art in Santa Fe has turned out a lot of really good artists. If I were to give advice to someone who wanted to go to school, it would be to go someplace that specializes in art training, versus going to the state university [and] getting an art degree. That's good [art degree] if you want to be a high school teacher. If you want to be a professional artist, you are a lot better off going to Chicago Institute of Fine Arts, the San Francisco Institute, or IAIA in Santa Fe. Everyone is an artist in these schools. So you feed off one another's energy. You will see what it really takes; you inspire one another. That is a lot better, I think, as far as training.

DEE: Is the Indian and western art and its popularity rising, declining, plateauing, and does it cycle?

WILL: Yes, there is definitely a cycle for it. The boom years in Indian art and Southwest art were from 1980 to 1995. Then there was a sharp decline, going down, down, down, until it finally plateaued. There are still people who appreciate it and have money, but at the same time, the people who were driving the market were older people who are not with us anymore. Their children got those huge collections and dumped them on the market. So for a while the market was flooded with so much art. It was a great time during those years. People don't realize just how much artwork was produced during those years. It was estimated that in just Southwest Indian stone sculpture during the years from 1985 to 1995 there was more stone being carved than at any other time during the history of the world in any place. That's more than Italy or ancient India. Artists were carving tons and tons of work, just in the U.S. Southwest. It was a phenomenon. It was helpful to me just being a part of that time with so many sculptors.

DEE: Have you seen over a period of time that American Indian artists have been accepted and come out over the last twenty or so years to be proud to be Indian?

WILL: Yes, I have seen a lot of that. It's a healthy thing. In 1992 the population of Indians doubled because they were willing to admit they were Indian. The numbers or birth rate didn't double; they were being re-born. It's still easier to be an Indian artist than any other ethnic artist. There are more Caucasian artists and a lot more competition because of the numbers. They have a lot harder time setting themselves apart.

DEE: I wish you the best, Will. Keep producing your fine art.

Oral history interview on December 7, 2005, at the Delaware Community Center in Bartlesville, Oklahoma, by Dee Ketchum, transcribed by Annette Ketchum.

Former chief Curtis Zunigha, a Vietnam veteran who serves on the Delaware Tribe Color Guard, at the 2006 Delaware Powwow near Copan, Oklahoma.

CURTIS ZUNIGHA

Tribal member, chief, 1994–1998
Born 1953 in St. Louis, Missouri

I reside in Bartlesville, Oklahoma, and currently serve as executive director of the Delaware Tribe Housing Authority.[1] It's interesting that from the office I occupy in the Delaware Tribal Headquarters I can look out my window and see the house that my father was born in. So, I've come full circle after being born in St. Louis at the time my father was in the United States Air Force. I was raised on air force bases all around the world. My connection with my Indian heritage, with my Lenape identity, was more or less through my dad's mother, my grandmother, Edna Wilson Zunigha, who lived in Copan, Oklahoma. Whenever we came to Oklahoma to visit my grandma and grandpa, she would tell me stories, and I would be in rural Copan, Oklahoma, where a lot of Delaware allotments were, and in some cases still are. So, my recollections of childhood, as far as my Lenape heritage, has to go back to that time and place and with that particular woman. Her husband was a Pueblo Indian. So, the Lenape, or Delaware, connection was through her and any of those stories. My father didn't pass a lot on to me, other than to be proud of my Indian heritage. But, I didn't know a lot about the customs and traditions of the Lenape.

In 1866 the Delaware tribe signed a treaty with the United States of America that was the last treaty in our historic record. In the treaty we promised to sell our reservation in Kansas and be removed to the Indian Territory. At the same time, of course, the Cherokee Nation had signed a treaty with the United States promising to accommodate tribes coming down from Kansas, making land available for sale. Delawares purchased that land and began to cross over the state line into Indian Territory beginning late 1867. It took a couple of years for everyone to come on down. My ancestors, who would really be my grandma's grandparents, were the ones that came down; that was the generation that came down. Her father, James Wilson, was born in, I believe, 1875, but he would have been born here in Indian Territory. He is buried up in the Dewey Cemetery. He and his wife lived in Copan and Dewey before they were really towns.

---

1. In 2002, Curtis Zunigha resigned to become an independent television producer.

As far as allotments, the agreement was that the Delawares would take the proceeds from the sale of their reservation in Kansas. Those proceeds would be used to purchase land in the Indian Territory on Cherokee Nation Indian Territory. The amount would be 160 acres for every man, woman, and child that came down. In addition to that, the allotment area began in the late part of the nineteenth century and the early part of the twentieth century. Those were endeavors to again provide individual allotments of land through government control, ostensibly to benefit individual Indians and to give them so-called more control over their own lands. But actually it was a prelude to abolishing tribal governments, tribal courts. Then, in the year 1907, statehood occurred, and Oklahoma became a state. With those allotments, however, ultimately any individual Delawares who were on an approved government roll had 160 acres of land allotted to them. For a lot of the Delawares around here it may not have been contiguous land. As an aggregate, you may have had 30 acres over here and then later on you'd have a little piece over here. As an aggregate, you were allotted 160 acres.

My grandmother's allotment, which she lived on until the 1960s, was just west of Copan, Oklahoma, not far from the Caney River. Today, in the year 2000, it is about at the site where the floodgates of the Copan Lake are. I still go up there often and look up in the hills and look off in the distance and remember times when I was a little boy playing with my cousins and playing ball and looking for frogs along the river and going out with my grandma and picking poke. [Pokeweed is a plant used in dyeing.] Those are some memories that I have. Through her dad, my grandmother has told me stories of what it was like to be an Indian person, and the Indian Territory and then later, the state of Oklahoma. That was still in days that they had wagons and horses, and the young Indian kids went to boarding school. So, as far as the move coming down from Kansas, I can say that there was first a small group of tribal leaders that were sent down as an advance party to negotiate the sale of this property and that they went to look for the best land. Heading due south out of what was the reservation, near approximately what is now Leavenworth, Kansas, they came into an area of what is now known as Washington County. When they hit the Caney River, knowing that they had just crossed the border, and we're talking about from the Kansas border now to the Caney River today, we're talking about twelve to fourteen miles, they hit the Caney River, looked around, and said, "This is a good starting spot." So those are the stories of leaders coming down to pick a place first, and then as establishing council with Cherokee Nation tribal leaders and negotiating some kind of an agreement on what they would purchase and what the price would be and those kind of things. Now, that's just a little bit of somewhat fleeting information. That would have occurred again with her grandparents' generation. Most of the stories that I remember from my grandmother had to do with her as a little girl and then growing up in this area around here.

There are a number of Wilsons, actually two strands of Wilsons, in among the Delawares around here. So many married into other tribes also, so the bloodlines become somewhat diminished as far as full-blood Delawares. We don't have many that are still around here. But, the extension of those Wilsons that came down, there are some records that has in parenthesis their Lenape/Delaware name, on some of those old enrollment forms, particularly for the full-bloods. However, right down the road from my grandma's house was a gentleman by the name of Reuben Wilson, a distant relation. Reuben was known not only as one of those traditionalists involved in the Big House church ceremony, but he was also pretty well known as an archer. He really knew how to shoot those arrows. They say that at a certain point in his life he lost a leg, so he would go around with crutches. And he would stand there and balance himself on a crutch and still shoot arrows with a bow, balancing himself on a crutch. I have relations today that might be three or four generations removed, second, third cousin, fourth cousin, that we've traced back to those Wilsons, names like Ice Wilson, Buffalo Wilson, those are common ancestors. My cousin, who is our tribal council member, Bucky Buck, he goes back to Wilsons also.[2] That's my connection with some of those folks.

The Indian boarding schools were set up regionally, and so you had a lot, remembering that we had over thirty tribes headquartered, removed, to the Indian Territory. Therefore, when the government boarding schools were built and young Indians were sent to them, you had them growing up into their teenage years and even later, and relationships were developed. That's what happened with my grandmother. She met Dedal Julian Zunigha at Chilocco Indian School. They eventually married in the early 1920s and that produced four children, my father Curtis being the third of four children. So, there are lots of Indians in my grandparents' and my father's generation who become multi-tribal in their heritage because of those marriages. It just had to do with the evolution of tribes moving and co-mingling with each other. The boarding schools were sort of a forced co-mingling. In many cases, with tribe's population being so decimated, you didn't have a lot to choose from, from your own people. And when your tribal population becomes diminished, it's kind of slim pickings. The pretty girl might be your cousin, so you start looking out there to other tribes. The Delawares,

---

2. In 2002, Bucky Buck was named chair of the Delaware Culture Preservation Committee.

too, married into the whites. Delawares and Cherokees do around here. The founding father, so to speak, of the town of Bartlesville, Jacob Bartles, married a full-blood Delaware woman, Nannie Journeycake. They were kind of like the first couple of Bartlesville. Later, their son, half-blood Joe Bartles, was the chief—well, they call it the chairman—of the Delaware Tribe for almost thirty years.

I've had opportunities over the last several years, in part because of my responsibilities as an elected tribal leader, to travel back to areas and along our historic migratory trail. So, I have been to Indiana, along the White River. I've been to Ohio along the Tuscarawas River. I've been to Pennsylvania along the Delaware River; New York along the Hudson River. It is what I call blood memory. There is a sense of belonging, a sense of there was something here that I'm connecting with. Later, that sense tells me that it's ancestral, it's passed down to me without even realizing it. I'm grateful for that. Most places, when I do go back to the east, I'm welcomed. There is a great interest in the Lenape heritage, the Delaware presence, historically. All too often those people's perspective of the Delawares at those spots is, in their minds, what it was like in 1780 or 1820. So, they want to know what the Delawares are doing today, and who are the Delaware people today? When I tell them about our development and what we're like today, they're quite amazed, because they kind of thought that the Delawares had more or less vanished or died out. So, they are quite pleased to hear our development. But again it's that feeling of I've been here before, somehow, and so therefore I feel at home and relaxed. And then to be on the shores of the ocean in New Jersey, that is yet another feeling; it is connected to the land. The Delawares are smart; they get around the water, too. And so there is that feeling of I was here.

The landscape may have changed for the Delawares during their historic migration from the East Coast. I think that the Delaware leaders were looking for, first of all, water, a place to set up a village near water; second, cover, mainly physical protection; and third, I think that they were always looking for a place to grow crops. With those things in mind, the rest of it was really more instinctive. When they first came down here [to Oklahoma Territory], the Delawares primarily settled in what's now Washington County. The only group that split off did so because of some cultural differences. History tells us that the Delawares had two decided factions. They had the traditionalists and they had the Christian Delawares. So, they kept somewhat apart as far as their socialization. Many of the Christian Delawares went over more east of here, toward what is now Nowata. Nowata, Alluwe, Armstrong communities, out in that direction. Nonetheless, as the Delawares went to look for a place to live, I think they were also looking at "what landscape is here that can help remind me just a little bit of back home?" Having lived in the forest with a vast ocean at their disposal back east, and then that pattern coming through Pennsylvania, Ohio, and Indiana with rivers and forests, if no ocean, I think that they were always reaching out for something that would kind of remind them of back home. Plus, to have the resources that they were used to, to do such things as constructing their long house, having enough room to pattern their village structure so it could be like it used to be back home. So, even though the landscape changed, I think that they actively sought out something that would, in their own mind, keep them grounded to the memories of the past.

I have no knowledge particularly of Wilson ancestry that goes back to a place location in Indiana along the White River. I can look at the family tree and go back to Ice and Buffalo Wilson, but you get a lot of Indian names and not Wilson names any longer. And records are imprecise at best.

The reason that I'm living in Bartlesville, Oklahoma, working for the Delaware Tribe Headquarters in Bartlesville, Oklahoma, probably goes back twenty-five years. It goes back to a time when I received my own vision of what it is that I had to do in life. I was given a certain directive, a certain purpose. It was not so precise that I could write it down on paper. All I know is that I was given a vision. It was not something I actively sought. It is not one that I even welcomed warmly. It was confusing. It was challenging. It was spiritual. It was ancestral. And it began me on a path of ultimately self-realization and a search for self-identity. And in doing so, [it] opened up my eyes to the fact that in this search it required that I invest my total conscience and my energy back into this tribe. In doing so, I have come up through the ranks, serving among other things as the manager of the tribal office and the tribal business capacity, serving as a member of the tribal council. Ultimately being elected to a four-year term as the chief of the Delaware tribe in the 1990s. So, that vision guided me here. Even beyond service as chief, I continue to be here, and I'm now working for the tribal housing authority as the director of the housing authority. All of this effort combined is to help rebuild our tribe. Not from a purely government and business standpoint, but the cultural heart of the Lenapes incorporated into all business decision making, planning. The best interests of the people are all the time considered in any decisions that we make. As I continue my endeavors in serving the tribe in these capacities, I have to go back and refresh myself in that self-identity; to go back and re-examine who I am, who my ancestors are, how I make decisions, and that they are done through a spiritual and cultural standpoint. In order to do that, I have to immerse myself in culture and spirit through my own worship and my own participation in cultural activities. When I do that, it refreshes me and helps me think like an Indian; it helps me think like a Lenape. So as I'm engaging in this modern conveyance through tribal government, as we build a community, I'm still thinking like an Indian even though I'm administering federal government money, in the form of programs through this institution called the Delaware Tribal Housing Authority.

In the 1970s, HUD [the Department of Housing and Urban Development] provided specific funding for Indian housing authorities. Public housing back in the sixties and the seventies was concentrated in urban areas; rebuilding the ghettos. But, there were a lot of more or less ghettos in areas that were thought of as mainland U.S. third-world countries. And that was the Indian reservations. So, much needed funding and legislative support was created with the Indian housing authorities. In the late 1970s, the Delaware Tribe created, with the allowance of the federal government, their own tribal Indian housing authority and have operated now for over twenty years to construct homes and make homes available for low-income Indian people. It has grown and developed over the years. We have a two and a half million-dollar fiscal operating budget for the current year. We probably have about nineteen million dollars in total assets that we're operating right now. I have a staff of eight people. We are doing everything from building a child-care center and homes to providing emergency assistance to people who are unfortunately displaced for some reason or another. We're helping out our elders with repairs to their homes and making safe, secure housing available to particularly low-income Delaware and other Indian people. The law allows us to give those kinds of preferences to, quite frankly, make up for decades of lack of services and lack of support to tribes, to provide safe and secure housing for their membership.

The development for the Delaware Tribe Housing Authority of homes is based on some long-range planning. That planning, when executed, starts off with the acquisition of land. In order to spend all of these federal monies through the housing authority, we have to have the land first. So we plan the first year of funding to buy land. The second year of funding we're going to do the infrastructure. Third year, we'll start building houses on top of that. In addition to that, our programming has expanded so that we can have some modernization or rehabilitation funds to help people who own their property, own their house. We can assist them to some degree, to bring their homes up to certain standards that are set in the modern sense. And now that the tribe has engaged in efforts to acquire more land, we continue our planning process to build on that land. The idea is that it is also to elevate the capacity of our tribal membership to get out of what is considered low-income housing and provide rental assistance. We want to lift up our tribal membership and get them to where socially and economically they can become homeowners and want to invest into the community. When it's their home, they take better care of it and they want to make their neighborhoods even better. That is the whole idea. We have special advantage direct funding to the tribe for that purpose, and in our planning and development that we look at, we are trying to re-create a sense of Delaware community with that.

I've always said we should reverse the process of the last several generations. In the earlier part of the twentieth century that affected my father, like the Depression era, what we call the dustbowl days, and WWII, Indian relocation policies and Indian termination policies had a devastating effect on tribal governments. All of that was preceded by the allotment era, which broke up the tribal community and focused on individual Indians. Then, in particular, in the 1920s, the demise of the Big House Church religion, which had kept the traditional Delawares together. All of those factors, combined, caused the Delaware population center to slowly disperse. Many Indians were involved in relocating elsewhere: California, Colorado, Texas, other places where there was more economic opportunity. Now, I think that if we rebuild that capacity, by buying the land back, building homes, building child-care centers, building elder centers, providing education, transportation, and jobs, that we can seek to attract people back and rebuild our community. In doing so, we create a greater likelihood that Delaware families will more and more be living amongst each other. It's hard to attract Delaware families back unless you have that. If you get people together more and more, then you can start including the cultural gatherings and teaching language and teaching all the cultural aspects. You're going to have a greater likelihood of little Delaware boys growing up around Delaware girls, increasing the likelihood—you can't legislate it, you can't mandate it—but increasing the likelihood that you're going to have Delawares marrying Delawares and having Delaware children. Then, and only then, will we address this assimilation, this diminishment of the bloodlines of the Delawares. You've got to change the social institutions first, reverse that process of the last several generations. Tribal government can do that, and I think that the housing authority is a great contributor to that capacity. Certainly, that is what I would like to see. As I said before, you can't legislate blood quantum. If we did it now, we'd legislate ourselves out of existence in about two more generations. So, we look ahead and change the whole social dynamic back to the way it was. We don't have to create anything new. Those ancestors, they already knew it. When we lost it, that's when it got worse. I think that it is indicative of the legacy of the Delawares who had European contact first, compared to a lot of tribes. We've been dealing with this for five hundred years. It shows, to be honest with you. I still feel confident, however, about the future of the Delawares.

The Lenape, historically among other tribes, have had this aura, this mystique, this image of being the wise and ancient ones. Stories of many other tribes call them the grandfathers; the Potawatomis and the Miamis, in their language, their word for who the Delaware are literally means "grandfathers." So, that identity of the ancient one and the wisdom and the religious, they were strong in their religious practice, their religion was very specific to their tribe and who they were, so they had an image among other tribes as the "old ones," the "ancient ones," the "spiritual ones." They were called upon at many times to serve as mediators among warring factions, or warring tribes, or whatever the case may be. Thus, they were known as peacemakers. Later on, as Europeans came, they were involved in helping to negotiate treaties. The United States of America signed the first treaty with an Indian tribe with the Delawares in 1778. Delawares were called upon to be negotiators and interpreters among other tribes of the Algonquian stock. To mediate a peace that eventually led to treaties that provided land cessions, but at least gave them some semblance of hanging on to something. With that historic identity of being the grandfathers, of being the peacemakers, of being very fervent in their religious worship and practice, as I began to study my own identity as a Lenape, I learned about these aspects of our historic identity. I found it to be tremendously ironic that in the 1990s, as I traveled back to the East Coast, and even went overseas, traveling to Sweden, and I recently took a trip to the Middle East, and I explained who the Delawares were to people, I would use this very phraseology that I just mentioned. I would stop for a moment and think, "Well, if we're peacemakers, if we're grandfathers, if we're strong in our religion, then I must conduct myself in that very same manner." And, low and behold, I was appointed to become the indigenous representative of the United States to the World Conference on Religion and Peace. The last conference was held in late 1999 in Amman, Jordan. Again, I found it to be tremendously ironic that as I was explaining to the people who the Delawares were and using those phrases to create a context, I found myself representing the Delaware people at the World Conference on Religion and Peace. I thought, how appropriate; therefore, I should re-examine my approach to conflict, to community service, to community development and continue to embrace the teachings and the historic identity of my ancestors. I get so caught up in a modern image, I need to go back more and more like the old-timers were and honor their identity and the legacy that was passed on to me. I already am doing a fair job of learning in the contemporary world. But I always want to keep one foot in the traditional world and achieve that balance. If I stay grounded into the traditional world, it will help me, guide me, as I seek to maintain a place in this contemporary world. By achieving that balance, I'm going to be able to survive, because it's not easy to be an Indian in the modern world.

My experience in any kind of traditional dances, powwow dances, ceremonials, anything like that, that's really gone on just about the last fifteen years of my life. I wasn't raised like that. My grandparents or even my parents didn't actively teach me as a young boy anything about the beat of the drum. It was only after, as an adult, that I began to learn that. But again, it's that blood memory. It's that natural understanding among all the Indian cultures, that drumbeat is one of the constants of what our culture is about.

It is the heartbeat of the Indian people, because the drum, the singing, that drumbeat, tells the story of the people. And those songs are giving honor to warriors, to ancestors, to tribal leaders. They are songs lamenting the loss of loved ones, particularly the loss of loved ones in battle, or in efforts to protect the people. But they are also songs that give thanks and praise to the Creator for the many gifts that we have. It is so instinctive to connect with that when those songs are sung. There are a variety of songs, different kinds of songs for different kinds of dancing. When I first came to the Delaware powwow, I sat up in the top of the bleachers. I might as well have been a civilian. I might as well not even have been an Indian because I didn't know my way around the powwow arena. I've been to some as a younger boy, but I kind of forgot all of that in my world travels. Coming back to Copan, Oklahoma, I watched it. I felt something there, and I didn't know how to connect with it. And as the years went by, I came down from the top of the bleachers and got closer and closer and closer, and the closer I got, I knew that there was something there for me. I asked for help, and I received help to come into that arena.

Now, today's modern powwow is a social event. It's for fun. It is a family event, and it's pretty healthy for families. It keeps Indian families together. You go out there around that powwow, you're going to see little children, and you're going to see all the way up to elders. We're all together, and we're enjoying ourselves. Where I get my true spiritual nourishment comes from ceremonies. Ceremonies are decidedly different from powwows. Ceremonies are meant for specific purposes. It is to replenish, renew, and rebuild the spiritual center of the people, and to give thanks in prayer to the Creator for the blessings that we do have, and to ask for help for the next cycle. It can be anything to asking for rain, to help out the crops, to strengthening our warriors before we send them into battle, to giving thanks for surviving another year. That's also meant to bring the people together and to put them in that circle so that the collective energy of all of those aspects of ceremony: the song, the drumbeat, the fire, the individual spirit of the participants; all of those things collectively when they're used in a certain order, an order that is ordained and given by the Creator thousands of generations ago, if we use it in that certain way there's a spiritual energy that comes up and blesses the people. That is why they are still alive. That's why there are still Indians on this Earth. So, I again derive my truest sense of Indian identity and connection from deep, deep inside my heart and my mind when I'm involved in ceremony.

Delaware ceremonies, they're pretty well gone. We lost our Big House church back in the 1920s. Today we're holding on just to the social dances and this traditional powwow, which is still spiritual in many senses, but it's pretty much social as very much inter-tribal anymore. We have non-Indians, we have spouses, and we have Indians from other tribes that we welcome into our powwows and our other social gatherings. I long for those days when we can have our own traditional Delaware ceremonies again. But I think it's going to have to be a gift from God again, that certain leaders would come forward. I do pray for that to happen again. In the meantime, I'm honored and blessed by having invitations to participate in the ceremonies of other tribes. The Osages, with their Eloshka dances, their war dances, among the Creeks and the Shawnees, when they have their ceremonial dances, I'm a guest in their camps. I'm a guest on that bench and asked to come out and dance with them, that my representation of the Lenape and my own personal identity help strengthen their endeavors. It's a high honor to have another tribe ask someone who is not of their people to join and participate in their ceremonies because they believe that I can bring a certain spiritual, a cultural addition to their strength of their ceremony. It builds good relations. So, I'm grateful for that opportunity. I find that more and more as I travel around Indian country. It practically lifts me off of the ground when I can participate in those things. It makes me want to continue to pray that one day, we'll have leadership, and we'll have specific Delaware religious ceremonies once again. I believe that it will happen.

Oral history on May 30, 2000, at Bartlesville, Oklahoma.

Curtis Zunigha's oral history also appears in
Always a People *(pages 278–286).*

ROUNDTABLE
DISCUSSION

Following a talk on Delaware history by Mike Pace, students show their appreciation.

ROUNDTABLE DISCUSSION ON THE LENAPE PROGRAM

AT CONNER PRAIRIE LIVING MUSEUM, FISHERS, INDIANA

Roundtable Interview (with Hugh Harrison's additions) includes James (Jim) P. Willaert, Hugh P. Harrison, Mike Pace, Annette Ketchum, and Dee Ketchum, at the home of Rebecca and James W. Brown on October 4, 2000, at Fishers, Indiana.

JIM: I'm going to go back a little bit further than the first [Delaware Indians] program because this actually started in 1991 with the program called "100 Years of Change in Black America," which was to be the first of a five-year rotation of programs. Year one we started "100 Years of Change in Black America." Year two was a program called "Indiana's Indians: Culture and Contrast," where we invited a group of folks from the Delaware as well as a group of folks from the Miami Tribe of Indiana. Year three was supposed to be "German Immigrants." Year four "The Utopian Societies." And I can't remember what year five was supposed to be because we never got past year two. The idea behind this was that each year we would add a new program until we had five of them, and we would have a progression for schools to go through over a five-year period. It was supposed to represent the different cultures that were in central Indiana or eventually came and settled in central Indiana. Well, we did the black history program for a couple of years, it changed names couple of times. And then we started the program with the Delaware and decided to stick with that one and develop it instead of going on to the other three. It's now been eight years [in 2000]. It's, in my opinion, one of the best programs we do. And the biggest reason for that is the people we deal with. I deal with a lot of people through the course of the year. This is the nicest group of people that I deal with. Not only on a personal level but with a commitment to education and a commitment to teaching the kids their history and culture. And with any luck they'll keep coming back for a long time.

The main thing that we are trying to do is introduce the students to not only the Woodland culture in general but the Delaware culture specifically so that they get an idea of what the Native peoples in this area were and are like. Most of the kids walk in the door with the expectation of what they have seen on TV, which is full-feather war bonnets, horses, tipis, buffaloes, and drums. That is very different from the culture of the folks that lived here. So if we get one thing through to them in the course of the program, I'm happy with it being what they're expecting to see is not necessarily the case. The second thing that we want them to gather is that Indians are not something of the past. It's a living culture, and while it is very rich in its history and traditions, there is also room for today. Over the course of the years we've had everything from second graders up through eighth graders at the school program, and probably people anywhere from about six months to eighty at the public program.

As a general rule we don't have to advertise this program too heavily. My phone starts ringing in May for an October program. We generally send letters out to the people that have come in the past and include one brief mention in our school brochure, but it's not heavily advertised. People come looking for us. Usually the question we get isn't, "Are you doing the program again," it's, "Are the Delaware coming back?" A lot of the times they'll call and ask, "Is [a specific person] coming back?" They often ask for Annette or Dee or Mike. The biggest chunk is probably fourth grade because that's when they do Indiana history. But I've noticed, over the past two years, a lot of schools seem to be adding a curriculum specifically about Woodland Indians. That's been seen in third, fourth, and fifth grade, depending on the school district. For many years we did take the program on the road. One day a week we went to several inner-city Indianapolis schools that traditionally can't get out for field trips. The program has always been well received there, and those schools are very culturally diverse. It didn't seem to matter what the kids' backgrounds were; they all seemed very interested and seemed to enjoy it quite a bit. I think they were probably some of the most interested audiences we've had in some years. Although, as a general rule, the kids that come to this program are some of the better behaved that we see during the course of the year. I've had a lot of good questions over the years, had a lot of fun questions.

ANNETTE: We had been going to Minnetrista Cultural Center [in Muncie, Indiana] for a couple of years before coming to Conner Prairie. And we've been over to Ohio before that. When we came that first year, in 1992, to Conner Prairie we had about five or six Delawares, and there were about five or six Miamis. We were mixed together with them, and we tried to be very helpful with them, and the Miamis were looking at our clothes. It was a cultural exchange just between our two tribes. I felt that a lot. We all came into the same session, and one of the things that I remember was that Mike [Pace] brought in Aunt Thelma [Pace] to the storytelling with me and Cathy Mowry. The children wanted to touch Aunt Thelma. They wanted to sit on her lap. They wanted to hug her and love her, like they had never seen a grandma before. It was such an incredible feeling. Cathy and I would each

Mike and Ella Pace and Don Secondine lead students and teachers in Bean dance, a Delaware social dance, at the 2005 Delaware Days at Conner Prairie. The line follows the leader.

tell our story, and then Aunt Thelma would tell her story, and the children just couldn't wait until they got through because they would touch her and hug her. It was very good feelings. It started out as only three days. We did three days and an evening. The evening one was outside on a nice evening. It was so nice. We just have such good feelings.

DEE: I wasn't part of that first trip up here. I passed on it. So Annette came back and talked to me about how wonderful of a time she had, and I didn't believe her much. She kept saying, "Well, Dee, you need to go, it's really a great experience." And I said that I didn't think I wanted to go. I wasn't too excited about it. I didn't believe her much in relationship to what she was talking about concerning the people and how receptive they were to our culture. So I guess in a weak moment I said that I would go, just to prove her wrong. I came up here [1993], and obviously I was wrong. I was never one as far as taking to culture and trying to go on the road with it. I

Bucky Buck is a favorite with students and teachers who attend Delaware Days at Conner Prairie. Bucky is frequently asked to pose for pictures and always makes them memorable.

wasn't a big advocate for that necessarily. But what I observed up here was the people like Jim [Willaert] and Hugh [Harrison] are sincerely involved in really wanting to know about a culture. That they weren't just putting on, like we weren't on stage. It was not play acting; they were sincerely wanting to know about our feelings and about our history and culture. I sensed that, and I guess that's why I have to come back. I also have observed that the kids that come into the program are, I don't know whether they have been tutored or what, but they have really shown a sincerity of wanting to know and learn about our culture. And, being an ex-schoolteacher, I appreciate that. They're very attentive and very appreciative of the things that we have to say. They are very respectful in that way. So I will continue to come back as long as that is the case. The friendships that we've made with the staff have been wonderful.

I have observed, from the first programs that were put on by Mike and Annette and some of the others from Bartlesville, and the programs that I first came to, that we've evolved into doing our real songs and dances of our Delawares. That's really been of importance to me. You can kind of pick up even in Oklahoma this pan-Indian thing where you can't really distinguish one tribe from another. Here, what we are showcasing is authentic Delaware. That's really where I'm coming from. I think that the emphasis on our songs and our dances that the Delaware did, that our ancestors did many years ago, is something that our program has developed into. To showcase that, and to be able to talk to the kids and say, "This is Delaware." It is a special time for us to come up here and to sing those old songs and dance those old dances.

MIKE: I don't think that I can add too much more to what Dee and Annette have said except that when we first talked about the idea of us coming to Conner Prairie we thought that would be an excellent thing. I think that we are all proud of who we are, and we're proud of our culture, and we do enjoy speaking out and talking to the people about it and showing it to them. There was a time when we spent a little more time doing the powwow aspect of it, but now it's moving into where we're actually showing them what we consider the real Delaware. We're talking about our own songs and our own dance. The other things, the clothing, the storytelling and history, have stayed the same, but now we've added this component of doing the Delaware songs and the dance. It has been very rewarding to us.

When we first came up here we did enjoy the fact that they did want us to come up here; they did want us to talk about what took place here from 1795 to the 1820s. We were certainly happy to do that because there is a great deal of mystery as to what happened to the history of the area. You certainly don't get it in normal public school American history. You don't hear about these things; you get a generalization of what existed just before Indiana became a state. There is very little American Indian history in American history. So there is that stereotype that you get, and that's what the kids show up with. This can affect children even if they don't understand what a stereotype is. They see these things on television, and they hear the music on television, and they have learned through a kind of osmosis, I guess, and they don't really understand it. We are able to talk to them about where we are coming from and what the real culture is. They do show a great interest in that because it's completely different from what their own idea was before they show up. And that's why the expectation is strange, and that's why some of the kids, when they come in, are saying, "How." So we try to change that attitude. I think we've been very successful with that. By the time they leave they have something that is completely different from what they thought, and we've taught them a few things. They've been able to look at the Delaware culture specifically, and it's much different than they

Two young men join the drum circle with Todd Thaxton and former chief Dee Ketchum at Conner Prairie Delaware Days in 2006. Chief Ketchum stresses the importance of learning to strike the drumhead in unison.

thought. They don't really realize how much or how important our presence here was at an earlier time. They're certainly surprised to learn about the towns that were here, and where they got their names, and that those were old Delaware villages at one time.

I've always been really happy to come up here. Over the years you work with people like Jim and Hugh, and Deb and Bob Cottrell. There is that friendship that we still have with them because you've worked that close together, you can't help but do that. We're interested in their welfare. They're interested in our welfare. So you naturally become close at that point. Everything that we do, that we try to do, as a tribe, is that we want to do the responsible thing. We want to act honorably in everything that we do, and we try to show respect to those people, and that's the way that we were brought up. If we can't do that, then shame on us. We try to show that, that there is honor there. We are proud of our heritage, and that's what we're trying to express here. Although we do change content from year to year, just slight things, I think we still accomplish the same objective. We're like everyone else; we don't want to do the same thing all the time. Actually we have a lot more to offer. We could probably do an hour- or two-hour program for each class and teach a lot more. However, in the time allotted we get a lot of information passed on. I think that the kids really enjoy what we've done and they do learn these things. In fact, we've had some classes where they come back the next year, a grade older, and they remember what they've learned the year before. So we do know that it is important to them and that they are learning from it. I'm very happy to come back up here and do it. We're proud of who we are and what we did. We're happy to express that, and we try to do that in an honorable way. If we can educate those young people and change those stereotypes that they've learned, then we've done our job.

HUGH: I joined the Conner Prairie Rifles about eighteen years ago and used to shoot in the village.[1] I wanted to work here, but I thought that I wanted to be a restorer of antique furniture, that sort of thing. But before I could do that I had to spend time in the villages and the tour group. I was intimidated. In fact, I had my application for two years before I turned it in. It came to a point, where I was working, that I had to retire whether I wanted to or not. And so I turned my application in, and John Schippers told me, "You got over in the village, and you never came out." So I never did get to restore the furniture. But that's how I started working at Conner Prairie.

At the time I didn't know that there was Delaware heritage in my family, but my father raised me using Indian principles for both my brother and myself. My wife (deceased) was part Indian. There's always been a deep respect for the Indian people, so I suppose that might have been one thing that kind of pushed me into it. When they [Delawares] came, I remember that they had the gift shop out there at Clowes Commons, outside the museum, and Mike was playing the drum, and they were selling fry bread. I came out after church, and I ate fry bread like it was going out of style. I started working with Becky Lauderbeck (on the Conner Prairie staff). The Delawares were presenting the various classes to the children inside the museum center. We had the class "natural resources." We had the children put cattail mats around a miniature wigwam, passed around furs and dried food, discussed hunting, fishing, gardening, gathering wild food, food preservation, etc. I just sort of keep coming back. This is my favorite program.

---

1. In 2002, the relationship between Conner Prairie Rifles, a black-powder shooting group, and the Conner Prairie Living Museum dissolved.

JIM: Probably what started the whole concept of the Lenape Village was that it was very much a part of not only the Conner story but the whole story of central Indiana. From what I understand, the idea of the village was on the drawing boards and the five-year plans off and on for probably fifty years before I ever came on the scene. It was just one of those things they never got to. Once we developed a relationship with everybody [Delawares] that we've been talking with in Oklahoma, it suddenly became a little bit more important to the Conner Prairie administration because they saw that there was a resource there and that there was interest from the Delaware side as well. So in August of last year [1999] the decision was made that we would actually go ahead and start this site and that we'd have it up on April 1 of this year [2000]. We got with an advisory committee made up of Mike, Dee, Annette, Paula [Pechonick], Jim Rementer. And then also John and Herbert Kraft in New Jersey. We sent some information out to everybody about what we wanted to do and got their comments on it. We had two or three drafts of information on history and culture that were reviewed again by Dee, Mike, Annette, and everyone. We made the changes that they asked us to make, and we started building. We started construction on February first and opened it to the public on April first with the dedication by Dee, Don [Secondine], Mike, Annette. They all came up and kind of got it kicked off for us. The Lenape Village is along the White River, representative of what life may have been like just prior to Delaware Indian removal from Indiana, set in approximately 1810.

HUGH: [Describing his participation at the Lenape Camp, as a first-person interpreter], "I'm Duncan McKinnen. Duncan McKinnen is an 1816 fur trader. He lives with the Delawares, as did his father before him. They are family. He is more Indian than white in the way he thinks, in the way he lives—and in the way he is. All he has ever done is trade furs with the Delawares. His wife was Lenape, but she died. He's looking for another Lenape wife. It's important to be part of the tribe, to be trusted and accepted—good for business, for the fur trade, from a commercial standpoint.

[Speaking as McKinnen] "The Delawares treat me as family, and I treat them the same way. I'm not trying to get wealthy. I don't like to sell whiskey or rum because you would not give something to your family that's going to cause them harm. I said when the government moves the Delawares west, I'll move with them. They have always done that—move the Indians west. The government never kept a treaty yet. And so I'll be going with the Delawares wherever they go."

OPPOSITE PAGE:

Annette Ketchum, tribal council member, performs "God Bless America" in Indian sign language at Conner Prairie Delaware Days, October 2006.

Duncan is based on a combination of William Conner and Gordon Saltonstall Hubbard, a fur trader among the different tribes in Indiana in 1816, 1817, as a sixteen- or seventeen-year-old boy, and information that we got from Dee, Annette, Mike, Paula. Paula told us a wonderful story that we use occasionally at the Lenape Village about how an ancestor of hers was a fur trader who kept his furs in a shed out back. The Indians would come in and trade with him. He would put them [the furs] in the shed. The Indians would go get the furs back out of the shed and then trade with him again. That one was just too good not to use.

ANNETTE: It's supposed to be a true story. We have it written in some of the genealogies.

JIM: And from there we developed the character; we developed his background, his attitudes. Jim Rementer worked with us on coming up with a name and a little bit of the story line on his wife so that we made sure that everything was appropriate, such as not using her formal name with anyone outside of the family. The reason that we have her as being deceased is we have no Delaware who could appropriately play the role [of McKinnen's wife]. One of the things we were asked to do early on was not to put somebody out there in costume that was not Delaware. There's no problem with that so we kind of fixed it so that there is the tie-in, but leaving it open should someone become available and interested that we can create a position out there [in the Lenape Village.]

ANNETTE: You can marry a few off!

DEE: The way that Conner Prairie went about creating the Lenape Village was quite appropriate as far as my perception was concerned. Mike made reference to the history of all Indian tribes and the other people, not being told correctly. It seems to me that the individuals that have been writing the history have put a lot of fiction in the writing, but that was not done in this case. They referred to some of the historians [John and Herbert Kraft] that understood and have done a lot of good research on the Delawares and then consulted with the tribe and the members of that particular tribe on their history so they would get it correct. What was impressive to me was that they were seeking input from the individuals who had a direct connection to the culture, and they were willing to make the changes and willing to write the script accordingly. Therefore, I fully endorsed it from that perspective. I have been at other places where this was not the case. Again it just ties the knot for me as far as the sincerity of Conner Prairie and the staff in what they're trying to depict in all of their projects that they do out there. I feel this is going to be very successful. I think it has been even today. They gave honor for my perspective and they have opened it up properly. They invited us to come and to speak and to look and to serve and to endorse, and what we have seen so far has been very good.

MIKE: While Dee was talking I was just thinking to myself, you know sometimes the old clichés that we use are certainly true, and this one is. The truth is stranger than fiction because to display these things is certainly more educational and more fitting, at least for us in this particular instance, because the truth is stranger than fiction. What happened in reality is much more fascinating than things that have been "created" or written. We found out not too long ago that there are some 730 references to Delawares, but a vast majority of those books were based on the research from other books, so it really wasn't done by actually coming and sitting down and talking to the real people about how they felt about these particular things. It was just kind of a self-renewing untruth that just passed on. A lot of things absolutely weren't true. Now we have an opportunity here to have input; we can actually tell them, this is the way it really was. That's the most important thing that we want to get across. They did take their time to come down and sit down and figure this out and present this the way it should presented, and we've been very, very happy with that. Yes, it's an evolving thing, but we were just talking tonight about how things evolve, just like clothing. So there is that evolving; I'm sure you'll see that in the village, too. There are many things still to be covered in the village. They'll get to them eventually as they add onto it. Then there will be change that will be made there eventually, but the important part, it is not a stagnant society. It evolves all the time. The basic part of our beliefs are still the same. The songs are still the same, but everything else is evolving. You couldn't help but evolve. But the Delaware people are still alive, and that's what we want to present here, and that's what's important to me.

DEE: One of the things that impressed me about this particular village first of all is that this type of village is not built in a day. It evolves over a period of time if you're going to do it correctly. Mike and I visited back in New York another supposed village, and it was made of concrete because they didn't want to go against fire codes. So, when the people came to see that, the kids and the private sector, they weren't getting the true representation of what it was like, it was just make-believe again. Our people didn't use concrete. Most of the children and a lot of the adults think that the Delawares lived in tipis. They did not. They lived in bark huts, called wigwams. Conner Prairie shows that not all the tribes necessarily lived in tipis. Visitors to Lenape Village can walk in and feel and touch and see the wigwam in person. So that's the one thing that I am really pleased with as far as Conner Prairie is concerned, that they are proper and putting the right stuff in it and not just building it with concrete or building blocks and then painting it over.

ANNETTE: Well, one of the things that I wanted to add was that we knew the integrity and the genuine sincerity of Jim, Hugh, and the historians at Conner Prairie. We didn't have to come in being really guarded. All we had to do is correct things so it came more from the Indian perspective rather than a white historical perspective, if they had gotten some information that wasn't correct. There is no time like today to correct the things that were errors in the past, because anything that is not corrected now will just go on as that myth. Many cultures die because they're nothing but a myth today. There's nothing there; it's just a big poof. But we're [the Delawares] really anchored out there. First of all it is the site. They chose the site right on the river, and the White River was where we were settled up there at Munceytown. We were settled in the forest in a very natural setting. There's not any paved roads or trails or cart paths that go to the Lenape Village. They're all paths that would be made natural. All these natural things. And then when they came to do the buildings, they were careful to authenticate the buildings. It's a real cabin where McKinnen lives and works. All of the Lenape Village looks so real, that in a few more years after it's aged, it's going to look worn-out in those buildings, and everything is going to get worn so they all look like they were the real thing. It's going to be a place that has life in it. It's almost like a time machine or something.

DEE: Some of the songs and dances that we do once a year are like what our old people did, in the latter part of September early October, to give thanks and to sing those songs. It just seems to be quite appropriate because that's usually the time we come up here, late September, October, so it fits with what has been passed on to me to show the appreciation of the year that just went by. The songs that we sing, while a lot of them are obviously social songs, they're spiritual songs, too. It gives thanks for the year that just went by. As to bringing some of our Delaware members from Oklahoma up here, I think it would be a wonderful experience. I don't think it would be easy because our people, like many other Indian people around the country, do live in two worlds. And so consequently they're having to maintain work. And this is an area that we fight all the time and that we really concentrate on, so that we don't lose out. We make an effort to sustain our work in private sectors, yet be this other part of our culture and our livelihood and our being and what's been taught us, to keep it alive. It's for our moms and dads and grandmothers and grandfathers, it's honoring them to do that. It's a commitment that I know Mike has made and I have made and all the other people have made to say that we're not going to let it die. They've already said, you've passed two generations and you've lost it, and we came close to that at one time, the Delawares, like many other tribes. But I think we're definitely on the upswing and making some real progress to retaining Delaware culture.

HUGH: Jim and Conner Prairie took several of us out to Bartlesville, Oklahoma, to the powwow. I'd like to say that the music and the drum beat gets "under your skin," and I was tremendously impressed. I continue to be impressed. I don't want to get too emotional, but these people are my dear friends. They're my best friends. I'm more comfortable around these people than anyone else. When we went to the powwow, of course, I took a lot of pictures, and later I felt maybe I shouldn't have, because I learned that some of the regalia (clothing) is original, and some of it has been passed down from generation to generation, and maybe they don't want a photograph taken. So I don't take pictures anymore out of respect. I was invited to come back. I've missed one year, but I've been back every other year since 1996. I stay at Mike Pace's camp. Last year Mike told me that I would be the elder of his camp, which is a high honor, and which I greatly respect. And I did take it. To be accepted by these people as family is such a good feeling; I can't explain it, but it's wonderful.

JIM: At the Lenape Village what we're hoping to do is have the interpretation and programming to where things change seasonally and focus on what would have been the appropriate activities for that season. Spring will be planting. Right now [2000] our focus is a little different. For the month of October we're trying to do some activities on a daily basis. And we're looking at a theme of crafts, orientation, that sort of thing. We're doing some work with natural dyes to show the dying process. [We are using] some of the native plants that were used for dyes, such as to dye the deer hair used for some of the dance roaches, and the traditional coil pottery when the Delaware were in the Pennsylvania, New Jersey area. Of course, [we demonstrate] cattail mat-making for lodges, because you constantly have to re-cover the wigwams. Cattails are a plant material, so they do weather a little bit. That's something that we found fascinates people, to watch a mat being made. Although they don't seem to want to get down there and help.

ANNETTE: They might make a mistake, that's part of the reason they don't.

JIM: We're going to focus heavily for November on preparing for winter and food and processing corn and making acorn flour, cooking a lot of the traditional dishes that Michael taught us about back in the spring. Mostly corn and pumpkin based. We dried some pumpkin and fish out there a few weeks ago, in the way it was described by Herbert Kraft, and it worked out very well. To be honest, I was a little leery of the concept of drying fish by a fire. But what we hope to do with this is get a seasonally accurate picture of what life was like for the Delaware in this area in the mid 1800s. As a basic rule we're not going to do anything that they say is inappropriate. And as Dee mentioned earlier, a lot of things come out of books, but that doesn't mean that the authors who wrote them know what they're talking about. I don't do anything that is not confirmed by at least two to three people. And then I send it out there [to Bartlesville] to find out if these people have any idea what they're talking about.

Mike taught the staff some [Lenape] language when he was here in March.

MIKE: I don't think that they've progressed a whole lot on that yet. But we're working on that. The CD-ROM actually has a lot of the vocabulary for the Lenape Village. I don't know how we can really expand speaking Lenape here except to make the CD-ROM available to volunteers that do come along. Out in the village I think once they begin to understand that, they can pass that onto the people that are there; he's going to get an understanding of what this and that is. There are some descriptive things that interpreters might have to remember. Delaware is a descriptive language, and some of the language that they might use in the village could grow. As Interpreters progress and they get better and better at it, I don't see why they couldn't eventually start having a lot more use of the language itself. And then, of course, it's really up to the people how much they can retain or whether they even want to retain it. So there might be a point where visitors to the village learn they can pick up a language CD-ROM in the gift shop and have the opportunity to take that home and learn Delaware. There are quite a few people who are interested in that sort of thing.

ANNETTE: There aren't going to be people in the village wearing Lenape clothes. When you start dressing up non-Indians in the traditional clothes it becomes a kind of a fairyland. It takes away that authenticity.

JIM: We have a set of man's clothing in the Lenape Village that visitors can see, and we have a series of programs throughout the museum called "Culture Look." They're ten or fifteen minutes. I was talking to Dee about this the other day. What we're going to do is have one of those about clothing so the interpreters can show the Lenape clothing. It's not a fashion show, but a demonstration of how to get dressed. We hope to get a set of women's clothing also so visitors see what the women's clothing at the time of the Lenape Village looked like.

ANNETTE: During that time [1820s], women were wearing cloth fabric over-aprons and skirts. They weren't wearing ceremonial clothes out in those villages. They wore what we call a day dress. And that started evolving, because the Delaware women looked at the non-Indian women and saw what they were wearing, and the motive, at the time, you had to be covered up. You better have long sleeves, long dresses, and you're not going to be wearing a dress that you weren't well covered. But because they're Delawares, they are going to be wearing Delaware tops, Delaware blouses, not what the white women were wearing. It's not the very same things, but it's similar.

JIM: When we first opened the site, both Dee and Annette came to me separately, and apparently they hadn't talked among themselves, asked if we could change Duncan's attire so that it was more representative of Delaware clothing. And we are going to do that; we're waiting for the broadcloth to come in. So Duncan will be wearing a pair of the broadcloth leggings, the long shirt, with the belt on top of the shirt and then some of the trade silver that he currently wears. The "Closer Look" program that I mentioned about the clothing is basically going to be how Duncan gets dressed in the morning.

ANNETTE: If he's married to a Delaware woman, he's not going to be wearing white man's clothes. He's going to wear whatever that woman makes him. That's the way I interpret it. I think that he probably had other clothes as well. He had a wife before he met her, his Indian wife, I'm sure.

JIM: Apparently it was very common, as Dee said, to live in two worlds even back then, so Duncan's top hat and waistcoat that he currently wears will still be hanging on the wall for those days that he does business with other European settlers. But the emphasis on his dress will be more on what his Lenape wife would have made him, which is what he would have been wearing. For our time period, from what we've been able to find out, it was a traditional style, but even the Delaware had pretty much gone to the cloth top. That was some information that we got from Jim Rementer.

JAMES BROWN: Did you already know about the Indiana part of your ancestry? Or did the relationship with Conner Prairie cause you to think more about that. Or did you already know that because things have been handed down to you?

ANNETTE: I didn't know too much about it because everybody is dead that was here in Indiana. In fact, all of our immediate ancestors came down from Kansas as young people.

DEE: All this has been an enlightenment of our history, personally. Because most of the stories that have been related to me primarily came out of Kansas, going back two more moves or so, Missouri, Indiana, was something that was never talked about much.

MIKE: I think that's certainly true. We know the language has changed, but we have retained words that go back a long way. But since we don't have a written language or even a written history, what comes down to us is fairly recent. We do know what happened back here in Indiana. We really didn't care about the historical part, what we cared about was the traditional things that passed on. History didn't make much of a difference to us; all we knew was that we moved to protect our own people. So that was what was important. I remember Lucy Blaylock [an elder] used to say, "Well, that was their life, this is my life. What I learn I learned from my grandmother or mother." And that was recent history; beyond that it was just a story. But the only thing that was important was, "What do we do now? What's going to happen in the future?" Yes, it is interesting to come back here; we do know what happened. But as far as passing down orally, I don't think we have much of that.

ANNETTE: You knew the highlights of the federal government history, too.

DEE: The point all of us are making is that the Indiana sojourn was not part of our daily conversation. Where the Delawares advanced in Kansas, the last move, was a lot more talked about and prevalent.

ANNETTE: I can remember Mother saying, "Oh, they came down from the north." Which meant from Kansas.

Dee and I were talking about it last week, that we need to prepare the next generation to be leaders. When we fade out, they can fade in. We're trying to pass on our culture and teach our kids.

DEE: My dad's generation, because of the time period that they went through, let it slip a little bit, and so we've really focused on the language and the songs and the dances, and it has made an impact surely on ourselves, but also I can see some impact on our youth. But that's a continuous thing. I do fear that my grandson, grandkids, will never have heard the spoken language of the Delaware tribe. So that's what motivates me. So consequently I am excited about the future of the Delawares. I think that the tribe and the awareness of the culture is on an upbeat. We started our Delaware Days back seven or eight years ago. It's successful; people come and enjoy themselves. The Delawares are different from a lot of people you talk to back east that thought that we were all dead.

Hugh P. Harrison died 2006.

REFERENCES

Adams, Richard C. *Legends of the Delaware Indians and Picture Writing.* Edited and with an introduction by Deborah Nichols. Syracuse, N.Y.: Syracuse University Press, 1997. Appendixes by James Rementer, Nora Thompson Dean, Lucy Parks Blalock. Original cover art by Ruthe Blalock Jones.

Barker, Herbert, Sr. *Paradise Remembered: A Lenape Indian Childhood and Other Stories.* Self published, 1991.

Benedict, John D. *Muskogee and Northeastern Oklahoma.* Vol. 1 of 3 vols. Chicago: S. J. Clarke, 1922.

Brown, Janifer, and Jim Rementer. *Conversational Lenape: Lenape to English and English to Lenape.* Bartlesville, Okla.: Delaware Tribe of Indians, 1999.

Carvalho, S. N. *Incidents of Travel and Adventure in the Far West.* Philadelphia: Jewish Publication Society, 1954.

Cranor, Ruby. *Kik Tha We Nund: The Delaware Chief William Anderson and His Descendants.* Bartlesville, Okla.: n.p., n.d.

———. *Some Old Delaware Obituaries.* Bartlesville, Okla.: n.p., n.d.

Delaware Trails: Some Tribal Records, 1842–1907. Transcribed by Fay Louise Smith Arellano. Baltimore, Md.: Clearfield, 1996.

Grumet, Robert S. *The Lenapes.* Indians of North America series. Frank W. Porter III, general ed. New York: Chelsea House, 1989.

Kohn, Rita, and W. Lynwood Montell. *Always a People: Oral Histories of Contemporary Woodland Indians.* Bloomington: Indiana University Press, 1997.

Kraft, Herbert C. *The Lenape-Delaware Indian Heritage: 10,000 BC to AD 2000.* Bartlesville, Okla.: Lenape Books, 2001. This publication contains an extensive bibliography (pp. 579–635).

Weslager, C. A. *The Delaware Indians: A History.* New Brunswick, N.J.: Rutgers University Press, 1996.

INDEX

Italicized page numbers indicate illustrations.